W9-CZU-915

18.45
54 ℞

A REFORMED, EVANGELICAL, CATHOLIC THEOLOGY

A Reformed, Evangelical, Catholic Theology

The Contribution of the World Alliance of Reformed Churches, 1875 – 1982

•

Alan P. F. Sell

•

WILLIAM B. EERDMANS PUBLISHING COMPANY
GRAND RAPIDS, MICHIGAN

Copyright © 1991 by Wm. B. Eerdmans Publishing Co.
255 Jefferson Ave. S.E., Grand Rapids, Mich. 49503

Printed in the United States of America

Library of Congress Cataloging-in-Publication Data

Sell, Alan P. F.
  A Reformed, evangelical, catholic theology: the contribution of the
World Alliance of Reformed Churches, 1875–1982 / by Alan P. F. Sell.
    p.   cm.
  Includes bibliographical references and index.
  ISBN 0-8028-0483-7
  1. World Alliance of Reformed Churches (Presbyterian and
Congregational)   2. Christian literature—Publication and
distribution—History.   3. Theology, Doctrinal—History.   I. Title.
BX9403.W6S45   1991
230'.5'0601—dc20   90-45927
                                                          CIP

*To
friends
and former colleagues
in the
World Alliance of Reformed Churches*

Contents

Preface

Important though individual theologians and prominent schools of theological thought may be, when the full story of twentieth-century theology is written, some attention will surely need to be paid to the theological contribution of the ecumenical bodies. The World Council of Churches and the several Christian world communions have played an important theological role, frequently calling upon the services of their most eminent scholars whose work, sometimes hidden within composite reports, has been of real significance. It will be interesting in due course to compare and contrast the theological contributions of the several ecumenical bodies; to see how far they have been occupied by the same, or by different, theological questions; to evaluate their findings; and to relate them to the general course of academic theology. None of this will be possible, however, until the required building blocks are available.

The present analysis of the theological writings engendered by one Christian world communion, the World Alliance of Reformed Churches, is offered both as a contribution to the larger task, and as a reminder of a considerable body of theological work which has interest in its own right. We shall draw not only upon official pronouncements and resolutions of the Alliance, but also upon material published in Alliance *Proceedings*, books, pamphlets, and journals.

It is by no means suggested that all of the Alliance's theological writings are of the highest caliber; but much is too good to be forgotten, and a good deal of it can still inform and nourish us today. Although most, if not all, of the Alliance's theological publications have been read in the course of writing this book, they will not all be mentioned in it. Some of the material is of transient interest only, and much of it is repetitive. Accordingly, we shall select what we take to be the major themes, and refer to what appear to be the most important writings.

The date in our subtitle is to be taken seriously. We have confined our attention to work completed, or nearly so, by the General Council of 1982, and have not commented upon new work published or in progress since that date. It seemed necessary to have a clear terminus, and undesirable to comment upon uncompleted projects, or upon work in which the writer was directly involved. A list of some of the Alliance's post-1982 theological concerns will be found in the antepenultimate note.

The history of the Alliance has been competently recounted by a former general secretary, Marcel Pradervand, in his book, *A Century of Service* (1975). There is no need to repeat what he has done. Our present objective is to analyze a large body of theological materials which actually exist, whatever the circumstances of their appearance. Our emphasis will be upon those analytical questions concerning internal coherence, the nature of the argumentation, and the adequacy of the claims made, questions which can be posed of any written text. In short, we wish to enter into critical dialogue with the corpus: to evaluate it rather than simply to describe its growth and contents. It is fully recognized, however, that theological issues do not arise ex nihilo. Accordingly, our first chapter will include a chronological synopsis, and within each succeeding chapter a broadly chronological approach will be taken towards each theme under review, with brief reference to prevailing circumstances as appropriate.

The conventions to be adopted reflect the fact that we are dealing with the World Presbyterian Alliance (1875), which united with the International Congregational Council (1891) in 1970 to form the World Alliance of Reformed Churches (Presbyterian and Congregational). The earliest *Proceedings* are of the first General Presbyterian Council; the second are of the General Council of the Presbyterian Alliance; the third are of the Alliance of the Reformed Churches holding the Presbyterian System—and thus the designation remained until 1970 (except that "order" was substituted for "system" in the 1954, 1959, and 1964 *Proceedings*). Our shorthand for all of this is "Presbyterian Council." Similarly, we shall use "Congregational Council" when referring to the International Congregational Council. This will enable us to use "Reformed" when referring to the entire family (though we should never forget that not all of the Reformed churches of the world belong to the Alliance). We shall speak of "the Alliance" when referring to the history of the two wings of the family from 1875 onward and, of course, when denoting the post-1970 body. The term "Alliance literature" will encompass the published work of the Alliance and its two parent organizations.

The complete list of Council meetings will be found in Appendix I. We shall not interrupt the flow of our argument in order to introduce biographical details even of the principal thinkers under discussion. Instead, in Appendix II we shall provide brief information concerning a few whose *theological* contributions to the Alliance were especially important. Since it would be invidious to select from the living, we note only the deceased. Finally, Appendix III is a bibliography of the major publications of the Alliance and of its Presbyterian and Congregational forebears.

In addition to the lofty reasons offered above for the writing of this book, there was the practical consideration that in 1983, as the then newly appointed theological secretary of the Alliance, I felt that I ought to review the literature in order to get my bearings. This attempt to meet that practical need developed into my major piece of research during my Geneva years. I am grateful to the executive committee of the Alliance for its willingness to regard this project as an integral part of my brief. I was greatly helped by Lukas Vischer, the then moderator of the Alliance's department of theology, who devoted considerable time to the reading and discussion of earlier drafts of this material. For this I thank him most warmly. The final draft was read by three scholars who have long and detailed knowledge of the Alliance: Arthur C. Cochrane, professor of systematic theology emeritus at the University of Dubuque Theological Seminary; Gabriel Fackre, Abbot Professor of Christian Theology at Andover Newton Theological School; and J. K. S. Reid, formerly professor of systematic theology in the University of Aberdeen. All of these suggested improvements and offered much encouragement: my thanks to them all. My then secretary, Mrs. M. A. (Dori) Noce, deserves hearty thanks for her patience and high praise for her typing skills.

My publisher and I acknowledge with gratitude that publication has been made possible, in part, by a grant from the endowment fund of the University of Calgary.

It was a real privilege—and a rich educational experience—to serve as the Alliance's theological secretary, and I have the happiest memories of those years. I take the liberty of dedicating this work to the many friends I made around the world, and to my former colleagues. I trust that this book will be taken as evidence of my continuing belief in the importance of the Alliance's theological work.

Among the many friends my wife and I made is Edmond Perret, the recently retired general secretary of the Alliance. He went out of his way to welcome Karen and me to Geneva, and throughout our time there he proved to be a most loyal colleague, whose kindness and commitment we shall never forget. We wish Edmond and Simone many happy years.

Alan P. F. Sell
The University of Calgary

1

Introduction: The Reformed Alliance and Its Theological Work

In each of the following chapters I shall take a specific theme, the sum of which will provide a general indication of what I have found in reflection upon the entire corpus of Alliance literature. The predominant overall finding will be that taken as a whole the corpus represents a theology which is catholic, evangelical, and Reformed. It is catholic both in the sense that it is in line with the apostolic faith of the ages and also in the sense that its objectives are not sectarian. It seeks to stand upon the message of the grace of God in Christ, as that has been given by the Spirit through the Word; and, challenged by that same Word and Spirit, it is conscious of needing ever to be reformed. The major points of Christian doctrine are expounded in the literature (chapter 2). The resulting ecclesiology is evangelical in that it starts from God's gracious calling of a people for his praise—a people who are covenanted to him and therefore to each other in a fellowship which is inherently and inescapably catholic (chapter 3). Consistent with this, the theology we find in the Alliance corpus responds to the vision of the modern ecumenical movement, to which it has made an important contribution (chapter 4). Again, the Alliance's theological corpus has something to say concerning the Christian response to the philosophical-apologetic climate (chapter 6), and rather more to say concerning an ethical-social witness (chapter 7).

Before proceeding to the themes, however, we must set the scene by asking three questions: What is the Alliance? What major theological issues have engaged the attention of the Alliance during the course of its history? What is the nature and status of the theological work which has been open to such a body as the Alliance? Only when an attempt

1

has been made to answer these questions shall we be able subsequently
to view our themes in historical perspective.

I. What Is the Alliance?

The simple, though relatively uninformative, answer to the question
"What is the Alliance?" is that in 1990 it is a family of 173 member
churches that are in accord with Article II of the Alliance's constitution
(1970, amended 1982 and 1989):

> Any Church which accepts Jesus Christ as Lord and Saviour;
> holds the Word of God given in the Scriptures of the Old and New
> Testaments to be the supreme authority in matters of faith and life;
> acknowledges the need for the continuing reformation of the Church
> catholic; whose position in faith and evangelism is in general agree-
> ment with that of the historic Reformed confessions, recognizing that
> the Reformed tradition is a biblical, evangelical and doctrinal ethos,
> rather than any narrow and exclusive definition of faith and order,
> shall be eligible for membership.[1]
> United Churches which share this understanding of the nature
> and calling of the Church shall be eligible for membership.
> Membership in the Alliance does not restrict the relationship of
> any Church with other Churches or with other inter-church bodies.

But at once the reference to "United Churches" alerts us to the fact
that we are here dealing with a body of mixed pedigree; and if we turn
to the full official name of the Alliance—The World Alliance of Reformed
Churches (Presbyterian and Congregational)—that impression is confirmed. The Alliance as we know it today results from the coalescence of
two international bodies. Of these the senior was the World Presbyterian
Alliance (1875) and the other was the International Congregational
Council (first meeting 1891; constitution and permanent secretariat
1949). The former body brought together churches of the Reformed and
Presbyterian polity, the latter those of the Congregational Way. The two
international bodies united in 1970. The United Churches to which the
constitution refers are a product of the modern ecumenical movement,
which has encouraged transconfessional unions in a number of countries.
Some sixteen such churches are members of the Alliance, and they
include the Evangelical Church of Czech Brethren (Lutheran, Reformed), 1918; the United Church of Canada (Congregational, Presbyterian, Methodist), 1925; and the United Church of Zambia (Congregational, Presbyterian, Methodist), 1965. To date, the widest confessional

convergence is found in the Church of North India (Congregational, Presbyterian, Anglican, Baptist, Brethren, Methodist, Disciples), 1970.

The factors of ecclesiological, cultural, and geographical diversity are implicit in what has already been said. What now needs to be made plain is the phenomenal growth of the Alliance membership during the past century. Although the Italian Waldensians look back to Peter Waldo in the twelfth century and the Evangelical Church of Czech Brethren honors Jan Hus (c. 1369-1415), and although the Reformed family as a whole is greatly indebted to the reforming movements of the sixteenth century, the fact is that approximately half of the member churches of the Alliance have been founded or have attained their present constitution since 1875, some thirty of them since 1935. Some of these churches have resulted from the union of pre-1875 traditions, but the majority are churches resulting *de novo* from missionary endeavor.

Thus, in 1899 the membership of churches belonging to the World Presbyterian Alliance was 4,852,096.[2] By 1952 the figure had risen to 40,041,995.[3] Today the Alliance (including now the bulk of the Congregational family, which in 1949 numbered 3,458,860)[4] is sometimes said to encompass up to 70,000,000 Christians. We cautiously use the words "up to" because it is notoriously difficult to secure accurate figures; moreover, churches do not all employ the same numbering criteria. Thus, for example, Congregational churches will tend to count communicants only; others may count entire church communities—that is, all of the baptized. Our own attempt to assess the membership of the Alliance community on the basis of returns made by member churches and comparison with published statistics yields a figure of some 55,000,000, though this is a conservative estimate.

Whatever the actual figure, it cannot be denied that the number of Reformed Christians in the world exceeds it. For there exists the Reformed Ecumenical Synod (1946), a conservative confessional grouping of some 30 Reformed and Presbyterian churches, two-thirds of which do not belong to the Alliance, and whose total membership is in the region of 5,500,000. There is also the International Congregational Fellowship (1977), a body designed to promote fellowship between Congregational individuals, some of whom belong to member unions of the Alliance, some of whom do not. Finally, there are Reformed churches, often resulting from local or regional secessions, which do not belong to any international organization. This state of affairs highlights the challenge to unity and union within the Reformed family at large—a perennial challenge which the Alliance is currently seeking to place once again before its own member churches. It also warns us to bear in mind the fact that when showing, as we shall, the ecumenical thrust of the Alliance's work, we are not referring to the position of *all* Reformed churches in the world. Indeed, not all Alliance member churches, and certainly not all local congregations, are at this point represented by the ecumenical thrust of the literature we shall review. This in turn raises a question (as yet scarcely considered by the Alliance): How far are Alliance statements truly representative of the Alliance constituency? This kind of question will not be unfamiliar to the several member churches of the Alliance; but it presses with particular force where international Christian affairs are concerned.

The upshot is that Alliance member churches are found in most parts of the world, with the largest number in developing countries. Some witness amidst Muslim, Hindu, and other majorities; and if in Scotland and in some of the Swiss cantons they continue as established churches, in other lands they have had to discover their roles within the parameters laid down by the various styles of communism.

So much for a general description of the constituents and diversity of the Alliance family as it is today. How did the institution itself originate? Since the story has been fully told by Marcel Pradervand for the Presbyterian Alliance[5] and by Albert Peel and Douglas Horton for the Congregational Council,[6] I may be brief.

By the beginning of the nineteenth century the colonizing activities of the Dutch, the Germans, the French, the Portuguese, the Spanish, and the British had already yielded ecclesiological outcrops that maintained more or less regular contact with the several "old countries." The modern missionary movement gathered pace during the century and numerous regions were reached with the gospel as a result of the sometimes heroic labors of missionaries from the older colonizing countries, and from America, Switzerland, and elsewhere. At the same time, in Europe, North America, Australia, and South Africa Presbyterian, Reformed, and Congregational churches were establishing their national and regional structures. Interestingly, in at least some cases it was the success of foreign missions that prompted the development of home missions and hence, in English Congregationalism, for example, of county unions,[7] and later of the Congregational Union of England and Wales (1831).[8] Transdenominational bodies, a term which aptly describes some of the missionary societies, were growing up. Prominent among these were the Evangelical Alliance (1848) and the Young Men's Christian Association. In 1867 the Lambeth Conference of Bishops met for the first time.

In view of this spirit of cooperation and association, and of their representation throughout the world, it is not surprising that both Presbyterians and Congregationalists began to think that the inauguration of some form of global fellowship was their next logical step.

Professor James MacGregor of New College, Edinburgh, was one of the first Presbyterians to express himself in print on the matter. In an article entitled "Our Presbyterian Empire" (May 1868), he advocated "a Council of Presbyterians who hold by the Presbyterian Standards." He thought that such a council should meet every five, ten, or twenty years, alternately at Edinburgh, London, and New York. The purpose would be that the churches "might confer for ecumenical purposes, while each Church, for local purposes, would always retain her own autonomy, and hold herself perfectly free to accept the decisions of the Council in the exercise of her own independent judgment under Christ."[9]

Meanwhile, in America the thoughts of James McCosh and Philip Schaff (a Swiss who became America's church historian par excellence), who had already collaborated to revive the (1846) Evangelical Alliance in America, were turning in a similar direction.[10] Like MacGregor, McCosh was a minister of the Free Church of Scotland. After parish experience he had served as professor of logic and metaphysics at Queen's College, Belfast, and there his most important philosophical works were written. By now he was president of the College of New Jersey (later Princeton University). In 1870 the reunion of the Old and New School Presbyterians was consummated at Philadelphia, on the occasion of the General Assembly of the Presbyterian Church in the United States of America.[11] McCosh used the occasion of reunion to call for a confederation of all Reformed churches. Among these who heard McCosh's address was William Garden Blaikie, a delegate from the Free Church of Scotland, who described himself as "an early and somewhat strenuous advocate of a General Presbyterian Council."[12]

In the following year Blaikie wrote an article entitled "Confederation of English-Speaking Presbyterians—A Proposal" in *The Presbyterian* (November, 1871). He afterwards explained that "the proposal was limited to 'English-speaking' Churches, simply because at that time it seemed too difficult to embrace all languages, though the writer has since become convinced that the comprehension of others in the scheme is one of its most interesting and hopeful features."[13] Blaikie's objectives for such a body were:

1. To foster the idea of a large brotherhood, or ecclesiastical family, with the stimulating influences which that thought conveyed.

2. To give to the various churches more of "the communion of the saints," more real fellowship in each other's gifts and graces.

3. To communicate to each other the results of experience in practical work.

4. To show how the elements of true conservation and legitimate freedom and progress might be adjusted to each other.

5. To divide foreign and other fields of labor among the various churches.

6. To give opportunities for united prayer.

7. To cultivate Christian friendship, bringing congenial souls into closer contact with each other, and deepening their interest in each other's work. It was added that the due result of such an alliance would not be an increase of sectarianism, because Christian brotherhood, as it enlarged its fellowship, enlarged itself; and possibly the final result might be a federal gathering together of all the evangelical churches, whether Presbyterian or not.[14]

Others who advocated a pan-Presbyterian council included the Scot, J. Moir Porteous, in his book *The Government of the Kingdom of Christ* (1872). In 1873 the Irishman Dr. Knox addressed an overture to the General Assembly of the Irish Presbyterian Church to the effect that an ecumenical council of churches which subscribe to the Westminster Confession of Faith be convened, and this was approved; and in the same year Dr. Niccolls of St. Louis addressed a similar overture to the General Assembly of the Presbyterian Church of the United States (North), and this was cordially approved.

Thanks in large part to the efforts of McCosh and Schaff, the Evangelical Alliance met in New York in the autumn of 1873. A meeting of attending Presbyterian ministers and elders was convened, and further steps were taken which led first to discussions in general assemblies and church courts, to much correspondence, and finally to an international preparatory meeting in New York on 3 December 1874. At this meeting McCosh presented twenty-two resolutions concerning the objectives and establishment of a council, and these were unanimously adopted. A similar happy overture resulted from the London Conference in July 1875, when the constitution of the Presbyterian Alliance and Council was agreed upon: McCosh was appointed president of the conference, and Schaff was among others in the American delegation. The original intention was to hold the first council in 1876, but owing to the subsequently discovered coincidence that on the day selected, 4 July 1876, the centenary of American Independence was to be celebrated, the council met in Edinburgh in 1877. Meanwhile, the concept of the council had been tirelessly advocated by McCosh, Blaikie, and others; Schaff took the opportunity of travel in Europe and the Near East to engage the interest of the French, German, Swiss, Egyptian, Turkish, and Syrian Reformed communities,[15] and Blaikie followed up this initiative by undertaking an extended tour in 1876.

We shall have more to say concerning the ecclesiological self-understanding of both the Presbyterian Alliance and the Congregational Council in chapters 2 and 3. Suffice it for the present to say that a fellowship rather than a supreme court was envisaged by both communions, and that the objectives were mutual support, concerted testimony, the encouragement of mission, the defense of the faith, and the avoidance of narrow sectarianism. Indeed, both sides would have sympathized with McCosh's letter to Blaikie of 17 June 1875: "We wish to make the movement evangelistic rather than ecclesiastic. . . . The Council is to have no power to order the Churches. Our power is the moral, persuasive. . . . We must avoid. . . .—being a mere talking body."[16]

We have already said that Congregationalists no less than Presbyterians were caught up by the movement towards cooperation, and by the growing mood of internationalism. The London Missionary Society, the Colonial Missionary Society, and the American Board of Commissioners for Foreign Missions had long fostered links with their respective extended families around the world; and there had been personal contacts between England and America extending back to the Pilgrims. But *official* transatlantic links took longer to forge. Americans attended most of the assemblies of the Congregational Union of England and Wales (1831); and at the 1835 assembly they lamented what they took to be their hosts' apathy vis-à-vis the Total Abstinence Movement (1832) and expressed concern that wine was available to platform speakers and to ministers on their descent from the pulpit.[17] Not all the traffic was in one direction. Andrew Reed and James Matheson's tour of 1834 to the United States and Canada was chronicled in a two-volume work, *A Narrative of the Visit to the American Churches by the Deputation from the Congregational Union of England and Wales* (1834). Some twenty years later, when the American Congregationalists held their national convention in Boston (1865), sixteen Congregational representatives from other countries were present. When at last in 1871 the American National Congregational Council was inaugurated, other lands were well represented; and a considerable contingent of Americans attended the Jubilee meetings of the Congregational Union of England and Wales in 1881.

It was against this background that an article by Hastings Ross published in the American journal *The Congregational Quarterly* (1874) excited considerable interest. The article, "An Ecumenical Council of Congregational Churches," was reprinted and circulated in England and Canada. At the meeting of the national council at St. Louis in 1880, the distinguished American Congregational historian Henry Martyn Dexter and Alexander Hannay, secretary of the Congregational Union of England and Wales, discussed the idea; and on 7 June 1884 the Congregational Union of Ontario and Quebec advocated a general Congregational council and requested the Congregational Union of England and Wales to consider the feasibility of such a meeting. The idea was affirmed and correspondence with Congregational unions around the world was undertaken. In 1888 Hannay and Mr. Henry Lee were in the southern colonies for the meetings of their unions, and at the Melbourne assembly of the Victoria Union they were asked to urge their home union to convene an international gathering. This action was endorsed by the New South Wales Union. The request was unanimously granted by the Congregational Union of England and Wales at its assembly in May 1889; in October Dr. Alexander Mackennal conveyed a formal invitation to the American National Council to attend an international council in London, and this was unanimously accepted. It was resolved to limit the number of delegates to one hundred from America, one hundred from England, and one hundred from the rest of the world. The Americans agreed to this, despite the fact that their numerical strength might have been thought to entitle them to a larger representation.

Thus the first meeting of the International Congregational Council took place in July 1891 under the presidency of R. W. Dale of Birmingham,[18] though an attack of influenza prevented his attending all of the sessions. Two of the pioneers were not present: Drs. Dexter and Hannay had died during the same week of November 1890.[19]

II. Major Theological Themes, 1875-1982

What major theological questions have engaged the attention of the Alliance during the course of its history? This is, of course, the theme of this book. But whereas in subsequent chapters I shall deal thematically and in detail with the published material, it may be of service here to offer a brief survey of major topics in chronological order. This will place the thematic discussions against their background. It will enable us to gauge the periods at which the several themes receive attention, to notice the points at which they are of real concern, and in some cases to note the points at which they drop from the agenda altogether. For convenience I shall divide the survey into four sections: 1875-1914; 1920-1939; 1945-1970; 1971-1982. Since the most concentrated and varied collections of theological writing are to be found in the Council *Proceedings*, I shall limit attention to those volumes in this rapid survey; and since the interests of the two sets of Council meetings were so nearly identical, we may treat them together.

1875-1914

In their early years both the Presbyterian and Congregational bodies were full of the enthusiasm of youth. At the first Presbyterian Council (1877) the attempt was begun, under the leadership of Philip Schaff, to determine a consensus of Reformed confessions; the principles of Presbyterianism were announced in five papers, and a further three papers were delivered on the eldership as a distinctively Reformed phenomenon. The Presbyterians attempted to devise a consensus confessional statement for the Alliance as a whole, but without success. Not surprisingly, the quatercentenary of Calvin's birth was marked by numerous papers at the ninth Presbyterian Council (1909).

For their part, the Congregationalists at their first Council (1891) devoted much attention to their heritage, polity, and witness vis-à-vis the state and the world. This concentration upon matters familial was quite understandable. These were, after all, the first gatherings of their kind, and the sense of corporate identity and of a common basis were important desiderata. It must be said, however, that for the most part the papers and discussions on confessional interests at the first and at subsequent councils were not triumphalist or narrowly sectarian in spirit.

With its considerations of unbelief, spiritual life, and Christian nurture, the first Presbyterian Council was introducing further subjects that were to feature largely in both Councils up to 1914, though in their concern for worship and the sacraments the Presbyterians outstripped the Congregationalists in the early period. At the second Presbyterian Council (1880) the themes of mission and the social witness of the church became prominent, the latter remaining so throughout the Alliance's history, the former being *theologically* raised throughout the history, though the hearing of reports from the mission fields ceased with the fifteenth Presbyterian Council (1937). No doubt in our first period the weight of Alliance opinion was on the side of those who believed that there was a world to be won, and that this entailed both mission abroad (and cooperation with others therein) and social witness at home. Under the latter heading came such themes as the temperance question and Sabbath observance, both of which scarcely survived on the Alliance agenda after the First World War (though both have continued to exercise some of the Alliance member churches). But questions of work and wealth, peace and war, politics and international relations were also given detailed treatment. Nor was the treatment of issues only in general terms. For example, the sixth Presbyterian Council (1896) recorded its protest against the treatment of the Armenians in the Ottoman Empire.[20]

Underlying all was the question "What is the heart of gospel, and how is the gospel to be related to contemporary thought and life?" On "life" we have already commented, but what of "thought"?

In the early years of the Alliance evolutionary thought and the question of the appropriate response to modern biblical criticism were high on the theological agenda. The prevalent post-Hegelian immanentism and the rediscovery in some quarters of Alexandrian Christology were prompting the modification (some said the erosion) of certain doctrinal formulations—especially those concerning soteriology (the penal substitutionary theory of the atonement came under increasing attack) and eschatology (the possibility of eternal punishment was dismissed by many). In certain liberal theological quarters an optimism in humanity and in human progress prevailed that in some cases not even the horrors of the First World War could entirely dispel.[21] This optimism was frequently accompanied by what now appear to be somewhat sentimental invocations of the Fatherhood of God and the Brotherhood of Man (capital letters being then much in vogue!). All of these matters were thoroughly aired up to the First World War.

Right through the First World War P. T. Forsyth was prominent in seeking to recall the church to the idea that God's love is *holy* love, and that sin has to be reckoned with. He spelled out the implications of this for doctrine, church order, and Christian living, using a veritable avalanche of aphorisms in which some delighted and under which a few were utterly submerged. Forsyth's Christological emphasis was echoed (at first unconsciously) by Karl Barth after the war. Although Barth's direct contributions to the work of the Alliance were few, his influence was great, and we shall need more than one occasion to note the increasing importance of the Christological motif in the Alliance's theological work.

Our reference to the First World War prompts a digression concerning both world wars.

We might have expected theological reflection from the Alliance in time of war. But precisely because of the wars the activities of such bodies as the Alliance were seriously curtailed, especially in the councils of the Presbyterian and Congregational bodies. Precisely from the councils we derive the bulk of the theological reflection of the pre-1970 Alliance. Thus, whereas the first ten Presbyterian Councils were held every three to five years, there was a gap from 1913 to 1921. A period of twelve years separated the Congregational Councils of 1908 and 1920. Again, the Presbyterians met in council in 1937, and not thereafter until 1948; while the Congregationalists did not meet in council from 1930 until 1949—a period of nineteen years. We by no means suggest that the respective international bodies were inactive during wartime. On the contrary, much was done to foster fellowship and to offer assistance during those dark days—and Marcel Pradervand has told the story. But the major theological platforms were removed by the wars, and this goes a long way towards explaining the paucity of *corporate* Alliance theological reflection at certain crucial points in this century's history.

1920-1939

Turning now to our second period, 1920-1939, we find that the fourth Congregational Council met in 1920, shortly after the signing of the Treaty of Versailles. Memories of war were fresh in delegates' minds, and questions of reconstruction were much debated. For the first time the council received reports from previously appointed commissions. Among these was one on "The International Obligations Laid upon the Church of Christ by Present Conditions and the Special Bearing of These upon Congregationalism." It was signed by J. G. Hurst and F. J. C. Hearnshaw, who argued that precisely because of its freedom from the state, Congregationalism was free to cooperate with such bodies as the League of Nations. A minority report was submitted by Leyton Richards, the pacifist occupant of R. W. Dale's old pulpit in Birmingham. Richards sought a much closer application of the principles of the Sermon on the Mount to the problems of the day.

Other commissions considered the contribution of Congregationalism to modern thought and to civil and religious liberty, and discussed Congregational polity—not a surprising conjunction of topics in view of the fact that the fourth council was meeting in Boston during the Pilgrim tercentenary. In the wake of the Edinburgh Missionary Conference of 1910 a further commission reported on "Congregationalism and Unity"—a theme which was to become increasingly important in both Councils during our second period, and which remains so to this day. This early Congregational commission on the subject was both cautionary and at the same time convinced that Congregationalism had something to offer: "If Church Unity is to be achieved in the near future, it cannot be on the basis of any single intellectual statement of belief, but may be achieved by some expression of common consecration and Christian purpose as is embodied in the traditional 'covenant' of Congregationalism."[22]

In the same month in which the Congregationalists met in Boston the Lambeth Conference met in London. The Anglican bishops issued an "Appeal to All Christian People" for reunion, and this appeal was much in the minds of the delegates to the eleventh Presbyterian Council

(1921). On the vexed issue of the ministry, P. Carnegie Simpson uttered what must rank as a prophetic word: "If we start by making the ministry the primary issue and if we say we cannot recognize the Church standing of communions which have not ministerial order as we hold it, then Reunion has no future." We must, he said, start with the church.[23]

At the twelfth Presbyterian Council (1925) a proposal to seek a common confession for the Reformed family was adopted, but as in the earlier years of the Presbyterian Alliance the attempt was subsequently abandoned. The theme of the unity was again to the fore at the thirteenth Presbyterian Council (1929), at which delegates heard reports on the Lausanne Conference on Faith and Order (1927). We shall later refer to the positive statement of Lewis S. Mudge, but in order to show that not all were starry-eyed about Lausanne we may quote from William E. Barton's address at the fifth Congregational Council (1930):

> Of the noble and scholarly and consecrated body which assembled in Lausanne, I wish to say only two things. The first is that while it called itself, and undertook to be, a World Conference on Faith and Order, it was not quite all of that. There was very little conference on Faith, for we found ourselves essentially agreed about Faith. It was not a conference on Order, for there we did nothing but to register our disagreements. It was not precisely a World Conference, for Rome hardly cast a contemptuous glance in our direction, and the Greek Churches withdrew as soon as they discovered what it was all about. It was a Conference of European and American Protestants, and of missionaries from those countries. . . . Our serious clashes were in the third and final week. Heaven alone knows how far apart we might have been had the Conference continued for a fourth week.[24]

This may be adjudged either a jaundiced or a swashbucklingly realistic response.

The question of Christian unity was raised again at the fourteenth Presbyterian Council (1933), especially by W. A. Curtis,[25] who in the wake of the recent commemoration of the Marburg Colloquy between Luther and Zwingli appealed for closer relations with Lutheranism. But the council was overshadowed by the menace represented by Hitler's rise to power and the plight of German Jews. Delegates were given the text of Karl Barth's "A Theological Declaration for the Form of the Church" which underlined the problems, and the council promulgated its own "manifesto and appeal on public questions in religion and morals," to which we shall refer on more than one subsequent occasion. Amid all of this urgent concern R. A. S. Macalister's address on "Early Metrical Psalmody in the Presbyterian Churches" (with musical illustrations unique in Alliance *Proceedings*) might well have appeared as an oasis of calm to some and as an irrelevant antiquarianism to others.

In even more forbidding circumstances the fifteenth Presbyterian Council met in Montreal (1937). The authority of the church and worship were treated, but there was special concern for the Confessing Church in Germany. Although Dr. Haitjema was able to present a paper on "The Bible and the Confessions as the Foundation of the Reformed Faith" without referring to the earnest contemporary confessing occurring so near to his native Holland, other speakers made good the omission. R. C. Gillie quoted part of the Barmen Declaration in his address,[26] and a resolution expressing solidarity with the Confessing Church was unanimously adopted.[27]

1945-1970

Our third period begins in 1945. We shall find that many themes—theology, ecclesiology, ecumenism, socio-political witness—are carried forward, but that others—temperance, Sabbath observance, the hearing of missionary reports, detailed reflection upon the thought of the age—are dropped. We shall reflect on possible reasons for these changes of agenda when we deal systematically with our themes. Suffice it now to ask: "What were the main emphases in the period 1945-1970?"

In 1948 the Presbyterian Alliance met for its sixteenth council in Geneva—the first council to be held outside of North America and Britain. Delegates were divided into six study groups as follows: (a) the historical confessions and the present witness of the church; (b) freedom and justice in the light of the Bible; (c) Presbyterianism and the present ecumenical situation; (d) the forms of Reformed worship; (e) what is fundamental in church order? (f) the church in the modern world. We might at first sight seem here to have "the mixture as before," but when we explore our themes in detail we shall note a marked change of accent. There is a *realism* about the hopes and fears of the age, and there is a Christological centering of much of the thought which is inspired by Barthian influence on the one hand, and by the "rediscovery" of Forsyth (especially in Congregational circles) on the other.[28] The council welcomed the forthcoming Amsterdam meeting (1948) at which the World Council of Churches was to be established, and resolved that its own stance vis-à-vis the World Council would be cooperative and complementary. As an earnest of its good intentions in this matter the same council resolved to remove its base from Edinburgh to Geneva. Since January 1949 the activities of the Alliance have been centered there. Further cohesion was given to the work of the Alliance by the council's decision to appoint an international executive committee under whose auspices the total program of the Alliance—including the contributions of its Eastern (that is, European) and Western (North American) sections—would be conducted.

The Congregationalists too organized themselves for postwar challenges. An international committee met in Bournemouth in 1947, and decided to hold the next council at Wellesley, Massachusetts, in 1949. It also agreed that an international office should be established in London, and it invited Sidney M. Berry to be the first permanent secretary. These plans came to fruition, and at the sixth council (1949) a constitution was adopted to govern the *organization* (where previously there had been a constitution for the ordering of the councils only). Among the papers were those on "The Gospel, the Church and Church Order," "The Gospel, the Church and the World's Disorder," and the "Congregational Contribution to World Order." For the first time in an Alliance council there was a paper on Christianity in what was explicitly designated "the atomic age." At the seventh Congregational Council (1953) papers were presented on "The Foundation in Christ," and on Congregationalism vis-à-vis the local church, denominational structures, catholicity, and Christian unity. Church and state issues were handled, and we have the first Alliance paper on the question of race: "The Middle Wall of Partition," delivered by Arthur D. Gray, a black American. Public addresses were given on "The Work of the World Council of Churches," by W. A. Visser 't Hooft, its General Secretary, and by others on "The Church and the Stateless" and "The Church in International Affairs."

The theme of the seventeenth Presbyterian Council which met at Princeton (1954) was "The Witness of the Reformed Churches in the World of Today." The themes covered were the ecumenical movement, the outreach of the church, the church's ministries, its freedom and responsibility, and the renewal of its inner life. The report of the discussions under the first heading declared that "as Reformed and Presbyterian Churches we bear witness to our fellow Christians that we recognize the ministry, sacraments, and membership of all Churches which, according to the Bible, confess Jesus Christ as Lord and Saviour. We invite and gladly welcome the members of all such Churches to the Table of our common Lord."[29]

At this council W. A. Visser 't Hooft delivered an address on work of the World Council of Churches, and it was resolved (in the wake of the Third World Conference on Faith and Order's "Lund principle" of 1952, which urged churches to do separately only what they could not in conscience do together) that the Presbyterian Alliance would not organize its own inter-church aid program as if in competition with that of the World Council of Churches. Though by no means the only factor in relations between the Alliance and the World Council of Churches (and on other aspects of the matter M. Pradervand's history has a good deal to say), the importance of the Lund principle for the Alliance's "complementary, not contradictory or duplicatory" stance vis-à-vis the World Council cannot be denied. The council further resolved to appoint a commission on ordination, and to appoint a committee to oversee the publication of Calvin's as-yet-unpublished sermons.

The eighth Congregational Council met at Hartford, Connecticut, in 1958, covering the themes of the witness of the local church and of the church to the ends of the earth, the nature of Christian unity, and the significance of the World Council of Churches for members of the Congregational Council. Area reviews covering the Near East, Africa, Europe, the Americas, and the Far East were presented. Of great significance for the future of the Alliance was the welcome given to an approach from the Presbyterian Alliance to discuss relationships between the two confessional bodies.[30] There had, of course, been numerous fraternal contacts between the two bodies, and as early as 1955 the moderator of the Congregational Council, S. Maurice Watts, had sent a letter to Marcel Pradervand, the general secretary of the Presbyterian Alliance, in which he asked: "Is there not some preliminary approach desirable between these two bodies?"[31] Pradervand broached the matter with his executive committee in 1956,[32] and in 1957 the first theological secretary of the Presbyterian Alliance, Lewis S. Mudge, wrote to the secretary of the Congregational Council, Ralph F. G. Calder, suggesting that conversations begin.[33] Thus was laid the foundation of the first union at an international level of two Christian world communions, an event effected and celebrated at the Uniting General Council which met at Nairobi in 1970.

On the way to Nairobi each world body held two further councils. In 1959 the Presbyterian Council met in São Paulo, Brazil, the first such council to be held in the southern hemisphere. The theme was "The Servant Lord and His Servant People," and the service of theology, the church, the Christian, and the state were treated in papers, many of which reflected the influence of the biblical theology of those years. It was this council which decided to create a department of theology. The decision to appoint a theological secretary had been taken by the executive committee in 1956, and Lewis Mudge entered upon the work in 1957. But now it was felt that the work should be advanced by the appointment of a department comprising members of the executive committee. This was done, and James I. McCord, the president of Princeton Theological Seminary, became the first chairman of the department.

Since the late 1950s councils have not had to provide such a large proportion of the Alliance's theological reflection as in earlier years, thanks to the work of the members of the department of theology and its secretary. This secretaryship and its associated department of theology (comprising approximately one third of the members of the executive committee) continues in the post-1970 Alliance. The department is charged with the responsibility of fostering theological sharing among the members of the family. This entails, first, assisting member churches as requested on theological matters; publicizing theological resources produced within the family—an important task given the relative lack of such resources in many of the member churches; maintaining links with the theological secretaries of member churches, and servicing a scholarship scheme for students. Second, the department is the vehicle for the representation of Reformed opinion in dialogues with other Christians and in consultations of various kinds. Third, the department's mandate requires that contact be maintained with Reformed theological colleges and faculties around the world—a requirement fulfilled by means of letters and lecture tours. Finally, and undergirding everything else, the department is expected to undertake and encourage research into the Reformed tradition, with special reference to its contemporary significance. As we shall see, the work of the department since its inception has resulted in a more continuous flow of theological material from the Alliance than was possible in the years prior to 1957. In this work a considerable number of theologians from all parts of the world have shared in a voluntary capacity. Apart from exemplifying good stewardship of resources, this method of working ensures that those engaged in the department's projects are people who are in constant touch with their own grass roots—an important dissuasive against ecumenical etherealism! Without doubt the most continuous and planned chapter in the Alliance's theological story opened with the appointment of a theological secretary in 1956 and the constitution of the department of theology in 1959. Among the early major studies undertaken by the department was that on "Catholicity," a study to which we shall refer below.

When the ninth Congregational Council met at Rotterdam in 1962 it heard a wide variety of addresses. The main theme was "Essentials of Faith," but papers were also delivered on "Science, Faith and the Church," "Erasmus," "The Remonstrants," "Worship in Contemporary Congregationalism," and "Faith and Despair in Modern European Literature" and in "Contemporary Literature."

Two years later the Presbyterian Council met, for the nineteenth time, in Frankfurt. The theme, "Come, Creator Spirit!" was treated under these headings: for the re-making of man, for the renewal of worship and witness, for the calling of the churches together, and for the redemption of the world. At Frankfurt a note sounded from the very beginning of the Presbyterian Alliance was struck once again: "We cannot treat as absolute any of the structures and confessions which we inherit; in our very loyalty, we must be ready to go wherever the Spirit leads, even if it be through that death which leads to new life."[34]

The tenth and last meeting of the Congregational Council took place at Swansea, Wales, in 1966. Its theme, significantly, was "A Reformed Church in a New Age: Reformed Faith and Congregational Churchmanship in an Ecumenical Era." John Huxtable spoke on "Congregational Churchmanship and Reformed Faith," and did not omit to mention the Anabaptist strand in Congregationalism's heritage. Ernest E. Long spoke on "The Council and the Alliance"—this with the forthcoming union much in view; and that Congregationalists were aware that others besides themselves and the Presbyterians were thinking ecumenical thoughts is clear from George Caird's paper on "The Second Vatican Council." By a happy inspiration the closing address of the tenth council was given not by one from those English-speaking lands which were always Congregationalism's major spheres of service, but by Olle Engstrom of the Swedish Mission Covenant Church. The tenth council resolved to proceed to unite with the Presbyterian Alliance, and in 1966 the executive committee of the latter body did likewise.

1971-1982

Thus we come to the period of the World Alliance of Reformed Churches (Presbyterian and Congregational), the new and official title. We shall later consider the grounds on which the union took place, though implicit in what has already been said is the ecumenical motivation of both partners, the growing feeling that no insuperable theological obstacles separated the two communions, and the significance of the unions—in Canada, Zambia, and elsewhere—which embraced both Presbyterians and Congregationalists. It remains only to mention the theological themes pursued by the Uniting General Council (1970), the Centennial Consultation (1977), and the Ottawa Council of 1977.

The theme of the Uniting Council (Nairobi, 1970) was "God Reconciles and Makes Free," and this was dealt with in four sectional study groups, which related the concepts of reconciliation and freedom to creation, humanity, society, and the church. A report was received on the study of "Episkope" which had been undertaken by the department of theology. But a successful motion calling for a consultation with all

South African member churches on the question of race proved impossible to implement "in spite of all the efforts of the Alliance."[35]

The centenary of the first Presbyterian Council was marked in St. Andrews in 1977 by a centennial consultation[36] under the title "The Glory of God and the Future of Man." The participants reflected upon the glory of God in Jesus Christ, in his people, and in his world. There was no triumphalism here, but a confident rejoicing in the presence of God with his people as they confront the options of renewal or chaos in the fields of economics, politics, culture, and ecology.

The concept of glory was explicit and the eschatological dimension implicit in the theme of the twenty-second (1982) council of the Alliance: "Thine Is the Kingdom, the Power, and the Glory." The chairman of the department of theology, Jan Milič Lochman, introduced the theme, and it was discussed in relation to "The Power of Grace and the Graceless Powers," and "The Theatre of Glory and a Threatened Creation's Hope." Important though this theme was, there can be no doubt that it was the Alliance's "Resolution on Racism and South Africa" which caught the eye of the world's press and, indeed, yielded publicity the likes of which the Alliance had never known before. The council's action in calling the colored South African anti-apartheid leader Allan A. Boesak to be its president increased the sense of drama. On the basis of the gospel, and in the wake of statements made at its Frankfurt (1964) and Nairobi (1970) councils, the Alliance declared that "apartheid ('Separate Development') is a sin, and that the moral and theological justification of it is a travesty of the Gospel, and in its persistent disobedience to the Word of God, a theological heresy."[37] Here is the paramount example in the Alliance's history to date of the application of theological principles to a socio-political situation which was deemed to be the more obnoxious because of its allegedly biblical undergirding. Here too, with its suspension of two white Dutch Reformed member churches, the Alliance acted in a decidedly *ecclesial*, church-disciplinary way, and this despite its traditional stance as a fellowship whose resolutions have moral force only. The Ottawa resolution not only challenged the suspended member churches—and, indeed, all member churches—in the matter of racism; it also challenged the Alliance to review its own status as an international communion of Christians. We may suspect that the implications of the Ottawa resolution on racism will occupy the Alliance for some time to come.

Among the most concentrated theological activities of the Alliance since 1970 has been its program of dialogues with other Christian world communions. These dialogues owe much to the impetus of the Second Vatican Council, which prompted the Roman Catholic church to initiate official conversations with other Christians. An international joint committee of Lutheran and Reformed theologians met in July 1975 and recommended that a number of steps be taken to foster Lutheran-Reformed relations in various parts of the world, and to "actualize past cooperation commitments."[38] Although neither the Alliance nor the Lutheran World Federation pursued these matters at the time,[39] intensive work had already and independently been in progress in the regions. Thus, for example, the U.S.A. National Committee of the Lutheran World Federation and the North American Area of the Alliance were in official dialogue in 1962-66, 1972-74, and 1981-83.[40] Conversations between the same communions in Europe led to the Leuenberg Agreement of 1973, which among other things revoked classical confessional doctrinal condemnations of one side by the other, and advocated "table and pulpit fellowship"—a recommendation which has yet to overcome the obstacles of church law in some places.

Conversations preparatory to an international Orthodox-Reformed dialogue were held between the Alliance and the Ecumenical Patriarchate of Constantinople in 1979, 1981, and 1983.[41] At a further meeting in 1986 between the Alliance and representatives of most of the autocephalous Orthodox churches it was agreed to recommend the convening of a full international dialogue commission in 1988.

We are thus left with four completed international bilateral dialogues in which the Alliance has been involved: those with the Roman Catholic Secretariat for Promoting Christian Unity (1970-77), the Baptist World Alliance (1973-77), and the Anglican Consultative Council (1981-84).[42] The fourth international dialogue (1971-77) was among three partners: the Secretariat for Promoting Christian Unity, the Lutheran World Federation, and the Alliance. The theme, different in kind from that of the other dialogues, is indicated by the title of the dialogue report: *Theology of Marriage and the Problems of Mixed Marriages* (1977). We shall discuss these international reports in detail in chapters 4 and 6 below.[43]

III. The Nature and Status of the Alliance's Theological Work

In view of the diversity of histories, cultures, and ecclesiologies represented within the Alliance family it might seem prima facie unlikely that such a body could foster serious and coherent theological reflection. Certainly neither the council, the executive committee, nor the department of theology could conceivably serve as the *magisterium* of the Reformed family (even if every Reformed church in the world belonged to the Alliance, which is not so). The polities represented in the Alliance family are such as positively to discourage any magisterial aspirations: whether Presbyterian or Congregational, the emphasis has ever been upon the catholicity of the *local* church; and although "local" means here the local congregation and there the presbytery, on all sides there has been an ecclesiologically inspired disinclination to think in terms of church structures which begin "from the top down," so to speak. For precisely this reason, as we shall see, both Presbyterians and Congregationalists were scrupulously careful to underline the voluntary nature of their international bodies, and to emphasize the role of those bodies as making for mutual fellowship and common (though not binding) testimony. What the Alliance will make of the ecclesiological implications of the "Resolution on Racism" of 1982 remains to be seen.

In chapter 3 we shall consider the attempts which were made in the early days of the Presbyterian Alliance to devise a confession of faith for the entire Presbyterian family. The distinguished church historian Philip Schaff was heavily involved in this enterprise, but the attempt failed. Some would not have objected to a confession designed to rehearse the beliefs commonly held by Presbyterians, but some wished to use the proposed confession as a test of Alliance membership. It eventually became clear that given the variety of prevalent theological opinions within the Alliance it would be difficult (and possibly disruptive) to devise one formula for common assent. It would be even more disruptive to require subscription on the part of those churches seeking membership in the Alliance. Indeed, any requirement of subscription would have been embarrassing in the extreme—after all, the church of Calvin's Geneva had no confession of faith, and the theological position of the Cumberland Presbyterian Church was deemed by some to be dangerously Arminian.[44] Above all, it was realized that the Alliance is not a church but a fellowship of churches, each of which must reach its own confessional conclusions in its own way.

It did not follow from this that the Presbyterian Alliance had no doctrinal coherence, or that a form of church government alone held its members together. On the contrary, a close examination of the major confessions and catechisms of the Reformed family would reveal that in both the Presbyterian and Congregational streams certain doctrinal emphases recur through the ages, and that these are held in common by both wings of the family.[45] This is not to say that a certain number of doctrines are exclusive to the Reformed tradition. Neither the Reformers nor the Puritans set out to devise a Reformed theology in that sense. Rather, their intentions were catholic, and they sought to provide biblically based teaching. Moreover, those who produced the confessions and catechisms did not regard their own work as sacrosanct. Still, certain doctrinal emphases characterize Reformed teaching: the priority of the free grace of God, who is sovereign Lord of church and world; the maintenance of the Creator-creature distinction; the desire to claim the whole world for God; the concept of the people of God as, by his initiative, covenanted to him and to each other. All of these points of doctrine are part of the heritage of both Presbyterians and Congregationalists.

But no amount of commonly held beliefs would suffice to turn the Alliance's council, executive committee, or department of theology into a teaching authority for the whole family, to whose findings assent was required and expected. The theological work of the Alliance, like its work in other fields, is done on behalf of the member churches, and any results may or may not be used by them, as they wish. There is, of course, a moral obligation upon member churches to pay some attention to work that they commission through their own representatives; but they cannot be required to endorse any findings in toto. The published theological work of the Alliance comprises articles, books, and pamphlets—some commissioned, some unsolicited—together with the reports of consultations and dialogues held under Alliance auspices. The participants who report do not normally serve as delegates mandated to advance the particular views of their churches, but as those who bring their best scholarship and experience to whatever task may be at hand.

What kind of theological work is possible by these means? Clearly there is not and cannot be any such thing as an Alliance dogmatics. What we have are theological writings published under the auspices of an international body representing a remarkably diverse, yet definable, family of Christians. The Alliance's published theological work reflects that variety—even if it is not yet as fully reflective of it as one could wish. But the published work does not only reflect to some extent the variety within the family; the publications themselves vary, as we have seen. Some are more official than others; some are unsolicited. In a word, we may say that taken over the whole period of the Alliance's history the theological work published has been of an occasional nature.

It could hardly have been otherwise. We have seen that as far as the Presbyterian Alliance was concerned no permanently directed policy for theological work existed until 1957, when the first theological secretary took up his duties. Indeed, it was not until 1888 that the third Presbyterian Council resolved to appoint a full-time general secretary: W. G. Blaikie served in a voluntary capacity until that time. After 1954 the American and European sections appointed theological committees, but there was not always coordination between them. From 1879, the journal of the Alliance provided continuity (though there was a break in publication between the end of 1883 and the beginning of 1886),[46] but, as we have said, the bulk of the concentrated theological offerings were prepared for the general councils until the late 1950s. This was even truer for the Congregational Council which, as we have seen, did not have a permanent office until 1949. Its councils were less frequent than those of the Presbyterians, and its journal, *World Congregationalism,* was published only from January 1959 to January 1965. What Albert Peel wrote of the Congregational Council was to a lesser extent applicable to the Presbyterian Alliance:

> The International Congregational Council is like a subterranean river: for long it disappears from sight, and then for a brief period runs its course in the light of day: at times, though invisible, the sound of its rippling can be heard—like that of the Lost River in the White Mountains of New Hampshire—mainly in the minutes of the National Union Committees of the country where it is next to appear. Here, no doubt, continuity could be traced, but such international activity as there was in the intervals between the Councils was often personal and unofficial as much as representative and official.[47]

Not surprisingly, therefore, as we examine the publications of the Alliance we shall from time to time have to advert to lacunae in the material. The Alliance is not culpable in every case, however. We have already noted the gap imposed upon the Alliance's corporate reflections by the two world wars. Again, the Alliance has tended to regard such questions as Christian-Marxist dialogue and dialogue with people of other faiths as matters which, in the spirit of its policy decision taken at Amsterdam (1948) and of the Lund principle, are best attended to through the World Council of Churches. The same may be said of the question of missiology in relation to people of other faiths. Here is a field of wider-than-Reformed interest, and Reformed theologians are able to make their contribution through the World Council of Churches. The Alliance is not, of course, precluded from reviewing such corporate work on Marxism, other faiths, and missiology, but it had not done so up to 1982.

In our opinion one of the most serious deficiencies in the material is represented by the dramatic decline since about 1930 in engagement with the prevailing philosophical climate. The brevity of the fifth chapter witnesses to this sorry decline—a decline which was not even checked by the more theological challenges posed by the secularization debate of the 1960s.

In the conclusion we shall enumerate the tasks which seem to arise from our consideration of the Alliance's corpus. We shall have to be realistic, for the Alliance's international office is modest, finance is scarce, and there are clear limits to what the permanent secretariat can undertake. But it has been ever thus, and, as we suggested earlier, the implications are by no means entirely adverse. We certainly hope, however, that the circle of voluntary helpers will become ever wider—and with this we come to our concluding introductory reflection.

Although "World" and "International" have been part of the official titles of the Alliance institutions from the beginning, it has not been easy to create the sense of a truly global, mutually supportive family. Distance and finance posed obvious problems, as did the logistical problems posed by the multilingual nature of the constituencies. Again, at the regional level members of the Reformed family have not always felt very close to each other, and the challenge of unity and union *within* the Reformed family has yet to be fully taken up around the world. Yet again, partly perhaps because over much of the period there has not been the sense of an ongoing theological policy with its own momentum, member churches have not always considered consulting with the Alliance in connection with their own theological concerns. Further, it cannot be denied that at least until the 1947 Presbyterian Council held in Geneva the Alliance appeared to be too much like an Anglo-Saxon club. After forty years of existence, the Alliance drew to its tenth council at Aberdeen (1913) only eleven delegates from the European churches (eight of them from Hungary); the same number appeared at the thirteenth council (1929), though none was present from Asia; and when he commented on the situation at the time of the Princeton Council of 1954 M. Pradervand could say, "The Alliance was not yet a 'world' organization in the full sense of the word."[48] There was soon movement, however. At the Presbyterian Council of 1964 over one third of the official delegates represented the younger churches, and in membership those churches now comprised more than fifty percent of the Alliance's ninety-five member churches. The movement to fuller participation has continued, and at Ottawa in 1982 delegates from 132 member churches were present.

The fact that global participation has come about only gradually (and it must be remembered that about half of the current member churches of the Alliance were founded since its establishment, most of them in Africa, Latin America, and Asia) has had clear implications for the theological work of the Alliance. It takes time for indigenous theological expertise to develop, but happily this has happened and is happening in many places. We may hope that such a consultation as that held by the Alliance at Bali (1985) on "Gospel and Cultures," though outside the scope of our present work, is a harbinger of much more theological participation and variety to come.

2

The Faith of the Ages

In this chapter the main lines of Christian doctrine are presented and discussed as they have emerged in Alliance literature. In the interest of clarity we shall classify our material under the traditional headings of systematic theology, though we shall reserve our major treatment of ecclesiology to chapters 3 and 4. Typically the trinitarian emphasis is implicit rather than explicit in the literature; certainly the concept of Trinity has not been subjected to detailed analysis under the auspices of the Alliance. We shall draw the trinitarian strands of thought together in our conclusion. Although in both Presbyterian and Congregational circles the use of creeds and the question of subscription have prompted the expression of divergent views (as we shall see in the next chapter), we have found nothing in the literature which does other than respect the creeds of the "undivided" church.

I. The Doctrine of God

On 4 July 1877 the first General Presbyterian Council considered the "Consensus of Reformed Confessions." We may conveniently use some of the sections of the paper by W. Krafft of Bonn to indicate the Alliance's terminus a quo. Krafft pointed out that whereas in some Reformed confessions—notably the Westminster—the doctrine of the holy Scripture is placed first because the Bible is the source and standard of Christian truth, the majority begin from the article "De Deo"; and that this is more in keeping with the ecumenical confessions of the catholic church. Krafft's consensus statements on God's being and revelation are as follows:

24

> We believe and confess that there is only one living and true God, to
> whom alone our worship is due, a simple, spiritual Being, eternal,
> infinite, unchangeable, immense, almighty, who is perfect, wise, good,
> and righteous.

> We believe that this living God has revealed himself to men, first, by
> his works in the creation and government of the world, but more
> clearly still by his Word.[1]

The traditional attributes are thus assigned to God in what is, properly, an affirmatory manner. Krafft's clause on God's revelation rightly
places the initiative with God, and traditionally asserts what has elsewhere
been called general and special revelation. That is to say, there is a general
revelation of God in all that he has made (*ex nihilo*—God does not make
out of anything: he *creates)*[2] and hence those who refuse this knowledge
of God are "without excuse" (Rom. 1:20). Special revelation is redemptive and is given through the Word. The question of interpreting special
revelation in this way is at the time of this writing coming increasingly to
the fore—not least within the Alliance family—as older missiological
thought and practice are giving way to a more sensitive, and at times
more ambiguous, stance vis-à-vis Eastern and other cultures.

As far as creation itself is concerned, this debate in the history of the
Alliance has gone through two main phases, and these are separated by
some seventy years. First, as the nineteenth century drew to a close
Alexander Gosman addressed the second Congregational Council (1899)
on the theme "Theology and the Order of Nature." The burden of his
message was that religion has nothing to fear from evolutionary thought.
The modern doctrine of evolution is not subversive of faith, for it is not
an account of origins; rather, it comprehensively illuminates the way in
which nature is ordered.[3] Like so many others of his age Gosman
construes "evolution" as "development" and reveals that to him it is far
more a *theme* than a scientific *theory.*[4]

The second phase of discussion is more significant from the point of
view of theological starting points. The Uniting General Council of 1970
took "God Reconciles and Makes Free" as its overall theme. Among the
topics considered was "Reconciliation and Creation." It was recognized
that whereas the message of reconciliation in the New Testament is
clearly addressed to man, "it is not addressed to him in isolation from his
fellows, or from his culture, or from the created world of which he is a
part."[5] Although the Genesis creation narratives have often prompted
systematicians and confessors to begin from creation, "the foundation of
Israel's faith was in the redeeming act of God, in the deliverance from
Egypt."[6]

In the report on "Reconciliation and Creation" creation and re-creation are universally construed, with re-creation taking precedence. The influence of the biblical theology of the mid-twentieth century and of the ecumenical (and biblical) vision of the reconciliation of the "whole inhabited earth" is clear in all of this. The methodological implication is that confessing Christ should begin not from the Bible as such, not from the doctrines of the being and attributes of God, not from the doctrine of creation, but from the fact of God's gracious redemptive act in Christ.

Concurrently, the ethical implications of this approach to creation received increasing attention. Thus, for example, the scientist John H. Reisner wrote a chapter on "Reconciliation and Creation" for the preparatory booklet issued prior to the 1970 Uniting Assembly. In a section entitled "The Stewardship of Creation," Reisner referred inter alia to the wanton exploitation of the world's wealth, claiming that "it is no exaggeration to say that, along with nuclear warfare and the population explosion, failure to care for natural creation has the potential to destroy man."[7] Again, the official study papers for the 1970 assembly included one by Hendrikus Berkhof on "Reconciliation and Creation: The Freedom of God's World." In it he chastised the churches of the Reformation for failing to hold "the personal and the cosmic elements of the faith together" in recent centuries.[8] Pietism and liberal individualism had been the order of the day. Nevertheless, "the reconciliation of men has priority over the reconciliation of structures" and as far as the former is concerned the reconciliation is costly to both God and man—it entails the payment of a price. Berkhof does not spell out the nature of this costliness in detail, though clearly the older understanding of God's impassibility is by implication ruled out, and the cosmic reference of reconciliation is clearly asserted.

The theme of the St. Andrews Centennial Consultation (1977) was "The Glory of God and the Future of Man." In a paper on "The Creation—God's Glory in His World" André Dumas related creation to eschatology: "The doctrine of creation points to the truth that everything comes from God, belongs to Him and lives by His grace, while eschatology, the doctrine of final redemption, announces the truth that everything moves towards God, and will be purified, liberated, and summed up in Him."[9]

In passing we may note an optimistic inevitability reminiscent of the evolutionary idealists of an earlier day, and we may justly remark that the apparent definition of eschatology as "the doctrine of final redemption" seems to leave out of account the more judgmental aspects of the four last things, thereby distorting the biblical witness, which gives no unqualified ground for the claim that all things (including all people) will be saved come what may. At the very least we have to place the parables of warning alongside the declaration that the exalted Christ will draw all men to himself. We may illustrate the movement (we do not use the judgmental term "progress") of thought during the century by reference to the following consensus statement presented by Krafft in 1877:

> We believe that God, to reveal his incomprehensible power, wisdom, and goodness, created all things out of nothing,—heaven and earth, and all that is therein; also the invisible spirits, of whom some have fallen away and perished, hence become the enemies of all good; the others have persevered in obedience and are glorified; and as the servants of God glorify him, and promote the salvation of his elect.[10]

There is an emphasis here upon God's motive in creation, and on the role of invisible glorified spirits in the promotion of the salvation of the elect.

It should be remembered that Krafft was asked to produce a consensus of Reformed confessional statements, and this he did. It is certainly not the case that all those who were present at the first Presbyterian Council meeting would have assented to every statement in it. But Krafft's work does provide a criterion for measuring the extent to which subsequent theological affirmations have modified, or even radically departed from, the traditional Reformed confessional position. In subsequent Alliance literature we do not find reference to the role of invisible spirits in the salvation of the elect.

The strength of Dumas's paper is that the created order is clearly seen as both the theater and the object of God's redemptive activity. The ethical implications of this were spelled out in the report of the group which discussed the paper. Economic, political, cultural, and ecological chaos were all attended to, and the prospect of renewal in each sphere was asserted. The report ends with this strong affirmation:

> "The world is the theatre of God's glory" (Calvin). He invites us to think of life and of history as a spectacle set within an arena prepared for it. Here human beings live as actors, but not as puppets. They live as performers who are watched by spectators with an interest either in promoting chaos or in promoting renewal for creation. God himself shares in the action, in addressing his sovereign concrete word to the Church and also by evoking from the world-wide range of actors the resolute contributions which serve his over-arching purpose. It is God himself who achieves the dénouement of the drama enacted in the vast theatre which is the world. We, therefore, must understand

ourselves neither as spectators nor as victims of a drama imposed upon us. We are actors, in the presence of interested observers to whom we often witness about the process of struggle between creation and chaos. In this drama God has already disclosed the full weight of his glory in the suffering endured on the world's behalf by Jesus at his crucifixion and in the beginning of deliverance for the world at his resurrection. For us, to live with the Holy Spirit is to accept, freely and communally, as our own the life of God which Jesus shares with his Father, where the suffering is put to the proof in history and the deliverance is tasted in joy.[11]

As we might expect, there is in the Alliance literature a considerable emphasis upon God's sovereignty, justice, and grace, though somewhat surprisingly it was not until the twelfth Presbyterian Council meeting (1925) that an entire paper was devoted to "The Sovereignty of God." It fell to John R. Mackay of the Free Church College, Edinburgh, to handle this "exceedingly lofty and solemn theme." Mackay defined sovereignty as God's "universal dominion, and, along with that, His absolute right to rule and carry out His own will in all His dominions," and declared that "His Sovereignty and His right to rule, are the crown and sceptre of the Living God. It has been the glory of the Reformed Church to have strained every nerve in order to do homage to this crown and sceptre of the Everlasting God."[12] He further explains that "the subject of God's Sovereignty is focused for us in the idea of an all-embracive plan, a plan which, because it is informed by His wisdom, is called His counsel; because it lies near His heart, is called His purpose; and, because it will all be assuredly realized, is called His decree."[13] God, says Mackay, is sovereign in creation, election, and redemption, and he claims with some justification that it was the personal experience of unmerited grace enjoyed by Paul, Augustine, and Calvin which histori-cally constituted the route by which the doctrine of "eternal Predestina-tion to life" came into the Reformed churches. Indeed, "there is nothing more characteristically Calvinistic than this insistence upon the need of regeneration, and the particularism of grace. Yet this particularism as with a view, not to isolation, but to union, association with the members of Christ's mystical body, and with that mystical body must we relate the ultimate renewal of heaven and earth."[14]

Mackay counters the objection that our free will is violated by the doctrine of the divine sovereignty by applauding "the doctrine of *concursus,* which renders Reformed teaching consistent with "the reality of secondary causes, the sincerity of the free offer of the Gospel, and the truth of free will in the sense in which free will is regarded as inalienable

(Westminster Conf. 10:1)."[15] Positively, Mackay finds that the doctrine of sovereignty gives humanity a worthy conception of what the universe is, and provides comfort, assurance, and encouragement to the saints. The knowledge that God has decreed that "righteousness, wedded to love, shall triumph on this earth" yields the only true ground for an optimistic outlook upon the world:

> The glory of the Mighty Lord
> Continue shall for ever,
> The Lord Jehovah shall rejoice
> In all His works together.[16]

In his address upon the same theme Eugen Sebestyén of Budapest agreed: "In our modern Calvinism we must bring back our great principle [that is, of the divine sovereignty], not only as a theological dogma, but as a *Weltanschauung* giving us a view of the world, and a programme for every phase of life." Every domain of life—the ethical, the political, the scientific, the social—is to be conceived from this perspective.[17]

No doubt, but much turns upon how this is done. The Reformed must confess that there have been and still are examples of the tracing back of all things into an inscrutable sovereign will which have obscured the fact that what Reformed theology—indeed, the Christian gospel itself—is primarily concerned with is an overflowing sovereign *grace* that fulfills but does not overturn the law. Our point was taken by W. A. Curtis in his presidential address to the fifteenth Presbyterian Council (1937):

> Let us in proclaiming the Divine Sovereignty and transcendence beware of enthroning in heaven the kind of despotism that in God's own name we abhor and resist on earth; of so disinheriting man and stripping him of the last vestiges of the Divine likeness and affinity as to refuse him even the character of the prodigal son, a son disillusioned of self-will, come to himself and fleeing from the swine-trough back to the father whose substance he had squandered in riotous living in the far country of his choice. Let us beware of formulating the standards of Divine judgment in such terms as to violate the compassionate mind of that Son of Man to whom the great white throne has been committed.[18]

These words constitute a plea for the priority of grace. Concerning that grace Malcolm Macleod had said this two Presbyterian Councils earlier (1929):

> Too apt are we to rob the word grace of its splendour. Not infrequently it has been used to denote something hard and narrow and

sectarian. So often we think of it as a perfumed sentiment, a smile of
amiability. But this is denuding the word of its glorious majesty. It is
denaturing it. Rather is it a forceful energy moving toward the race
with the might of the ocean tide. . . . Grace, like the ocean tide, is an
irresistible energy. It is an omnipotent thing. It can do what nothing
else can do. It can be merciful to the sinner. Grace is a great love that
enswathes humanity. It is grace that proclaims the forgiveness of sin.
Law cannot do that. Jesus Christ has made atonement for the world's
sin. The Church is commissioned to proclaim a full and free pardon
to every sinner.[19]

There is an omission of crucial importance here, however, and P. T.
Forsyth made good the deficiency in a major address to the Congregational Council of 1908. He here struck the note of the *holiness* of grace,
and related it to judgment and atonement:

> Christianity is concerned with God's holiness before all else; which
> issues to man as love, acts upon sin as grace, and exercises grace
> through judgment. The idea of God's holiness is inseparable from the
> idea of judgment as the mode by which grace goes into action. And
> by judgment is meant not merely the self-judgment which holy grace
> and love stir in man, but the acceptance by Christ of God's judgment
> on man's behalf and its conversion in him to our blessing by faith.[20]

We stand here at the threshold of the next of those traditional
"departments" of systematic theology: the person and work of Christ.
We shall, however, reverse the familiar order, first, because in the order
of our experience a satisfactory Christology is achieved only via a
satisfactory soteriology. No doubt Christ can only do what he does
because he is who he is, but we (like the apostles, for example, whose
use of the name "Lord" is largely post-resurrection) come to see who he
is through what he has done and still does. Second, we wish to redress
the balance of some modern Christological discussion and incarnational
theology which seem almost to divorce Christology from soteriology, the
incarnation from the atonement, leaving us with a "Christ-idea" and
with a Christianity which have lost their historical rootedness. The
scandal of particularity, we are convinced, is not thus to be avoided.
Elsewhere we find somewhat arid discussion of the two-nature doctrine
of the person of Christ which brackets the doxological motif in theology.
Nor will it be forgotten that *Soli deo gloria* is a perennial theme in
Reformed theology.[21] Therefore, since, as George Yule has said, "The
glory of God is grace, so *sola gratia* must be at the centre of the Church's

existence and not merely one of a number of doctrines,"[22] we turn to God's sovereignly gracious work in Christ.

II. The Work and Person of Christ

We may begin with Krafft's consensus statement "Of the Showing of God's Mercy in Christ toward Us":

> We believe that God has demonstrated His unbounded love and mercy to us by showing forth his righteousness on his own Son, when for our sin and guilt he gave him even to the death, and for our justification raised him up from the dead, that we through him might obtain immortality and eternal life.
>
> We believe that Jesus, our one only Mediator, by his voluntary obedience and his one sacrifice, which he offered to God in the death of the Cross, has fully satisfied the justice of the Father, and accomplished our reconciliation, so that we are accepted as righteous before God, though we are yet sinners, and therefore every other way of reconciliation with God, save this sacrifice offered once for all, is to be rejected.[23]

These are full-blooded statements, most of them echoing the biblical text, which make plain:

(a) That the redemptive initiative lies with God.

(b) That something had to be *done* at the cross, not simply *shown*. In a word, we have more than an "Abelardian" moral influence theory of the atonement here. (We place "Abelardian" in quotation marks to acknowledge the increasingly recognized fact that the moral influence theory of the atonement does not exhaust what Abelard had to say on the subject.)

(c) That although God gave up his Son to death, Jesus' obedience was voluntary. Here is an aspect of the mystery of the cross which must forever elude our attempts to "explain" it. However, the consensus statement rightly rules out any setting of the allegedly angry Father over against the compliant Son.

(d) That God's justice required to be satisfied. That is, he cannot, qua God, behave as if sin were of no account.

(e) That because of the action of God-in-Christ at the cross sinners are accepted as righteous.

(f) That every other route to salvation is to be rejected.

The last point here requires further comment, for it is less biblically defensible than the others. One would have expected, given that there is said to be "only one Mediator," that a consensus statement of Reformed confessions would categorically have asserted that there is no other way of salvation—just as in Krafft's consensus clause on prayer we are advised that "Christ is our one only Intercessor, through whom alone we have access to the Father." The majority of the textual references which Krafft cites without any difficulty affirm the exclusivity of Christ as Savior, and of them all Zwingli is the bluntest: "Christ is the only way to salvation for all who ever lived, do live or ever will live."[24] Could it be that Krafft was influenced at this point by the relatively recent Western scholarly "discovery" of the great religions of the world that prompted many to modify older statements of Christian exclusivity?[25]

Be that as it may, the early Alliance literature contains some impressive affirmations concerning the atoning work of God in Christ. At the meeting of the Presbyterian Council in 1880 both John Cairns and A. A. Hodge spoke on "The Vicarious Sacrifice of Christ." In a concise statement that defies summary the former put the matter in perspective thus:

> The atonement of Christ comes in as connected with the fall of man, and the gracious purpose of redemption. It presupposes on the one hand justice, and on the other mercy. There is a moral character and government of God to be dealt with, and a righteous sentence of law binding over the transgressor to penalty. Any scheme which does not recognize and proceed upon this moral order of the universe, is not in any proper sense atonement, but displacement of law; and in like manner any scheme which does not start with a merciful design and purpose of God, but brings in the atonement first to create this in the Divine mind, equally misconceives the question by attempting, and necessarily in vain, to produce that which, if it did not already exist in God, would preclude the whole saving process.[26]

Cairns further explains that, although in the last resort the elect only are saved, this does not make the offering of the gospel redundant, and he quotes the second series of Dort articles to prove it: "men do not perish in unbelief through any defect or insufficiency of the sacrifice of Christ offered on the cross, but through their own fault." He proceeds to argue that the idea of vicarious sacrifice harmonizes with humanity's universal sense of the need of expiation as evidenced by natural religion, with the Old Testament revelation, with the rest of Christian doctrine, and with Christian experience. His penultimate point is of great importance both for Christian doctrine and for our present ecumenical activity:

Now, there is one doctrine which above every other is correlative to atonement, and which seems to lose its place in the grand structure when this in the proper sense is denied. It is the doctrine of the divinity of Christ, or what indeed is but a deeper and wider foundation of the same doctrine—the Trinity. These doctrines, setting forth the necessity of so great a work and of so great a person to do it, disappear alike from modern Judaism, from Mohammedanism, and from a Socinianized Christianity. But can Christianity survive the extinction of mediation and the loss of a divine Mediator?[27]

This is a question which expects a resounding "No!"

In his paper Hodge draws the ecumenical implication. He claims that the doctrine of vicarious sacrifice is catholic. For however much the contending parties might differ over justification and the personal application of redemption, the doctrine of the vicarious sacrifice of Christ has been held in common by Roman Catholics and Protestants from the Reformation to the present day (that is, to 1880).[28] It is, moreover, the only view of Christ's work which makes such "subsidiary" lines as the moral influence theory in the least credible.[29]

At the third meeting of the Congregational Council (1908) P. T. Forsyth gave what in the present writer's opinion is the most substantial address delivered on any subject so far under Alliance auspices. His theme was "Forgiveness through Atonement: The Essential of Evangelical Christianity." We have already considered Forsyth's emphasis upon the holiness of God's love. In the same context he criticizes much Christian thought and worship: "What is lacking to current and weak religion is the very element supplied in the atoning cross as the reconciling judgment of the world."[30]

To Forsyth the way in which the death of Christ is interpreted is of crucial importance. He sets out from some of the deficient views of his time:

> To treat that death as more than a martyrdom, or to allow it more than a supreme degree of the moral effect upon us of all self-sacrifice, is called a gratuitous piece of theology. To treat it as anything more than the seal of Jesus's own faith in the love of God, or in his prophetic message of reconciliation is to sophisticate. To regard it as more than the closing incident in a life whose chief value lies in its history (which all the time criticism slowly dissolves), is a piece of perverse religious ingenuity much like the doctrine of Transubstantiation. To regard it as having anything to do with God's judgment on man's sin, or as being the ground of forgiveness, is a piece of grim Judaism or gloomy Paulinism. The death of Jesus had no more to do with sin than the

life of Jesus; and Jesus in his life made no such fuss about sin as
Christianity has done. The death of Jesus had really no more to do
with the conditions of forgiveness than one of Fox's [*sic*] martyrs.
Every man must make his own atonement; and Jesus did the same,
only on a scale corresponding to the undeniable greatness of his
personality, and impressive accordingly.

Such teaching removes Christ from the Godhead of grace and
makes him but the chief means of grace. It is not ours. In my humble
judgment it is quite foreign to Congregationalism, and incompatible
with it. For a Congregational church is not a band of disciples or
inquirers, but a community of believers, confessors, and regenerates
in Christ's cross. Congregationalism, as an evangelical body, has
stood, and stands, not only for the supreme value of Christ's death,
but for its prime value as atonement to a holy God, and as the only
atonement whereby man is just with God.[31]

Like Hodge, Forsyth emphasizes the catholic implications of the
doctrine of the atonement, and hence its ecumenical import; but whereas with Hodge it was a question of observing the continuity of belief as
between Catholic and Reformed, with Forsyth it is not so exclusively an
intellectual matter. Far from it. It is *vital* in the strictest sense of the word:
"To bring *sin* home, and *grace* home, then, the *Holy* must be brought
home. But that . . . can be done, on the scale of the church and the world,
only by replacing the *cross* at the centre of Christian faith and life, as an
atonement to this holy love. The centrality of the cross belongs to it only
as an atoning cross."[32] In Forsyth's view the very unity of the church
depends on the doctrine of the atonement:

It is here that the evangelical issue lies. It is here, and not upon the
nativity, that we part company with the Unitarians. It is here that the
unsure may test their crypto-unitarianism. I would unchurch none. I
would but clear the issue for the honest conscience. It is this that
determines whether a man is Unitarian or Evangelical, and it is this
that should guide his conscience as to his ecclesiastical associations.
Only if he hold that in the atoning cross of Christ the world was
redeemed by holy God once for all, that there, and only there, sin was
judged and broken, that there and only there the race was reconciled
and has its access to the face and grace of God—only then has he the
genius and the plerophory of the Gospel. If he hold to Christ on this
head, then whatever views he may hold on other heads, he is of the
Gospel company and the Evangelical pale.[33]

Still further, God's grace in atonement is constitutive of the church:
"The doctrine of the incarnation grew upon the church out of the

experience of Atonement. The church was forced on the deity of Christ to account for its saved existence in Christ. We can experience the redemption as we cannot the incarnation."[34] It follows that the church's

> witness to the divine act which called it into being and made it what it is, is on another footing from any matter of its polity of speculation. The church might have gone widely wrong on grave points like these without wrecking its own existence; but to have gone so widely wrong on the point I am treating would be for the church to commit suicide, to cease to be the thing that God once made, and practically to deny the Lord that bought it. For that there would be no repentance. The church of the papacy and the mass was reformable; but a church that renounced universally its atoning redemption would not be reformable. It would be extinct, however long it kept the name to live. All turns on the cross (i.e., the total person of Christ put into the cross) being the power creative of the church, and on the church's relation and witness to this source and secret of its life.[35]

This theme will recur in our work, especially when we come to consider the concept of "catholic," the sacraments of the church, and the basis of the Christian view of the world.

For the present, however, we prepare to pass from the work of Christ to his person. But before doing so we would make three points. First, it is disturbing to note that nothing as substantial as Forsyth's 1908 paper has subsequently appeared on the doctrine of the atonement in the Alliance literature. It is true that the theme of reconciliation has recurred, and in recent years. "God Reconciles and Makes Free" was, for example, the title of a paper presented on the council theme to the Nairobi meeting of 1970 by Jürgen Moltmann.[36] But here as so often the emphasis was upon God's reconciliation prompting us to walk the way of reconciliation, which in a divided world is also the way of suffering.

We in no way question this emphasis as such: it is integral to Christ's challenge to his people. But the question "What has God-in-Christ done for our redemption?" demands a clear and joyful answer in every generation. Here and there attempts have been made to supply the answer. For example, in a preparatory booklet to the Uniting Council of 1970 we read that "reconciliation defines the entire existence of the Church in the world: her origin in the saving work of Jesus Christ *and* her calling both as witness of God and as servant of mankind."[37] In the same book Donald G. Miller (with acknowledged indebtedness to Forsyth) declared of God that "He is reconciler solely as redeemer through his Son. The distinctive role of the Church in being a reconciling community . . . is to remind men that they may be truly reconciled to each other *only* as they are first reconciled 'to God' (Eph. 2:16)."[38] The striking of these notes is welcome, but, especially in view of the tendency we noted earlier for some theologians to employ "incarnation" almost as an atonement-avoiding concept, there is room for fresh major attention to the work of Christ, which would draw upon the rich cultural experience of the Reformed family.

Second, if as with Forsyth we believe the church is the creation of the atoning God, then the doctrine of the work of Christ ought to be more prominent in ecumenical discussions than has sometimes been the case. We record the point here, and shall resume it in chapter 4, where we shall be alive to the possibility that technical ecclesiological discussion has been less than clear on the divine work without which there would be no *one* church at all.

Third, the full-orbed Christian understanding of reconciliation through atonement needs to be reasserted against humanists and other competitors for the human mind, whose prescriptions for personal and social amelioration are not radical enough. This consideration will occupy us further in chapter 6.

The Person of Christ

In a characteristically crisp way Forsyth underlines the methodological point we made above: "It is the cross, then, that is the key to Christ. None but a Christ essentially divine could do what the church beyond all other knowledge knows the cross to have done for its soul. The divinity of Christ is what the church was driven to to explain the effect on it of the cross."[39] When he further points out that "the great question of the hour for the church's belief is Christological," he could almost have been speaking to our own times; Western theologians, for example, have, by ways as various as those of the post-Barthians and the investigators of *The Myth of God Incarnate* (1977), been raising afresh (if not always freshly) the question of the person of Christ. But in declaring that Christology was the question of the hour Forsyth made an important qualification which we *almost* wholeheartedly endorse: "The question of Christ is not the question of a divine hypostasis, but of a divine Saviour."[40] With the main point we are in sympathy; our hesitation arises from Forsyth's too strongly disjunctive mode of expression. From the fact that the happiest route to Christology is via soteriology it does not follow that the question of a divine hypostasis has no place in Christological discussion.

These considerations notwithstanding, the traditional creeds and confessions place the incarnation before the atonement, and Krafft's consensus of the Reformed confessions follows suit:

We believe that God's Only-begotten Son voluntarily took the form of a servant, became even as other men, and truly took to himself our human nature, with all its weaknesses, yet without sin, when he was conceived by the power of the Holy Ghost in the womb of the Virgin Mary.

We believe that by this conception the Divine and Human natures are truly and indissolubly joined and united in one person, Jesus Christ, though each of the two natures retains its own properties, so that the Divine nature remains, uncreated, infinite, filling all things; and the human nature has remained finite, retained form and dimensions, and, though the body of Jesus at his resurrection became possessed of immortality, yet it lost not its true human nature.[41]

As we examine these statements a number of points come to mind. First, there are clear echoes of biblical terminology here. For example, the clause, "truly took to himself our human nature, with all its weaknesses, yet without sin" is manifestly a conflated paraphrase of Philippians 2:6, 7 and Hebrews 4:15. Second, in the words on the two natures of Christ we have a summary echo of the Chalcedonian formula, and evidence that tradition as well as Scripture has shaped the Reformed testimony. Third, and most importantly from the standpoint of the obligation to confess the gospel in every age, we are prompted to note the distinction to be drawn (a) between the church's confession and the believer's testimony, and (b) between the church's confession and the theologian's system.

The church's confession of faith is always intended as a declaration of the things commonly believed by its members. (How confessions should be used is another matter, and it will occupy us later.) In the words quoted above, Krafft was quite correct in recording belief in the virgin birth of Christ as being an integral part of the consensus of Reformed confessions. However, we know quite well that at the time he wrote, that very doctrine was under attack in some—not least Reformed—quarters. According to one's point of view the "culprits" or the "saviors" were the higher criticism of the Bible and the new historical methodology.[42]

The pastoral implications are important at this point. The church must, on the one hand, deal sensitively with those of its members to whom parts of its teaching are difficult or even impossible to grasp (yet, sadly, even the Reformed have sometimes given the impression that a detailed "plan" of salvation has to be swallowed whole in order to receive salvation—a thoroughly "worksy" attitude!); on the other hand the church may not properly expunge the strong meat from its official declarations in the interests of those who can only digest milk. Even Forsyth, persuaded as he was of the centrality of the atoning cross, could say

> The saving action of Christ for many individuals begins there—in his life; especially to-day, and it only attains late unto the resurrection of the dead. We do ill to force the ripe experience of the cross on those who can as yet feel but its dawn. Any theology of atonement must be adjusted to the indubitable fact that Christ's forgiveness may and does reach personal cases apart from conscious reliance on his atoning work or grasp of its theology. To do otherwise would be to show ourselves the victims of a pedantic dogmatism or a theological papacy. To preach Christ is indeed fundamentally to preach his atonement, but it is not incessantly to preach about it.[43]

As to the relation between confess*ing* the faith and theological systems (of which confess*ions* of faith constitute summaries), we may note that these are different in kind, and that their starting points differ. On the same day on which Krafft's consensus was presented, Philip Schaff was found explaining that "the Reformed system went back to the ultimate source of free salvation in the ante-mundane eternal act of election, upon which the historical process of salvation in all its stages depends."[44] It must in fairness be pointed out that Schaff's context here is anthropology and soteriology; but even so we wonder whether it would not be clearer to say that the Reformed system on these points ultimately grounds upon the doctrine of the Trinity. But the main point is that however it may be vis-à-vis its confessional *system*, the Reformed tradition, when confess*ing* its faith in the sense of witnessing before the world, does not naturally *begin* either from an ante-mundane act of election or from the Trinity. In the order of Christian experience and proclamation these may be logically prior, but they are not the first matters to claim attention: and the primary need of humanity is not of correct doctrine but of new life. From the point of view of confess*ing*, therefore, the Alliance's 1982 study booklet, *Called to Witness to the Gospel Today* (to which we shall refer in more detail later), does well to express its "Central Affirmation" that Jesus Christ is Lord and Savior in the following terms:

> The message of Jesus Christ is the Good News of God's love. God sets us free. Despite our disobedience he does not abandon us to destruction and death. He has given his son Jesus Christ who died and rose

again so that we may have life. As we trust him in faith and live in communion with him we discover that we have been forgiven and can live life in thankfulness and praise. There is no other purpose for our life than to "glorify God and to enjoy him for ever."

Here is God's supreme revelation of his active grace and mercy, and of his judgment too; and no doubt our recent writers would agree with Thomas G. Apple who declared more than a century earlier that "we mean not to undervalue the universal, intuitive consciousness of God in man, nor the revelation in nature, reason, and conscience, but the knowledge of God obtained from this source does not support the revelation in Christ, but the revelation in Christ supports it."[45]

The fact that a church's confession is one thing and its act of confessing another does not, of course, absolve theologians from the challenging task of reflecting upon the person of Christ and the meaning of his incarnation. On the contrary they should be stimulated by the need to ensure that the confessing is not altogether out of accord with the confession. The Declaratory Acts of a number of Reformed churches bear witness to this kind of stimulation among theologians.

The remarks just made were prompted by Krafft's consensus of Reformed Christological affirmations. What else does Alliance literature reveal concerning Christology? In 1899, for example, we find Alfred Cave distinguishing between the Christ of history, the Christ of dogma, and the Christ of experience. In view of all the lives of Christ that had appeared—by Paulus, Strauss, Renan, Farrar, Edersheim, Didon— Cave could not resist the conclusion that the question of the historical Christ was of paramount importance in his day. He was concerned, however, that "in the search after the Christ of history you may divert attention from the Living Christ. . . . Settle the precise date of our Lord's birth, you have done interesting archaeological work, but your argument has brought no man nearer the kingdom of heaven."[46]

It cannot be denied that Cave helps his case by fastening upon a relatively insignificant detail. But if it could conclusively be demonstrated that Jesus never lived, or that having lived he was not raised from the dead, would these findings be simply the results of "interesting archaeological work," or would they be destructive of the Christian faith? Moreover, to complain that the demonstration of the exact date of Jesus' birth would not bring anyone nearer to the kingdom is a rhetorical non sequitur; for the objective of the historical investigation would not be evangelistic, and hence to complain that the fruits of evangelism were not forthcoming would be out of order. Nevertheless Cave declares that there is a Christ of history.

There is also the Christ of dogma. This

is a Christ of two natures, human and divine, but of one Personality. The Christ of Dogma is a Christ of three states—his state of preexistence, and his state of incarnation, and his state of glory. The Christ of Dogma is a Christ of three offices—in each of his three states he is our Prophet or Divine Teacher, our Priest or Divine Mediator, and our King or Divine Ruler. Now, I have no word to say against the Christ of Dogma. The theological attitude is inevitable. Nay, I have always found that those who object to doctrine in religion always do so for doctrinal reasons.[47]

However important the Christ of history and the Christ of dogma may be, the one indispensable Christ, says Cave, is the Christ of experience:

Know Christ historically and you know a picture of him more or less accurate. Know Christ doctrinally, and you know a definition of him more or less exact. Know Christ experimentally, and you know Christ himself. The Christ of History is man showing Christ; the Christ of Dogma is man showing Christ; the Christ of Experience is the Living Christ declaring himself.[48]

Undeniably many have a genuine experience of Christ (though the question of what the nature of such an experience is may be begged here) who are given neither to historical research nor to dogmatics. Undeniably there is more than one way of approaching the person of Christ. But to dissociate Cave's "three Christs" from one another is a temptation resolutely to be resisted. (We do not charge Cave with succumbing to this temptation, though the lack of qualification in his schema is disturbing.) Thus, we have already alluded to the indispensability of the historical for the "living Christ" if we are not to land in an idealized gnosticism or a sentimental religion of warm feelings. Again, the temptation to divorce "belief in" from "belief that" must be shunned—"anyone who comes to God must believe *that* he exists" (Heb. 11:6) (and this with questions of the logical placing of "God" and "exists" notwithstanding). Finally, if dogmatics be not permeated by vital experience its perspective will be awry and it will be arid indeed.

The fact remains that dogmatic questions need to be addressed, not least concerning the person of Christ, and Alliance literature provides no evidence that these have been studied in depth under Alliance auspices. No doubt in the later years of the nineteenth century and the early years of the twentieth century Cave's Christ of experience was much in vogue; in more recent years the theme of the servant Christ, with its implications for the church's mission, has received a good deal of attention in Alliance circles.[49] But of published Christological debate in its more technical and analytical sense there has been little. Now it might be objected that the assemblies, and even the publications, of Christian world communions are not the most appropriate contexts for such discussion. However, the member churches of the Alliance have received a tradition concerning the person of Christ which is, as we have demonstrated, Chalcedonian. Are not the representatives of those churches under some obligation to review such an important part of their confession from time to time— even if its terms are in the first instance remote from the actual act of confes*sing*? Is not this obligation the more weighty given the open denial of the worth of the Chalcedonian formula by many theologians, including some of the Reformed family? Is it conceivable that a large Christian world family has tacitly shelved Chalcedon? If this were the case would not the integrity of the family be at stake? These questions no doubt are overdramatized, and I do not actually believe that all is lost! But that there is a case for sustained reflection upon the person of Christ whom we confess—reflection in which the multicultural insights from within the Reformed family would now be clearly articulated—cannot be denied.

There are of course numerous Christological *assertions* in Alliance literature. Thus, for example, at the tenth Presbyterian Council (1913) W. Radcliffe declared that

> there can be no logical revolt against the doctrine of the Two Natures. That is but another expression for the Incarnation. If there be no Two Natures there can be no Incarnation, and if there be no Incarnation there can be no Christianity.[50]

In speaking thus Radcliffe was in opposition to those who would press the Christian faith into

> the crucible of a laboratory. The Word of God cannot be compressed into a philosophic formula, or a syllogism of the schools. The new phrases of today—"the mythical Christ," "the earlier Jesus," "the Progressive Incarnation," "the human legend," "the deified man," "the God in humanity," "the multiple personality,"—are but echoes of the Arian controversy, and repetitions of Pilate's irony, "Art thou a King, then?"[51]

This is lively swashbuckling rhetoric. Radcliffe perceives the way in which Chalcedon can serve to block off undesirable exits from orthodoxy; but he does not really make out a sustained case.

In our own time Hendrikus Berkhof has challenged Chalcedon on a broad front, offering two technical considerations in support of his view. His perfectly proper concern is that Christians today shall give their own answer to Jesus' question, "Who do you say that I am?" (Matt. 16:15; Mark 8:29). Berkhof's general point is that "we cannot refer back to the answer of our Hellenistic ancestors We live in a different world."[52] We cannot but feel that this is too strong a statement, and that its implications are damaging to the faith. First, if a statement of A.D. 451 can in no sense be authoritative for us because its framers inhabited "a different world," then a fortiori the New Testament documents cannot in any sense be authoritative for us because they are even older; and as for the Decalogue. . . .

Second, we may not deny that God the Holy Spirit has addressed his people through the Word in every age, even if they expressed what they understood him to say in their own terms and not ours (and what else should we expect?). We should deny God's providential leading if we were to take no notice of their conclusions. There is no reason at all why we should not adjust and refine our own doctrinal stances in relation to those of the fathers; indeed, when Christians have spurned the guidance implicit in this activity and have embraced the novel, the result has more frequently been the multiplication of idiosyncrasies (some of them destructive of faith) than the increase of truth. Third, there are problems in the phrase "a different world." As it stands it has too absolutist a ring. Of course in many ways the circumstances and habits of thought in A.D. 451 were different from those of our own time. For these reasons a measure of historical sympathy and ideological adjustment is necessary when reading Chalcedon—or any other literature from an earlier time or a different culture. But to recommend no contact with the past not only raises huge questions concerning the problem of time and the possibility of doctrinal development, but it also calls into question the possibility of universals in the gospel concerning man's need and God's gracious provision which are perennially—even eternally—relevant. Our own view is that, especially as far as the challenge of the gospel is concerned, there is not an absolute discontinuity between our time and former times. Even Chalcedon may yet have things to teach us, and among them may be the importance of the distinction to be drawn between a novel and a rooted theology.

When Berkhof proceeds to dissent from Chalcedon because of its language of "substance" and two natures, we sympathize with him given our much greater interest in Christ's work for us than in his personal constitution. We also agree that Chalcedon bequeathed numerous thorny problems to subsequent theologians; notable, as Berkhof declares, was the problem of dualism in the person of Christ. Concerning language we may say that however foreign talk of substance and two natures may be to our ears we should do the Chalcedonian fathers the justice of recognizing that they were using terms available to them to insist upon facts and realities, not imaginative constructs. As to the dualism, we ought in fairness to recall that the Chalcedonian phrase to the effect that "the Son and our Lord Jesus Christ is to be confessed as one and the same" was at least designed to exclude dualism. It is also helpful, when confronted by puzzling theological formulations, to ask the question, "What were these writers seeking to guard *against?*" In the case of Chalcedon we can then begin to see that the four famous adverbs which state that the Son of God has two natures—unconfusedly, immutably, indivisibly, and inseparably—stand as bulwarks against Eutychianism, Apollinarianism, and Nestorianism and that the affirmation that the Son is eternal and of one substance with the Father excludes Arianism. In this way, without solving all the problems and while giving rise to fresh ones, Chalcedon does indicate what needs to be maintained (however we do it) concerning the one competent to be our Savior, and it does set up warning beacons against inadequate views.

III. The Doctrine of Humanity

In older systems of Reformed dogmatics we often meet the doctrine of humanity before that of the person and work of Christ. The object was to show clearly the stages in the "plan of salvation": creation, man and the Fall, salvation accomplished and applied. There is, no doubt, something to be said for this arrangement, though it has too often been followed through in such a way as to exalt law above grace, and to separate the Father from the Son. To put it simply, God is the sovereign law-giver; man disobeyed, and God saved the situation by sending the Son in order to fulfill the penal requirements and to preserve a predetermined number of the elect. There is, however, much to be said for the view that we only really begin to see who man is when we have seen what God has done for him in Christ: the first word of the gospel is grace. As Johann Tibbe said in a 1964 Bible study paper on Romans 8:1-11:

> *In Christ* we can now be what we actually are, in truth: men whom God loves . . . the greatest service we owe and should perform for each other . . . is simply to remind each other, again and again, that the only place in God's sight where we can really live as human beings is *in Christ,* under his rule. For here we are no longer left to our own

devices. . . . Here we find our life firmly grasped by One who will not reject us. . . .

This also means, of course, that we are at last liberated from all our illusions about man. To minimize sin, to regard it as a merely relative imperfection, is now impossible. . . . That man should bend all his energy and effort to dispute the truth that God has already provided for man in the best possible way, that God has indeed already conferred great dignity on him—this is our sin.[53]

What, then, does the Alliance literature have to say concerning humanity? We may return in the first instance to Krafft's consensus of Reformed confessions:

We believe that God created man, male and female, perfect after his own image, gave him wisdom, righteousness, freedom of will, which was subject to change, and clear self-knowledge; that man, tempted by Satan, fell by his own guilt from the divine favour, and his nature is so wholly corrupt, that he cannot, by his own power, reason, and will, draw near to God.

We believe that this corruption as a debt (guilt) has descended as an inheritance to Adam's posterity, and this original sin is really sin, which manifests itself from youth upwards as evil concupiscence, and makes man wholly incapable of good, so that he can do nothing but sin.[54]

It is possible that there has been more "softening" of doctrine here than at any other point in the life of the Alliance. As Philip Schaff pointed out, the Reformers' anthropology was "entirely under the spell of the anti-Pelagian writings of St. Augustine."[55] Hodge underlined the point: Presbyterianism teaches that man's "apostasy was complete, and the spiritual depravity of his nature total."[56] All of this may be contrasted with the section on "Man" in M. J. Macleod's Presbyterian Council sermon of 1929. The everlasting gospel, he declares, teaches us that man *is* material, but not only material. He is a spiritual being, made for fellowship with God: "We can not only think God's thoughts after Him with the scholar, we can repeat His acts after Him with the saint."[57]

Undeniably man's dignity as a child of God, and the inference to be drawn as to man's worth from God's sending of his only begotten Son, could be, and often were, underplayed by Reformed anthropology of the stricter kind—and this in opposition to, for example, Calvin's *Institutes* II.i.11. But in Macleod's words there is no inkling that man needs help from his fellows—still less from God. We might diagnose Macleod's position as an optimism undeterred by the Bible, the Re-

formed tradition, or even World War I. Josef Hromadka in 1964 knew
better:

> The Gospel of Jesus of Nazareth reveals two aspects of humanity. On
> the one hand, the fact of the Incarnation points to a great mission and
> destiny of man. . . . In Jesus was integrated the integrity of man
> created unto the image of God, the supremacy of Holy Love and of
> loving holiness, on the one hand, and on the other, an unrestricted
> readiness to descend to the very depths of human depravity and
> corruption, of human shame and helplessness, of human misery and
> forlornness. And it was exactly this approach to men that revealed the
> way in which we should understand ourselves and our fellow men.[58]

Jesus as proper man is at once the revelation of true humanity and our
only hope.

We thus begin to see that only if we are realistic concerning our
nature, need, and potential can we explain the dogmatic necessity of an
atonement which was provided not for our instruction, not as an
example, not to be aesthetically appraised, but in order to rescue us.
Twenty years before Macleod's optimism, and six years before the First
World War, Forsyth lamented that "we have lost the sense of sin. . . .
And apart from sin grace has little meaning. The decay of the sense of
sin measures our loss of that central Christian idea; and it is a loss which
has only to go on to extinguish Christianity."[59] To Forsyth, as we have
seen, the disease was a result of the loss of the sense of the holy, and in
the end this loss makes God appear to be using a sledgehammer to crack
a nut when he provides atonement. If he is not holy and sin does not
matter, something much less dramatic would have sufficed. Later Alliance writers have underlined the point. For example, Donald G. Miller,
writing amid the fashionable humanism of the 1960s, has this to say:

> One does not quarrel, of course, with a Christian "humanism" which
> places the Christian on the side of true human values. Nor, for that
> matter, does one quarrel with a non-Christian humanism insofar as
> its aims are concerned. What one does stumble over, however, is the
> theory that humanistic goals may be ultimately achieved by forces
> generated purely within man. Essential humanism is man's rebellion
> against and alienation from God. This is man's slavery. How can that
> which has produced man's slavery set him free from that slavery? . . .
> All of man's efforts to possess a self-contained freedom, to find the
> meaning of life by his own wisdom, to build a worthy human society
> without God, are self-defeating, for they are a denial of man's essential
> nature.[60]

The word of the gospel is, however, that God does not leave us to our fate; that in Christ he provides for atonement; and that by the Holy Spirit sinners are regenerated, called to repentance, renewed, and united with the family of Christ, the church. It is this last clause which must now be developed further.

IV. The Holy Spirit

The Alliance literature is full of references to the regenerating work of the Holy Spirit. The Spirit takes the scales from our eyes so that we may see God in Christ; he unstops our ears that we may hear the Word of God. Although in his consensus Krafft did not devote an entire paragraph to the Spirit we may extract the following clauses: we become partakers of Christ's righteousness "only by faith, which the Word of God and the Holy Spirit awake in the hearts of men";[61] the catholic church is a "communion of all believers . . . who are . . . sanctified by his Spirit";[62] the communion of saints "by faith are united with Jesus Christ, their only Head, by his Spirit";[63] through the church's sacraments "God himself works in us by the power of the Holy Spirit."[64] These points are amplified in the literature, and, as we shall see, the discussion has been extended along a line *not* found in Krafft's consensus, namely, in relation to the Spirit and the world. It will make for clarity if we classify our remarks under the headings, "The Person of the Spirit," "The Spirit and the Believer," "The Spirit and the Church," and "The Spirit and the World."

The Person of the Spirit

In an article of 1963 entitled "Humanity and the Spirit" Jean Bosc makes a very important point:

> The earthly activity of the Spirit does not begin with the work of reconciliation, with the history of salvation. To suppose so would be to endanger the very unity of God, since the one God is at the beginning as well as at the end and at the centre of history, is Creator as well as Reconciler and Redeemer, and is always thrice the same Lord. Just as we are pardoned and regenerated in Jesus Christ through the Holy Spirit, so too it is in Jesus Christ and through the Holy Spirit that all things exist and we are men.[65]

Bosc thus cautions us against thinking of God the Holy Spirit *only* in connection with what older divines called "the application of redemption," crucial though the Spirit's work in that matter is. Accordingly, we shall first consider the Spirit per se.

In 1908 W. L. Walker addressed the third Congregational Council on "The Holy Spirit." This, it will be recalled, was the council that Forsyth addressed on the fundamental importance of forgiveness through atonement. When we place Walker's and Forsyth's addresses side by side we cannot but be struck by the difference in accent and by a crucial omission by Walker.

To Walker the Spirit—whose identity is developed in both the Old and New Testaments—is "the very inner life of God Himself, the source of the new holy life of the sons of God . . . an abiding presence."[66] This presence "in divine fulness came to men through *Christ*."[67] Hence the Bible identifies the Spirit with Christ as well as with God. The Spirit then is *"God himself in one of the modes of the divine being and manifestation."*[68] Though personal *in God*, "the Spirit *of* God cannot possibly be a separate person in the individual sense. The Holy Spirit is a 'Person' in the *Theological* sense, which is practically a *mode* of the divine being and manifestation." As if in anticipation of an objection Walker continues, "This is not Sabellianism, and *Tri-unity* must be kept clear of that virtual *Tritheism* which has been such a hindrance to the due recognition of the nature and work of the Spirit."[69]

According to Walker the Spirit is a spiritual influence who always requires a medium of manifestation, and "everything in creation and providence is to some extent a manifestation of God and, therefore, a medium of his Holy Spirit."[70] But the Spirit is supremely manifested in Christ:

> The great Christian truth is this; That the Holy Spirit that God is has been manifested in the fulness of ethical grace and truth in the life and work of Jesus Christ, and has gone forth therefrom in all the plenitude of divine spiritual power, and so that every human being may become its temple and live in spiritual and eternal unison with God. This is the consequence of the incarnation of God in Christ and of the at-one-ment of humanity to God in his Person and Cross. . . . In the Holy Spirit we have the consummation of Christianity, which is, therefore, distinctively, "the dispensation of the Spirit."[71]

The Holy Spirit, Walker continues, is the life of the individual Christian and of the church. The Spirit desires to reveal himself through us—indeed, "It is only *through us, and in no other way,* that God can act in the world or be manifested as God."[72] Walker here overlooks the fact that the church may become apostate, and if it does God will not be held ransom by it. But the gravest difficulty lies in Walker's appeal:

I know of nothing more solemn, more urgent than this "call of the Spirit." Only think! God is longing and waiting, God is moving within us, to do what he fain would do, but which he cannot effect except through us, any more than you or I could move without limbs or speak without vocal organs. If we are irresponsive to his Spirit we are not only hiding from men the God in whom we profess to believe, but we are making his manifestation in the world of the present impossible—impossible to God.[73]

Here we have the voice of liberal Arminianism. No doubt Christians need to be challenged to witness and to serve, but the gospel is that the *tragic* in our condition has been dealt with, and that our witnessing is not all our own work. Walker's last clause is uncomfortably close to the liberal slogan, "God needs you as much as you need God"—but what price a God who cannot move unless or until we give him permission? Even more serious is Walker's failure to take sufficient account of the Spirit's regenerating work. This deficiency runs through the address, and its root cause is that the doctrine of the Spirit is not sufficiently closely related to the doctrine of the atonement. Walker virtually forgets what Forsyth roundly declared elsewhere: "Christ's was a death on behalf of people within whom the power of responding had to be created."[74] This point leads us to consider regeneration.

The Holy Spirit and the Believer

"Regeneration" was John H. A. Bomberger's theme at the second Presbyterian Council, and he spoke in graphic style:

Redemption is not an economy or a covenant of grace which deals with man in a *merely* forensic, formal, commercial way, offering and applying salvation as it were *ab extra*. On the contrary, its great ultimate purpose with regard to man is [in the Reformed theologies] rightly conceived and claimed to be to beget and build up in him a *life* in essential correspondence with its own living heavenly source and nature. Under this economy, true godliness is not, primarily and chiefly, a dead name, but a vital power; not a sensuous form, but a spiritual fact. Its Christianity is not a sarcophagus, however elaborately hewn and gorgeously decorated by religious art. Its church is not a charnel-house of baptized corpses, though most profusely adorned with floral crosses, fragrant wreaths, and thornless crowns. It is a living temple, and as such must be built of "lively stones."[75]

The Spirit is he who quickens, begets, creates, renews; and in a passage which is so concisely written as to defy summary Bomberger declares that these different ways of speaking of the work of the Spirit agree on the following important points:

> First, that the change wrought in Regeneration affects the inmost vital spring and centre of man's being as a spiritual, rational, ethical person. Secondly, that it is a change wrought in full harmony with the original generic constitution and ethical nature of man as a distinct order of created being. Thirdly, that it is a change wrought by God, by his supernatural divine influence operating upon man in harmony with the ethical personal character he possesses by the design and will of his Creator. And finally, that whilst the grace effecting this result works an illumination of the understanding, turning its natural darkness into light—a cleansing of the heart, turning its carnal lusts into holy love, and a conquest of the rebellious will, bringing it into glad submission to the will and law of God—it does so by reaching back of these faculties of the human soul into the basis and centre of their unity and life, into man's inmost personality, and renewing, spiritually reviving, or resuscitating, recreating, re-begetting and regenerating that—but doing what is thus done on and in that human personality. Hence, it is *not* the purpose or aim of gospel regeneration to beget a new order of beings in the intelligent universe of God.[76]

In the prosecution of his work, Bomberger continues, the Spirit normally uses means, supremely that of the preaching of the gospel, for the Word and the Spirit who gave it are inseparable.[77] The sacraments are confirmatory signs and seals of the covenant of grace into which the believer has been called. Care is needed, however, in speaking of the new life of the Christian:

> Christ is *not* our life in any pantheistic sense. Nay, the mystical union established between the regenerated soul and him is not even a hypostatical union of their two natures. Man is not deified by regeneration. In it men become Christians, but are not made Christs.[78]

Bomberger sums matters up in a quotation from Ursinus. Regeneration "consists in a change of the corrupt mind and will into that which is good, produced by the Holy Ghost through the preaching of the law and the gospel, which is followed by a sincere desire to produce the fruits of repentance, and a conformity of the life to all the commands of God."[79]

We have dwelt at some length on the Spirit's regenerative work not only because of its importance in the Reformed tradition, but even more because of the relatively scant attention paid to it in Alliance literature in more recent years.[80] Of its practical importance for the believer there can be little doubt—we *cannot* take the credit for our own salvation;

unless the Spirit removes the scales from our eyes we cannot see. But if
this is true the implications for evangelism are clear. First, there can
properly be no "decisionism" which neglects to point out that those who
"decide for Christ" do so only by the Spirit's enabling. To overlook this
proviso can be almost cruel, for it means that people are being challenged to believe when that is the very thing which, unaided, they cannot
do. Again, unless we acknowledge the Spirit's sovereign freedom in his
regenerating work we run the risk of developing a breed of neurotic
evangelists who, having burned themselves out can only cry in despair,
"We piped and you did not dance!" In circles in which the evangelist's
success is computed (sometimes literally computed) in terms of the
number of decisions achieved, the danger is compounded, for this is an
unwarranted application of the sanctions of the marketplace to the
realm of grace. In the Alliance's most considerable collection of studies
on the Holy Spirit—those presented at the nineteenth Presbyterian
Council (1964)—Johann Tibbe struck the right note:

> When God does something, he does it thoroughly. He does not place
> this alluring hope of deliverance before us to shine like some distant
> dreamy object, leaving us to solve for ourselves the problem of how
> we are to reach it. He removes every justification for the plea that
> ultimately we are left to our own resources in this trackless wilderness
> of our life—a desert in which we shall finally perish. . . . We are
> deprived of all ground for complaint that we are incapable of hoisting
> ourselves up to God (though this is true enough) by the very fact that
> God himself comes to the aid of our weakness by his Spirit.[81]

Many other aspects of the Spirit's work are treated in the Alliance
literature. For example, William Caven addressed the fifth Presbyterian
Council (1892) on the Spirit as teacher, and David G. Wylie spoke to the
tenth such council (1913) on the fruits of the Spirit.[82] Again, the
nineteenth Presbyterian Council report (1964), "Come, Creator Spirit
—for the Remaking of Man" contrasted the "new man"—that is, man
renewed by the Spirit—with the "old man";[83] and frequent reference
has been made to the Spirit as sanctifier. But what is striking in more
recent Alliance publications on the Spirit is the increasing emphasis
upon the Spirit and the church and the Spirit and the world. To these
themes we now turn.

The Spirit and the Church

What brought the church into being? What made the legacy of Jesus
not simply a corpus of moral teachings, but a faith? Forsyth had his

answer, as we might expect: "It was the cross, when it came home by the resurrection through the Spirit."[84] The act of redemption and the calling of a renewed people into being—these twin and inseparable acts of God constitute the church. We here reaffirm the conviction which will underlie all that we shall later say concerning ecclesiology, and the intellectual and practical articulation of the faith.

As we have seen, the nineteenth Presbyterian Council wrestled with the theme "Come, Creator Spirit." In J. Tibbe's illuminating set of Bible studies on Romans 8, to which we have already referred, and in a wide-ranging if uneven collection of papers on the subject, many points of importance were made. Thus, for example, in a variety of ways the inseparable relation of the Spirit to the Word was emphasized. In his council sermon W. A. Visser 't Hooft said, "We have good reason to worry about the communicating of the Gospel to a rapidly changing world. But that must never become our deepest concern. The primary question is whether we have a living Gospel to preach . . . the word of divine authority which only the Holy Spirit can give us."[85] Albert Curry Winn dwelt on the Spirit as interpreter of the Word,[86] and T. F. Torrance declared that apart from "the one Word or self-revelation of God in Jesus Christ" the Spirit is not knowable at all.[87]

A recurrent theme is that by the Spirit believers are grafted into community: Otto Weber was among those who lodged a protest against a wrong individualism at this point.[88] There can be no doubt, however, that if Forsyth the Congregationalist gave the deepest and most challenging paper in the Alliance's corpus on the atonement, the Presbyterian T. F. Torrance was equally deep and just as challenging vis-à-vis the Holy Spirit. His paper "Come, Creator Spirit—for the Renewal of Worship" is not entirely unproblematic, however. Thus he asks,

> Does Pentecost mean that the Church is endowed with the Spirit as a gift for its possession and as the animating principle of its develop-ment? Or does it mean that, through the coming of the Spirit, the Church, in its earthly and historical pilgrimage, is made to participate in a perfected reality so that it lives out of a fulness above and beyond itself? Put bluntly and crudely: Does the Church possess the Spirit or is the Church possessed by the Spirit?[89]

Torrance opts for the second alternative, declaring that the first lands us in "a doctrine of the Church as the extending of the Incarnation, a Church that is still evolving and is yet to reach its completeness and will do so only when it brings to completion the redemptive work of Christ."[90] We likewise have no interest in defending the notion that the church is the extension of the Incarnation—"That which owes itself to a rebirth cannot be the prolongation of the ever sinless"[91]—and we do not think that Torrance's first alternative need lead in that direction. Indeed, we cannot accept the disjunction proposed here. Where Torrance says, "either . . . or" we wish to say "both . . . and," and we feel that this is consistent with the Bible and with that Christian eschatology which proclaims that the church lives between the times. Christ does give the Spirit to his people (though not because his work is unfinished), and they do participate in (that is, have a foretaste and pledge of) a perfect reality and live out of a fullness above and beyond themselves.

For Torrance the Spirit is constitutive of the church: "In coming upon the Church, the Holy Spirit constitutes it the Body of Christ on earth in union with its Head, the risen and ascended Lord."[92] Moreover, "It is [the Spirit's] office constantly to call the Church out of the world and to create it as the sphere within which He realizes and perpetuates among men God's own witness to Himself."[93] As to the Spirit and the renewal of the church, we are left in no doubt as to Torrance's prescription:

> Let it be said quite bluntly that what we need urgently is a renewal of faith: of belief in Jesus Christ as, in reality, God Himself incarnate among men, of belief in the Cross as indeed the objective intervention of God in human existence for the salvation of mankind, and of belief in the resurrection of Jesus Christ from the dead in body as the first-fruits of the new creation. The renewal of our witness will only come as we surrender ourselves to the miraculous divine power of the Creator Spirit, and commit ourselves to faith in Jesus Christ as God and Saviour.[94]

The Spirit and the World

The witness, of course, is in the world, and in 1964 the nineteenth Presbyterian Council gave much attention to this fact. The church is to be in, but not of, the world: "It does not exist so that the world will become Church. It exists so that the world will be renewed, will become God's new creation."[95] This, as a report to the following Uniting Council (1970) made plain, is an implication of trinitarian doctrine.[96] God is at work outside the bounds of the church. By the Spirit he is permeating, lifting up, glorifying, and transfiguring the whole creation. Here is the eschatological note once more: "it is the *creature* which is being perfected, not transmuted into something divine, and . . . this is something for which we wait in hope and experience only in foretaste. In this way, the work of the Father in creation and sustaining, the work of the Word in reconciling and renewing, and the work of the Spirit in leading the creation to its future are all affirmed as symbolizing the work of the one God in relation to his creatures."[97]

This is plainly a deliverance of faith. The question, "On what grounds may we pronounce that action *a* or incident *b* are signs of the Spirit's activity in the world, whereas action *y* and incident *z* are not?" does not admit an easy answer: "One cannot speak of the signs of the Spirit as unambiguously present in human life, whether the life of the individual, or of the Church or of the whole world. The signs themselves are normally visible to all. But in a profound sense, this new life is discernible only by faith."[98] We cannot declare that such and such activities, or effects, are God's without reference to what we know from revelation of his will: "When we see something that accords with God's known will, then we confess his operation in and with the ordinary processes of human activity."[99]

This statement leaves many questions unanswered. To take a stock case, we may say that God's known will is for peace. However, on this basis one *believer* will take up arms in time of war, while another *believer* will not. In absolute terms they cannot both be right; they may both be wrong; or one may be right and the other wrong. The point is that amid the ambiguities of this world, and given the varieties of religious experience and cultural formation, those who attempt absolute diagnostic precision are verging upon the incautious. In some of the most important matters we can but walk by faith.

But the main thrust of the Alliance's testimony on the Spirit and the world was crisply expressed by Lewis Mudge in *One Church: Catholic and Reformed,* a book written under the auspices of the department of theology: "If we are renewed by the Spirit of Jesus Christ, we are taken up into the cosmic work of renewal being carried on by God."[100] Something of what this means in practice was suggested in *The Creator Spirit in Secular Society* (1966). This pamphlet comprises reports of task forces set up by the North American Area Council of the Alliance with a view to pursuing the theme of the 1964 council further. Laymen with theologian abettors asked how the Spirit could be discovered in the areas of science and technology, the professions, business, social structures, and community relations. The reports contained valuable insights and suggested lines of desirable action. Though thin in size this volume is a testimony to the Reformed desire to claim the whole world for God, whose it is; and it exemplifies the ways in which theology may come alive in the situations of life. We in no way deny the importance of technical theology, but if there is no overflow from theology to world then the

Spirit has become the theologian's bread and butter, but not his life; and the attempt to "use" God is the oldest sin of all.

Though we have considered the Spirit's relation to the church and to the world, we have by no means exhausted Alliance deliverances on either church or world. The former will occupy us further in the next two chapters, and the latter in chapter 6. We conclude this chapter by rounding out the broad spectrum of the faith of the Christian ages to which, we maintain, the literature produced under the auspices of the Alliance has, on the whole, been faithful. This entails a few further remarks on eschatology, and the culmination of the whole in a note on the trinitarian thread which runs through Alliance literature.

V. Eschatology and Trinity

Taking the Alliance literature as a whole one must confess that neither eschatology nor the Trinity have received much detailed discussion. These doctrines, despite their admitted importance, have not aroused controversy in Alliance circles.

From time to time particular aspects of eschatology have been reviewed. Thus in the early days William Caven contributed an article on "The Immortality of the Soul and the New Testament" to *The Catholic Presbyterian*.[101] He here contended (in contrast with later biblical scholars who have dwelt on the Hebrew understanding of the person as a unity) that the Bible affirms a soul/body dualism. He argued against annihilationism (the then fashionable retreat from the alleged crudities of Calvinism), and he declared (innocent of the latter-day distinction drawn by biblical theologians between eternity and everlastingness) that both saved and lost souls "shall continue to exist for ever and ever."[102]

From the same period comes Krafft's Reformed consensus statement on eschatology:

> We believe and confess that our Lord Jesus Christ, when the number of the elect shall be completed, will come again to judge the quick and the dead, that the quick shall then be changed, the bodies of the dead raised up by the power of Christ, and that then all shall appear before the judgment-seat of Christ, to give account of their thoughts, words, and deeds, to receive, each according to the good or evil which he has done during his life in the body, the righteous, eternal life, but the godless, who have been disobedient to God, the punishment of everlasting suffering.[103]

As a consensus statement this is accurate enough: indeed, it says rather more on the subject than a number of early Reformed confessions do. On the other hand, it omits the emphasis on the perseverance of the saints found in the Westminster Confession (1643-47). Is it possible that a relative lack of detailed consideration of eschatology is characteristic of the Reformed tradition as such, and not simply of the literature written during the last 110 years under the auspices of the Alliance?

On a number of occasions those who have addressed councils have speculated upon the dearth of eschatological thought in the Reformed tradition. H. P. van Dusen offers two possible reasons: first, the Reformers' confidence in "the Sovereign God Himself, Creator and Ruler of men and of nations, who holds history as He holds the heavens in His omnipotent and omnicompetent control" was such as to inhibit futuristic exposition: they knew that all would be well and that sufficed. Second, since the Reformers had experienced "a fresh outpouring of the Living Spirit of God into their midst . . . they cherished good hope of a larger fulfilment of the Divine Intention for their societies here and now."[104] To these reasons Visser 't Hooft added a third: the fear of the wilder eschatologies of Reformation times.[105]

If not elaborated to any great extent in Alliance literature, changes (a less emotive term than "developments") in eschatological doctrine were noted. Thus the committee instructed to report in 1920 on "the contributions of British Congregationalism in the field of religious thought" observed that the poet Tennyson's *In Memoriam* "gave the signal for revolt" in eschatological matters. North of the border the Scottish Episcopalian layman Thomas Erskine of Linlathen remained with the Congregationalists in Dumfries until his views on universal salvation "became too advanced for our brethren to endure."[106] The influence of F. D. Maurice was pervasive on the question of eternal punishment, and such Congregationalists as Baldwin Brown and Caleb Scott stood in his line. Meanwhile Edward White became an exponent of conditional immortality, and to this cause R. W. Dale gave his considerable support. For his part, A. M. Fairbairn stood firmly against annihilationism: he announced in his determined fashion that "'Deity *could* not' annihilate rational creatures who were his very children. Another way of escape was chosen. On speculative and moral grounds, without claiming any direct support from Scripture, Fairbairn taught that there will be indeterminate punishment for sin in the hereafter, with endless opportunity for repentance and for return to God."[107]

But, to repeat, none of this discussion was seriously aired within either the Congregational or the Presbyterian Councils. Some, among them H. A. Stimson in 1891, were quite happy that this should be so:

You men of the schools are speculating upon the possible conditions of immortality by-and-by; the men at the front are labouring to awaken their fellows to know that they have souls now. You are dallying with hypotheses of a second probation; they are fighting a defiant, all-destroying, present devil.[108]

It would, however, have taken more than the relative silence of the Reformed ages to inhibit T. F. Torrance. In three pages of highly concentrated dogmatics he made a powerful plea that we recover Calvin's Christo-eschatological emphasis. For Calvin

> eschatology is the application of Christology to the work of the Church in history. . . . Because we are united to Christ who is bone of our bone and flesh of our flesh, and participate in the risen humanity of Jesus, that eschatology is essential to our faith. Union with Christ means union with the Christ who rose again from the dead, who ascended to the right hand of the Father and who will come again; and therefore union with Christ here and now carries in its heart the outreach of faith toward the resurrection of the dead and the renewal of heaven and earth at the Second Advent of Christ. The crucial issue in Calvin's eschatology is *the humanity of the risen Christ,* and our actual participation in his humanity through Word and Sacrament.[109]

Torrance is rightly convinced that weakness at this point is fatal to the gospel: "Here, then, is the chief point of controversy, both with the demythologisers, and with the millenarians: a weak and docetic view of the humanity of the risen and ascended Jesus. Weakness at that vital point destroys the Christian hope both for the future and for the present. Let the Reformed Churches of the Alliance learn again the meaning of the WORD MADE FLESH, and the RESURRECTION OF THE BODY."[110]

The Christian hope—yes. But heaven, hell, death, judgment? As we have said, and possibly for the reasons offered, these themes have not been extensively treated in Alliance literature. Neither has much *detailed* attention been paid to the Trinity. As with eschatology, so here current debate was noted. Thus we are reminded that in 1920 R. W. Dale held that "the Godhead means three personalities who are in some ineffable sense one," while D. W. Simon believed that God is "one personality who in some ineffable sense is three."[111] The positions are not further analyzed.

There was, however, a flutter in the dovecotes when the Church of England paper *The Guardian* reported that "Presbyterians and Congregationalists in the U. S. are largely Unitarian, regarding the Trinity and the Incarnation merely as pious opinions and not necessary beliefs." *The Quarterly Register's* editor, J. R. Fleming, countered that "random and baseless accusations of this sort are among the worst and least excusable hindrances to true unity."[112] No doubt there was no smoke without fire, but the *scale* of the fire was much less than *The Guardian* supposed, and most Presbyterians and Congregationalists would have affirmed Krafft's consensus statement on the Trinity:

> We believe, according to the Holy Scriptures, that the one Divine Being consists of three persons, the Father, the Son, and the Holy Spirit. The Father, the first cause, or ground and origin of all things; the Son, his eternal word and his eternal wisdom; the Holy Spirit, his eternal power and energy. The Son is begotten from eternity of the Father; the Holy Ghost, from eternity, proceeds from the Father and the Son. These three persons are not divided, but completely the same in substance and glory.[113]

From many trinitarian testimonies we may select the following as characteristic of the early (1891) and later (1962 and 1964) periods of Alliance history:

> It is the life of the Son that God has made the inheritance of our race, and we know for ourselves that this life reaches its complete union with the Father, and its perfect blessedness through the communion and grace of the Divine Spirit. Our relations to God as His sons are grounded on the eternal relations of the Son to the Father, and the life of the Son and the communion of the Holy Ghost have been made ours that we may realise our sonship.[114]

> The Bible provides us with no systematic doctrine of the Trinity. This only appeared as the outcome of the doctrinal development from the second to the fifth centuries. But the Bible does afford clear statements about the Spirit of God, the Holy Spirit, the Lord who is Spirit. The mystery of the Trinity is no abstract riddle of three-in-oneness, demanding a *sacrificium intellectus*. On the contrary, it points us to the mystery of height and depth, majesty and communion, holiness and love in God. It does not present us with a logical contradiction, it reveals the profound richness of the Godhead in the revelation in Jesus Christ. The doctrine of the Trinity simply reproduced the biblical witness to God as the Almighty Creator, Judge, and Lord, to God's self revelation in the midst of human history, to his presence in the very depths where man is, to his dwelling in the heart of a man, to his penetration and permeation of this world and human history.[115]

And, from Torrance:

> By His very nature, the Holy Spirit not only proceeds from the Father
> but lifts up to the Father. He is not only the Spirit sent by Christ but
> the Spirit of response to Christ, the Spirit in whom and by whom and
> with whom we worship and glorify the Father and the Son. Not only
> is He God the Holy Spirit descending to us, the Spirit by whom God
> bears witness to Himself, but God the Holy Spirit lifting up all creation
> in praise and rejoicing in God, Himself the Spirit of Worship and
> Witness, by whom the Church lives and fulfils its mission to the glory
> of God.[116]

Could any work be more ecumenical?

VI

In this chapter we have sought to show that through the Alliance corpus
runs a thread of doctrine in which the major themes of the church's
faith of the ages are represented. But the catholic doctrine we have
reviewed has been catholic doctrine as perceived and appropriated by
the Reformed. But who are the Reformed? This question will occupy us
in the next chapter. As we go we take with us the powerful emphasis we
have detected upon the centrality of God's atoning work in Christ and
its coming home to sinners by the Spirit. We shall claim that this evangel
is at the heart of catholic doctrine and that the Reformed *at their best* are
among those who will permit neither biblicism, sacerdotalism, nor
ecclesiasticism to stand in judgment upon, or in any way to sectarianize,
this glorious gospel of the free, redeeming grace of God.

3

The Evangelical-Catholic Heritage

The tradition to which the member churches of the Alliance are heirs is that which is generally, and to some extent confusingly, associated with the name of John Calvin. The confusion arises in both factual and theological terms. Factually, certain member churches—the Italian Waldensian Church and the Evangelical Church of Czech Brethren—look back to "Reformers before the Reformation": to Peter Waldo (twelfth century) and Jan Hus (c. 1369-1415) respectively. Nor does Calvin stand alone in his own century. We may not overlook the work of Bullinger, Farel, and especially Zwingli, all of whom, together with such catechists as Ursinus and Olevianus, nourished Reformed roots in decisive ways. Neither in its Reformed/Presbyterian aspects nor in its Congregational aspects, does the Alliance family acknowledge one founder only. In this it is unlike the Lutherans and the Arminian Methodists.

To oversimplify a complicated story we may say that the major emphasis of the German, Swiss, and Puritan Reformation was Pauline, while that of the Waldensians and Hussites was grounded in praxis derived from the Sermon on the Mount.[1] Again, the Congregational stream brings into the Reformed family an Anabaptist influence which goes far towards explaining its attitude towards the status of confessional texts—an attitude which some Presbyterians have found more than a little irksome.[2] However, and here we come to the major theological consideration, any tradition which stands upon the platform *semper reformanda*, as the Reformed tradition does (however much its several strains may devise a diversity of ploys designed to *resist* reformation—the Presbyterians referring matters to apparently endless successions of committees, the Congregationalists brandishing local autonomy in an improper, anti-catholic way), is irremediably disobliging to those who wish to have all things cut and dried once and for all.

As soon as this point is made, however, another must at once be added. All strands of the Reformed tradition have, at their best, denied that *anything* qualifies as reformation under the Spirit. Here the checks provided by the other Reformation watchwords—*sola scriptura, sola gratia*, and *sola fide*—come into play. In his classic treatment of Christian freedom the Congregationalist P. T. Forsyth declared that the genius of his tradition lay in its possessing a "founded freedom."[3] Nothing could be further removed from this than license. The way in which the appeal to the Spirit, to the Word, to the testimony of the fellowship, and with reference to empirical factors in the situation, is characteristic of Reformed methodology and provides built-in checks and balances against bibliolatry on the one hand and the private mysticisms of individuals on the other will become even clearer as we proceed.

I. Traditional Reformed Emphases

We may begin to elucidate further some characteristic emphases of the Reformed tradition by attending to a powerful utterance of E. P. Goodwin delivered at the first Congregational Council (1891), and to a symposium presented at the fifth Presbyterian Council (1892).

Goodwin extols his Pilgrim ancestors while agreeing with Dr. Storrs that "it is easier very likely to honour some of them *now*, than it would have been to live with them *then*."[4] Their supreme confidence, and that of the biblical writers, is that

> man proposes, but God disposes. One Divine plan, perfect, absolute, carrying one Supreme end and aim from the beginning, includes all, interpenetrates and shapes all; and one Divine, absolute, all-controlling sovereignty steadily and irresistibly carries the plan on to its consummation. Explain it or not, fight it or fall in with it, the one great truth written in this book, illustrated everywhere in the history of the race, so far as the book records that history, illustrated past doubt, equally by that which is unrecorded, is this—THAT GOD RULES.[5]

Further, the Congregational fathers were for the most part content with the doctrine (if not with the polity) of the Westminster Confession. Indeed, says Goodwin (with some exaggeration), questions of polity alone distinguish Westminster from the (Congregational) Savoy Declaration of Faith and Order (1658).[6] He declares that the men of Scrooby and Leyden were men of the infallible book in a way that Luther was not—though "From Augsburg to Westminster is more than 100 years; time enough for Luther, had he lived, to correct a number of his mistakes!"[7] Moreover, those who have understood John Robinson's confidence that "the Lord had more truth and light yet to break forth out of his holy Word" as a protest *against* an infallible book or a rigid creed have failed to appreciate that in thus speaking Robinson had *church polity* in mind.[8] Robinson, like Goodwin's other heroes, were made what they were by Dort.

Just when we are expecting Goodwin to take the direction of those in the present-day "inerrancy camp," he reveals that he is, after all, a child of his own age, and that liberal influences driven out of the front door come in again through the back. He grants that the world has moved on since the fathers' day; that because they gibbeted those they believed were in league with Satan we need not believe and act accordingly; and that the Bible is not a fetish containing infallible affirmations about everything. Then it comes: "We must not trust the words of the Book alone, but test them by our inner consciousness."[9] One is tempted to reflect that the Pilgrim fathers would never have said that—even though it was what they did all the time.

On the question of the relations of science and religion Goodwin denies the necessity of conflict and rises to the heights of rhetoric:

> Let the pickaxes and spades dig on! Let the decipherers of obelisks and cylinders and tablets read on! He who hung the stars in the sky, and laid the foundations of the earth, and fashioned the flower, is He who made the Book. They who dig in His works, or dig in His Word must, therefore, inevitably find one and the same God. Specially, my brethren, have we no need to fear the assaults of the so-called HIGHER CRITICISM.[10]

Returning to his Puritan ancestors Goodwin explains that they were not only men of the Book, they were men with a creed: "They believed in a creed simply because they believed in the book. That Book taught, as they held, certain great truths important for God's people to know and to teach."[11] Moreover, their creed was not any creed; it was a *Calvinistic* creed. At this point Goodwin's awareness that he is charting choppy waters becomes clear:

> This word Calvinism is, of all theological words, the one just now in worst odour. It stands with many for ecclesiastical sackcloth, thumb-screws and straight-jackets. It suggests, popularly, dungeons and fagots. It raises chiefly a vision of a grim-visaged, pitiless Genevan tyrant gloating over the fire that burns to cinders the man who denies

the Trinity and the dogma of the Divine decrees. The sooner it is blotted out from text-books and thrust out of our pulpits, the sweeter, more rational, and more Christ-like our theology.

But say what we may we cannot deny our paternity. If anything stands proved in our Congregational history it is that the fathers were Calvinists. Most of them past doubt shared John Robinson's fond conviction that the deliverance of the Synod of Dort, that supreme embodiment of Calvinism—was so perfect a symbol of the faith that it would endure unchanged.[12]

There follow concessions: we are not bound to the *words* of the past; we may not burn those who do not agree with us (and at this point Goodwin defends Calvin while not condoning his action vis-à-vis Servetus). Men as various as Hume, Paine, and Froude have admitted that to the ancestors of Congregationalism we owe religious and political liberty. For if God alone could command the conscience, who *else* could?[13]

Goodwin next surveys the moral weakness of the day as seen in personal, national, and international life, and he recalls his hearers to the old paths:

> Over against this I now lift up this old Puritan life. The family altar with the fire never suffered to die out; the covenant which made the children of believers sharers through the parents' faith in the grace of God, scrupulously observed; the Lord's day rigidly kept and hallowed; the house of God preferred above all others; the giving as regular as the worship, and as joyful as the songs of praise; Christian stewardship indeed recognized and honored by all; simplicity of dress and life a part of everyone's faith and practice; personal responsibility for all Christian duty profoundly felt; and, on the part of all, an earnest and prayerful longing for the establishment everywhere of the Kingdom of Christ. If a baptism of that spirit were to come upon the Churches of our polity great results would come of it to the glory of God and the good of men.[14]

In a nutshell,

> The peril of the time and the peril of the Church is a Bible with its infallibility, its divineness struck out, a theology with sin minimized or apologized for, with the Cross reduced to an object lesson, with culture substituted for the work of the Spirit, with saintship made a matter chiefly of self-development, retribution a figure of speech, and the pit of perdition either filled up or spanned with a bow of hope.[15]

To read Goodwin is to feel the desperation of a man attempting to hold back the tide, and this feeling is confirmed by the remarks of the chairman of the first Congregational Council, R. W. Dale, who, in the introduction to the *Proceedings*, reflected thus:

> Judging from the speeches alone, one would infer that among modern Congregationalists decisive theological ascendancy belongs to the "left centre"; all other parties were most inadequately represented. I should like to know whether this gives a true impression of the facts. I had supposed that both in this country and in America there is no inconsiderable number of ministers whose theological position is far more remote from the traditional creed than that of any of the English or American speakers. On the other hand, I think it certain that in America Calvinism retains an authority which received no sufficient illustration except in the powerful sermon of Dr. Goodwin. By that sermon Dr. Goodwin laid the Council under great obligation. It revealed, I suppose, to many English Congregationalists that the Calvinism of the Puritans and the early separatists still retains among American Congregationalists much of its old power. For Dr. Goodwin does not stand alone. He is not a man whose theology is tolerated for the sake of his high personal character and his effectiveness in the ministry; he represents a strong section of American Congregationalism. Nor should it be forgotten that the theology of the City Temple sermon was the theology which was the glory, the strength, and the solace of Congregationalist in the days of heroism and martyrdom. For myself—though I finally broke away from Calvinism very soon after I entered the ministry—I can see that its conception of the infinite greatness of God and of man's absolute dependence upon Him for all righteousness are necessary to correct some of the characteristic tendencies of modern thought and life. If we could but recover the faith of Calvinism without its speculative theology the gain would be immeasurable.[16]

We shall return in due course to the specific issue of science and religion. For the moment, en route to the Presbyterian symposium on the Reformation, we must hold in mind the two major issues raised by Goodwin: the place and authority of the Bible, and the place, authority, and use of creeds and confessions within the Reformed family.

Professor T. M. Lindsay addressed the fifth Presbyterian Council on "The Protestant Reformation: Its Spiritual Character and its Fruits in the Individual Life." Against those who argue that the Reformation was simply a political, an intellectual, or a social movement which exalted the individual, Lindsay claims that such matters constituted the environment of the Reformation only. At its heart the Reformation was a revival of religion, one of the many fulfillments of the promise of the outpouring of the Spirit of God upon His waiting Church. The great movement will always be misread if any other theory of its nature be taken. The revival fired the masses; the revival lit up the individual souls; the revival laid hold on the political revolution, sanctified the intellectual movement, and consecrated the intense individuality of the time.[17]

Thus it was that "men who knew that grace was sovereign, that they themselves were, body, soul, and spirit, directly dependent on God and on God alone, could treat Church censures and papal frowns in a way that would have made a medieval saint shudder."[18] It was not that the Reformation enunciated truths that were absolutely unknown to the medieval church, but it rediscovered them in their evangelical import. Above all, the Reformation was an answer to

> earnest, long-sustained prayer. . . . Shortly after the traces of the pray-ing-circles of the Gottesfreunde and the Brethren of the Common Lot died out, the careful reader in the byways of later mediaeval religious life, can discern the slow growth and quiet spread of little communities, who met to pray for an outpouring of God's Spirit on His faithless Church. . . . They were called in the times immediately before the Reformation, the Old Evangelicals, their immediate descendants were the despised and slandered Anabaptists. Their leaders were not the outrageous, ignorant fanatics they have been so frequently described, but gentle, pious men, whose rare scholarship won them entrance into the famed Erasmus' circle. They welcomed the revival when it came. But, alas! the Reformed leaders refused their friendship. For these Old Evangelicals held three things that the majority of the Fathers of the Reformation either could not accept, or had not the courage to face. They held that Infant *versus* Adult Baptism might be an open question in the Christian Church; they pled for a free Church in a free State, and repudiated both State support and State control; and above all, they insisted, that the realm of conscience was inviolable, and that no man should suffer civil pains or penalties for his belief.[19]

In the ensuing discussion of Lindsay's paper Thomas G. Apple remarked that whereas Lutherans lay most emphasis upon justification by faith, the Reformed (the personal religious experience of Calvin and Zwingli notwithstanding) emphasize the formal principle of the Refor-mation: "the Scriptures as the only infallible rule of faith and practice . . . this we must cling to, and keep on our banners, as in the Reforma-tion."[20] Here is Goodwin's emphasis once more.

A further contrast between Lutheranism and Calvinism was drawn by H. Bavinck in his paper "The Reformation and Morals." Whereas the Lutheran Reformation changed only the inner man, the Calvinist went out to claim the whole of life for God. In either case the sovereignty of God was the key, and sovereignty is the foremost Reformed doctrine. Bavinck underlined the contrast:

> In the mighty mind of the French reformer, regeneration was no system, which filled out creation, as among Romanists; no religious reformation, which left creation intact, as among Lutherans; much less an entirely new creation, as among the Anabaptists;—*but a reformation and a renewal of all creatures.* Calvin traced the working of sin wider than Luther, deeper than Zwingli. But, on this very account, grace is narrower with Luther and poorer with Zwingli than with Calvin. The Calvinist, therefore, is not satisfied when he is personally reconciled with God and assured of His salvation. His work begins then in dead earnest, and he becomes a co-worker with God. . . . The family and the school, the Church and Church government, the State and society, art and science, all are fields which he has to work and to develop for the glory of God. The Swiss Reformation bore thus not only a religious, but also an ethical social and political character.[21]

Hence,

> we must not forget that Calvinism, even in its strictest form, differs on principle from the Romish asceticism and from the Anabaptist "avoidance." These originate in despisal of the world; in the thought that the natural life, as being of a lower order, cannot be sanctified. But the Calvinist rigorism was born from the desire to consecrate the whole of life to God. Rome tries to bridle the natural man, Calvinism tries to sanctify him.[22]

We shall return to the social thrust of the Reformed tradition in chapter 6. Meanwhile we resume the issues bequeathed to us by Goodwin: the nature and authority of the Bible, and of creeds and confessions.

II. The Bible and Its Authority

Dr. Krafft summed up the consensus of the Reformed confessions on the Bible thus:

> We believe that this living God has revealed himself to men, first, by his works in the creation and government of the world, but more clearly still by his Word.

We confess that the one only source and standard of his divine revelation is Holy Scripture, the contents of all those books which God has caused to be written by the instrumentality of men enlightened by the Holy Spirit—prophets, apostles, and evangelists.[23]

Many passages in Alliance literature reveal that contentment with the position stated here was widespread among both Congregationalists and Presbyterians. What few advocated, and what is here ruled out by the reference to the Spirit, was a crude biblical literalism. James Eells reminded the first Presbyterian Council that Presbyterians rule out other things too:

They deny that human reason and conscience can decide what God may reveal, for then there would be as many revelations as there are men. They deny that each one has an inner and superior light, independent of the Bible, for his guidance in truth and duty, for then there would be an open way to fanaticism and superstition. They deny that the Bible, though once sufficient, has become effete, and the advance of the race demands that it be supplemented or superseded. . . . Others may permit some invasion of philosophy and speculation on the positive authority of the Word, but Presbyterians must regard this as a direct attack on the very citadel of their system.[24]

Dr. Schaff was as earnest as any in contending for the infallibility of God's Word, but he was thinking of it over against "the pretended infallibility of the Vatican." He went on to distinguish clearly between the fact of the Bible's inspiration and the mode of it. Against any mechanical or magical theories of inspiration he declared that "the written Word is all divine and all human, and reflects the theanthropic character and glory of the personal Logos who became flesh for our salvation"; and he reminded the assembly of Luther and Calvin, who, "with the profoundest reverence for the divine substance of the Bible, had a very liberal view of its human form"[25] (a point not made by Goodwin). Dr. Apple was to observe at the second Presbyterian Council (1880) that when the letter of Scripture was substituted for the living Christ the Bible is reduced to a dead letter and reverence for it becomes bibliolatry.[26] But the great weight of opinion in that council was on the side of plenary inspiration. Major papers on this theme were delivered by E. P. Humphrey and Robert Watts. In discussion the only caveat was one introduced by John Cairns who, while himself asserting biblical infallibility, did not think that the doctrine of inspiration should be introduced in the early stages of apologetic endeavor.[27]

Underlying some of the strenuous defenses of plenary inspiration in the early days of the Alliance was a profound hostility to the so-called higher criticism of the Bible. At times this hostility surfaced. In his opening sermon at the seventh Presbyterian Council (1899), John De Witt warned that "the intellectual duty which presses most severely on the Reformed Churches today is not the duty of concessive apologetics, but the cheerful and by no means difficult task of pointing out to the new Biblical critics the very serious limitations of their method as an instrument of knowledge, and its more serious limitations as a power to compel general or permanent conviction—limitations which they, like most of their predecessors, appear to have ignored or forgotten."[28]

On the other hand, less than ten years later, W. H. Bennett was found lecturing the third Congregational Council on "The Positive Value of Criticism to the Bible." "By the aid of modern criticism," he argued, "the church confronts the world with a more assured faith in the Bible and in God. We put no fence round our law, it can defend itself." And he invoked no less a person than Calvin in support: "Scripture, carrying its own evidence along with it, deigns not to submit to proofs and arguments, but owes the full conviction with which we ought to receive it to the testimony of the Spirit. . . . We feel a divine energy living and breathing in it—an energy by which we are drawn and animated to obey it."[29]

Debate was not altogether silenced, however. As late as 1925 Clarence Macartney sought to recall his Presbyterian hearers to the traditional way. He attacked the concept of progressive revelation which was used as a pruning knife to excise "redundant" passages of Scripture: "A deleted Bible means a diluted Gospel."[30] In the address immediately following Daniel Lamont took a more flexible approach. Attempting to steer a course between the Scylla of fundamentalism and the Charybdis of modernism, he defended the Bible as "the original and normative testimony of the Church" in that it testifies to "Jesus Christ as the Son of God, our only Lord and Saviour." Herein resides its authority.[31]

We may gauge something of the extent of the change of attitude towards the authority of the Bible if we contrast the relatively "loose" view of Lamont with that enunciated a generation earlier by A. A. Hodge. The latter spoke in 1884 on "The Authority of the Holy Scripture as Taught in the Reformed Confessions" and declared that

> The ultimate authority justifying or requiring the assent of the under-standing to asserted truth must lie either (a) in the *intuitions*, mental or physical: as where a thing is seen to be true; or (b) in the *deduction of the reason*, where one truth is seen to be certainly involved in another which is already known to be certainly true; or (c) in the *testimony* of a

witness, at once competent and veracious. Conditioned as men are in this world, this last mentioned ultimate ground of belief, *i.e. Testimony*, is unquestionably the foundation of by far the greater part of our knowledge, and universal experience proves it to be not less practically trustworthy than either of the others. It is evident that the *Testimony of God*, if that can be assuredly pledged is, because of His absolute and infinite competency and truthfulness, more ultimate and more certain than any other belief-compelling authority in the universe.[32]

He then proceeded to argue that the Reformed confessions take their stand on the Bible as God's own testimony which is as such supremely authoritative.

In order to illustrate further the *variety* of views within the Reformed family in this crucial matter we may cite Alexander Stewart, who in 1913 adopted what may be described as a psychological stance. For him Christian experience is the arbiter. It is the verdict of the saints of the ages that the Bible is the authoritative Word of God, and this verdict must be pronounced voluntarily: "To put my thought in the briefest possible words, I would say that the rule of religious life, the authority in matters of faith, is not Scripture alone, or Reason alone, but Scripture understood and assimilated by Reason, Reason enlightened and stimu-lated by Scripture."[33] We note in passing that the internal testimony of the Spirit is here conspicuous by its absence.

However much they might differ on the place of biblical criticism and the nature and authority of the Bible, all—both Presbyterian and Congregational—would have endorsed these words spoken at the fifteenth Presbyterian Council (1937): "God has spoken to us in Jesus Christ. He is the living Word. To Him the Scriptures bear witness."[34] This Christological emphasis became ever more prominent as the influence of Barth increased. The distinction between the Word written and the Word embodied in Jesus was employed, inter alia, to undergird much of the biblical theology of the 1950s and 1960s. This theology (too easily, some have subsequently said) characteristically viewed Christ the Word as the one to whom both testaments testify, and therefore as the source of the unity of the Bible. That Hubert Cunliffe-Jones is within this tradition is clear from his paper on "The Word of God" delivered at the ninth Congregational Council meeting of 1962.[35]

Cunliffe-Jones begins from the recognition that Christians have no option but to take account of the deeply skeptical nature of the environ-ment in which they have to speak of the Word of God. Two types of skepticism prevail. The first is a deeper skepticism than was held by those who understood the Word of God as a transcendent reality forever beyond our knowing. The present skepticism denies meaning and relevance to the concept "Word of God." Second, there is the skepticism of those who point out that to speak of the "Word of God" in a Christian sense wrongly implies that Christians alone are religious people, whereas this is manifestly not the case.

These varieties of skepticism notwithstanding, Cunliffe-Jones contends that "the Word of God is expressed finally, conclusively, uniquely in the man Christ Jesus in whom the everlasting God is incarnate, in whom the everlasting God claims the world as His own. In our personal relationship with Jesus Christ in the fellowship of all who belong to Him, we know in deed and truth the Word of God."[36] Only by trusting Christ can we accept him as Savior and Lord: neither the Bible nor the church can provide external guarantees of this. Nevertheless, "The Bible declares the Gospel by which the Church is bound and to whose authority it is subject. And by the Church the Bible has been transmitted from generation to generation, and in the context of the life and fellowship of the Church the Bible is most truly known."[37]

Here, more clearly than previously in the literature, we have the emphasis upon the importance of Christian fellowship as the locus for the discerning of the Word. This is crucial to the congregational ecclesiology, as we shall see. We have here also the recognition that the Bible is the church's book. To say this is to recognize that it is part of the Christian *tradition*. In this recognition we have one of the main motives underlying the fresh analysis of *sola scriptura* which was undertaken by the European Committee of the Alliance and published in *The Reformed World,* March 1986. We have learned that for many *sola scriptura* came to be both a positive and a negative slogan; it meant "for the Bible, against the Roman tradition." In fact, however, the Reformers were never innocent of traditional presuppositions; they were simply selective concerning them. Nor, in their exegetical and expository work, did they hesitate to draw largely upon the tradition of the ages. When we further consider the advent of modern biblical criticism and hermeneutics—factors which cannot be passed over as if they did not exist—the wisdom in viewing *sola scriptura* afresh is undeniable.[38]

The next question to arise is, "How far is it appropriate or even desirable to seek one criterion only for the truth of theology?" This question has been raised in Alliance circles by D. W. D. Shaw. He refers to a colleague's unpublished paper which listed fifteen samples of criteria in theology:

These ranged from traditional philosophical categories, like "coherence" and "correspondence," through traditional theological criteria,

"scripture" and "tradition," in general, "Jesus Christ," "Word of God,"
"Revelation," in particular, to various interpretative categories which
have assumed the role of criteria, e.g., "existential significance,"
"logical performance," dominant motifs such as "covenant," "eschaton," "Heilsgeschichte," and finally, "historical authenticity."[39]

Shaw properly notes that because of its interwovenness with tradition
Scripture cannot be regarded as the sole criterion of theological truth.
Neither can tradition, for there is not one Christian tradition. Neither
can religious experience, because of its irremediable subjectivism which
rules out its usefulness as *evidence*. He concludes that the quest of a single
criterion is doomed to failure. It does not follow, however, that all is lost:

> Some criteria will be more basic than others and will feature in all
> Christian theologies. As long as Christian faith is to be centered on
> Jesus Christ, as long as it is a community faith (though the question
> "which community?" will continually arise), the criteria, for example,
> of "scripture," "tradition," "experience" will always be with us, though
> these will need to be supplemented by other criteria. So too, I suspect,
> will the criterion of "history" endure, as preserving the historical basis
> of faith. The truth of the Gospel is not to be "proved" by historical
> study any more than by philosophical speculation.[40]

But what is the "truth of the Gospel"? At this point once again P. T.
Forsyth, speaking with specific reference to "The Evangelical Principle
of Authority" comes to our rescue. He is in advance of his time in
reckoning with the fact that the Bible is the church's book; and theology
at large—not least ecumenical theology—has yet to catch up with him
in respect of the way in which he sets the gospel above both Bible and
church. He contends that the seat of authority is historic, not mystic;
social, not individual; and ethical, not merely rational:

> it must stand forth either as an institution or as a person in an act. As
> a matter of fact it is between these that we are compelled to choose—
> between a church and a person. And history has written in the career
> of Catholicism the result of placing the ultimate ethical authority in
> the church as an institution. It is Jesuitism. The conscience of human
> society is not another society. The church is not the conscience of the
> state; nor is the conscience of the church the kingdom of God even.
> The kingdom itself is first constituted by the king; and the conscience
> of society is a personal holy will. . . . Holy and blessed as the church
> may be, it is but the channel of grace, and therefore only the organ
> and not the seat of authority.
>
> But if the final authority be not an institution, then it cannot be

a canon, which is in the nature of an institution. It cannot be the Bible. The canon of Scripture was the work of the church, and if the church's work be final for conscience then the church must be. . . . The final authority is the Gospel in the Bible, which is Jesus Christ and him as crucified. . . .

The Gospel must do for the Bible what the Bible did for the church. The Bible has an authority that judges the church; and the Gospel has an authority that judges the Bible. The Gospel made the Bible and the Gospel must rule it. . . .

The touchstone of every book and passage is Christ, as Luther said; but it is Christ, not as the perfect character, but as the sole theme that Paul would know, Christ as the crucified Redeemer. "Back to Christ" is a sound call; but it would mislead us if it meant merely back to his teaching as our norm and his character as our ideal. His teaching, as precept at least, does not cover all the moral ground, even where it is clear; and his character means for modern ears such a biography as we have not and never can have. Back to Christ means back to the Gospel as it is in Christ, and especially in his atoning death. The supreme commentary on the Gospels is the Gospel, as the key to Christ's life is his death. . . .

The Reformation was not the rediscovery of the Bible chiefly, but of the Gospel in the Bible. And it stood not for the supremacy of conscience, but for the rescue of conscience by the supremacy of Christ in it. And of Christ in it, not as the supreme Rabbi to solve cases, but as the author and principle of a new life and spirit which solves cases age after age by an indwelling grace, and truth, and love, and light and power.[41]

III. A Confession for the Alliance?

We now turn to the question of the place and purpose of confessions and declarations of faith within the Reformed family. At the very beginning of its life the Presbyterian Alliance faced this question for itself. On the second day of the first Council meeting (1877) Philip Schaff spoke on "The Consensus of the Reformed Confessions." He recalled that in 1552 Cranmer invited Melanchthon, Bullinger, Bucer, and Calvin to a conference to form an evangelical union creed: "But the conference was frustrated by political events, and a formed union creed remains a *pium desideratum* to this day."[42] He pointed out that while the preliminary meeting held in London on 21 July 1875 specified "the Consensus of the Reformed Confessions" as the doctrinal basis for the

projected Alliance, it did not define the consensus as such. There were
thus a number of options open to the council. It could leave the matter
open, or it could formulate the consensus either (a) by listing cardinal
doctrines to which the assent of member churches would be required;
(b) by summarizing without addition the old confessions along the lines
of Krafft's work which was before the council; or (c) "By a new ecumenical Reformed confession. By this I mean the Consensus of the old
Reformed Confessions freely reproduced and adapted to the present
state of the Church. . . . It ought to be truly evangelical-catholic in
spirit."[43] Schaff cautioned that it would be calamitous if a new confession
had the effect of intensifying Presbyterianism at the expense of loosen-
ing the ties which bound Presbyterians to other Christians: "We want a
wall to keep off the wolves, but not a fence to divide the sheep; we want
a declaration of union, not a platform of disunion."[44]

Schaff went on to say that although the right to frame new confessions, or to revise old ones, was beyond dispute, confessions could not
be made to order. He did not think that the time was ripe for confession
making: "The new *formula concordiae* might become a *formula discordiae*,"
for the continental members would be content with a minimum of
orthodoxy whereas the Anglo-American representatives would require
more orthodoxy.[45] His hesitations notwithstanding, Schaff was appointed chairman of a committee on creeds and confessions. This
committee produced a lengthy report on Reformed confessions for the
second Presbyterian Council (1880),[46] but made no comment on the
desirability or otherwise of attempting a new consensus statement.
Accordingly, a new committee was appointed to examine this question.
The members held their first meeting during the second council session
and decided to work in three groups: British, Continental, and American. The report to the third Council (1884) revealed the Americans as
being in favor of a new consensus, the British (with Robert Watts
dissenting) declaring that "it is scarcely possible to formulate such a
Consensus as will determine all cases which may arise, or prove helpful
to the Alliance in regard to the admission of Churches,"[47] and the
Continental group as being divided on the issue. After long debate the
report was adopted and no further action was taken. Dr. Calderwood's
subsequent motion to draft a formal statement of consensus not as a test
of Alliance membership but as an aid to Christian testimony and
Reformed unity was defeated.

The inherent difficulty of arriving at a consensus statement to which
all could agree was a determining factor in the case; but there was also
the feeling that the Alliance was a *fellowship* of member churches, and
that it must not appear to claim an ecclesial status to which it was not

entitled. Thus, in the conclusion of the report the difficulty is raised that

> it is not easy to distinguish in idea and in fact, two kinds of definition, the one which would be merely historical, and the other the utterance of a new and living Creed by the Alliance. The last kind of definition it would be hard so to limit beforehand in its use and application as to disarm the uneasy feelings of the separate Churches: for such is the earnestness with which each guards its own Creed and the right to alter or interpret it, that the work of the central body in this field, even though its aim would be different, would almost certainly arouse susceptibilities not easy to be allayed.[48]

There the matter rested until John M'Naugher raised the question once again in his presidential address to the twelfth Presbyterian Council (1925):

> Were it not well that such a doctrinal consensus be at least attempted—something more distinctive than the ancient creeds and less extreme than the Reformed creeds? . . . Why might not a proper Committee be charged with the framing of a concise formulary which should be a reflex of apostolic teaching and have its baseline in the Second Helvetic Confession, the Canons of Dort, the Heidelberg Catechism, and the Westminster documents. . . . With a common testimony like this, the Churches connected with the Alliance would have a binding tie such as has never yet been known in the history of the Reformed kinship.[49]

Later in the session M'Naugher introduced a full-scale discussion of the matter. There were, he said, two preliminary questions: Is a creed desirable for a church? May a creed be amended? He answered both questions affirmatively and then inquired whether a creed was (a) desirable and (b) practicable for the entire Presbyterian world.[50] In his address to the question Alexander Martin said that it would be much more difficult to frame a confession today than in the past; for then the existence of a finally revealed doctrinal system was universally presupposed, whereas now it was not. Nevertheless he felt that the attempt should be made, provided that it were not done in the interests of cultivating Presbyterian distinctiveness.[51] J. M. Shaw argued that the devising of a common statement of faith for the Presbyterian world was both desirable and practicable.

The most substantial contribution to the discussion was a lengthy paper by Karl Barth. In his absence, the first and second sections of the paper were summarized, and the third was read, by A. Mitchell Hunter.

Barth began by reviewing the history of Reformed confessions. He noted that they were statements of God's revelation in Jesus Christ which comes through the Scriptures; that they were provisional, spontaneous, and practical; and that they invariably sprung from locally circumscribed Christian communities. He noted that Calvin and other Reformers did not go in quest of a general Reformed confession: they recognized a unity among themselves which required no paper bond. The real question for the Alliance was whether there is that grasp of God's revelation and degree of fellowship among the member churches which would make the devising and articulating of a confession a general and not simply a formal act. An affirmative answer would supply the only possible basis for proceeding.

But then, Barth continued, the question would arise: What is to be said? What has happened in theology or in the world to constrain the Alliance to confess its faith? He seriously questioned whether the theologians of many countries were in any position to articulate a common confession, and whether the "ethical aimlessness" in the evangelical church would permit a clear prophetic word. Representatives of the Alliance's member churches might on reflection be inclined to answer either "yes" or "no" to the question of a confession for the whole family; but the primary consideration was, "What is the good pleasure and perfect will of God in this matter?"[52]

In the ensuing discussion some warned of possible division within the Alliance were the attempt made to draft a common confession; but the business committee's motion that a drafting committee be appointed was in the end unanimously adopted.[53] The appointed committee found that it was impossible to discharge its task, for its Eastern branch desired only a brief statement of vital evangelical truths, while its Western branch was unable to consider such a statement sufficiently Reformed. This was the report to the thirteenth Council.[54] The matter was not allowed to drop, however, being resumed at the fourteenth Council (1933) and finally evaporating before the fifteenth (1937). The quest for a common confession for the Alliance as a whole had failed for the second time, and the matter has only recently been raised anew.

The upshot is that, unlike the Lutheran World Federation, whose members regard the Augsburg Confession as their doctrinal marker, the Alliance, like its counterparts the Baptist World Alliance and the World Methodist Council, has no one confession to which all its members subscribe and which all agree may be used as a test of membership in the global family. It is for each member church of the Alliance to adopt a past confession or confessions, to revise older standards, to compose new statements—or to do none of these things, according to its own choice. Clearly this makes for a measure of doctrinal variety within the Alliance family (and, as is well known, variety of interpretation is not precluded *within* the most strongly confessional bodies); but it does not signify lack of concern for doctrine. As for those churches which prefer not to elevate one historically conditioned form of words as their explicit and formal confession—they might claim that their understanding of *semper reformanda,* and their quest for that *founded* freedom of which Forsyth spoke, makes them more eager than some to ensure that in each successive age the activity of confessing the faith takes priority over adherence to past confessions.[55] This consideration brings us back to the way in which Spirit, Word, and fellowship—together with the reality of the contemporary situation—are all together involved in discerning the faith to be confessed at any time. The Reformed, claiming the whole world for God as they do, cannot justifiably overlook the world as it is at the point of testimony.

Ideas such as these come increasingly to the foreground as our period draws to a close. The Alliance's executive committee responded in 1980 to a memorandum from the Swiss Federation of Protestant Churches which urged reflection upon these "theological issues which challenge the life of the Reformed." An international group of theologians worked upon a document which eventually became the study booklet *Called to Witness to the Gospel Today* (1983; promulgated in draft form by the 1982 general council). The booklet begins from the central affirmation that Jesus Christ is Lord and Savior, and it then invites reflection by member churches on such themes as rethinking the Reformed heritage, catholicity, racism and South Africa, the community of women and men, the family and marriage, witnessing amid a diversity of cultures, peace, human wealth and power, and human rights. We have already referred to this booklet, and shall do so again.

Meanwhile, another group prepared the document *Confessions and Confessing in the Reformed Tradition Today* (1983). Here, as we have already noted, reference was made to the newer confessions emerging from many parts of the Reformed family and to the question of the relation between the Bible, creeds, and confessions. At the time of writing the questions are still under review, as an Alliance international consultation on "Confessing the Faith Today" (1986) indicates. In all of this reflection Lukas Vischer, who became moderator of the Alliance's department of theology in 1982, has been heavily involved.

It is not at all coincidental that the most dramatic stand ever taken by the Alliance—that on racism and apartheid in South Africa in 1982—should have occurred in the context of the question "What does it mean to confess Christ today?" Indeed, the raising of that question was by no means an academic matter: it was thrust upon the Alliance by world events and the obligation to testify. Also noteworthy is the suddenness with which some issues have appeared on the Alliance's agenda. For example, whereas in the case of racism and South Africa more than twenty years of conversation had taken place with the Alliance's white Dutch Reformed South African member churches and the general councils at Frankfurt (1964) and Nairobi (1970) had pronounced upon the matter, the "community of women and men" was hardly mentioned in Alliance literature prior to the one-and-a-half pages devoted to it in *Called to Witness to the Gospel Today.* Women had been mentioned from time to time—their church work and the question of their ordination— but of *theological* reflection upon the relation of man and woman there had been little in Alliance literature prior to 1982. Similarly, although in the early Presbyterian councils reports on mission were presented, the question of gospel and cultures, with all its implications for mission, has likewise been central to the Alliance's agenda only since 1982. The Taiwanese theologian Choan-Seng Song has been especially active in this aspect of the work.

IV. Creeds and Confessions in the Presbyterian Alliance

Despite the proven impossibility of the Alliance devising a confession of its own, a considerable amount of time was devoted to the question of the place of creeds and confessions in the Reformed tradition.

First, as to the motive behind the writing of confessions. The Reformed fathers, declared Pierre Maury in 1948,

> felt themselves *obliged* to confess Jesus Christ—first of all, because they believed in Him; further, because they were accused of perverting the Christian faith; and lastly, because they wanted to call other men to the joy of their own salvation.[56]

They thus made "the response required of them by a previous act of God in their behalf."[57] Nor did Maury and others overlook the paradoxical stance of those who framed the older confessions. At one and the same time they announced their convictions with assurance and declared that their written findings, far from being absolute, were under the judgment of Scripture and subject to revision by their descendants.

In a word, confessions are held in the literature of the Presbyterian Alliance to be both necessary—for testimony and clarity, and against heresy—and revisable—in new circumstances, or in response to fresh

insights. In 1904 John Patrick had gone further: not only were creeds
and confessions desirable and necessary; they were unavoidable:

> For the negation of creeds is itself a creed, in some respects the most
> dogmatic of all creeds; and it has behind it a theory of God and of
> revelation, a theory of the relation of doctrine and ethics, just as much
> as the most rigorous Confession. It takes for granted that definite
> Christian truths do not exist, or that they are relatively unimportant,
> or impossible of attainment, as if the essence of Christianity were
> something impalpable, which can be separated from any embodiment
> in Church or creed and even vanishes when it is so embodied.[58]

Professor William A. Curtis admitted in 1913 that confessions could
be employed legalistically, but he maintained that the rejection of
confessions was not the way to meet this abuse, for while "knowledge of
doctrine is not experience of faith . . . faith is notwithstanding inseparable from doctrine. We cannot trust God without believing that God
is."[59] N. B. Van Zandt drew the ecclesiological inference as early as 1880:
"The Church, as an organization, could have no existence without some
defined standards of doctrine,"[60] and the provision of such standards
enabled one to walk the middle ground between a chaos of biblical
interpretation on the one hand and subservience to an infallible church
on the other.

In his 1948 address Maury (a close associate of Barth) further
observed that creeds (and confessions) cannot be written to order, so to
speak. Rather, they "are given by the Holy Spirit out of the pressure of
a living, historical situation. It was in this fashion that the Barmen
Declaration was given to the hard-pressed German Church."[61] He also
noted that the mere possession of a confession does not automatically
lead to true acts of confessing, as has been recognized in one of the
Alliance's more recent statements on the matter.[62] The truth would
seem to be that the writing of a confession generally follows the act of
confessing, and that while a written confession may express, or challenge, the testimony of those who come after, it will not by itself preserve
the testimony in the hearts of those whose minds have departed from
it—as, for example, in the way in which most of the heirs of the older
English Presbyterians became Unitarian.

This last point was prominent in the early days of the Alliance when
the popular mood inclined some to believe in any doctrine which could
be called "progressive" and to reject any which could not be so called.
Facing this peril, and in relation to the question of the revisability of
confessions, James Orr was reported to declare in 1904 that Presbyterians

must protect themselves against [the danger of whittling away the substance of truth] by relying on Christ's own presence and the Spirit of God in His Church, to maintain the testimony of His truth in His Church and in the hearts of His people. If it did not rest on that foundation, there was no letter of the Confession that would ever keep it there, and if it did rest on that ground, then there could be no fundamental departure from it. The only thing we could do if a Church became utterly apostasized and corrupt was—to do as our fathers did—walk out; but in order to preserve ourselves against the danger, we must not deprive ourselves of our Christian liberties, which were inherent in the nature of the Church. He therefore did not think it could be for a moment argued or contended, that any step that the Churches in Christendom had been taking in the way of re-adjusting their standards to their doctrinal relations, and making clear their attitude to those, could be called a departure from their inherent powers.[63]

Dr. S. J. Niccolls reminded the tenth Presbyterian Council (1913) that the revision of creeds was justified by our growing knowledge of the Word of God, when the need to take account of changing conditions of life was clamant, and under the necessity of countering "changing forms of error and new assaults upon the truth."[64] To which W. A. Curtis added the consideration that "the elaborateness of our statements has made them peculiarly liable to disintegration by the hand of time."[65] In 1966 the executive committee of the Alliance summed matters up thus: "We cannot treat as absolute any of the structures and confessions which we inherit; in our very loyalty, we must be ready to go wherever the Spirit leads, even if it be through that death which leads to new life."[66]

So far, so good; but there are profound questions raised by the number and variety of the confessions which have been written over the last thirty years: "These new confessions vary in purpose and in form. Some seek to summarize the faith; others to provide a song of praise; some have been written for catechetical purposes; some are responses to crises which call into question the integrity of the church's witness; some are the results of union negotiations in which Reformed churches have been involved."[67] A brief analysis of some of the newer confessions has shown that although, for example, they insist upon God's activity in contemporary affairs, the doctrines of predestination and providence are played down or omitted altogether. At the same time, God's sovereignty is affirmed, as is his covenant in Jesus Christ. Moreover "the strong ethical and political note that is often heard, especially in statements from Asia, Africa and Latin America, stands in direct relation to the close connection between theology and ethics (and politics) in the older Reformed tradition."[68] No doubt, but how little of the ethical and the political found its way into the classical Reformed confessions.[69]

Despite the present variety of confessional expression within the Alliance family it remains possible to characterize the tradition as a whole in terms employed by Philip Schaff at the first Presbyterian Council: "The Reformed Confessions are Protestant in bibliology, oecumenical or old catholic in theology and Christology, Augustinian in anthropology and the doctrine of predestination, evangelical in soteriology, Calvinistic in ecclesiology and sacramentology, and anti-papal in eschatology."[70] Had Schaff lived he would have had to modify his ecclesiological statement in deference to those of the Congregational Way who came together with Presbyterians in 1970 to form the Alliance as we know it today.

V. Creeds and Confessions in the Congregational Council

In our last chapter we presented sufficient evidence (except on the doctrines of the church and the sacraments) to show that the Congregationalists fit easily (ecclesiology apart) under Schaff's rubric as just stated. So far, however, we have not mentioned the Congregationalists in relation to creeds and confessions. It is almost paradoxical that despite such a collection as Williston Walker's *The Creeds and Platforms of Congregationalism* (1893, 1960); despite the fact that, as we saw earlier, the Savoy Declaration of Faith and Order (1658) follows the Westminster Confession in most important respects; despite the fact that the Declaration of Faith (1967) of the Congregational Church in England and Wales is one of the most substantial works in this genre to have been written in this century, the impression lingers that Congregationalist liberty sanctions a cavalier disregard of doctrinal matters and an abhorrence of confessional statements. Some Congregationalists actively foster this impression. We may suspect that such Congregationalists are under the influence of a wrongly atomistic understanding of the priesthood of all believers, the roots of which may be traced to a nineteenth-century individualism of which John Owen and John Robinson were happily innocent, and which P. T. Forsyth went to strenuous lengths to rebut. Had there been no such Congregationalists how could one so eminent as Barth have made such an ignorant statement as this in an otherwise helpful article on "The Idea of a Reformed Confession of Faith": "The attenuated, anthropocentric notion of a Confession held by the Congregationalists, ancient and modern, with its over-emphasis on the human origin of the Confession to the detriment of its divine content, is in this respect sectarian and not Reformed."[71]

We shall do well to take careful note of what the Congregational Council literature has to say on the subject. But first let us prepare ourselves to grasp the paradox that Congregationalism has been very productive of confessional material, and very reluctant to make use of it—even in worship, and never as a test of membership. Geoffrey Nuttall has suggested that "perhaps few Christian communions can offer so much confessional material of a communal character as Congregationalists can," and he cited in evidence local church covenants, the ordination statements of ministers, hymns (pre-eminently those of Isaac Watts and Philip Doddridge), confessions of faith, and summaries of doctrine taught at the dissenting academies and colleges at which Congregational ministers were trained.[72] On the other hand, the reluctance to use confessional statements had in the earliest days to do with the desire to avoid "man-made" forms of words in worship (a rubric which does not seem to have applied to free and extempore prayer!). More generally, the following points were urged:

1. That it is not confessional subscription (any more than it is residence in a parish) that makes the individual a Christian.
2. That credal subscription shall not be a test of membership, because to ask for anything other than a profession of faith in Christ is of the essence of sectarianism.
3. That creeds and confessions may, unhappily, encourage assent to extra-scriptural authority on the one hand, and the fossilization and cerebralization of faith on the other.
4. That it is by the Holy Spirit and (humanly speaking) by their devotional life that churches are kept true to the faith once delivered to the saints: "to call it a safeguard is to speak on too mean a level. It is of the essence of our existence."[73]

The Congregational Way presupposes and demands a high quality of church fellowship, and, as W. Gordon Robinson pointed out, those who do not impose credal tests need to ensure that their hymns, their gathered life in Church Meeting, and the caliber of their covenant life are such that minister and people continually confront one another with the heart of the gospel—and all in a spirit of humble waiting upon the Spirit.[74]

At the ninth Congregational Council (1962) James M. Gustafson presented the alternatives which Congregationalists at their best have always found unacceptable:

What is our rightful relation to the great Christian tradition? We do not want our churches to be museums of medieval ways, in architecture, in vestments, in liturgies, in doctrines, and in ethics. But on the other hand we do not want to act as if contemporary church life is to be created *ex-nihilo* (out of nothing) or out of the mid-twentieth century patterns of thought, or out of the overwhelming anxieties of the century in which we live, or out of the present institutional forms given in Western culture. We desire, above all, congregations that are filled with the Holy Spirit of God, that make the presence of the living Christ known in the world, that are obedient servants in the calling to which God has called his people—in evangelism, in moral witness, and in praise and worship.[75]

The former error alluded to by Gustafson had earlier been denounced by F. J. Powicke, and by the entire Congregational Council in two statements drafted respectively in 1908 and 1949 to explain the stance of Congregationalism vis-à-vis other Christian bodies and the world at large:

We see that, if the constitutive principle of a church, what makes it a church, what forms and holds it together, is the abiding presence in and among its members of a living Spirit, whose holy task it is so to inspire the love of truth and so to cleanse the inner eye as that knowledge of Christ and the things of Christ shall be growing perpetually clearer and fuller, then for a church to fancy it possible that the sum of Christian truth has been compressed into the phrases of an ancient creed, or that its present apprehension and statement of the truth can be more than partial, is self-destructive and even a sin against the Holy Ghost.[76]

While Congregationalists do not require subscription to any man-made creedal statements, they have never differed from other Christian communions in respect of the great doctrines of the Christian faith and have always claimed their place in the witness of the evangelical reformed churches. At the same time they have stood, and still stand, for religious liberty under the Gospel and in obedience to the Gospel.[77]

In the latter quotation we have a clear echo of the warning contained in the preface to the Savoy Declaration:

Whatever is of force or constraint in matters of this nature causeth them to degenerate from the *name* and *nature* of *Confessions,* and turns them from being *Confessions of Faith,* into *exactions* and *impositions of Faith. . . .* The *Spirit of Christ* is in himself too *free,* great and generous a Spirit, to suffer himself to be used by any humane arm, to whip men into belief; he drives not, but *gently leads into all truth,* and *persuades* men to *dwell in the tents* of *like precious Faith;* which would lose of its preciousness and value, if that sparkle of freeness shone not in it.[78]

Gustafson's opposition to the misplaced attempt to invent the gospel *de novo* in each successive generation was anticipated by J. D. Jones and G. H. Wright in 1930:

> We have consistently declined to bind ourselves by any written formulary or creed. . . . This spiritual freedom of ours—in such an age as this—is a great asset. Perhaps we need the reminder that the freedom we enjoy is not freedom to indulge our individual fancies, but freedom to listen to the guiding voice of the Spirit of God.[79]

> As Congregationalists, then, let us rejoice in our freedom, but let there be no abatement in our loyalty to truths that matter most. . . . The Church's belief is most living when, rooted in its experience of God in Christ, it grapples with the thought of its age, and ceaselessly manifests its spirit in new ventures of faith. A Living Church will know that the great heresy is to be behind the time. Not to be behind its fashionable, fluctuating modes of thought—these soon vanish, we stand above them—but to lag behind in trusting and using a gospel that has resources equal to every emergency, is the worst heresy.[80]

In this connection we may recall E. P. Goodwin's praise of the Puritans for being "men with a creed," and we now note his insistence upon the fact that "every man's value, his worth to his fellows, will depend first on the correctness of his creed, and then on his pertinacity in sticking to it and using it, or working it out."[81]

The matter was judiciously summed up by A. E. Garvie, who in 1925 was invited to explain the Congregational position to the Presbyterian Council meeting in that year:

> What Congregational Churches have objected to is an elaborate confession, to which individual subscription is required as a condition of ministry. This is not due to theological laxity, but to the conviction that the Spirit of God is still with the believer, and the congregation of believers to guide into all truth, and that one generation must not impose the beliefs which it holds on the conscience of another generation as a restraint from the free following of the guidance of the Spirit. A common declaration of what is generally believed, when such a testimony seems necessary to meet the doubt, unbelief, or difficulties of any age, Congregationalism would be prepared for . . . What it

would never, as at present advised, consent to would be an intellectual bondage to the theology of any past age.[82]

The most sustained onslaught against the use of credal or quasi-credal statements as tests of membership came at the first Congregational Council (1891) in papers by Amory H. Bradford against subscription and Thomas Green against the doctrinal clauses in trust deeds.[83] At which point it is interesting to recall Philip Schaff's reminder to the first Presbyterian Council that

> the Reformed (as also the Lutheran) Confessions were not intended by their framers to be binding formulas for subscription and checks upon theological progress. Otherwise they would have been made much shorter and simpler. They were originally apologetic documents or vindications of the evangelical faith against misrepresentation and slander.[84]

The upshot is that in matters of basic Christian doctrine Presbyterians and Congregationalists have been at one; that both have been more than willing to set down the faith commonly held among them; that neither has contended for the irreversibility of confessions—on the contrary; and that in *practice* their theoretical difference in the matter of confessional subscription has been mitigated by the limited extent of formal subscription in Presbyterianism at large, and by the terms of such assent as have been widely if not universally required during the last hundred years. Nor need Congregationalists be too eager to look for inconsistencies in Presbyterian practice at this point, for at the first Congregational Council Amory H. Bradford produced evidence to show that some Congregational churches in the United States were imposing confessional tests upon those who sought church membership.[85]

The major remaining difference is *polity*. We shall attempt to elucidate Presbyterian and Congregational self-understanding of this in Alliance literature, observing Presbyterian and Congregational opinions of one another and reflecting on the implications of diverse polity for the being of the Alliance; and, before turning in the next chapter to the dealings of the Reformed with those of other Christian families over such matters as the sacraments and the ministry, we shall see what understanding of the church as catholic emerges from the Alliance corpus.

VI. Presbyterian Polity

Let us first note some areas which have not generally been at issue between Presbyterians and Congregationalists. Here, once more, Krafft can help us:

We confess that this true Church is thus distinguished from the false:
(1) that she busies herself with the pure preaching of the Gospel;
(2) observes the pure administration of the sacraments according to
Christ's institution; (3) practises Church discipline for the removing
of scandals; in general does everything according to the direction of
God's Word, abhores everything opposed to it, and acknowledges the
Lord Christ as her only Head; and therefore can in no sense regard
the Pope of Rome as her Head. From this true Church it is unlawful
for any one to separate himself.

We confess that there is a communion of saints, who by faith are united
with Jesus Christ, their only Head, by his Spirit, and who join one with
another, according to the Word of God, to shun sin and pursue
righteousness; so, to love God and their neighbour, and to serve one
another; and though they make constant progress in sanctification,
do ever again turn to Christ as their refuge, to obtain from him alone
forgiveness of their sins. The wickedness of hypocrites, who are found
among the saints, cannot annul their title to the name of the true
Church.

We confess that the office-bearers of the Church (pastors, elders,
deacons) should be called thereto in a lawful way by the Church, that
they should be set apart to their offices by the laying on of hands, in
the manner prescribed by God's Word, that those office-bearers form
no essentially distinct class from believers generally, and have all, in
whatever place they may be, equal authority and power, under Christ
their one Head.[86]

The first of the three articles designates the characteristic marks or
notes of the church which have traditionally been maintained by both
Presbyterians and Congregationalists (though discipline was not mentioned in either the Westminster Confession or the Savoy Declaration,
and has, in many places, not least under modern social conditions, fallen
by the wayside in practice if not in theory).[87] Equally common to both
traditions is the firm insistence on the visibility of the saints. This is not
to deny the concept of the invisible church, but this requires to be
carefully stated—as by John M'Naugher in his presidential address to
the twelfth Presbyterian Council (1925):

The Outer, or Visible, Church, along with its covenanted and ac-
credited membership, has a variable minority which is only adherent.
It is this untrue element that compels a distinction between the Outer
and the Inner Church.

Notwithstanding, we are not to think of two divorced Churches, but of one Church in two reciprocal aspects. The Visible Church enshrines the Invisible and gives it concrete expression. It is the servant Church, the auxiliary Church, ministering to the Church of the first-born who are enrolled in heaven. . . . On the other hand it is the resultant of the Invisible Church. Its vigor and its continuance depend on the sanctifying leaven of the household of God inside its borders. Through ages of vicissitude, of storm and stress, this has never failed, so that the fitting emblem of the Christian Church has been the Burning Bush with the encircling legend *Nec tamen consumebatur.*[88]

It is perhaps an interesting sign of M'Naugher's times that he does not overtly relate the concept of the invisible church to those of predestination and election. Neither did G. H. C. Macgregor make the link when he pointed out that "on the one hand, it will always be true that not all outwardly professing Christians are true members of the spiritual and invisible Church. . . . On the other hand, it is also true that the real Church of God can never be equated merely with the faithful members of the visible Church. We are but part, and the lesser part, of a greater Church which transcends the limits of earth."[89]

Krafft's articles omit any suggestion that the church is the continuation or extension of the Incarnation. This omission would be approved of by most Presbyterians and Congregationalists, while G. H. C. Macgregor's assertion that the church *is* the extension of the Incarnation is uncharacteristic of the tradition as a whole.[90] Most would have endorsed P. T. Forsyth's pungent remark, "That which owes itself to a rebirth cannot be a prolongation of the ever sinless."[91]

In connection with the government of the church, however, differences between Presbyterians and Congregationalists begin to emerge, and two in particular must be considered. First, the Presbyterians advocate the offices of pastor, elder, and deacon (and to these Calvin added teacher—an office still to be found in some Reformed churches to this day); the Congregationalists normally admit only the deacon, whose role is here more pastoral, there more "managerial." Second, the Congregationalists emphasize the catholicity-particularity of the local gathered church, and have normally accorded wider church councils advisory status only; whereas in Presbyterianism the consistorial order, moving (typically) from the local church session through presbyteries and synods to the General Assembly, has engendered the feeling of a hierarchy of progressively more authoritative church courts. The first Presbyterian Council (1877) received a "Report on the Statistical and General Condition of the Presbyterian Churches throughout the World" which summed matters up:

> These elements distinguish Presbyterianism, more or less, both from Episcopacy and from Congregationalism. That the Church should be governed by a body of elders; that in every congregation, besides one or more men set apart to labour in word and doctrine, there should be several appointed to aid in ruling, though not separated from the ordinary employments of life; and that the proceedings of these bodies of elders should be subject to the review of courts of elders, rising one above another, and culminating in a supreme court or synod,—are the fundamental principles of Presbyterian Church-government.[92]

Numerous writers and speakers developed this theme (and we shall contrast with it the Congregationalist understanding of the Church Meeting when we turn to the self-understanding of that tradition), but few were more comprehensive than D. Van Horne, who in 1892 listed six characteristics of Presbyterianism:

1. A high, yet discriminating estimate of the value of the Holy Scriptures.
2. A spiritual, reverential, and dignified form of worship, not anti-liturgical but anti-ritualistic.
3. A decided position in advocacy of civil liberty and the rights of conscience.
4. Adherence to a Scriptural form of church government, as understood by them, uninfluenced by views of mere expediency.
5. Adherence to the Scripture doctrine of the Divine Sovereignty, and believers' right to come directly to God in Christ without other mediation.
6. A testimony to the fact of man's fallen condition, and his possible salvation only through a crucified Redeemer, and regeneration by the Holy Spirit.[93]

Earlier Presbyterian contributors went to considerable pains to demonstrate the biblical origins of the Presbyterian system. Thus, in 1880 William P. Breed was confident that "no intelligent Bible student needs to be informed that . . . an eldership has existed in the Church, at least from the time when that Church was held in Egyptian bondage. Out of the burning bush came the command, 'Go, call the elders.' . . ."[94] That others had been more influenced by modern biblical criticism is clear from an article of the previous year by J. A. Wylie, who wrote of the Reformers:

> They found no "cut-and-dry" plan of Church government in the Bible. . . . No ecclesiastical fabric stood ready reared for the reformers, but the materials for constructing such lay all about.[95]

The view which many came increasingly to hold (though some might question the exegesis offered in support) was that expressed at the end of a 1901-5 series of articles under the title, "Whence Came Presbytery?": "We can come to no other conclusion than that that polity, or Plan of Church Administration which we call Presbyterian, is most conformable to the mind of the Head of the Church as made known to us in Providence, in Scripture, and in the experience of the Church."[96]

If at the first Presbyterian Council (1877) John Cairns found it necessary to question the suggestion in Robert Flint's opening sermon that the Bible does not recognize Presbyterianism as a distinct system, by 1952 J. Y. Campbell could only declare that "a Presbyterian who turns to the New Testament for information about elders and the presbyterate in the earliest days of the Christian Church can hardly but be disappointed by the meagerness of what he finds there, and it will be small comfort that even less is said about bishops and the episcopate."[97]

On several occasions emphasis is laid upon Calvin's initiative in church government theory, a theme prompting lyricism from Samuel M. Smith at the ninth Presbyterian Council (1909):

> Though in the strict sense of the term, [Calvin's] church government was no more original than his theology—both being clearly contained in the New Testament—yet, while others before him, notably Augustine, had plainly taught the Pauline theology, it was left to Calvin to redeem church polity from the tyranny of human tradition, virtually to rediscover the New Testament Church, until, rescued from the rubbish of centuries, it stood revealed in all the stately simplicity of a Greek temple.[98]

(We need not stay to consider how clearly Calvin's order is seen in the New Testament, or to point out that Pauline theology was not *all* that Augustine taught.) Later during the same Council meeting A. S. Martin compared and contrasted the supernatural, authoritative, sacramental, and hierarchical notes of the medieval church with Calvin's church:

> Mediaeval Church development culminates in the imposing institution of the Papacy. Its characteristic "Notes" are the supernatural and authoritative nature of the Church, the sacramental nature of its ordinances, and the hierarchical basis of its visible unity. Calvin cordially accepts the first two points, endeavoring merely to cleanse

them from popish corruption. He rejects the hierarchy with its temporal head the Pope as the visible basis of unity, and returns to what he pleads is the primitive constitution, the Presbyterate as the Unit of the Ministry, as set forth in the Scriptures, and to the parity of presbyters, and the voluntary character of their association in Courts, Synods, and Councils.[99]

Important though church organization was, Presbyterians for the most part granted that it was not of the essence of the church.[100] They realized that to have held otherwise would have placed them with Rome. They could also admit that "Presbyterian Church courts are not always nurseries of the highest style of Christian character."[101] Few, however, went so far in the direction of the invisible church as Harold Crosby in 1883: "On looking at our Presbyterian Church, and endeavouring to satisfy ourselves of its Divine authorisation and right, we are to leave all external order and profession out of the account, and turn our attention to the consideration of the spiritual life."[102]

After the Second World War we detect a more Christocentric note in the discussion of church order. Dr. Berkelbach van der Sprenkel invited the sixteenth Presbyterian Council (1948) to consider "What is Fundamental in Church Order?" He answered, *"fundamental in church order is the reign of Jesus Christ, is Christocracy."* From this the following points are deduced:

1. The *continuity* of the acts of the Church rests in the Lordship of Christ who is with His people always. . . .
2. *The entire Church* is called to serve the Lord in the world.
3. Christocracy enrolls *all members* in the prophetic, priestly, and royal office of Christ.
4. Christocracy carries with it the idea that all *organs of the Church* are instruments of the Lord having a serving function.
5. The Church appearing in the *plurality* of local congregations is a unity in her Lord who works through His *one* Word and through His *one* Spirit.[103]

In the second of Sprenkel's points we have a Christo-soteriological theme which was to become increasingly important, namely, that of the church as the servant of the Lord. Indeed, the theme of the eighteenth Presbyterian Council (1959) was "The Servant Lord and His Servant People." Lewis Mudge wrote a prefatory study guide under this title in which he diagnosed the current situation and proposed the remedy: "Man has numbly withdrawn into himself, and in his empty individuality he has become a featureless granule in a shapeless mass. . . . We become true men only when we discover that we are God's men, and that we are in the world to serve him."[104] In his pre-council reflections James I. McCord took the New Testament understanding of Jesus Christ as his starting point:

> The relationship between Jesus and the Covenant, Jesus and Israel, Jesus and his servant people, becomes clearer when we see four aspects of the New Testament's understanding of Jesus Christ. In the first place, he comes as the Son of Mary, a true Israelite, a Jew of the first century. . . . But, and this is the second aspect, he is also the Son of God and stands in radical discontinuity with anything that Israel could produce. . . . The third aspect involves the act of identification itself. In Christ God identifies himself with human nature, not at its highest as if, at this point, deity and humanity coalesce, but at its lowest, with man in the depth of his need, where he stands under the curse in rejection and despair. . . . The fourth aspect . . . relates to the stake that God now has in human nature. . . . God in Christ has disclosed his will and purpose for mankind finally and completely.[105]

Richard Shaull, while granting that "the Word of God must be prior to and determine all forms,"[106] took careful account of the empirical context in which the church must fulfill its servant role. He urged that we must not acquiesce in past patterns of church order, but must "attempt to do for our world and generation what Calvin did for his."[107] This entails the recognition of five factors:

1. The social sciences are confronting us today with grown evidence of what Toynbee has called "the intractability of institutions."
2. The Church today finds itself in a new situation in which the old forms of life are appearing more and more inadequate. As all illusions about the *corpus christianum* are now being shattered, the question arises how far church life based on this assumption can serve the needs of a post-Christian and post-Constantinian era.
3. Our confidence in the form of the Church's life is being shattered, from within the fold, by the experience of the Younger Churches and the rise of the Sects.
4. Recent Biblical and theological studies have given us a clearer picture of the nature of the Church: its essentially missionary character, its calling to live as pilgrim people in the world, to suffer with and for the world as witness to God's redemptive work.
5. Our study of church history shows the significance of new

religious movements as a protest against obsolete patterns and a search for new ones.[108]

In his council address James S. Thompson encapsulated the theology underlying the concept of the servant church:

> The decisive re-formation of the Church was the act of God in which the Word became Flesh. God became his own Servant in the Person of his Son. He took our place, he came among us as the Son of Man, to be his own Israel, the True Vine, the Light of the World, the Way, the Truth and the Life. He is at once the Head of the Church and its Reformation. For, he also became our Servant that by his sacrifice, our sins of disobedience might be forgiven and by union with him, we might become his faithful people of the New Covenant.[109]

He then went on to argue that the servant church is to be prophetic, priestly, and regal—though all in the manner of the Shepherd-King.

We may conclude our remarks on the Presbyterian self-understanding by quoting the full and eirenic statement on Presbyterian order agreed to by the seventeenth Council (1954):

> Our adherence to the Presbyterian Order is inspired by the fact that it expresses certain fundamental aspects of the nature and life of the Church. The Presbyterian Order bears witness (a) to the sole headship of Jesus Christ in and over His Church: (b) to the Church as a community of brethren to whom manifold gifts and services have been given; (c) to the relation between the Lord of the Church and the community of believers as a covenant relation in which men become children of God and find the way to trust one another; (d) to the perils of any authority which could lead to tyranny and the peril of such an absence of authority which could lead to anarchy, in the household of faith; (e) to the necessary participation of all members of the Church in the conciliar and representative government of the Church, and to the responsibility of the governing bodies within the fellowship of the Church; (f) to the conviction that the Holy Spirit guides the Church not only in the local congregation but also in the larger Councils of the Church. We believe the Presbyterian form of government is agreable [sic] to the Word of God, but as we do not consider Presbyterian Church Order as the one indispensable governmental structure of the Church, neither can we regard any particular existing form of episcopacy or other form of church order as a fundamental condition of the restoration of the unity of the Church.[110]

The reference here to "the necessary participation of all members of the Church in the . . . government of the Church" and to *larger* rather than *higher* "Councils of the Church" could only assist those Presbyterian Congregational conversations which had already begun in many parts of the world, and which were to increase in number as the years progressed.

VII. Congregational Polity

We turn now to the self-understanding of the Congregationalists, and we shall not be surprised to find considerable emphasis upon this in their Council literature. For the raison d'être of Congregationalism was its insistence upon the fact that the church catholic is local; that to be a Christian is to be a saint gathered in company with others in the covenant family of Christ; and that the priesthood of all believers (when *properly* construed collectively) imposes pastoral, administrative, and missionary obligations upon every member. In the words of Norman Goodall at the last Congregational Council (1966):

> The Church is more than local. The classic phrase *the focal point of the Church universal* should be read as having its climax in the last word *universal*. Christ has gathered to himself a people of all nations and tribes and peoples and tongues, and these, under Christ's Lordship and in his presence, constitute the Church. But it is our conviction— our wondering confession—that this universality is, by grace, made manifest in every particular company of Christ's people. Where the Word faithfully preached and the bread broken in his Name and men and women are committed to one another to live and serve under his rule, there he is, the creator and sustainer of the Church universal. Being one with him in a particular place we are one with all his people in every place.[111]

Although as late as 1948 the historian Albert Peel could write, "If we desired to be provocative—and strictly accurate—we should begin a Congregational martyrology with James, the Lord's brother, Peter and Paul, and the heroes of faith in *Hebrews* xi, for they were members of 'gathered churches.' "[112] Congregationalists had long since ceased to believe that the Bible revealed their pattern of church order and no other. At the same time, especially over against Anglo-Catholic ideas on ministerial orders, they were not averse to insisting that Congregational orders antedated other orders, and that the New Testament bishops were Congregational ministers.[113]

In fact, however, by the time the International Congregational Council came into being Congregationalism was no one thing. In America its structure was more synodical than in England and Wales, and everywhere there were varieties of interpretation of the congregational principle.[114] The alternative designations of the tradition from the time of the English Civil War are indicative of this. In the report of the commission appointed "to review the history of Congregational polity, to appraise its present features, and to make a forecast of the developments yet to come," which was presented at the fourth Congregational Council (1920), the terms "Congregationalism" and "Independency" are discussed: "The former is positive, suggesting by its very etymology the essential constitutive principle of a true church as 'gathered' *round* the Master *from* the world; the latter is negative, asserting that the church is *not* dependent on, or under the authority of, Bishop or Priest, State or King, or even of any Committee, Council, Presbytery, Union, Convocation, or Parliament."[115]

Again, the oscillation between the "spiritual cement" theory of Congregationalism and the "local autonomy" theory continues throughout the history, proponents of the former placing more emphasis on visible sainthood, proponents of the latter emphasizing questions of polity; and just as the former could lead to doctrinal idiosyncrasy in the name of freedom, so the latter could lead to isolationism and to the misguided view that Congregationalism was democratic—one man, one vote and government by the majority—rather than Christocratic and intent on unanimity in Christ. Nothing did more to foster the democratic ideal than the Enlightenment, with its implications concerning human autonomy and human rights. At the seventh Congregational Council (1953) Lovell Cocks made the point with reference to the philosopher John Locke (1632-1704), himself a son of English Dissent:

"A Church," he writes, "I take to be a voluntary society of men, joining themselves together of their own accord, in order to the public worshipping of God, in such a manner as they may judge acceptable to Him, and effectual to the salvation of their souls." Locke then proceeds to draw from his definition certain inferences which are familiar to us. (a) He had in view the Independent Churches of his own day. And if we are looking from the outside and with secular eyes at churches that still retain the Independent polity, there is much to be said for Locke's definition. From the standpoint of the lawyer and the sociologist, an Independent Church is merely one among other voluntary societies. It ranks with the trade union and the tennis club, is structurally similar to these, and like these enjoys the rights that belong to all lawful associations and groups in a democratic community. When the question at issue concerns legalities—title deeds, trusts and the rest—Locke's definition is very much to the point. But when we are defining the Church theologically—when we are exhibiting its nature as a religious reality—John Locke has nothing to contribute to the discussion. (b) The qualities of being a voluntary covenanted association and having a democratic constitution may be inseparable accidents, but they are not the essence of the Church as Congregationalists understand it.

The Church is the Church God gathers. Its foundation is in His free grace, and its beginning is in His saving Word. It is from above, not from below; from heaven, not from men. . . .

Of course there is obviously a sense in which the Church is an institution among other institutions. This is one side of that ambiguity which is inseparable from the historical existence of the Church in the world. But the essence of the Church is not to be sought in its institutional aspect. That is why we rejected John Locke's definition. And the institutionalism that stems from the conversion of the organic analogy into an identity we reject too, not only because pushed to extremes it menaces us with the totalitarianism of the papacy, but also because, even in more moderate form, it transfers the entire discussion of the nature of the Church from the appropriate religious context to that of legalism and legalistic conceptions.[116]

In a word, Congregational sainthood is (logically) given before it is earthed; or, to put it in another way, the one church is logically prior to its local manifestations.[117]

The local churches live by grace and gather in the presence of Christ around the Word of God; they are nourished by preaching, sacraments, and fellowship. The first thought is not of legalism or of structure, but of the call of the covenant God and the free response to free grace. In this order the "liberty of the Christian man" is explored ecclesiologically. But, as Bernard Lord Manning reminded the fifth Congregational Council (1930), it is necessary to define Christian liberty carefully. In answer to his question, "What *is* our peculiar sense of churchmanship, our peculiar doctrine of the Church?" he said,

You will not think far on that line before you mention the word *Liberty*. Liberty: that is the native air of Congregationalists. Agreed: but what sort of liberty? Freedom from all those things that used to arouse violent emotions in our liberty-loving breasts: freedom "from the Bishop of Rome and all his detestable enormities"; from hierarchies, from priestcraft, from councils, from creeds, from tradition, from dogma? You know the whole bagful of bogeys whom we habitually deny. But when, to-day, you say that liberty is the distinctive possession of us Congregationalists, do you seriously mean liberty from these things and the like? If so, you have no liberty but such as falls to the lot of all men. If this be your liberty, it is the liberty of the beasts that perish. Why, it is the freedom of Mr. Bertrand Russell, of Mr. Joad, of Mr. Llewellyn Powys, of Mr. Mencken: they all enjoy this freedom, with a freedom from all knowledge of Church history thrown in. This is a freedom enjoyed by all this sad, despondent, dying world. It is a freedom that leaves the man in the street exactly where you found him. Freedom from dogma, from tradition, from priestcraft, from creed, from an infallible Book: with a small price he has obtained *this* freedom, with the price of a two-seater car or a Sunday excursion ticket. If this freedom be our distinctive contribution (and men who sit in Moses's seat hint sometimes that it is) our contribution is worthless, for it is already, like most worthless things, "in widest commonality spread."

No: our distinctive contribution is liberty, but it is Christian liberty: liberty not from the Church, but in the Church. It is the combination of liberty with the highest, fullest, most rigid churchmanship . . . full liberty, undiluted churchmanship. . . .

What was it that made us assert the rights of individual independent congregations . . . ? Was it a love of petty societies, of primary assemblies, of theoretic democracy? Nonsense: it was a doctrine of grace. . . . We had not begun with some notion about the excellence of independent congregations, and from it deduced that what such congregations supplied must be grace. We found grace in the independent congregations to which (if the Church were to rule its own house) historical accident had driven us. We found grace; and we adored. Where we found grace we recognized the one catholic and apostolic Church which with all Christians we confessed. That is our position still.[118]

The same conclusion was reached by Truman B. Douglass in 1958. He quoted such Congregational fathers as Henry Jacob, John Robinson, and John Owen, and such documents as the Savoy Declaration and the Burial Hill Confession to show that

while Congregationalists have typically insisted that the local fellowship of believers possesses all that is needful for it to be *a* church in that place, we have seldom been willing to say that this local fellowship is the only possible form of *the* Church. It is, we believe, an *expression* of the Holy Catholic Church, and we claim for it all the *authority* of

that Holy Catholic Church, in its particular place. But we do not insist
that this is the only way in which the Universal Church can articulate
its life.[119]

In face of those who might *perversely* exalt individual liberty Daniel
Jenkins wrote that

it is this emphasis on the particularity of the Church, more than its
emphasis on freedom, which is the greatest contribution of Congregationalism to the life of the whole Church. It takes the Church
seriously, not by developing a "high" doctrine about it whose character
may be largely symbolic, nor by magnifying the power and dignity of
the hierarchy in such a way that the weakness of the believing fellowship
is concealed by its strength, but by insisting that every believer must
come to terms with it in its most concrete form, the local company of
Christ's people gathering together into church order.[120]

Dr. Lovell Cocks drew the confessional implications:

There are many still who say that we Congregationalists have no
creed. Never was there a greater mistake or a more serious misunderstanding of our witness. A Congregational Church fellowship, so far
from not having a creed, is a creed made visible. . . . Not only in the
preaching of the Word and the administration of the Sacraments, but
in the very structure of its ordered life, in the profession of faith it
requires of its catechumens, in its sacred and joyful Church Meeting,
and in every detail of its work and witness—a Congregational Church
proclaims that Jesus Christ is the risen Lord Who lives and reigns in
and among the two or three gathered in His Name, and by His Spirit
guides them into ever closer communion with Himself and ever wider
and deeper unity with His people everywhere.[121]

The Congregational understanding of the status of church members
follows naturally from this, and it was expressed by Douglas Horton in
1953:

Of the Lord of the Church all the members stand equally in need. In
point of spiritual status they are on a parity. Constitutionally there is
no difference between clergy and laity. There are clergy and there are
laity, and different kinds of each, but all occupy a ministerial status to
Christ and the entire Church: the differences between them pertain
to what they do, not to what they are. . . .
    If polity is designed to be a reflection of spiritual relationships,
and there is no such status as that of most-ransomed sinner or
more-ransomed sinner, over against that of most of us—plain ran-

somed sinner—the true, heavenly, polity provides for only one order
of membership.[122]

From this flows the Congregational hesitation over the terms "laity" and
"layman/laymen/laywoman/laywomen." Glynmor John spelled it out at
the last Congregational Council (1966):

> Characteristic of the present age of the Church is the recognition made
> of the importance of the "laity." There is a fundamental sense in which
> Congregationalism *rejects* the notion of the "laity": it cannot properly
> think or speak of any church-member as a lay person. For the use of
> the term "laity" (intended and still current) is *over against priest*. Repudi-
> ating sacerdotalism, Congregationalism repudiates "lay." The word
> has crept into usage amongst us only since and from Methodist
> "lay-preachers"; the historic Congregational term is "gifted breth-
> ren"—both words being significant: as *gifted*, recognized by their
> brethren as fitted by the Lord of the Church for a particular service;
> as *brethren*, because all are church members, our "officers" and "minis-
> ters" as much as those not in a particular office. If "laity" is now to mean
> the whole church, this is something which Congregationalism has
> always understood and sought to put into practice, but on its own and
> different grounds from those of sacerdotal distinction. Congregation-
> alism holds it to be truer Christian understanding to begin with the fact
> of believers constituting the people of God, within which community
> some are given special tasks.[123]

Institutionally, the Church Meeting proclaims the Lordship of Christ
over the whole fellowship.[124]
At the sixth Congregational Council (1949) Charles S. Duthie applauded Karl Barth

> for restating our position with great clarity and for pointing its
> significance for the whole Church. The principle to which we have
> sought to bear witness is the principle that the Church is constituted,
> in essence, by the presence of Christ in His kingly rule among His
> people. . . . While others have stood with us on this high ground, we
> have shown ourselves rather more obstinate than others in the refusal
> to allow any secondary principle to displace or obscure this fundamen-
> tal principle. . . .
>
> The Church is where Christ is because where Christ is He gathers
> His people into a distinctive community, in which they belong to each
> other because they belong to Him. It is the principle by which we reject
> any claim by the State to control the life and witness of the Church or
> make individuals or groups, whether Christian or non-Christian,

subordinate to ends which outrage the dignity of man and flout the law and will of God. . . . It is the charter in which is written the right, but also the duty, of the individual to be subject to Christ alone and only to the Church as under Christ. It is the ground of our catholicity.[125]

At its best Congregationalism has ever been Christocentric, and this has tempered any anthropocentrism which the devising of local covenants might have implied—as if the *people decide* to be the church. Thus in 1920, before Barth's thought had taken root, Albert Peel contended that

> the little communities in Ephesus or Philippi knew that they were independent of all but Christ, but still they knew too that, with Him, they were the One Church, Catholic, Universal.
>
> The history of Congregational polity is the account of the decline and fall of this conception, and of recent attempts to revive it, and the problem of Congregationalism in the future is how to recover this Apostolic sense of the church, so that our local churches realize that they are subject to no Lord but Christ, and at the same time feel, as did their Lord, that the Church is one.[126]

In view of this the last point in the "bookkeeping" statement of a committee including P. T. Forsyth, R. S. Franks, Robert Mackintosh, and W. B. Selbie seems, in its simple pragmatism, to be woefully inadequate: "We do not now stress our coincidence with the external machinery of the primitive churches, for we recognize the right of development. We rather claim that our system has some peculiar advantages for doing the work of Christ today."[127] A gallery of nodding Homers!

The Congregationalists, no less than the Presbyterians, were more than aware of the "shadow" side of their ecclesiology. At the first Congregational Council (1891) G. S. Barrett warned of the peril of individualism:

> You see it in the selfish isolation of many church members. . . . You see it in the small place the church meeting holds in the affection and honour of some who are members of the church, in its sterile monotony of form; so that when it is not a prayer-meeting it is often a purely business-meeting of the church.
>
> You see it wherever there is a carnal dependence of the church on the minister. . . . You see it on a larger scale in the exaggerated and unlovely independency of some churches. . . .[128]

Six Councils later John Huxtable pleaded for realism and nipped Congregational triumphalism in the bud:

You cannot say that the local Church is the outcrop in Bradford or Baghdad, St. Andrews or St. Louis, of the Church Universal, that to this covenanted fellowship of Christians is committed all Church powers and authority, that the Risen Christ is with them and presides over them, and that they reach their corporate decisions under the guidance of the Holy Ghost, without laying yourself open to the entirely natural and legitimate question: does it work out like that? Is this mere theory? Or is it a fact of experience? Does your experience, even if it lags behind the ideal, confirm or shake your faith in the ideal?[129]

From the first Congregational Council onwards the bane of individualism was denounced, as by Barrett. John Brown did not mince words:

While maintaining that internal freedom necessary to true church life, no church has a right to do just as it likes—to be as isolated, as angular, as contentious as it pleases. If it is a church of Christ at all it is a member of the body of Christ, and therefore what it does affects the character and reputation of the whole.[130]

Thirty years later Douglas Horton reminded his hearers that "it is not our right of private judgment that makes us a Church. The bootlegger and the assassin enjoy that right";[131] and, like Brown before him, he later argued that "the reason we cannot blame the non-Congregationalist for thinking that we believed altogether in freedom and not at all in fellowship is that we have not developed to the extent required the agencies and symbols of fellowship."[132] Lovell Cocks concurred, and drew the conclusion that: "if, as we maintain, the local fellowship is the catholic Church of Christ outcropping at a particular place, so also is the synod and any other fellowship of Churches gathered through their responsible representatives under the authority of the Lord Christ and in order to do His Will."[133]

Dr. Russell H. Stafford dissented from this view, and with reference to Horton said in 1953,

I must dissent soberly from his thesis that a Council of Churches is itself a Church of any sort. . . .

Every local Church is a family. It is the fact that it is a society of brothers living together under God as their Father that makes it a Church. It is this gracious intimacy of familiar relationship which is the principle of regular Christian association. That principle is the Church, an essence existing without remainder in every local congregation of such fellowship, and nowhere else.

But a Council is not a family. Its members do not dwell together. . . . Hence a Council is not a Church.[134]

But the tide was already flowing against Stafford, and in many parts of the world Congregationalists were coming to see that wider associations were not only *useful* (and there was good evidence of this from the burgeoning of the modern missionary movement, and from the regional and national unions of churches), but *right,* and that councils possessed a *churchly* authority not dissimilar to that of local Church Meetings.[135] No doubt some Congregationalists were reassured when Terence N. Tice, the second theological secretary of the World Presbyterian Alliance, wrote as follows in *World Congregationalism,* the journal of the International Congregational Council: "The congregation is the primary and indispensable form of the Church not simply because it is a place where people are listening together for the Word of God in Christ and are celebrating the sacraments, but because and insofar as it is gathered under the call of Christ to engage in Christ's mission to the world."[136]

The most mature statement of Congregational ecclesiology was presented to the sixth Congregational Council. It sets out from God's gracious, redemptive act in Christ, and continues:

As Congregationalists we stand in the central Christian tradition, acknowledging the living faith first delivered to the saints and rejoicing in our oneness with Christ's people everywhere. God, in His grace, has created the Church by calling men into fellowship with Himself and with each other in order to realize in the world His Kingdom of truth, righteousness and love. While Congregationalists do not require subscription to any man-made creedal statements, they have ever been loyal to the great doctrines of the Christian faith and have always claimed their place in the witness of the evangelical, reformed Churches. At the same time they have stood, and still stand, for religious liberty under the Gospel and in obedience to the Gospel.

We acknowledge Christ to be the sole Head of the Church. We believe that where He is present among His people there is all that is essential to a Church. Thus each community of believers is the Catholic Church in essence and is empowered by Christ to govern its own life under the guidance of His Spirit. Its members are ministers to each other of the grace of God and may perform such functions within the Church as may be committed to them by the Church. Within this priesthood of believers some are called by God to proclaim the Word, administer the Sacraments, tend the flock of God, build up the household of faith and win men to Christ. Ordination is to the ministry of the Universal Church. Therefore we cannot contemplate any form of union which would call in question the validity of our present orders.

We believe that the rule of Christ in His Church is by persuasion and not by coercion. In the assembly of Christ's people, authority is always spiritual, working through brotherly love. This principle applies throughout the entire government of the Church, from the local Church Meeting to the most inclusive Council. We consider it to be the root principle by which the World Council of Churches may draw the separated branches of the One Church out of their shameful division into closer unity. We acknowledge with penitence that we ourselves have often failed to walk by this light. In the setting of the ecumenical movement we long to discover how the authority of the Spirit may be brought more effectively to bear upon the widest reaches of our common life and upon the government of our Churches. We rejoice both to give and to receive within the world-wide fellowship of the Church of Christ.[137]

This quotation reveals how Congregationalists were beginning to apply their inherited understanding of catholicity to the realities of the ecumenical age, and into this matter we shall inquire further. First, however, having seen how during the lifetime of the Alliance Presbyterians and Congregationalists have viewed themselves, we must now turn to their perceptions of one another.

VIII. Mutual Assessments

At the first Presbyterian Council (1877) John Cairns distinguished Presbyterianism from both Episcopalianism and Congregationalism. Congregationalism, he said, makes each worshipping assembly independent, "while Presbytery carries out to the widest limits desirable the principle of subordination and centralization."[138] He also found that Presbyterianism was more in harmony with the biblical testimony—and numerous Congregationalists could be found at the time to contradict him. But the main point is that (perhaps because Congregationalists had been less than competent witnesses to the fact) Cairns failed to appreciate that it is by virtue of his *local* church membership that the Congregationalist becomes a member of the *catholic* church. Not even at their most catholic, however, would Congregationalists relish Cairns's term "subordination." Rather, they have sought to develop a mutual *episkope* at and between all foci (the word "levels" is not normally favored) of churchly activity.

Later in the same Council session Stuart Robinson compounded Cairns's error:

It would be supposed that any intelligent Presbyterian would see so clearly the incongruity of Presbytery with Independency as not to fall into the error of seeking to blend them. For Independency in reality recognises no organic Church visible. . . ."[139]

A sufficient retort is that however inadequately Congregational catholicity had been *expressed*, any intelligent Presbyterian should have known that Congregational sainthood has ever been *earthed: "visible* saints" was the self-description of the earliest in that line.

As if to tease Cairns and Robinson, the Congregationalist S. M. Newman greeted the seventh Presbyterian Council (1899) in these terms:

Of course, we feel with a bit of pleasure that, in entering upon these Council experiences, where a large number of the different branches of the Church come together, you adopt our principle, and are standing on Congregational ground in the fellowship which you express here for one another. . . . When you come here, you drop all legislation; you enter that higher realm, where discussion and deliberation and fellowship move the heart and the mind for the toil and the struggle which lie equally before you and before us.[140]

If Newman had a caricature of Presbyterianism in mind perhaps he was not altogether without excuse.

A slightly different, but fundamental, misunderstanding was purveyed by Andrew Thompson at the fourth Presbyterian Council (1888):

The Congregational or Independent system emphasises . . . the human side. Each individual is equal in authority and privilege, and government is entirely by the consensus of the people.[141]

We have provided enough evidence already to show that in Congregationalism the initiative in church-gathering lies with God; that the *status* of all believers as redeemed sinners is equal; that the authority is Christ's; that the privilege of being under grace is shared by all; and that the government is to be not democratic, but Christocratic.

When the Congregational Union of England and Wales appointed its first nine provincial moderators in 1919, J. R. Fleming observed that this

reveals a striking approximation to the old plan of John Knox . . . the superintendent was a practical necessity in 1560, and an answer to the needs of the country. So our Congregational friends seem to feel such action to be called for today to give cohesion and driving force to their system. If Episcopalians see in it a partial compliment to their form of

polity, we Presbyterians recognise a link with our historic past which
may prove a bond of future unity.[142]

The most significant political distinction between Presbyterians and
Congregationalists was referred to by K. L. Parry at the fifth Congregational Council (1930). He had attended a meeting called to discuss
the possibility of Presbyterian-Congregational union. On more than one
occasion Presbyterian speakers referred to the "mere congregation," in
contrast to the general assembly, where for them all authority lay:

> As they spoke of the Session, the Presbytery, the Assembly, they spoke
> with increasing solemnity and reverence. The General Assembly
> seemed to them an august body, near to the ultimate seat of authority,
> the great Head of the Church. I was constrained at last to protest. I
> spoke as if the mantle of Dale was upon me. " 'The mere congrega-
> tion,' my dear man, you do not know what you say. You speak of an
> ascending authority. . . . With us it is exactly the opposite. We move
> from the centre to the circumference as we go from the local church
> to our Union Assembly. 'The mere congregation,' as you call it, is to
> us the thing itself, the Church of Jesus Christ, the household of faith,
> the Body of Christ, the two or three who being gathered together in
> His name claim His promise. He is there. What you call 'the mere
> congregation' is to us the most august society on earth. Oh yes, I know
> that they are mere nobodies, just a little group of middle-class trades-
> people, servants, labourers, and the like. But these are the redeemed
> of God."[143]

But while numerous comparisons and contrasts—some more ignorant than others—might be drawn between the two traditions, it was
not until the tenth Congregational Council (1966) that, following P. T.
Forsyth's *Faith, Freedom and the Future* (1912), John Huxtable spoke
specifically on "Congregational Churchmanship and Reformed Faith."
He here drew attention to the fact that Congregationalists do trace their
origins to Geneva, but that they also have "an admixture of Anabaptism"
in their pedigree. His suspicion, moreover, was well founded: "I suspect,
though I have not the historian's expertise to make me sure of it, that
the Evangelical Revival struck our Anabaptist chord and found it in
harmony with the excessive individualism which it encourages; while in
an ecumenical age, when we are inclined and encouraged to think in
world terms and of confessional groupings, we are more and more
aware of and grateful for our Reformed inheritance. To put it crudely,
sometimes we feel nearer to the Baptists and at others to the Presbyterians."[144] To summarize a complicated story we may perhaps say that

from Geneva comes traditional Congregationalism's interpretation of central Christian doctrines and its emphasis upon the necessity of keeping Word and Spirit in close association; from the Anabaptists comes the protest against hierarchical orders and legalistic discipline. In its emphasis upon the locality and the visibility of the saints gathered, and in its view of church-state relations, Congregationalism resembles Anabaptism.

The Presbyterian and the Congregational world bodies came together in 1970 on the basis of a statement drafted in 1966 in which the following important points were made:

> We can regard ourselves, taken together, as in large part Reformed, not because of any single historic norm of either faith or order but because our internal histories have overlapped to such a great extent, beginning with our common point of departure in the Reformation, and indeed have come to such a culminating point of common life in our time. The name also indicates the priority we give to matters of faith, while also suggesting the great stress we lay upon the integrally related task of forming and re-forming the Church's order. . . .
>
> As world families of Churches, we do not claim to contribute any "special doctrines" to the rest of the Church . . . we do, however, at this time tend to lay emphasis upon the ministry of the whole people of God, upon the diversity of gifts which are to be shared within the one fellowship of faith, upon the responsibility of the Churches to provide that God's Word shall be preached and that the sacraments of baptism and the Lord's Supper shall become a vital force in every congregation, and upon the task of letting our common worship and witness penetrate into the whole present life of humanity. We also lay emphasis upon the primacy of fellowship within the whole order and service of the Church, upon the participation of the whole people together in the government and ministry of the Church, upon the sovereignty of God over the whole society of man, and upon God's call upon the Church to attest that sovereignty before the State and within all the structures of society, not only in the interest of its own liberty but also on behalf of that responsible freedom God wills for all men. Such emphases do not stand for the whole of our faith or even for the substance of our program, but rather spotlight the meeting-place of our several traditions at this time. . . .
>
> Neither body requires a strictly defined confessional position of its members. . . .
>
> Oversight (*episkope*) within the Church is basically a corporate task. . . .

The local congregation is the primary and indispensable form of
the Church not simply because it has a place where people are
listening together for the Word of God and are celebrating the
sacraments, but because and insofar as it is gathered under the call of
Christ to engage in Christ's mission in the world.[145]

There can be little doubt that their increasing—or rather their
recovered—sense of the churchly nature of the wider fellowship enabled Congregationalists to move closer to Presbyterians in many parts
of the world. The forming of the Alliance in 1970 was the natural
consequence of this movement at the international level. It may, however, be suggested that the ecclesiological implications of this union have
not yet received sufficient theological attention. What ecclesiological
insights are presupposed by, or result from, such a union? How far can
the regionally united churches guide us in this matter? On what grounds
have Congregationalists found it possible to accept a wider *episkope?*
How far has the Church Meeting come alive in erstwhile Presbyterian
(or even in erstwhile Congregational!) churches? Ought the discovery
and practice of mutual *episkope* at and between the several foci of
churchly life—an *episkope* grounded in the view that all alike are under
the governance of Christ, the one head of the church—to be commended more ardently in ecumenical dialogue?

Such dialogue is a fact of our time, and in the next chapter we shall
attempt an analysis of those parts of it which involve the Reformed
family. But as a prelude to this it will be well for us to see how
Presbyterians and Congregationalists have understood "catholic" and
how their ideas on the subject have developed since 1875.

IX. Catholicity

"Catholic" is a slippery term. In common parlance it means "universal,"
its original connotation in ecclesiastical usage. The term was applied to
all Christians everywhere, in contrast to those who formed a local
church. Soon "catholic" came to have reference to doctrine and unity:
the catholics were orthodox believers, over against the heretics who were
not. Moreover, the chief officers of the orthodox were deemed to be in
temporal succession to the apostles. It thus became possible to speak of
the catholic *faith*—that is, of the doctrines held by the orthodox believers. By subscribing to these doctrines one could call oneself a catholic.
After the Great Schism the Western church adopted the term "catholic"
as its own self-description, while the term "orthodox" was taken by the

Eastern. At the Reformation "catholic" came to designate those who continued in obedience to Rome, over against the Protestants and the Reformed who did not. Not to be deprived of the term, however, Protestants maintained their continuity in a spiritual sense with the faithful of all ages and concluded that they were as catholic as anyone else. The Scots Confession is but one of a number of Reformed confessions to underline this point, as G. H. C. Macgregor reminded the fifteenth Presbyterian Council (1937): "We most constantly believe that from the beginning there has been, now is, and to the end of the world shall be, one Kirk . . . which Kirk is Catholic and Universal, because it contains the elect of all ages, all realms and nations and tongues . . . out of the which Kirk there is neither life nor eternal felicity."[146] In more recent years the idea of the church's election in Christ has been influential in modifying earlier expressions of catholicity, as we shall see.

We may yet again take our bearings from Dr. Krafft's consensus of Reformed confessions:

> We acknowledge and confess one Catholic or Universal Church, which is a communion of all believers, who look for their whole salvation from Jesus Christ alone, who are cleansed by his blood, and sanctified by his Spirit; that his holy Church is confined to no special place, or limited to special persons, but is scattered over the whole earth, and yet is united in one and the same spirit by the power of faith.[147]

In January 1879 the first issue of the Presbyterian Alliance's journal appeared under the revealing title, *The Catholic Presbyterian*. In his first editorial William Garden Blaikie affirmed that "Catholic Presbyterianism cannot be a very exclusive Presbyterianism . . . we regard other evangelical communions as parts of the one Church catholic."[148] Here is the universal connotation—and the Alliance was already a fellowship of churches in more than fifty countries around the world; but the doctrinal qualification is also here—at least negatively—in the apparent restriction of the term "catholic" to those of the evangelical communions. The balance was redressed elsewhere by the realization that those whose lives are hid with Christ in God, whoever they are, wherever they are, and under whatsoever ecclesiastical label they travel, are all of the church catholic.

The point was forcibly put by M. D. Hoge at the first Presbyterian Council (1877):

> While our Church is thus distinguished by its loyalty to its doctrinal standards, it is equally conspicuous for the *Catholicity of its spirit*. It is

not a broad Church in the sense of embracing a Calvinistic creed with
an Arminian clergy; or, in a sense of believing in a trinity of persons
in the Godhead—the same in substance, equal in power and glory—
and then fraternising with those who deny the divinity of Christ. It is
not broad enough to believe that there is but one name given under
heaven among men whereby we can be saved, and then, to escape the
charge of narrowness, conceding that there may be other ways of
salvation provided those who walk in them are only sincere. It is not
broad enough to teach that there is a system of Church government,
discipline, and worship, derived from the Bible, and then to admit
that these things are matters of human devising, or of mere expediency; but it is broad and liberal enough to recognise the fact that,
notwithstanding the differences existing among Christians of other
denominations as to forms of government and modes of worship, that
a true Christian unity may exist even where there is little outward
uniformity, and that this unity not only may, but does, and must exist
among those whose lives are hid with Christ in God.[149]

At the first meeting of the Congregational Council (1891), H. R.
Reynolds gave the communion sermon. Riding on the crest of the
nineteenth-century evolutionary wave he waxed lyrical:

The dawn is breaking. The Holy Catholic Church is realizing itself,
notwithstanding all disclaimers to the contrary. . . . We have gathered
from many lands because God wills it, not because some principle is
at stake, not because some dear idea, some august truth, some hal-
lowed ritual is in peril. We have pressed over land and sea, and
gathered here for counsel and common prayer, not to inaugurate a
new dogma, or bind ourselves by a new rubric, or submit to a new
infallibility, but because the Lord has been lifted up and is drawing all
men unto Himself.[150]

Rhetorical this may be, but be reminded that catholicity has more to do
with Christ's work and the *eschaton* than with our past history or current
ecumenical ploys.

With sure if heavy-footed authority A. M. Fairbairn addressed the
same council on "Congregationalism and the Church Catholic." He
launched forth from the credal affirmation, "We [*sic*] believe in the Holy
Catholic Church"; and he continued, "It is because we so believe that
we are neither of Rome nor Canterbury, neither of Augsburg nor of
Geneva, but simply and solely of Christ. . . . The Church Catholic is the
communion of saints—find the saints and you have the Church!" It
follows that just as "the history of a State is not the history of its

statesmen," and the "record of a people is not the story of its monarchs," so "the being of the Church is not the same as the action, often malign, of its officials or ministers. Its true history is contained in the holy hearts . . . of a far-diffused, divided, yet united people." The upshot is that "The Church Catholic is and must be Congregational"—and Fairbairn spells the word with a capital "C"![151]

Six Councils and sixty-two years later Leslie Cooke resumed the theme of "Congregationalism and Catholicity." He declared that Congregational catholicity turns upon the fact that Congregationalists share with all Christians the faith once delivered to the saints, and that they stand in the unbroken succession of fellowship with all who hold the apostles' doctrine.[152] But here Cooke omits a dimension of crucial importance. It is not enough to speak of sharing the faith and standing in unbroken communion with the faithful of all ages. What is *basic* is the *gift* of union with Christ—a union which is grounded in the gracious purposes of God and in his redemptive, victorious activity at the cross and in the Resurrection. This was clearly seen by B. H. McVicar in his address on "Presbyterian Catholicity," delivered at the second Presbyterian Council (1880).

McVicar begins negatively. To be catholic does not entail ignoring our or any branch of the organized church: down that path lies sectarianism. Rather, we foster catholicity by discovering and enhancing the good in all. Second, catholicity does not require the endorsement of all forms of religion or of church government as equally true. Third, catholicity does not necessitate the cessation of theological conviction or formulation. Lastly, catholicity does not demand the fusion of all the churches into one visible mass.

Positively, "true catholicity must be regulated by a supreme regard to the honor and glory of our Divine Saviour, as well as a tender concern for the members of his body."[153] The Presbyterian view of catholicity is derived from the Presbyterian conviction that God has determined to have a people for his own possession; that Christ's atoning work is catholic in intent—it is with a view to one flock; that the work of the Holy Spirit in quickening the soul cannot be restricted—least of all by selected church orders and ordinances.

What, on this basis, should Presbyterians do? They should uphold the principle of the headship of Christ against "the dogma of the supremacy of the Pope." They must show how their system of church courts works out "with beautiful simplicity, harmony and clearness the unity of the whole Church" (well, perhaps it does ideally—and even empirically here and there, and from time to time). Third, they must maintain the parity of ministers called by God and resist any "man-made sacerdotal caste." Lastly, they must demonstrate that Presbyterianism is competent to secure both the purity of the Church and the liberty of the people.[154] As R. H. Fleming later declared, Presbyterianism "finds its utterance in the liberty of the people, it rests not until every man, simply *because he is a man,* is recognized, respected, and dealt with as a creature made in the image and likeness of God. Presbyterianism is Catholic not only in its interpretation of the relation of man to God, but also in its interpretation of the relation of man to man."[155]

All of this carries a tinge of triumphalism that nowadays may cause us to squirm a little. It may be, however, that a certain definiteness of conviction is of much greater service to the ecumenical cause than the sentimentality that would collapse all Christians into an aesthetic conglomerate, thereby eradicating history and the providential leading of God at a stroke. It is in any case pleasant to note the ways in which the triumphalism of Presbyterian and Congregationalist mutually cancel each other out.[156]

The most sustained analysis of "catholicity" prior to the union of the two international bodies was provided by the Presbyterians under the inspiration of Lewis Mudge.[157] From Mudge's articles and the responses to them we may distill the correction of an earlier error, the underscoring of the point of importance in the matter of catholicity, and the remedying of an omission.

The earlier error supposed that a church's order provided evidence of its catholicity. In 1880 Samuel J. Wilson clearly thought so:

> If Presbyterianism be *jure divino,* it is and must be Catholic. . . . Our catholicity is not to be maintained by a dilution of our Presbyterianism. Let us not be ashamed of our birthright. . . . Boast they of apostolical succession! We claim patriarchal succession. Presbyterianism is older by millennia than the apostles. . . . Jehovah sent Moses down to Egypt to convene the Presbytery.[158]

But this overlooks the fact that it is quite possible to envisage order in the absence of a lively relation of the people to God. Such a church might have a method which was in principle catholic, but not actually catholic. Thus, in the more recent study of catholicity T. F. Torrance strongly made the point that whereas the Reformers regarded the notes or marks of the church as evidencing its whereabouts, these notes did not, for them, *define* the church. "The Reformation," he says, *"defined* the Church by *reference to Christ and his saving work."*[159]

This point, made earlier by McVicar, needs to be underscored. The once-for-all sacrifice and victory of Christ is the ground of our redemption and the basis of the church, the reconciled people of God. Torrance concurs, and he draws the ecclesiological inference: "It is because justification by Christ alone is so central, and concerns everything in theology and Church order, that we must set aside the question of the recognition of orders from any starting point in ecumenical relations."[160]

John Macquarrie's contribution to the debate on catholicity begins an attempt to remedy an omission detected in earlier Alliance contributions to this subject. Writing in his Presbyterian days, Macquarrie says, "My own church's Confession of Faith says that 'The Catholic Church hath been sometimes more, sometimes less visible,' that 'particular churches are more or less pure,' and that 'the purest churches under heaven are subject both to mixture and error.' "[161] The more frequent recognition of these truths (some of which are reproduced in the Savoy Declaration) might have saved Presbyterian and Congregationalist alike from undue triumphalism. But we write with the benefit of hindsight. What is more important is that these words indicate the way in which the empirical condition of the church necessitates recourse to the eschatological content of "catholic." Alliance material continues to be deficient at this point, though in his review (published elsewhere) of the Anglican Evangelical volume, *The Fulness of Christ, The Church's Growth into Catholicity*, T. F. Torrance demonstrates the importance of the eschatological reference. He commends the authors because "they give a convincing exposition of their findings that the Church's unity is to be apprehended only in the fulness of Christ which is the destiny of the Church, and to be realised by growth into that fulness." He continues:

> Whereas the Anglo-Catholics in their document *Catholicity* work with a structure of catholicity embedded in the stream of history and interpret the development of the Church and understand her unity in terms of that ideal pattern which they claim to discern in the undivided Church of the early centuries, these Evangelical Churchmen interpret the development of the Church in terms of her divine destiny which is only imperfectly apprehended in history, and understand her unity in terms of her growth into the fulness of Christ. To be sure, the Church has an unalterable and static element which is her apostolicity, the faithful standing upon the teaching of the Apostles, but her faith is always proleptic, looking forward to a fulness which has not yet been made manifest. . . . The deepest difference between "protestant" and "catholic" theology in regard to the Church is to be found here, in the insistence that the Church, her life in the tension of history, her growth toward Fulness, are to be understood exclusively in terms of Christology, while eschatology is simply a thoroughgoing application of Christology to history.[162]

Sadly, this eschatological emphasis is conspicuous by its absence from the most comprehensive summary statement on catholicity, which the Presbyterians devised at their last pre-union Council (1964):

> We believe in the Holy Catholic Church which proclaims Jesus Christ the Lord, Lord not only of the Church but also of the creation. Since the grace of God in Christ is the good news for all the world, the Church, which is bound to Christ in faith and obedience, is called to show by its life that it has a complete gospel for all sorts and conditions of men. It is this essential aspect of the Church which is indicated when we say that the Church is catholic. Catholicity is not the exclusive possession of any one of the divided Churches.
>
> We are incorporated into the Church catholic through Christ's death and resurrection for all men, proclaimed in the Word and Sacraments. We recognize Catholicity in those churches also which are divided from us, in that they too bear witness to the one Lord and the one faith. Our baptism signifies our oneness in Christ, in His death and resurrection. The toleration of disunity denies the meaning of our baptism. Inflexible ecclesiastical institutions, rigid formulations of doctrine, racial and class divisions in the Church deny its Catholicity.[163]

Fortunately a more rounded statement appears in the Alliance's more recent study booklet, *Called to Witness to the Gospel Today:*

> Proclaiming the Lordship of Jesus Christ implies a vision of and a commitment to the catholicity of the church. The church is catholic because Jesus Christ, the Saviour of the whole world, is present in its midst. It is catholic by witnessing to his work of salvation. It is catholic by embodying in its life the message addressed to all people: be reconciled with God. It is catholic by being a sign of the communion to which all people are called. To this catholicity the church is committed. Its vision embraces the promise of God in Christ for the whole world. It may not be narrowly concerned with itself. It must be open to all people in their aspirations and in their sufferings. The church is a wandering people who look forward to the fulfilment of history in the kingdom of God.[164]

This clear statement not only keeps the *eschaton* in view, but also makes it plain that catholicity entails mission. For our part we would add one sentence to this statement. The church is not catholic simply because it witnesses to Christ's salvific work. It is catholic because it owes its very existence to that work as "applied" (to use the old term) by the Spirit. As well as bolstering the content, such a sentence would have introduced the third person of the Trinity into the passage by name.

One way of summing up the developing understanding of "catholic" in Alliance circles—a development which is marked from the time of the 1960s' catholicity study to the present, and which was fueled by Lewis Mudge's *One Church: Catholic and Reformed* (1963)[165]—is to say that it has become much more Christological. The church is elect in Christ, and its members gather under his Lordship. That the Presbyterians were not alone in making the Christological emphasis is clear from Lovell Cocks's address to the seventh Congregational Council (1953):

> When we are asked what is the objective element, the massive, unchanging Fact which manifests the reality of the Church, we point to the Word preached and the Sacraments administered. For behind the Word so preached and acted stands the Incarnate Word, at once historic and contemporary—Jesus Christ, the same yesterday, today and for ever. The Word that creates and guarantees the Church can be no other than the object of the Church's faith and the content of its message. When we say "Jesus is Lord" we are at one and the same time proclaiming the Gospel, avowing our faith in it, and claiming our inheritance as true and obedient subjects of the King. The objectivity of the Church is the objectivity of the Gospel it proclaims and to which its life is conformed. If anyone would see the catholic Church, let him look at the two or three gathered in Christ's Name, preaching His Word, administering His Sacraments, and walking lovingly together in His way. And as for their authority, warrant, or title deed, where can there be authority more decisive, guarantee more secure than the promises of God declared in His Word?[166]

When reading these words the thought occurs that as the present century progressed the Congregationalists *recovered* the Christological emphasis which had always been inherent in their ecclesiology. Nor did the Presbyterians lag behind, as T. F. Torrance made clear with reference to Calvin: "It is around this doctrine of *union with Christ* . . . that Calvin builds his doctrine of faith, of the Church as the living Body of Christ, and his doctrines of the Christian life, Baptism, and the Lord's Supper. Apart from *union with Christ*, Calvin says, all that Christ did for us in His Incarnation, death and resurrection, would be unavailing."[167] We shall draw out the implications of the Reformed understanding of catholicity for inter-confessional dialogue, with special reference to the sacraments and the ministry, in our next chapter.

Meanwhile we conclude this chapter by admitting that some readers may be puzzled by certain omissions from this chapter. What the omissions are, and why they were permitted, will be explained shortly.

4

The Ecumenical Vision

In view of the emphasis within the Reformed tradition upon the catholicity of the church, upon the fact that God will have his covenant people, and upon the once-for-all redemptive work of God in Christ as the ground of reconciliation, it is not surprising that Reformed theologians and churchmen have been leaders in the modern ecumenical movement. It would have been surprising if they had *not* been active in that movement. (We do not say that *all* Reformed theologians and churchmen have been active in or even committed to the ecumenical movement, as represented, for example, by the World Council of Churches; and even the friends of the movement may be critical of some of its manifestations. Some Reformed people are actually opposed to the movement, though for the most part these do not belong to the Alliance's member churches. As always in this book we have in mind *Alliance* literature, and that is overwhelmingly sympathetic to what may loosely be termed mainline ecumenism, however much that may fail to represent every possible and actual view entertained by Reformed Christians in the world.)

Recognizing that unity in Christ is God's gift and not a human achievement, Reformed ecumenists concur with all who believe that the goal is the *manifestation* of this God-given unity so that the world may believe. The church is called to be a sign in the world of that ultimate reconciliation of all things to God. Accordingly, the Reformed today typically maintain that the catholicity of the church entails its visible unity, which does not mean uniformity of expression, liturgy, and practice. On the contrary, it is recognized that differences of individual temperament and of cultural heritage are themselves gifts of God to be accepted gladly. But it is keenly felt that the proclamation of God's reconciliation by a manifestly unreconciled church is inherently incongruous and detrimental to mission. The goal, therefore, is the mutual recognition of ministries and memberships and, above all, the removal of those barriers dividing Christians at the Lord's table when certain doctrines of the ministry and of the sacraments cut across commonly held beliefs concerning the Trinity, the person and work of Christ, the work of the Holy Spirit, and the nature of the church as the people of God.

As already implied, the Reformed do not limit their understanding of "ecumenical" to the ecclesiastical realm, but share with others the vision of the whole inhabited earth—the *oikoumene*—as reconciled by and to God-in-Christ and living under his Lordship. Like others they differ among themselves as to how far the fulfillment of this vision is a matter for the *eschaton;* but even those who expect the fulfillment then do not, at their best, allow the eschatological consideration to dampen their ardor for that gradual progress in ecumenical matters which is the order of the day in many places. Some have been (perhaps unduly) optimistic concerning the apologetic utility of church union, as in this early example: "The Church Union movement is important for the enlightenment of non-Christians everywhere—the earnest doubters who will be deprived of one chief cause of their disgust with the Churches; the careless scoffers who will be deprived of their readiest criticism and simplest excuse; and the heathen, who now survey us so closely, and know us better than we do ourselves, and will quickly recognize the spiritual significance of [steps now being taken]."[1]

At the first Presbyterian Council (1877) Philip Schaff spoke a prophetic word: "The problem of Christian union and brotherhood is one of the great problems of the nineteenth century, and will work itself out in various ways until the great prophecy of the one Shepherd and one flock be fully realized."[2] That day is not yet, but in working for it the Reformed are in no sense stepping outside of their tradition.

The evidence in favor of this assertion has been produced time and again in Alliance circles (though we cannot say that all Reformed Christians would endorse it). It is consistent with their understanding of the catholicity of the church that the Reformed should strive for the fuller manifestation of Christian unity. George Yule summoned Calvin himself as a witness on this point: "For to what end did Christ come except to collect us all into one body from that dispersion in which we are now wandering. Therefore the nearer his coming is, the more we ought to labour that the scattered may be assembled together that there may be one fold and one shepherd."[3] Again, Calvin writes to Sadolet in the following terms:

God grant that thou, Sadolet, with all thine, mayest see that there is no other bond of Church unity than the fact that Christ, the Lord, has reconciled us with God the Father and has gathered us out of the dispersion into the communion of His body, that so we may grow together through His word and spirit into one heart and soul.[4]

Calvin regarded the division in the church as a "frightful mutilation of Christ's body," and he sought "to maintain the Church universal in its unity, which malignant minds have always been eager to dissever."[5] He longed for the unity of the churches of Germany, France, Switzerland, England, and Scotland, and would have tolerated (though he would not have advocated) episcopacy to secure this end. This was the theme of letters he wrote to Melanchthon and Bullinger. To the former he lamented, "O God of grace, what pleasant sport and pastime do we afford to the Papists, as if we hired ourselves to do their work."[6] And in a letter to Cranmer he wrote: "The members of the Church, being severed, the body lies bleeding. So much does this concern me that, could I be of any service, I would not grudge to cross even ten seas, if need were, on account of it."[7]

That the framers of the preamble and articles of the Presbyterian Alliance were well aware of their heritage is clear: "In forming this Alliance, the Presbyterian Churches do not mean to change their fraternal relations with other Churches, but will be ready, as heretofore, to join with them in Christian fellowship, and in advancing the cause of the Redeemer, on the general principle maintained and taught in the Reformed Confessions that the Church of God on earth, though composed of many members, is one body in the communion of the Holy Ghost, of which body Christ is the Supreme Head, and the Scriptures alone are the infallible law."[8]

For their part the Congregationalists had no difficulty in demonstrating from their classical and more recent documents that their order was more than open to church unity. Thus, for example, a commission on "Congregationalism and Unity" led by Willard L. Sperry showed that the vision of Christian unity is present in John Robinson's farewell speech to the Pilgrims (1620) and in the Cambridge Platform (1648) and the Savoy Declaration (1658), and that it had preoccupied national councils in America from 1865 to the present (1920).[9] At the same Council an English commission on "The Influence of Congregationalism in Promoting Christian Unity, and the Lines upon which It Should Use that Influence" quoted two crucial Savoy propositions:

1. "As all Churches and all the Members of them are bound to pray continually for the good and prosperity of all the Churches of

> Christ in all places, and upon all occasions to further it. . . . So
> the Churches themselves (when planted by the providence of
> God, so as they may have opportunity and advantage for it) ought
> to hold communion amongst themselves for their peace, increase
> of love, and mutual edification."
>
> 2. "Such reforming Churches as consist of persons sound in the
>   Faith, and of conversation becoming the Gospel, ought not to
>   refuse the communion of each other, so far as may consist with
>   their own principles respectively, though they walk not in all
>   things according to the same rules of Church-order."[10]

Against any who might suppose that the inspiration of international
consultative confessional bodies was triumphalistic, we may note the
considerable space given to the question of Christian unity by the first
Congregational Council (1891). In his address Edward White said,
"We are called to unity, to mutual forgiveness and mutual toleration";
and he reminded his hearers that the early Independents "did not
hold the now common notion that as soon as ever a difference arises
between Christians worshipping on one spot they have a right to go
out and set up another tabernacle and found a completely independent society."[11]

In addition to such references as this the *Proceedings* of the first
Congregational Council contain twenty-five closely printed pages of
addresses on, and discussion of, "The Unity of the Church. How far
does the desire to discover some means of outwardly expressing this
unity prevail? How far is it possible to gratify the desire, especially in
co-operative work?" (Latter-day ecumenists may feel unsatisfied by
mere cooperation, but in 1891 the Congregationalists were out ahead.)
Henry Allon opened the symposium thus:

> It is not only fitting, it is imperative that this congress should affirm
> the relations of Congregational churches to all other Churches of
> Jesus Christ. Silence concerning our common relations to the Divine
> Head of the churches would be an indication of culpable indiffer-
> ence to the intense and persistent sentiment of Christian unity, and
> of yearnings for its manifestation, which have characterized all ages.
> From the beginning unity has been a distinctive note of Christianity.
> It was indicated in the carol of the Nativity, it was a predominant
> sentiment in our Lord's teaching and prayers. . . . It is the assump-
> tion of all apostolic writings, it is an article of every Christian creed,
> it enters into every Christian prayer, into every anticipation of the
> Christian millennium on earth, and of the Father's house in
> heaven.[12]

Allon went on to speak of "Hindrances to Unity," and came very close to home:

> It is not merely—perhaps not even mainly—in diversified forms of church organization, that disunity has developed. It is seen in schisms within the churches, as well as sectarianism without—in internal antipathies, rivalries, and selfishness; in some Diotrephes "loving to have the pre-eminence"; in some Judaizing apostle seeking to impose a yoke of ritual; in some passionate partisan of Paul, or Apollos, or Cephas, or even Christ: for often the greatest evils are wrought in the holiest name.[13]

Among *secondary* hindrances to unity are questions of church order and worship. Allon can understand why people should deem their own order the best, but

> when . . . claims of Divine and exclusive Church prerogative are asserted, our reply is—First, that the *onus probandi* necessarily devolves upon those who make them; and next, that they are unsupported by any Scriptural authority; that the claim of a so-called apostolical succession . . . has not only many broken links in ecclesiastical history, but it is broken in its very staple ring; that there is no proof that the validity of the Christian sacraments, in any sense, depends upon the official authority of their administrator; and that, therefore, it is in the highest degree unchristian, and presumptuous, to unchurch the various and multitudinous communities of Christendom which refuse to admit such unwarranted assumptions, and upon which the abounding tokens of God's spiritual blessing so manifestly rest.[14]

We shall see later that this is still the position of those in the Reformed family who deny the *necessity* for the existence in the church of the threefold order of bishop, priest, and deacon. The question of the desirability of such an order with a view to the church's mission is a different, and a disputed, question.

Returning to Allon we find him declaring that uniformity is not a viable goal in churchly matters, for all analogy contradicts it, human consciousness resents it, and history testifies against it.[15] He concludes by asking: "Who is the schismatic?" His answer is that the schismatic is one who denies visible fellowship: " 'As if,' says Robert Hall, 'those whom He forms and actuates by His Spirit, and admits to communion with Himself, were not sufficiently qualified for the communion of mortals.' "[16] "It is," says Allon, "with a feeling of positive pain that, in connection with such a theme, I have felt constrained so to speak. There

seemed no alternative. If we really desire Christian union, we must first
and faithfully speak of the causes which hinder it. The evil is not in
diversified church organizations, it is in the exclusive spirit which
refuses to recognize them."[17]

As time passed the idea of the stewardship of resources was introduced as a motive for unity. Thus at the ninth Presbyterian Council
(1909) F. H. Henderson asked,

> Is the craving for Church Union a mere stirring of the commercial
> waters, a "Combine" for purposes of economy, a prudential shift for
> the prevention of waste and the husbanding of resources? Even if it
> were only a movement on this lower plane of existence, it would not
> be a movement to be despised, but one to be respected. . . . The
> Churches are feeling their impotency in a separated and divided
> state. . . . In other words, the desire for Union springs from a con-
> scientious and worthy desire to win the battle for the Lord and
> Master. . . .[18]

The same speaker went on to counter the notion that á "spiritual"
unity will suffice:

> but, apart from the fact that spiritual without corporate union in those
> who are bidden to live a corporate life is not clear enough to the mind
> to be intelligible, it is not easy to see how the unity of Christians is
> fitted to have the effect desired by our Lord in His prayer, that, viz.,
> of winning the world to Christ, unless it be a union that is not merely
> spiritual, but both corporate and spiritual, "that the world may believe
> that Thou hast sent Me."[19]

Later during the same Council session Ross Stevenson, speaking on
"Christian Fellowship and Future Opportunities," welcomed the following signs of growing unity:

> Sunday-school Conventions have been teaching children that all,
> regardless of credal name, belong to the same fold of Christ. Young
> people's Conferences are emphasizing only the essentials of Christian
> faith. The college student, in Christian Association work, does not
> think of enquiring whether the man who sits next to him in the Bible
> or Mission Study-class is a Baptist, or a Methodist, or a Presbyterian.
> Great inter-denominational Conventions at home and abroad make
> the different Churches sit at each other's feet for instruction.[20]

We may note in passing the view widely held in American "mainline"
churches that what are nowadays designated para-church organizations
are by no means necessarily an unmixed blessing where church unity is

concerned. For one thing, they are often not accountable to the churches either in respect of their policies and activities or in respect of their finances. Again, many would now feel, against Stevenson, that those who are *content* to gather on common ground only to return afterwards to their divided ministries and tables are opting too easily for a too shallow—sometimes a too sentimental—unity.

Twenty years earlier than Stevenson (1888), Moses D. Hoge had detected favorable signs of a different kind:

> There is not only a growing realisation of the essential unity of all who constitute the true indivisible Church, but a growing manifestation of that unity. We see it in the changed style of controversy on the part of those who, in earnestly contending for the truth, conduct the contest in love, avoiding the vituperation and shameful personalities which once disfigured and disgraced Church polemics. . . . We see it in the growing toleration of others who hold the views of doctrine which they believe to be Scriptural, without branding them with ignorance or insincerity.
>
> That is not the toleration of those who say it makes no difference what doctrinal system you hold, or what form of Church government you maintain, or what modes of worship you prefer . . . but it is the true, rational, Scriptural toleration of men who have positive convictions of their own . . . yet who believe those who differ from them may be equally loyal to the truth, equally honest in striving to discover it.[21]

When the subject of the proposed World Conference on Faith and Order was discussed by the tenth Presbyterian Council (1913), caution prevailed. A resolution commending the idea was modified, and it was simply agreed to convey the invitation to the proposed conference to the member churches of the Alliance, together "with such information as shall secure an intelligent consideration of the whole matter."[22]

Eventually, in 1927, the First Faith and Order Conference was held at Lausanne, and two years later Lewis Seymour Mudge reflected upon it (much more positively than the Congregationalist William E. Barton, to whom we referred in our first chapter) at the thirteenth Presbyterian Council. He said that the conference was Christian, able, thorough, courageous in its selection of topics for consideration; its spirit was good; and almost one quarter of its delegates (92 out of 399) were connected with the Presbyterian and Reformed family. The conclusions were:

1. That every Churchman should be deeply and prayerfully interested in the reunion of Christendom.

2. That every Churchman should be actively engaged in the promotion of the reunion of Christendom.
3. That a great step forward in the reunion of Christendom will be the reunion in every land of the Reformed Churches there located which hold the Presbyterian System.[23]

On the last point Mudge continued,

Why should this be considered by any of us an impossible task? . . . We are whole-heartedly agreed as to what is the Church's message to the world. We are at one as one to the nature of the Church. We should have no difficulty in deciding what are the essential elements in the Church's Confession of Faith. As to the Church's ministry, we have no need to decide as to whether the historic Episcopate is of the *esse* or of the *bene esse* or the *non esse* of the Church. As to the sacraments, our situation is not rendered more complex by the existence among us of any problems as to the Real Presence in the Holy Communion, or as to the particular form of ordination which is required to give validity to the sacraments when administered. Why, then, should not the reunion, nationally, of the Reformed Church be considered our immediate duty?[24]

At the fourteenth Presbyterian Council (1933) a "Declaration on Outstanding Matters of Religious and Public Moment" was made, of which the first point was:

Christian Unity.—While loyally adhering to the principles and the tradition of the Presbyterian Churches, the Alliance is in cordial sympathy with the world-wide aspirations and movements towards reunion in Christendom and rejoices in their progress. It believes that the sacred end in view will be best promoted through the attainment of a common understanding of the nature of the Christian Church, the Christian Ministry, the Christian Sacraments, and the Christian Message, based upon the inspired teaching of the Scriptures interpreted in the Creeds of the Ancient Church and in the standards of the Reformed faith.[25]

The point was reaffirmed at the next Council:

The unity of the Church is spiritual, but it needs to be made visible to the world. The witness of the Church has been gravely hindered by persistent divisions. While we acknowledge that from time to time, in obedience to conscience and for the good of the whole Church, it has been deemed necessary that Christian men should separate themselves from one another, we believe that God is ever calling us to seek ways of reconciliation within the essential unity of the Church.[26]

The implications of Reformed catholicity underlay all discussions of church unity, and to these were added, as we have seen, considerations of the stewardship of resources in the interests of God's work. The statement of the Princeton Council (1954) on "The Reformed Churches and the Ecumenical Movement," bears witness to this.

As the century proceeded a more intensely Christological-missiological note began to be struck. Thus the message of the eighteenth Presbyterian Council (1959) includes the following paragraph:

> *The ecumenical responsibility of the Church.* Viewed in the light of reconciliation, all forms, orders, traditions and doctrines of the Church become subject to renewal. Jesus Christ himself is the only criterion of the integrity of the Church, and he is only served when the Church, in every aspect of her life, is subordinate to him alone. The Reformed Churches must bear witness in ecumenical discussions to Jesus Christ the Lord and Head of the Church.[27]

At the next Presbyterian Council (1964) a study group declared in its report that

> we were baptized into Christ and therefore made members of the Holy Catholic (Universal) Church but we received this baptism through the ministry of a particular, historical Church: we could not avoid this. . . . Nevertheless the truth, recognized by the Reformers, that there is only one Church extended throughout the world, remains valid today and the present disunited state of the Church is sinful in that it obscures this truth and our reconciliation with one another in Christ.[28]

Here the concept of catholicity, Christologically conceived, is directly related to the question of church unity.[29]

The same council also heard the missiological challenge: "It is because of Christ's mission, in which we are called to share by the Spirit, that the unity of the Church is not only a given gift but also *a sacred task*."[30] These words of C. H. Hwang were matched on many occasions, but never as strongly as by the president of the Presbyterian Alliance, John A. Mackay, in 1955:

> The unity of the Church is for the sake of the mission of the Church. The health of the Body of Christ is fulfilled only when all the members, acting in perfect unison, obey the missionary mandate of the Head. Christians have no right to regard themselves as ecumenical unless they are prepared to do two things: first, to carry the Gospel and the

fruits of the Gospel into all the world, and secondly, to do this together. For us who belong to the Reformed tradition the mission of the Church and the unity of the Church are inseparably bound together.[31]

The next president, Wilhelm Niesel, returned to the theme:

The word of God, the good news of God's descending to seek the lost and strayed in the person of his Son, the Gospel of Jesus Christ and his blessed lordship over us, won through his death and sealed in his resurrection—this is the great discovery that the Reformers were enabled to make. This Gospel is the centre of all mission and all concern for the unity of the Church. Where there is no concern with this Good News, then, in spite of the greatest zeal, there is no mission; and where the word of the crucified and risen Lord is not the governing principle around which all crystallizes, then despite carefully prepared union schemes, there can be no uniting of Christendom. This can only lead to further confusion.[32]

An associated appeal was to the dire need of the world. As Henry Smith Leiper told the seventh Congregational Council (1953): "A responsible and intelligent attitude towards world community in such a time as this involves recognizing the degree to which the Christian Churches of the world are failing it in this time of peculiar crisis through their failure to provide the unifying factor which ought to manifest itself as the peculiar gift of those who worship God in Christ and depend for their inspiration upon His Holy Spirit."[33] Nor did J. L. Hromadka allow the Presbyterian Council members of 1954 to forget the kind of world in which they must prosecute their mission:

We have to sense the imperceptible, and yet real, shifting of the centre of gravity from the Christian nations to the non-Christian world. . . . The nominally Christian nations started and carried the two great, disastrous wars. . . . Christian nations are ceasing to lead the world, the so-called Christian civilization finds itself in disintegration. Christian countries are becoming a missionary field. Christian churches are getting more and more paganized. The process of secularization is proceeding and can hardly be halted.[34]

In debates and papers on church union an optimistic note was frequently struck vis-à-vis the Presbyterian and Congregational contributions. Dr. Mackay, for example, regarded the Reformed churches as suitable bridges between other communions: "The Reformed Churches, because of Calvin's high doctrine of the Church, and the anti-hierarchical and democratic spirit which tends to prevail in these churches, occupy a strategic mediating position in the ecumenical movement of today, between the Episcopal Churches on the one hand, and those churches which have a Congregationalist Church polity."[35] Cooperation was by now deemed insufficient; indeed, J. Hutchison Cockburn declared in 1948 that cooperation could actually *impede* union: "It is unfortunate that many Churches consider co-operation a sufficient step towards unity, and are unwilling to go further, because they think no more is required. They point to the things that the Churches do together, as if that were proof of their ecumenical outlook, whereas co-operation may only be a kind of inoculation against union, and may satisfy Churches which ought not to be satisfied; but co-operation is entirely to be encouraged so long as it is recognized as a first and not as a last step in ecumenicity."[36] On the other hand, a note of caution was struck by W. Niesel to the effect that zeal for unity can blind the eyes to other concerns: "A good aim can become an idol. Unity of Christendom can only mean unity in Jesus Christ."[37]

This is the basic point; and against any who might wish to hold that questions concerning papal primacy, apostolic succession, the sacraments, and the like must be settled prior to unity, George Yule contended that such people "have failed to see that a much more fundamental truth is denied by our disunity. It is the truth of the sheer grace of God in the incarnation who accepts us all though unacceptable and does not proffer us reconciliation and make us members of his family only when we have fulfilled certain conditions and seen certain doctrines in the right way."[38]

Lest it be thought that unity was simply a matter of talk and not of action, we may cite Glynmor John's address to the last Congregational Council (1966): "One quarter of all the Congregational communions in the world have already moved into united Churches, and . . . an exceptionally high proportion of Congregationalists find themselves congenially engaged in occupations in which the ecumenical movement expresses itself."[39]

I. Ecumenical Words and Deeds

Despite the clear and unbroken catholic-ecumenical thrust of Alliance literature the complaint is sometimes heard that Christian world communions, by their very existence, are an *impediment* to Christian unity. It is not normally suggested that it would have been better had there *never* been such bodies, for most recognize that but for the activities of those who were keenly connected with confessional bodies (notably the

Anglican and the Reformed—including the Congregational) there would be no World Council of Churches as we know it today.[40] Indeed, the first general secretary of the World Council said that "without the Reformed Alliance, there would have been no world Council," while the second secretary described the Council as "the child of the Reformed Alliance."[41] It is worth recalling that the sixteenth Presbyterian Council welcomed "as a manifestation of the Spirit and will of Jesus Christ" the "prospective formation of a Council of Churches," and urged its members to "give serious and prayerful consideration to applying for membership" of it.[42]

We have already provided evidence to show that the founders of the Presbyterian and Congregational world bodies were not narrowly sectarian, but it cannot be denied that at the first Presbyterian Council (1877) W. G. Blaikie had a global ecclesial structure in mind: "Besides the obvious desirableness, on general grounds, of a General Council of the whole Church, there are special reasons in the very nature of the Presbyterian system pointing us toward it as the cultural apex of the whole structure. The Presbyterian system is remarkable for its unity of organization; yet that feature is wanting where it is most natural to look for it."[43] This vision has not become a reality, and most member churches have been content with the "general ground." Indeed, at their preliminary meeting held at Edinburgh on 13 November 1874 the British delegates agreed that the Council's "powers should only be those of a deliberative body, and should carry only moral weight."[44] This became the prevailing opinion, and thus the objectives have consistently been fellowship, common testimony, and cooperation in mission.[45] The aim, to repeat what we noted earlier, was not to vitiate successful fraternal relations between the Presbyterian churches and other Christian communions.

The spirit of the Alliance was enunciated time and again—as by the general committee to the first Presbyterian Council: "Important though we deem our Presbyterian organization, it is but as the outer case of an inner treasure, our supreme regard for which will, it is hoped, be apparent throughout, nor ought it to be forgotten that there are many from whom we may differ as to the structure of the case, but with whom we are at one as to the value of the treasure."[46] The Alliance sought to be ecumenical in the geographical sense too. When R. M. Patterson introduced the *Proceedings* of the second council he could hardly contain himself: "How truly ecumenical the concourse was! How suggestive of the Catholicity of Presbyterianism! . . . The white, the black, the copper coloured races were all there."[47] Our familiarity with modern transport should not blind us to the fact that in 1880 this was a very considerable achievement.

That the objectives of the Congregational Council were equally broad, and exactly comparable with those of the Presbyterian, is clear from the following clause in the constitution: "The purpose of this International Council is to foster and express the substantial unity of the Congregational Churches in faith, polity and work; to consult upon and devise measures and maintain agencies for the advancement of their common interests; and to do and to promote the work of the Congregational Churches in their international and interdenominational relations."[48] The moderator of the ninth Council (1962), Russell Henry Stafford, could hardly have been clearer: "This Assembly is not a legislature or a court of law. It is a consultation among colleagues. Its only tone must be persuasion. Nor is the persuasion we would exercise aimed at extension of Congregationalism at cost to other Christian Communions, or in rivalry with them. The International Congregational Council is not a sectarian promotional agency."[49]

By the time Stafford spoke both Presbyterians and Congregationalists had come to see their role as being *within* the growing ecumenical movement. Thus at their seventeenth Council in 1954 the Presbyterians reaffirmed their executive committee's statement of 1951: "Just as it is the true nature of the Christian Church to be an instrument of God's glory, it is the true nature of Presbyterianism never to be merely an end in itself, but to serve the Church Universal of Jesus Christ, the Church which is His body."[50] At the same council John Baillie, noting that both Anglicans and German Lutherans were becoming more confessionally self-conscious, remarked that

> to many of us . . . the new confessional movement appears to be far from an unmixed blessing. A return to the creeds of the undivided Church is one thing, but a return to the confessions born of the fragmentation of the Church is quite another. If the latter were to mean only that each denomination sought a clearer mind as to the true genius of its own heritage, and as to the essential nature of the contribution which it can make to a reunited Church, then it would be a thing to be cordially welcomed; but if it means that each is digging in, entrenching itself more firmly than ever, along the old lines of battle, it can only spell disaster.[51]

Two Councils later (1964) a report affirmed that "the truth, recognized by the Reformers, that there is only one Church extended throughout the world, remains valid today and the present disunited state of the Church is sinful in that it obscures this truth and our reconciliation with one another in Christ."[52] The same Council received a further report which contained the following declaration:

The modern ecumenical movement is probably the most significant development in 20th century Christianity, affecting as it does, not only all the member Churches of the World Council of Churches but also influencing all denominations large and small, and now manifest within the Church of Rome through the Second Vatican Council. This situation requires the Alliance to integrate all its study and action in the ecumenical movement in general and in the work of the World Council in particular. This policy has emerged in all the recent General Councils, but its practical implications have to be continually reviewed. The continued association of the Alliance office with the World Council, now located in the new building at Geneva, promotes this close association and cooperation.[53]

For an example of similar Congregational statements we may turn to Douglas Horton's address to the sixth Congregational Council (1949):

To the strengthening of this [Congregational] association all of our churches are called. . . . By this means we shall be able to cast lines of Christian understanding and good will across international boundaries and so make our contribution to the peace of the peoples. By this means we shall be able to make effectual our witness to freedom and fellowship through Christ in the councils of the developing Ecumenical Church. We may dare to pray that power be given to our new endeavours not for their sake or ours but that through them the world may be blest.[54]

In the light of the background thus sketched the "Message to Member Churches" from the Uniting General Council of 1970 is in no way surprising: "We pray that God will not let us rest at ease with our common identity but will use us, as we hope he will use other world confessional bodies, not to retard but to hasten the wider unity which he wills among all Christians."[55]

So much for affirmation. What of practice? In the first volume of the *Quarterly Register* the editor answered his own question, "Is a Presbyterian Alliance necessarily sectarian?" with a resounding "no." Not all today are convinced of this, however, and so we shall present some evidence of the way in which, true to the foundations laid in both its parent bodies, the Alliance seeks to fulfill its ecumenical objective.

First, the Alliance contributes towards the manifestation of Christian unity by not doing what it need not do, and by encouraging its member churches to work together with Christians of other communions wherever possible. In a word, a real attempt is made to apply the principle underlying the question posed by a member of the third World Confer-

ence on Faith and Order (Lund, 1952): "Should not our Churches ask
themselves whether they are showing sufficient eagerness to enter into
conversation with other Churches, and whether they should not act
together in all matters except those in which deep differences of conviction compel them to act separately?"[56] This question received official
affirmative answers from both the Presbyterian and the united Alliances.
Thus the seventeenth Presbyterian Council (1954) unanimously resolved that "The World Presbyterian Alliance is not organised for the
administration of Inter-Church Aid, and does not propose so to or-
ganise, because of the conviction of many of our Churches that the
giving and receiving of Aid has ecumenical implications beyond our
Reformed family."[57] The principle was underlined with reference to a
wider range of issues by the Presbyterian executive committee in 1966:
"It is our principle in relation to the World Council of Churches to do
nothing separately which can be done in cooperation, and to enter as
fully as facilities allow into its program, especially in the area of studies.
We do not wish to administer Inter-Church Aid or other similar funds,
but prefer to support the aid programs of the World Council of
Churches, providing special counsel on the situation of minority
Churches."[58]

Second, the Alliance is committed by its own resolutions to promoting
the ecumenical cause by encouraging unity and union within the
Reformed family itself. This may appear a paradoxical statement at first
sight, for it might be thought that such nurturing of the confessional
family could be undertaken only by the irremediably clannish. But in a
threatened and divided world the church is called to proclaim a gospel
of reconciliation which cannot but sound hollow if the church remains
divided. If particular Christian communions remain internally divided,
a fortiori the proclamation of the reconciling gospel is further compromised. In many parts of the world more than one Alliance member
church occupies a given region. In some cases the confessional separation between Presbyterians and Congregationalists (or their united
heirs) persists. Elsewhere earlier internal confessional secessions are
perpetuated to the present day (and perhaps the Reformed heritage of
secessions—reunions notwithstanding—shows more clearly than anything else what can happen when those who claim both Scripture and
Spirit fail to "discern the body"). Yet again, distinct member churches
within a given region may be the children of different mission boards—
and to this consideration are sometimes added tribal and linguistic
factors, or both. Still, if "unity begins at home," the Alliance is challenged
at these points.[59]

Again, over against those who would regard the fostering of Reformed unity as a sectarian pursuit we would set "ecumenical man," who despises all confessional groupings and seeks membership of the one, holy, catholic, apostolic, visibly united (and thus currently non-existent!) church. Less extremely, "ecumenical man" may accuse Christian world communions of *impeding* local efforts towards union among Christians. We have seen no evidence to suggest that the Alliance has been a complicating factor of this kind, though the fact that the Alliance is itself a union of two confessional families and that nearly twenty of its member churches represent transconfessional unions would seem to tell against the allegation.

The fact remains, and Reformed ecclesiology insists, that to be Christian is to be called by grace and engrafted into the people of God. The Christian cannot avoid being ecclesiastically anchored somewhere within the present divided church. President Mackay resorted to a Spanish proverb in explication of this point: "A bird may fly to the ends of the earth but only in a nest can it raise a family."[60] He continued, "Christians can not belong to the Church in general, any more than they can belong to humanity in general, or be Germans, or French, or British, or Americans, or Japanese in general."[61] Mackay was here in the line of G. D. Henderson, who in 1929 had sought "to emphasize two things at once—width of comprehensiveness and maintenance of principles. I think Churches not prepared to combine these should not attempt Church Unions."[62] Henderson's address prompted an interesting discussion, in the course of which J. M. Wells said that Henderson "tells us that we can have a comprehensive Church as to the great doctrines; but he declines, and so far as I can find out all decline, to say just where the lines of comprehension end or begin. In other words, where is it that the limits of truth lie?"[63]

In all of this certain points need to be clarified. It is legitimate to say that to be a Christian entails ecclesiastical anchorage somewhere; and it would be a denial of the providence of God to complain that we had been permitted to hear the gospel somewhere and not somewhere else, and through some lips and not through others. Again, since there is a gospel to be proclaimed we do well to guard against notions of an ecumenical aesthetic conglomerate into which people slide simply because nobody believes anything in particular. But the view that if the Reformed, the Anglicans, the Roman Catholics, the Baptists, and all the others will only bring their individual bricks, then God the Holy Spirit will take them and cement them together to form the one Church of Christ is very wide of the mark—happily so from the Reformed point of view.

It is not simply that as well as being concerned with our own insights we have to hear those of others.[64]

The point is that *we* do not provide God with the ingredients for making his church—and least of all by offering our partialities. God gives unity in Christ on the basis of his finished reconciling work at the cross and in the Resurrection. The church is called into being by the Spirit through the preaching of the word of reconciliation, and Christ is its only head—hence all that was said earlier concerning catholicity. It follows that the Reformed and those of other Christian communions are challenged to testify to what they have seen and heard *within* the *one* family of Christ. Thus when the Alliance executive committee's Basel statement of 1951 declares that the Reformed must "emphasize aspects of the Reformation heritage which are of permanent significance for the Christian Church,"[65] this can only be because those aspects are Christian and not because they are Reformed. The church is already catholic.

Moreover, the reason why the Reformed should be happy with this state of affairs is that, strictly, they have nothing else to say: "The confessional conflict does not consist in putting a Scriptural, theological or interior security over against a hierarchical, doctrinal, or sacramental security. It consists in putting the consciousness of being able to live only by faith and grace over against every security, whether of a Catholic or of a Protestant type."[66]

At this point we return to the cryptic remark made at the end of the last chapter. In that chapter some readers may have detected certain omissions. We expounded the Reformed heritage without mentioning (except by implication) what are compendiously known as the doctrines of grace. Where was predestination? Where was election? Our justification is that such doctrines are by no means the exclusive possession of the Reformed. Hendrikus Berkhof spoke in no uncertain terms on this matter:

> What would Calvin think of this enumerating of "special" Reformed doctrines? In my view it would sound to him like the very worst affront to his life work! Nothing was further from his intention than such "an enrichment" of the Universal Church with "special doctrines." . . . The doctrine of Election is certainly the plainest instance of a Reformed "special" doctrine. It played a great role in Western thinking from the time of Augustine onwards. In most of Calvin's writings it plays, however, only a marginal role, even in the *Institutes*. . . . But the idea of "special doctrines" and "partial truths" is untenable not merely historically but also in principle. What sort of quantitative thinking is this? Is revelation then a number of separate truths? And even if it were, would not the maintaining of particular special truths mean the betrayal of the Church and a deliberate decision in favour of sectarianism?[67]

It is quite wrong to suppose that Calvin and the other Reformers set out to contribute certain doctrines to a "coming great Church," or that they intended to found new confessional groupings on the basis of a certain number of underplayed doctrines. Rather, they sought to reform the existing church according to the Word of God, and to encourage its continual renewal under the Spirit; and all of this in the interest of *catholic* truth. The precise place of regeneration in the *ordo salutis*, or the analysis of "total depravity," or even the desirability of the presbyterial or congregational orders—these were not the motivating considerations of the fathers of the Reformed family. If the Reformed feel the need to offer insights on such matters within the catholic church it must be because those insights are biblical, not because they are uniquely Reformed—otherwise the Reformed are as sectarian vis-à-vis truths of the faith as they suspect others of being vis-à-vis ministerial orders.[68]

The Reformed protest is in the interests of the catholic gospel and of the church as already one in Christ. The visible manifestation of that unity is to be a sign of the ultimate goal: the realization of the unity of the *oikoumene* in Christ. A Christian world communion which embraces such a hope cannot justifiably be accused of being anti-ecumenical.

A specific way in which the Alliance works for the manifestation of the unity of the church is by participating fully in inter-confessional dialogues. (We use the customary shorthand "inter-confessional" while feeling uneasy with it because [a] any contribution we make is intended to be catholic, not sectarian, and because [b] the Alliance as such does not have one confession to which all its member churches adhere.) International dialogue has increasingly become a feature of church life since the 1970s. It was indeed partly with a view to this work that the Alliance constituted its department of theology with a permanent officer in 1957.[69]

The value of inter-confessional dialogues has sometimes been questioned. No doubt much of the effort towards church union must be expended locally and regionally, but the findings of international commissions may help to prevent insularity. Further, they take seriously the reality of the present situation which is that the Christian world communions exist, and that some of them (more than others) will press only for solutions which are global in scope. The question of how the findings of dialogue commissions are to be received by the Alliance's member churches is an abiding challenge; but to any who may wonder how far it is possible for dialogues to be conducted vicariously and representatively on behalf of others, and how far dialogue results can be absorbed by those who were not existentially involved, Nils Ehrenström and Günther Gassmann have made reply:

These problems cannot be solved by a devaluation of world-wide conversations and a one-sided emphasis on national or regional encounters. These more limited encounters are very often in danger of a provincialism which may occupy itself too exclusively with domestic problems and partial solutions, thereby losing sight of the universal dimension of the Christian faith and the world-wide community of the Christian Church. The world-wide conversations, if properly based and conducted, serve as a reminder and a sign of this wider dimension. Yet if they are to be an "effectual sign," their relation to the encounters on these other levels needs to be reconsidered and forms and structures developed which will enable a more effective two-way communication and mutual enrichment.[70]

The authors specify the following benefits, "obviously varying in substance and precision," which have resulted from bilateral dialogues:

(a) Agreements on eucharistic doctrine. . . . (b) Agreements on the nature of the ministry and/or full or partial mutual recognition of ministries. . . . (c) Full intercommunion. . . . (d) Partial intercommunion. . . . (e) Agreements concerning the relationship of Gospel, Scripture and Tradition. . . . (f) Discovery of profound affinities in spirituality and concern with sanctification. . . . (g) Agreement on "church fellowship" (full pulpit and altar fellowship) on the basis of a common understanding of the Gospel, invalidation of the mutual condemnations of the sixteenth century, and mutual recognition as Church of Christ.[71]

It need hardly be said that although the World Council of Churches may and does encourage multilateral and bilateral dialogue, the Christian world communions must themselves initiate dialogues directed to the mutual clarification of issues between them, fulfilling a role which they alone can fill. Indeed, the Alliance was not first in the field of bilateral dialogues. The possibility of conversations with the Baptist World Alliance, which was mooted by Marcel Pradervand at the 1968 executive committee meeting, was shelved until after the Uniting Council of 1970; and a certain early caution resulted from unwillingness to appear to be vitiating the Lund principle by "going confessional."

II. The Bilateral Dialogues

Against this background we may view the dialogues in which the Alliance has been engaged. We shall confine our attention to international work completed, or near completion, by 1982. This means that we have three documents to consider: *The Presence of Christ in Church and World*—the report of the dialogue between the Alliance and the Secretariat for Promoting Christian Unity of the Roman Catholic Church (1970-77); *Baptists and Reformed in Dialogue*—the report (with supplementary material) of the conversations sponsored by the Alliance and the Baptist World Alliance (1973-77); and *God's Reign and Our Unity*—the report of the Anglican-Reformed International Commission (1981-84).[72] (We shall note the document, *Theology of Marriage and the Problem of Mixed Marriages*—the report of Lutheran-Reformed-Roman Catholic conversations, 1971-77—in chapter 6 below.) Our consideration of these reports will enable us to highlight the ecclesiological issues that gather around the topics of baptism, eucharist, and the ministry, thereby completing our consideration of doctrine.[73] It would be untrue to say that the completed dialogues have by themselves made for change at the grass roots of the churches' life. The ideas enunciated have, however, been propagated to a reasonable extent—through consultations, publications, and personal contact. We dwell on the reports in some detail not because they are in themselves a panacea for all the ecumenical ills of the Reformed family, but simply because they represent the most protracted and thorough (and the most expensive) theological study sessions in the Alliance's history to date.

Before proceeding it is necessary to record with gratitude the quite remarkable change in spirit marking inter-confessional relations since the 1960s, a change that has had not a little to do with the Second Vatican Council. It is symbolic of this change that the Reformed and others are no longer deemed by Roman Catholicism to be heretics, but are now regarded as separated brethren. On the Reformed side attitudes have changed noticeably since the parent bodies of the Alliance were founded. It would nowadays be most difficult for a speaker at an Alliance council to make the points and use the language of A. A. Hodge in 1877:

> By the definition of the Immaculate Conception, the Syllabus, and the Dogmatic Constitutions and Canons of the Vatican Council, the true character of our great adversary is uncovered, and the pending controversy reduced to its ultimate terms. The Virgin has been practically substituted for the Godhead as an object of worship, and for the God-man as a source of redemption. The Word of God, as the supreme rule of faith and duty, has been rendered obsolete by the Papacy.[74]

Points of disagreement would today be stated with greater care, and in a less pugilistic way.

In 1964 the nineteenth Presbyterian Council received a report of its standing committee on Roman Catholicism in which the "new climate" was welcomed, with its promise of cooperation and dialogue.[75] Ten years later the first phase of dialogue was more than half completed. We shall introduce the reports of the dialogues with the Roman Catholics, Anglicans, and Baptists, making brief comments *en passant*, and then turn to a thematic treatment of the sacraments and the ministry.

The introduction to *The Presence of Christ in Church and World* contains an account of the background to the dialogue and describes the process leading to the report itself. The first main section is entitled "Christ's Relationship to the Church." "The starting-point of these discussions," we are told, "was the recognition that, in Jesus Christ, God has made joint cause with sinful humanity and aims at the renewal of the world. Therefore all those who are connected with the name of Jesus Christ have the joint task of bearing witness to this Gospel."[76] There are many witnesses to Christ in the New Testament, and norms for the belief and practice of the church are not to be found "in isolated proof-texts or in clearly discernible primitive patterns, but in the New Testament considered as a whole and as testimony to the divine purpose and mission for Israel, the Church and for all humanity."[77] There is agreement that "the Church Catholic is really represented and exists in the local Church," and that the church is to serve in the world for Christ's sake.[78]

The following sentence is intriguing: "There was complete agreement in presenting ecclesiology from a clear christological and pneumatological perspective in which the Church is the object of declared faith and cannot be completely embraced by a historical and sociological description."[79] In response, the first point is that the Reformed might have been expected to have had reservations concerning the *church* as the object of faith—the more so when in the next paragraph the report declares that, whereas the church may (after Paul) properly be described as the body of Christ, such images as that of the bride "warn us against any absolute identification."[80] Second, the phrase to the effect that the church "cannot be completely embraced by a historical and sociological description" is of considerable importance, given the catholic claim of the Reformed that their churches are ecclesial realities. The phrase is unexceptionable if we are to understand a reference to the entire church, visible and invisible. Clearly the church triumphant is not susceptible to ostensive definition or to sociological or historical description. The question is, however, whether the visible Reformed churches are deemed to be ecclesial realities in anything other than a sociological sense. The Vatican Fathers' own definition reveals, among other things, a profound misunderstanding of the Reformed claim: " 'Ecclesial communities' is the phrase adopted by the Council when the Fathers wish to refer to those christian bodies which would reject the name of church for themselves, yet retain many of the Church's practices and beliefs."[81] Paolo Ricca has reminded us that

> in introducing the second part of the 3rd chapter of *De Oecumenismo* . . . Cardinal Heenan . . . explained that, in choosing the expression "Churches and Ecclesial Communities" to describe the Protestant Churches, "it was not our intention to deal with the question of the conditions which a Christian community must fulfil in order to be a Church in the theological sense." It is not clear, therefore, that the terms "Churches" and "ecclesial" have any theological significance here, in the mind of the drafters of the Decree at least.[82]

He also notes that in the *De Ecclesia,* the dogmatic basis of the *De Oecumenismo,* the phrase "Churches and *ecclesiastical* communities" is used. This "seems to indicate that in the *De Ecclesia,* the sociological view prevails over the theological view of the Protestant Churches. It also strengthens the doubts about the theological significance of the term 'ecclesial' used in the *De Oecumenismo.*"[83] The impression is reinforced in the document itself: "It gives us joy . . . to observe that our separated brethren look to Christ as the source and centre of *ecclesiastical* fellowship."[84]

The underlying consideration is that the Roman church, though its self-understanding is more dynamic than hitherto, regards the ecclesial status of the separated brethren as deficient because they are not in communion with the bishop of Rome, a claim supported by a remark of a modern-day pope. When he preached in the Ecumenical Centre, Geneva, on 12 June 1984, Pope John Paul II said "to be in communion with the Bishop of Rome is to give visible evidence that one is in communion with all who confess that same faith, with those who have confessed it since Pentecost, and with those who shall confess it until the Day of the Lord shall come. That is our Catholic conviction and our fidelity to Christ forbids us to give it up."[85] It would be simply a cheap point of debate to retort that *some* of those who have been in communion with the bishop of Rome through the ages have not in fact been noticeably caught up by the matter or the spirit of the apostles' doctrine—no church should be judged by its more wayward elements. The main point is that the pope's words sound—to use Forsyth's term—monopolist, not catholic.[86] The negative inference to be drawn from these words is that if one is not in communion with the bishop of Rome one is not giving (any? the best?) visible evidence of catholicity. Such a charge the Reformed, from the depths and reality of their ecclesial life, can only deny.

The question implied but not addressed in the main sections of the

Roman Catholic/Reformed dialogue report is, "How far is a particular church structure given in and with the gospel?" The section entitled "The Teaching Authority of the Church" records the agreement that "the Church has its authority to the extent that it listens to the Word Christ speaks to it ever afresh."[87] The significant point is made that "historical researches have shown not only how the New Testament writings are themselves already the outcome of and witness to traditions, but also how the canonisation of the New Testament was part of the development of tradition."[88] It is further agreed that "for its witness in the world, the Church must always express its faith by confessions in which it interprets the Word of God in the language of today."[89] The respective positions of either party vis-à-vis the confessional statements of the past are accurately stated: "For Catholics, the affirmations of the past are normative as guides for subsequent reformulations. For the Reformed, they have a real positive value which is nevertheless subordinate to the authority of Scripture."[90] A crucial sentence follows: "So far as instruction is concerned, for the Reformed it is the community as a whole which is responsible and which delegates qualified people; whereas for the Catholics there is a distinctive responsibility of the pastoral ministry: the latter is rooted in the believing community but does not derive its authority from an act of delegation on the part of the latter."[91]

We are thus led to statements concerning infallibility which are accurate as far as they go, but, as we shall suggest, are incomplete:

> Catholics hold that God's faithfulness to his Church necessarily means that when the People of God unanimously declares that a doctrine has been revealed by God and therefore demands the assent of faith, it cannot fall into error. And in particular that those who have been specially charged with the teaching mission are protected by a special charisma when it is a matter of presenting the revealed message. . . . This is equally the case when the bishop of Rome, in the rare cases specified by Vatican I, expresses himself *ex cathedra*. Nevertheless, what has just been said does not imply that all the expressions chosen are necessarily the best available, nor again that the ecclesial authorities enjoy this charisma in a permanent manner or that they cannot be mistaken in a certain number of affirmations on which they do not commit themselves fundamentally.
>
> The Reformed rejection of any infallibility which is accorded to men derives from a repugnance to bind God and the Church in this way, in view of the sovereignty of Christ over the Church and of the liberty of the Spirit, a repugnance strengthened by the experience of

frequent errors and resistances to the Word on the part of the church. In addition there is a fear lest confidence in the infallibility of a formulation should distort the personal character of faith in the living Christ; further, the fact that many Reformed take the resistance of man to the Spirit of God so seriously today that any assertion of the infallibility of the Church becomes impossible. Apart from that, for Reformed sensibility, any claim to infallibility in the modern world represents an obstacle to the credibility of the proclamation.[92]

The conclusion is that for the Reformed "what alone is infallible . . . is God's fidelity to his covenant, whereby he corrects and preserves his Church by the Spirit until the consummation of his reign."[93]

The preceding statement of the Roman Catholic position is incomplete in that no mention is made of the apparently monopolistic claim of *De Oecumenismo:* "When Christians separated from us maintain the divine authority of the Sacred Books, they think in a different way to us—and differ among themselves—about the relation of the Scriptures with the Church; for in the Church our Catholic faith asserts that the true magisterium enjoys a unique position when it comes to the exposition and preaching of the written word of God."[94] Since this comparison with separated Christians was not made in the Roman Catholic/Reformed dialogue report, the Reformed were not able to reply to it.

The report next considers "The Presence of Christ in the World." The contention is that

the presence of Christ in the world is a consequence of the continuity of God's action in creation and redemption. . . .

It is through the Spirit that Christ is at work in creation and redemption. As the presence in the world of the risen Lord, the Spirit affirms and manifests the resurrection and effects the new creation. Christ who is Lord of all and active in creation points to God the Father who, in the Spirit, leads and guides history where there is no unplanned development.[95]

The presence of the Spirit of Christ may be sought "in the plan or purpose which God is realizing through all the complexities of history"; "in those movements of the human spirit which, with or without the assistance of the Church, are achieving the ends of his Kingdom"; and "in those values and standards which owe their origin to the Gospel, but now have become embedded in public conscience and institutions."[96] These affirmations are informed by a number of convictions, including the following:

"In the Cross Christ identifies himself with men in their sin (cf. Isa. 53:4f., 11f.; John 1:29; 2 Cor. 5:21) and need in order that they might be identified with him in the new victorious life of his resurrection (cf. Rom. 6:4f.; Col. 3:1-4). The first identification remains true and effective even where it is not recognized. Christ is present in the poor and helpless who cry for liberation."[97] However, to say that "Christ himself is the carrier of the message of the rule of God and the *liberation* of mankind"[98] can, in view of the way in which "liberation" is currently employed in connection with the acquisition of national independence—by force if need be—unwittingly encourage the proclamation of a truncated gospel. This is not, of course, to deny that "the challenge of the world to the Church and its appeal for help may be at the same time a challenge and appeal from Christ, who in this way judges his Church, demands obedience and calls it to reformation."[99] How can the church respond to this? "The Church can . . . correspond to its calling if its structure and its life are fashioned by love and freedom. Accordingly the Church does not seek to win human beings for a secular programme of salvation by propagandist methods but to convert them to Christ and in this way to serve them. In its proclamation of the Gospel there is at the same time a powerful creative cultural dynamic."[100] Hence the church may legitimately claim that in its endeavor "to realize more justice, more conciliation and more peace" it is "only following its Lord into domains that, unbeknown to men, already belong to him and where he is already anonymously at work."[101] But the fundamental work of rescuing us from the malaise empowering the obstacles to justice, conciliation, and peace is his and his alone.

The report goes on to expound "The Church, as the Effective Sign of Christ's Presence in the World." The church, which "exposes its fundamental orientations and loyalties by the way it lives, no matter what it says to the contrary," bears witness that "Christ is Lord over the world as well as the Church."[102] The church cannot be static but must listen to the Word of God in order to discover what transformations may be required of it. A statement of the utmost significance for the Reformed (and especially for the Congregational) family follows: "The localness and the catholicity of the Church are to be kept in perspective. It is only by participating in the local community that we share in the life of the universal Church, but the local community without universality . . . runs the risk of becoming a ghetto or being arbitrarily dominated by individuals."[103] The assertion that we belong to the church catholic by virtue of our local membership will be reiterated in the Reformed/Baptist dialogue report.

The report continues: "Practical changes must take account of the great variety of situations confronting the Churches and these changes presuppose both a de-centralization of the Church and a larger participation on all levels, quite especially on what is commonly (and perhaps misleadingly) called the laity."[104] Ecclesiologies diverge in the way the words in parentheses are cashed, and the underlying question is, "How far is the 'both'–'and' ecclesiology of the Roman church acceptable?" The problem was posed by Vittorio Subilia: "If we were to interpret Catholicism solely in the light of chapter II (On the People of God) and chapter IV (On the Laity) of the Constitution *De Ecclesia* the inescapable conclusion would be that Catholicism had adopted a lay ecclesiology of the universal priesthood of all believers. On the other hand, if we were to interpret Catholicism in the light of chapter III (On the Hierarchical Constitution of the Church), it would be correct to conclude that the Church of Rome has not abandoned its traditional clerical, hierarchical ecclesiology."[105]

It remains to be seen whether the second phase of Roman Catholic/ Reformed dialogue will be able in any way to resolve this difficulty. The present report closes with a section on "The Eucharist" to which we shall return when offering our thematic treatment of sacraments and ministry. But first we must introduce the other completed dialogue reports.

III. God's Reign and Our Unity

God's Reign and Our Unity—this title aptly catches the spirit of the Anglican/Reformed International Commission's dialogue. It is a dissuasive against suspicious and premature thoughts of "ecclesiastical joinery"—"Have the Reformed embraced a variety of episcopalianism congenial to the Anglicans, and if so what have the Anglicans espoused or relinquished in return?" The undergirding motifs in this report are that God reigns whatever we do, and even if we do nothing; that he has a purpose for his entire cosmos; and that he calls a people to himself that he may dispatch them in mission. Here is an attempt to set the familiar ecclesiological themes of baptism, eucharist, and ministry within the context of God's saving purpose and the church's role as witness and servant.

As well as having breadth, this report is marked by realism. The authors agree that the unity sought is ultimately that of all Christian people, but they face the fact that progress is more likely to be made by "small advances," and they urge the churches to work for these.

Moreover, the report attempts to be practical. The authors have no wish to have their work reviewed—perhaps even praised—and then shelved. They are well aware that all too often theological agreements reached by international commissions have no perceptible results at the front line of Christian life and mission. Accordingly, they have included a number of practical recommendations which range from a suggestion that Anglicans and Reformed pray systematically for each other (which surely should not be beyond the most tender conscience), to the challenge that "member churches in each place explore seriously the possibility of moving towards the formation of united churches"[106] (which may, here and there, hurt a little more).

Chapter 1, "Our Task," is a description of the relations between the two communions in various parts of the world and a consideration of the question, "What keeps Anglicans and Reformed apart?" A number of answers are suggested:

1. The two traditions have customarily defined themselves in different ways: the Reformed in terms of confessional subscription (though with the recognition that those of the Congregational Way who are within the Alliance, "though never reluctant to devise declarations of the faith commonly held among them, have not made confessional subscription into a test of church membership");[107] the Anglicans by reference to a communal liturgy, and the common adherence to the threefold ministry.

2. While both communions affirm the centrality of Word and sacrament, "the accent falls differently."[108]

3. "The role of the bishop in Anglican piety and churchmanship has no exact parallel in Reformed experience."[109]

4. The establishment question awaits resolution.

5. The "bonds which tie our two communions to the national feeling and the folk religion of the people of whom we minister" constitute subtle obstacles.[110]

More general obstacles include the fear of losing one's confessional identity, apprehension concerning organizational "bigness," and false understandings of the nature and calling of the church. Of these the last is the most important. Hence a major, urgently reiterated aspiration of the authors is that "our quest for Christian unity is seen steadily in the context of God's purpose to reconcile all people and all things in Christ."[111] The relation between Christian unity and human unity, with all that that entails concerning such issues as peace and justice, is central to this report.

With the foundation laid, the report assumes the character of a "communal autobiography," with the authors recording how missiological and cultural considerations led them corporately to restore the concept of the reign of God as an impelling focus for ecclesiology. They came to realize that "the most effective way of overcoming the apathy which is threatening the ecumenical movement is to put much more closely together concern for the unity of the Church and for the unity of humanity in the purpose of God."[112]

The second chapter, entitled "The Church: God's Apostolic People," draws readers back to the sheer grace of God. Our God, "whose being is holy love, uniting the Father, Son and Spirit, draws us by the work of the Spirit into participation in the Son's love and obedience to the Father. This same holy love draws us to one another. This is grace, and to reject one another is to reject God's grace."[113] Thus the gospel contains both promise and judgment.

The church is to be "a sign, instrument and firstfruits of a reality which comes from beyond history—the Kingdom, or reign of God." It is "a provisional embodiment of God's final purpose for all human beings and for all creation,"[114] provisional because only part of the human family has been brought into its life, and those so brought are only partly conformed to God's purpose.

The authors reject the view that concern for evangelism, social justice, and church unity are competing claims set over against one another. On the contrary, they "are complementary aspects of the one mission of God in which we participate as accountable stewards. To restrict our concern to any one of them would be to abridge the gospel."[115]

The third chapter, "The Life of the Church," begins by discussing the relationship between orthodoxy and orthopraxis: the action of the Alliance in suspending two white South African member churches over apartheid is cited as an example of the pronouncement by Christians that their fellows have failed in orthopraxis.[116]

A discussion follows of baptism and the Lord's Supper. Though more shall be said about these in due course, for the present we note that the Reformed have welcomed the emphasis upon the fact that "Baptism and Eucharist rest alike upon the finished work of Christ in his incarnation, death, resurrection and ascension."[117]

"Ministry in the Church," the title of chapter 4, once again strikes the evangelical note: "Only in this double perspective of mission and of the new life in Christ experienced as the free gift of grace can ministry in the Church and the ministry of the Church be adequately understood."[118] Against this background ordination, authority, and continuity are considered: "In the act of ordination, the Church in Christ prays to the Father to grant his Spirit to the one ordained for the office and work to which that person is called, accompanying the act with a sacramental sign which specifies by the imposition of hands the one for whom the prayer is made, and—in faith that the prayer is heard—commits to the person ordained the authority to act representatively for the universal Church in the ways proper to that particular office."[119] The underlying issue is spelled out:

> We confess one holy catholic and apostolic Church. In the ordination rites of both our traditions we make our invocation to the Father in the name of Christ and therefore intend that the ordination is to the ministry of his universal Church, carrying an authorization universally valid. In fact, because we are divided, the prayers are not the prayers of the whole Church, and the authorization is not acknowledged by the whole Church. In particular our two communions are divided at this point because of different views about the role of the continuity of ordination in signifying and safeguarding unity.[120]

Still, we cannot say that God's answer to our less-than-unanimous prayers is defective. What is required is "(a) that the reality of God's gift of ministry to the churches in their separation is unambiguously acknowledged; and (b) that the continuity of succession in ordination with the undivided Church is—so far as lies in our power—visibly restored and maintained."[121]

As the parties to the Anglican/Reformed dialogue work towards the meeting of these requirements some all too familiar discussions will resume, and it will be interesting to see whether the missiological-eschatological emphasis of this report will be sustained.

Under the heading "Patterns of Ministry" we are invited to consider ministry as personal, collegial, and communal; and one of the concluding recommendations urges churches of both communions to reflect on the extent to which their structures give due place to these three aspects, and to take remedial action where necessary.

The fifth chapter, "Our Goal," contains a reaffirmation of what was said at the outset concerning God's purpose for his people, together with a number of practical suggestions. In the latter connection the authors put their point bluntly: "If our two communions are to become one, Reformed churches will have to face the question of bishops, Anglican churches will have to reconsider the diaconate and take into account the Reformed experience of the eldership, and both communions will have to take more seriously the role of the whole membership in the governance of the Church."[122]

The final chapter of the report contains nine recommendations, three of which we have already mentioned. The fifth recommendation bears closely upon the challenge to the Reformed churches to which we have just drawn attention: "We recommend that where churches of our two communions are committed to going forward to seek visible unity, a measure of *reciprocal* communion should be made possible; for communion is not only a sign of unity achieved, but also a means by which God brings it about."[123]

A Reformed suggestion is that the crucial question does not concern bishops as such—the Reformed Church of Hungary, for example, has had bishops for centuries. Everything turns upon what bishops are supposed to be able to do, especially in ordination. Do they or do they not transmit a special *potestas*? Are we invited to embrace sacerdotalism? To both questions the majority of Anglicans say "no." In view of this, in view also of the doctrine that episcopacy is said to be of the *bene esse* of the church and not of its *esse*, and in view of the ecumenicity of every Lord's Supper, it has often seemed strangely sectarian to the Reformed that Anglicans should balk at reciprocal inter-communion—especially since canon law promulgates no prohibition. For some years now Christians who are in good standing with their own churches have been welcomed at the eucharist in the Church of England. Will Anglicans, in response to the recommendation now before the churches, come with untroubled conscience to the Lord's table in Reformed churches? If they do not, will it not appear that despite denials that episcopacy is of the *esse* of the church, those concerned are behaving as if it were? Nothing would do more to draw the sting of the "bishops" controversy than that this recommendation should be adopted by both parties to the dialogue.

In this connection we may note that the Roman Catholic/Reformed report, which claims that the church as a whole is apostolic or "sent," has this to say on "special Ministry":

> Within apostolicity in general there is a special ministry to which the administration of Word and Sacrament is entrusted. That special ministry is one of the charismata for the exercise of particular services within the whole body. Ordination, or setting apart for the exercise of these special services, takes place within the context of the believing community. Hence, in consultation with that community, profession of faith before that community, and liturgical participation by that community belong to the process of ordination. This is important to underline because we need to go beyond an understanding of ordination which suggests that those consecrated to the special ministry are given a *potestas* and derive a dignity from Christ without reference to the believing community.[124]

But did not the Reformed wish to say that they do not understand themselves as receiving a special, sacrament-validating *potestas* at all?

God's Reign and Our Unity does not treat every issue in equal depth, and much work remains to be done. For example, the question of the ordination of women (a question, indeed, for the Reformed family as well as for the Anglican) is posed but not resolved; and that of the establishment of religion is but briefly mentioned in the text and is implicit in five of the thirty questions which are offered for discussion at all levels, and bilaterally where possible. Both questions are nonetheless important, and of the two the former has received more attention of late than the latter. When we reflect, however, that behind establishment theory and practice there lie the questions "Who is a Christian?" and "How are we to honor Christ's Lordship over his Church?" we see at once that this is not a matter which can be shelved forever.[125]

Again, a significant question of language requires further consideration. On two occasions the sacraments are said to be "constitutive" of the church.[126] From such language it may be but a short step to *ex opere operato* views of the sacraments and to a minimizing of that catholic-evangelical claim which it is in the supreme interest of the Reformed to maintain—namely, that God constitutes his church by the Spirit through the Word on the basis of the once-for-all reconciling work of Christ. In a word, the church is constituted by the Trinity. To this the sacraments bear witness. It is not, of course, suggested that the authors of the report would deny this; neither is it supposed that those who may wish to question the bald assertion that the church is constituted by the sacraments intend to deny that the sacraments are a mode of Christ's presence with his people. What the questioners require, and what the authors need not hesitate in, is the conjunction of Word and sacraments at this vital point. It is, furthermore, in the interest of both to maintain that those who humbly and obediently hear the Word and participate in the sacraments will be blessed far beyond their deserving, for God in Christ has acted first, and he is faithful to his promises.

We shall have more to say shortly concerning the sacraments and the ministry, but first we shall introduce the third completed dialogue report and its attendant materials.

IV. Baptists and Reformed in Dialogue

Baptists and Reformed in Dialogue contains the dialogue report itself, the report of the group which evaluated the dialogue findings, a statement of the actions of the executive committees of both bodies, a letter to member churches, some suggestions as to how to proceed, and an appendix in which Larry Miller offers a Mennonite perspective on Baptist-Reformed relations.

The reason for the original conversation is clearly stated: "Because of the deepgoing divergence in theology and practice between Baptist and Reformed traditions *and* because of our close kinship it would seem very important that we explore together the nature of our disagreement and how best we may overcome our differences."[127] Further stimuli are the review of baptism in Reformed circles,[128] and the existence already of one united church—that of North India—in which Baptists and Reformed are fully involved.

The report of the conversations sets out from the shared emphasis upon "Holy Scripture as the normative source for faith and practice,"[129] and describes the discussion which took place on the themes of the people of God, the new covenant, the status of children in the church, the "holiness" of children (cf. 1 Cor. 7:14ff.), the understanding of the church as mission, and the boundaries of the church.

As with *God's Reign and Our Unity*, so here: the missiological note is loudly struck. "We must," declare the authors, "seek ways for our churches to work together in the common mission of Christ."[130] Where these two communions are concerned this means confronting

> the difficult question whether Christians of Reformed and Baptist convictions who are members in good standing in their churches could recognise one another as both occupying the position of those who have received and responded to the grace of God in baptism as this grace is understood in the New Testament. Such a mutual recognition could only arise from:
>
> (i) an agreed understanding that a complex of elements, including baptism with water in the name of the Trinity, public profession of faith and admission to the Lord's Supper, are all parts of the reception of and response to this grace of God;
>
> (ii) the acceptance (still problematic) that this complex of elements could find place in the life of any individual *either* contemporaneously in the act of believer's baptism, where profession of faith, water baptism and communion come together in time, *or* over a period of time, short or long, in which (infant) baptism, profession of faith (at "confirmation" as it is often called), and admission to communion follow one another as separable stages in a process.[131]

Here is the crux of the report, and the authors affirm their own position in the eighth of twelve theses on "The Holy Spirit, Baptism and

Membership in the Church of Christ": "While we affirm the New Testament view of baptism as a once-for-all incorporation into the Church, the body of Christ, we propose to view baptism in the context of the Spirit's total action upon the total life of the individual and the Christian community."[132]

On the question of ministry, and at an important point of contact with *God's Reign and Our Unity*, this report is uncompromising:

> Both Baptists and Reformed are averse to the sacramental concept of a ministerial priesthood and rather put the emphasis on the functional nature of the pastoral office and of the particular ministries. Together they reject the doctrine that a particular understanding of spiritual office and succession in office, bound with the historic form of the episcopate, belongs to the being of the church and is therefore essential to it.[133]

As we have seen, the Anglican/Reformed report does not defend what is rejected here. To reiterate the point made above, responses to its fifth recommendation concerning reciprocal inter-communion will be highly informative.

As to the church, the Baptist/Reformed authors make a number of affirmations, of which the following three constitute a bulwark against congregational excesses on the one hand and presbyterial ones on the other:

> The one holy universal Christian church becomes concrete in the local congregation. [This sentiment, as we saw, is echoed in the Roman Catholic/Reformed report.]
> At the same time the local congregation is necessarily related to other local congregations.
> The wider church relationships (area, national, regional, world-wide) have ecclesiological significance.[134]

In all of this the term "congregation" has a rather Presbyterian ring. If it is understood to mean "the congregation of the saints" there should be no difficulty; if it were (wrongly) taken to mean "all who comprise a worshipping congregation—members, adherents and passing atheists alike"—then Baptists, and Congregationalists within the Reformed family would feel an ecclesiological threat.

Twenty-two (only) responses to the Baptist/Reformed report were received and evaluated. The evaluation report clarified a number of points, and the following is underlined: "To overcome the impasse created by an exclusive insistence on infant baptism or believers' baptism, we have tried to approach the problem in the light of a comprehensive understanding of Christian initiation."[135]

The Mennonite commentator, Larry Miller, detects three deficiencies in the report: its virtual silence on church discipline (with which our own question concerning the "matter" of the church is inextricably interwoven), on the nature of discipleship, and on church-state relations (of which the establishment question is one aspect).

Two comments may be made on Miller's response. First, in raising the establishment question he fastens upon a weakness common to both the Baptist/Reformed and the Anglican/Reformed dialogue reports. Second, his three points are linked by the question, "Who is a Christian?" Is this not a question which the confessing church in exciting and dangerous times needs to address with renewed vigor?

Clearly, all three completed dialogue reports leave us with further work to do. Additional matters emerge when we recall that Roman Catholics, Anglicans, and Baptists have been and are in dialogue with others as well. Thus, for example, we have *The Final Report* of the Anglican/Roman Catholic International Commission (ARCIC I). The most striking point of difference between what Anglicans and Roman Catholics said to each other and what Anglicans and Reformed said to each other is encapsulated in ARCIC when, with reference to the ordained ministers, it is said that "their ministry is not an extension of the common Christian priesthood but belongs to another realm of the gifts of the Spirit."[136] The Roman Catholic/Reformed report leaves the matter on the table in the form of a question: "What is the meaning of the laying on of hands: mission, transfer of a *potestas*, or incorporation into an *ordo?*"[137] It may be that the second phase of this dialogue, now in progress, will address this question directly.

Again, ARCIC I has things to say concerning the primacy of the bishop of Rome—and they were not overenthusiastically received by the Vatican's Sacred Congregation for the Doctrine of the Faith.[138] This matter is not raised in *God's Reign and Our Unity*, no doubt because it is not a point of difficulty between the majority of Anglicans and Reformed Christians. But now that the Reformed are in further conversations with the Roman Catholics, this issue, which has arisen between them and their Anglican dialogue partner, cannot responsibly be overlooked. Furthermore, the North American Lutherans and Roman Catholics have published the results of their dialogue under the title *Differing Attitudes toward Papal Primacy* (1974), and this will surely not go unnoticed in the forthcoming international Lutheran/Reformed dialogue, not least because the Americans, distinguishing between the "divine institution" and the "divine design" of the papacy, have agreed to opt for the latter.[139]

The moral is that while in bilateral conversations issues of concern between the partners expectedly loom largest, the fact must not be overlooked that frequently the partners are partners of someone else as well. Since different teams have different players, a real effort must be made to ensure consistency of play and to obviate the perpetration of "own goals." Thus cautioned we shall proceed to relate the wider Alliance literature to the three completed dialogue reports on the subjects of the sacraments and the ministry.

V. The Sacraments in Alliance Literature

An initial caveat is needed here: as a plain fact the vast majority of the Reformed do not find it natural to *begin* ecclesiological discussion from the sacraments. For them the action of God the holy Trinity, expressed in the Word, is prior to, and illuminative of, the sacraments. In the absence of the Word the latter are but dumb witnesses. G. D. Henderson was being no less than truthful when in 1929 he said

> the Reformed Churches speak of the Word and Sacraments, and not of the Sacraments and Word; and I feel that here we discover one limit to union which, for a long time, will remain final and definite. *Ex opere operato* views of the Sacraments place them in the centre of worship, and are bound up with that view of Episcopacy which alone has made Episcopacy a difficulty and a danger, the doctrine of Apostolic Succession (not necessarily involved in Episcopacy itself), and as a result the Catholic or Anglo-Catholic is separated from us by much too wide a gulf meantime for us even to think of gathering the materials for a bridge.[140]

Sixty years later we may say, to continue the analogy, that the materials are now being gathered, but the feasibility studies are by no means complete.

The underlying and as yet unresolved question is, "How far is a particular church structure given in and with the gospel?" The evangelical view, though by no means inherently averse to good church order—especially in its Reformed mode—places grace above order and requires the latter to be judged by the gospel. But let us proceed carefully and examine first what Alliance literature has to say concerning the sacraments.

Dr. Krafft's 1877 consensus statement on the matter says this:

We confess that the Sacraments are instituted by God as sacred pledges (seals) of the divine covenant of grace, to support our faith, that they are outward signs of invisible blessings, whereby, as means, God himself works in us by the power of the Holy Spirit. There are, however, corresponding to the Sacraments of the Old Testament, Circumcision and the Passover, only two in the New Testament instituted by Christ himself, Baptism and the Lord's Supper.[141]

In his paper at the same Council Schaff distinguished the Reformed from other views:

The two sacraments of the New Testament are significant sealing ordinances, whose efficacy depends on the faith of the recipient. The *opus operatum* theory, the necessary connection of water-baptism with moral regeneration, and all materialistic conceptions of the real presence, whether in the form of transubstantiation or consubstantiation, are rejected.

Here lies the only serious doctrinal difference between the Calvinistic and Lutheran symbols. The former make spiritual regeneration independent of water-baptism, so that it may either precede or succeed it or coincide with it, according to the divine pleasure; and they teach a spiritual real or dynamic and effective presence of Christ in the Eucharist for believers only, while unworthy recipients receive no more than the consecrated elements, to their own judgment. The latter teach unconditional baptismal regeneration, and a corporeal real presence of the true body and blood of Christ in, with, and under the visible elements, for all communicants, worthy and unworthy, though with opposite effects. The Lutheran theory of the real presence and oral manducation requires for its dogmatic support either a perpetual miracle (as the Roman theory of transubstantiation), or the hypothesis of the ubiquity of Christ's body (taught by Luther and the Formula of Concord). This hypothesis is rejected by all branches of the Reformed Church as being inconsistent with the limitation of all corporeal substances, and with the facts of Christ's visible ascension to heaven and future return from heaven. . . .

The Church of England teaches in her formularies the Calvinistic theory of the sacraments in general, and of the Lord's Supper in particular; but in the baptismal service of the Book of Common Prayer she clearly teaches baptismal regeneration without qualification, and in practice she gives larger scope than the Presbyterian Churches to the sacramentarian principle.[142]

In a paper presented to the sixth Presbyterian Council (1896), W. G. Blaikie distinguished some Reformed views from other Reformed views. He referred to Dean Stanley, the Anglican broad churchman, who "reduced [the sacraments] to the baldest possible form, and disconnected them wholly with Divine grace and the blessings of grace." The late principal, John Cunningham of St. Andrews University, "took up a position akin to Dean Stanley's but even on a lower level; while Dr. John Macleod . . . and other members of the Scottish Church Society, have advocated views not far removed from those of the Tractarian School."[143]

The literature of the Congregational Council reveals divergent viewpoints within that fold, though here the higher criticism of the Bible plays a larger part. Thus Frank H. Foster presented the third Council (1908) with as reductionist a view as we have seen, positive and pragmatic. Congregationalism "may be comparatively indifferent to the question whether Jesus ever designed that the sacraments should be perpetually observed in a church built upon him as its foundation stone. The church has observed them: that is enough. Congregationalism will continue to observe them as long as they are found helpful."[144] Negatively, "We are quite able to discard the sacraments if they prove harmful anywhere and for any reason."[145] Foster grounded his words on a highly skeptical view of the reliability of the gospel texts, on which the judgment of W. Adamson was terse: "I should like to say that if his paper accurately represented Congregationalism I should cease from being a Congregationalist."[146]

Returning to Blaikie, we find that his opinion is that "essentially, the Sacraments are to be regarded as encouragements to the exercise of faith in the Lord Jesus Christ, and as bringing to faith, in a very special degree, the benefits which it derives from union and communion with Him. . . . We do not conceive that there is anything essentially different in the nature of the blessings which faith derives through the Sacraments from those which it derives through the preaching of the Gospel. Whatever difference there is must be in degree, not in kind."[147] He proceeded to lament the slipshod treatment accorded to the sacraments in some Presbyterian circles, and advocated a reemphasis upon the true doctrine of sacramental grace: "It rests on two great truths: the objective presence of Jesus Christ, with all His benefits, in the Sacrament, and the subjective operation in the heart of the communicant, through the influence of the Holy Spirit, of the faith that sees in Christ a blessed provision for all its needs, and draws from His fulness, even grace for grace."[148]

Blaikie's position was widely shared in both Presbyterian and Congregational circles. First the emphasis is upon the fact that sacramental blessings are not different in kind from other blessings received at the

Lord's hands. So convinced was Ivor J. Roberton of this that he could contemplate a reappraisal of the place of the sacraments in the life of the church:

> If *we* maintain, as I incline to think we do, that there are not two kinds of saving Grace but only one, that there is and can be no Grace given in the Sacrament—especially where penitence and prayer are absent,—that cannot also come without the Sacraments to simple penitence and prayer; if we also think it clear that there is and can be no living Christian experience without such things as penitence and prayer, whereas it is solid unshakeable fact that we can have living Christian experience and fellowship, beautiful and fruitful, without any observance at all of fixed external Sacraments; if we call to memory that the Apostles' Creed has nothing about Sacraments in it at all; must we not, some or many of us, re-think the order of value in which we set the means of Grace?[149]

The Congregationalist Robert Mackintosh took much the same line in 1930:

> A sacrament is not completed *ex opere operato* (baffled only by the *obex* of deliberate, deadly sin). . . . Not faith in the ordinance saves or blesses—not a correct and worthy theory regarding the ordinance, highly desirable though such may be—but faith in Christ. With or without sacramental vehicles, faith blesses, enriches, and saves the soul of a Christian man.

> Accordingly, what as Protestant evangelicals we Congregationalists stand for is the twofold assertion—the Christian sacrament is truly a means of grace; but the sacrament bestows nothing which is not accessible to simple faith—which is not pledged, and granted, to Christian prayer. . . . Sacramental grace—yes; special sacramental grace—no. Sacramental grace—yes; because salvation is of grace; because it is the gift of God; and because sacraments are a standing witness to that great truth. Special sacramental grace—no; for the assertion of a special grace peculiar to sacraments means the denial of the spirituality of the Christian salvation and the sufficiency of the gospel of the Lord Jesus. So we appear to stand midway between those who would suppress or belittle the sacraments and those who attach to them an excessive and unworthy significance. We have to fight a battle on two fronts.[150]

Despite this Mackintosh can say of baptism that, "however inevitable as a rite of dedication," it "ought not to be called a sacrament."[151] What is

missing here is what Blaikie referred to as "the objective presence of
Jesus Christ, with all his benefits, in the Sacrament."[152] Missing too is
the idea that infant baptism signifies incorporation into the covenant
God has graciously made with believers and their children.

Blaikie's further point, which was also endorsed by other Presbyterians and Congregationalists, is that there can be no place for sacramentarianism in Reformed ecclesiology; and from the Congregational
side Frank H. Foster said that his church order

> protests against sacramentarianism of every sort, whether Roman or
> Anglican, against the conception, that is, that by the outward admin-
> istration of the elements of a sacrament grace is infallibly communi-
> cated, so that the sacraments, merely as things done, are means of
> grace. This is dignified with the designation of an "objective" Chris-
> tianity; but Congregationalism finds in it nothing but a mechanical
> Unchristianity. It is the idea that something spiritual can be done for
> man without his own spiritual activity. It makes Christianity a collec-
> tion of nostrums rather than an abundant life.[153]

VI. Baptism

Turning in more detail to baptism, we find the following in Krafft's 1877
consensus statement:

> We confess that baptism, in which water is to be used as the external
> element, is administered to the baptised catechumen in the name of
> the Father, Son, and Holy Ghost, not only as a sign of his reception
> into the Church of God, but also as a seal of the covenant of grace,
> that he has thereby been ingrafted into Christ, cleansed by his blood,
> and renewed by his Holy Spirit; also, we hold, that because God in his
> Church receives the children with the fathers, the children of believers
> are to be baptised.[154]

The lack of balance which we noted in passing in Mackintosh's view is
here made good, and the Congregationalist Lovell Cocks was among
others who presented a more rounded doctrine of baptism:

> The sign of this free, electing grace of God is our baptism. The
> ordinance proclaims the Gospel of a divine grace that set us apart from
> before the foundation of the world, called us in Christ, and in His
> Cross wrought the "finished work" of our salvation. It speaks of a
> Father Who loved us while we were yet sinners, and of a Christ Who
> for our sakes conquered sin and broke the power of death before we

were born. Baptism declares that the child of Christian parents is already within the Covenant, and it is the visible sign of his incorporation into the people of God.[155]

We are a long way here from the view of baptism as the dedication of infants, with the emphasis being on the promises made by the parents. But Mackintosh was not the only one to feel ill at ease with what may be termed the "higher" view. In the early days of the Presbyterian Alliance T. P. Stevenson rejected the emphasis in baptismal doctrine upon the imagery of dying and rising with Christ. To him such imagery complicated the otherwise simple symbolism of cleansing and it was, he declared, unacceptable to make baptism partly the symbol of a symbol (dying and rising), and partly the symbol of a spiritual fact (being cleansed).[156] We have found no others in Alliance literature who shared this particular scruple.

Thomas F. Torrance, characteristically, pulls no punches in his statement of 1954:

> I believe it to be extremely important for us to recover again in all its magnitude the Biblical and early Christian teaching about Baptism. In the New Testament there are whole books which have nothing to say about the Lord's Supper, and a great deal to say about Holy Baptism; while in the Early Church it was Baptism that was the prime mystery of the Church, and the Eucharist had its significance within baptismal incorporation into Christ. It is our weakness in regard to Baptism, and our reducing it to a rite of small and even petty dimensions, in which its supreme significance is betrayed, that gives rise to so many of our difficulties—particularly in questions like intercommunion, marriage and divorce, as well as evangelism and Christian nurture. Let us have again the full Biblical teaching about Baptism as involving death and resurrection in Christ, and incorporation into His living Body, the sphere where the mighty salvation-events are operative by the power of the Word and Spirit for our salvation, and we shall strike at the heart of many of our difficulties and divergencies, not least in regard to the nature of the Church and Ministry, and their continuity.[157]

In both Congregational and Presbyterian writings we have found the assertion that baptism is not a sine qua non of church membership. Thus the Congregationalist Foster: "Congregationalism has no doctrine of the sacraments which will erect them into a condition of fellowship";[158] and the Presbyterian P. Carnegie Simpson: "No Presbyterian Church— so far as I am aware—would or could exclude a man from communicant membership because he does not accept Infant Baptism. Even an office-bearer might have his conscientious judgment in this matter, provided, of course, he did not thereby disturb the peace and unity of the church."[159] By contrast, the Anglican/Reformed dialogue report— especially with its use of "constitutive," to which we earlier objected— appears to make baptism the criterion of church membership: "Baptism, by which Christ incorporates us into his life, death and resurrection, is thus, in the strictest sense, constitutive of the Church. It is not simply one of the Church's practices."[160]

With one voice (though the Anglican/Reformed dialogue report is silent on the matter) Presbyterians and Congregationalists alike have protested against the doctrine of baptismal regeneration. Thus in 1880 Stevenson took E. B. Pusey to task, illustrating his point by reference to Nicodemus:

> The doctrine of baptismal regeneration stands or falls with our understanding of John iii:5, "Verily I say unto thee, except a man be born of water and of the Spirit, he cannot enter the kingdom of God."
>
> These words were uttered in answer to the question of Nicodemus, "How can a man be born when he is old?" And when, to this reply of Jesus, the inquirer still responded, "How can these things be?" the divine Teacher answered him with words not of further explanation, but of reproof: "Art thou a master in Israel, and knowest not these things?"
>
> The new birth of which Christ had spoken was a subject with which Nicodemus ought to have been familiar. And so, indeed, he ought, if Christ's words denoted simply that moral and spiritual change which the truth, made effectual by the Spirit, works in the soul enlightening the understanding, quickening right emotions, and renewing the will. This change was indispensable to salvation under the Old Testament as well as under the New, and it behooved every "master in Israel" to be able to point it out to others. But if our Saviour was here expounding the value and significance of the new, and, in this respect, altogether unprecedented ordinance of Baptism as an "overwhelming mystery" and "miracle," having a specific reference to his own incarnation, so that thereby we are made "members of the body of our incarnate Lord," even as he was made partaker of our humanity by the power of the Spirit in the Virgin's womb, then was the Lord indeed setting forth new truth, of which it was not strange that Nicodemus should be ignorant, which, until now, it was impossible for him to know, and the reproof of the Master was not deserved.[161]

Similarly, Blaikie briskly urged five points against the Tridentine position towards which he thought his colleague Dr. John Macleod was veering:

> With great deference to this very earnest and confident divine, we would submit, first, that his view, like the decrees of the Council of Trent, limits and disparages the function of *faith,* for Scripture always teaches us that it is through faith that we are vitally united to Christ and become sharers of His life—His resurrection life—and of all the grace and all the blessings that flow from Him. Second, it elevates baptism to an importance which neither its place in Scripture nor its declared purpose warrants. Thirdly, it makes entrance into a glorious and spiritual condition dependent on a mechanical act, contrary to the spiritual character of the scheme of grace. Fourthly, it introduces an element of uncertainty into the child of God's position and prospects that conflicts with such statements as this: "Moreover, whom He did predestinate, them He also called; and whom He called, them He also justified; and them He justified, them He also glorified." And fifthly, the connection of baptism and regeneration is not in agreement with the state of the fact, as witnessed in the godless lives of many baptized persons.[162]

To Robert Mackintosh, as we might expect, baptismal regeneration was a fiction, and he illustrated the point with reference to a convert on the mission field:

> Are we to say that as the convert approaches the font he is an unforgiven soul? And that he returns from the font forgiven? That he approaches the font unregenerate, and returns from it born again for the first time into a wholly new life? I cannot say that. It would be unreal. If the convert is fit for baptism he already knows what God's friendship means, and being justified by faith he already has peace with God through our Lord Jesus Christ. Baptism will assure him afresh of these highest of all blessings, but it does not create them, though it movingly symbolizes them.[163]

Our review of Alliance material on baptism prompts two comments. First, it is surprising that those earlier Congregationalists who wrote on the subject did not make more of the covenant idea, which was so much a part of their local (and hence catholic) ecclesiology. Second, the content of the Baptist/Reformed dialogue report and the language of the Anglican/Reformed report challenge the Reformed family to appraise afresh the entire process of Christian initiation (including as it does baptism, nurture, conversion, profession of faith, and reception as an enrolled saint) in relation to the doctrines of regeneration and of the nature of the church. It will be especially interesting, from the other side, to discover whether the Baptists can allow for a church which includes others than *professed* Christians.

VII. The Lord's Supper

Concerning the Lord's Supper we may once again launch out from Krafft's 1877 consensus statement:

> We confess that the Lord's Supper, which our Lord Jesus instituted that night on which he was betrayed, as the Sacrament of his body and blood, serves in the case of those already received into the Church of God, to seal their communion with Christ, inasmuch as they who come truly believing to the Table of the Lord are spiritually fed by Christ, though he sits at the right hand of the Father in heaven, —yea, as truly as they partake bodily of the outward signs, bread and wine, so certainly, by the power of his Spirit are they spiritually fed by him, on his real body and blood; but the unbelieving receive, indeed, the elements of the Sacrament, but not the thing itself, and are therefore guilty of the body and blood of the Lord to their own condemnation.[164]

One class of persons is omitted here—understandably enough, for the Reformed confessions do not mention them—namely, those who would like to believe, and for whom the sacrament, since it witnesses to the gospel, may be a converting ordinance. This possibility was raised at least once in Alliance literature—by D. D. Bannerman at the second Presbyterian Council (1880):

> About the beginning of last century a theory of this kind was propounded by Mr. Stoddard, the grandfather of President Edwards, and himself an eminent and pious man. He taught that "unconverted people, as such, had a right in the sight of God to the Lord's Supper"; that "those who really rejected Christ, and disliked the gospel way of salvation, and knew this to be true of themselves, might and should come to the sacrament, and be admitted by the church," on the ground that it is a converting ordinance, and that they desire to get a blessing from it. . . . In 1750 Jonathan Edwards himself was actually deprived of his charge at Northampton for opposing this theory and urging greater purity of communion. . . . [This] gave us his great

treatise of "Qualifications for Communion in the visible Christian Church," and it helped at least to make him a Presbyterian.[165]

So all was not lost! The majority opinion in the Reformed family has been on Bannerman's side, namely, that the Lord's Supper is a sacrament of the church and is for those whose Christian initiation is complete. No doubt there were always those who would receive the elements prior to making their profession of faith, but this would have been taken as indicating a desire for that closer fellowship which completed initiation implies and would have brought the pastoral forces of the church into play. It must be said, however, that in recent years, partly because of the increased emphasis upon baptism which the Anglican/Reformed report underlines, and partly because of the influence of Orthodox teaching on the matter, the reception of children at the Lord's table is becoming increasingly common, and the reception of infants is not unknown. The ground is that all the baptized are of the family of Christ.

This development has caused most soul-searching within those Congregational circles where reception as a member has traditionally been associated with receiving communion and with taking one's place at Church Meeting (though in some places *voting* rights have been withheld until the member has attained the age of eighteen or twenty-one). The Anglican/Reformed dialogue report recognizes the problem and seeks to meet it: "It is indeed difficult to defend the practice of admitting children to baptism while denying them the Eucharist. However, all of us would wish to affirm the need for a rite in which those baptized as infants, whether they have been accepted as communicants or not, are enabled, after due preparation, to make their own confession of faith and commitment to Christ, and are renewed by the grace of God through a further invocation of the Spirit, so that they can commit themselves freely and deliberately to share in God's mission to the world."[166]

Insofar as the Lord's Supper is a declaration in word and action of the gospel of the grace of God, the possibility that it may be the means by which God the Holy Spirit intervenes in a person's life may not be ruled out. Moreover, Calvinists may reassure themselves that but for the regenerating work of the Spirit a person would not come sincerely to the table. The trouble is that a hypocrite might come—but then even the most doctrinally correct Calvinist must leave some matters for the Almighty to unravel.

This last consideration, however, leads to the connection between admission to the Lord's table and church discipline. D. D. Bannerman framed two questions: "We may ask—1st. What sort of persons are the office-bearers justified, before God, in receiving to baptism or to Lord's table. Or, 2nd. What sort of persons are *themselves* justified before God in coming forward? The two questions are quite distinct."[167] Bannerman was sure that discipline ought to exist in the church, and equally sure that there could be an excess of it. Furthermore, "it may be exercised even from praiseworthy motives, on wrong principles and by incompetent hands, and the result be evil in the Lord's eyes."[168] He observed two extremes in the course of church history: one tending towards laxity, the other towards "purity," and he sought a middle way. In answer to his original question, he said this:

> What according to Scripture will fully justify *the Church, or its office bearers,* in admitting a man is one thing; what according to Scripture will justify the *man himself* in the sight of God in asking for admission is another and quite a different thing.
>
> As to the *first,* I believe that what Scripture requires is a serious and intelligent profession of faith in Christ and obedience to him, with a corresponding conduct; as to the *second,* the *real existence* in the man of what he professes—a true faith and sincere obedience.[169]

Enough has been said to show that over and above the "converting ordinance" possibility, the question of admission to the Lord's table requires fresh consideration vis-à-vis both baptism and church discipline. In such a consideration the possibility that some more recent, no less than some older, interpretations are open to question on exegetical grounds should not be overlooked.[170]

The onward march of the modern ecumenical movement required the clarification of the Alliance attitude towards other Christian communions on the question of admission to the Lord's table. The Presbyterian Alliance was the first world communion to speak, as it did in the message sent by the sixteenth Council (1948) to the first meeting of the World Council of Churches: Our "constituent Churches welcome to the Lord's Supper those who are members of any branch of the Holy Catholic Church, and recognize as valid ordinations carried out, with prayer, according to the established order of every such branch."[171] The point was underlined and further expounded at the next Council (1954): "We cannot proclaim the Gospel of reconciliation without demonstrating at the Table of the Lord that we are reconciled to one another."[172] The president, J. A. Mackay, threw his weight and that of Calvin behind the position and also outlined the meaning of the Supper:

> We alone of the three great Reformation communions have written into our Constitution the general invitation to all believers to sit down with us at the Lord's Table. Calvin believed, and we his successors

believe, that the Table of the Lord is the supreme meeting place of
Christians. Why? We have a high view of the significance of the
Supper, the Eucharist, the Holy Communion. The Living Lord
Himself is present in the Sacrament; there is a real Presence. Not as
transmuted into something, but as a living invisible Presence, Jesus
Christ makes Himself real to those communicants who worthily partake of the holy symbols of bread and wine in the Communion. There,
in the supreme and unique manner, they have fellowship with Christ
and with one another. I entirely agree, therefore, with Professor
Torrance when he says that the Lord's Supper belongs not to any
ecclesiastical body, but to the Lord of the Church.[173]

As with baptism, so with the Lord's Supper: Robert Mackintosh was
one of the few in Alliance literature who (in 1930) brought exegetical
considerations to bear upon the matter:

There is some room for doubting whether our Lord gave the injunc-
tion to repeat the acted parable—i.e., whether he precisely and
literally founded a sacrament. One Gospel says so—St. Luke; but the
text even there is uncertain. Otherwise we are thrown back upon the
evidence of St. Paul, in I Cor. xi, and the doubt forces itself upon many
minds whether St. Paul has kept separate what actually was said in
that upper room from what he is convinced, in his heart of heart, was
God's purpose in connection with the events of that hour. And so
today, by general admission—unless in quarters where candour is
overborne by dogmatism—a certain element of doubt exists whether
Jesus literally founded either of the two New Testament sacraments.
    Certainly a much stronger case can be made out for Christ's
institution of the Eucharist than for His institution of baptism. Plainly
our Lord was looking forward to a time of separation from His
disciples which was to be for them a season of trial and danger. He
may well have desired to leave with them not merely the recollection
of that eternally memorable gathering in the upper room under the
very shadow of His cross, but a repetition of the same acted parable
with its ever renewed testimony—Christ is the food of our souls;
Christ's death is our life. So long as it is even a possible opinion that
Jesus really said, "This do in remembrance of Me," I do not envy those
who deliberately turn a deaf ear to that request.[174]

Whatever they may have thought concerning the scriptural authority for observing the "dominical" sacraments (and, to judge from
Alliance literature alone they did not think much about it—such is the
weight of tradition), Alliance speakers and writers have for the most

part adopted what might be termed a central position with the memorialism of Foster the Congregationalist on the one side and the quasi-Tridentine views of Macleod the Presbyterian on the other. This prompts us in passing to recall Dale's question concerning the representativeness or otherwise of the first Congregational Council. We have a suspicion that in some Presbyterian and Congregational circles there were, and are, more sacramental "Zwinglians" than the written materials would suggest (we surround Zwingli's name with inverted commas by way of indicating that he was by no means the Zwinglian memorialist that some have made him). Be that as it may, the central thrust is plain in the literature of the Alliance, and J. M'Naugher's careful communion address at the fourteenth Presbyterian Council (1933) typifies it.

M'Naugher begins by pointing out that baptism and the Lord's Supper are "the oldest witnesses to the Gospel. Both antedate the written word of the New Testament."[175] (With the latter sentence we agree; but was not the preaching of the gospel the earliest witness, consequent upon which people were baptized?) He goes on to explain that the Lord's Supper is

1. a commemorative ordinance which brings home to us the cost and benefits of our salvation;
2. an ordinance which seals the benefits of Christ to his followers;
3. a special way of receiving Christ as food for the soul—worthy recipients are nourished because of the real presence of Christ;
4. a foretaste of the heavenly banquet;
5. a means of communion with "the entire family of grace."

M'Naugher movingly concludes thus:

> The Sacrament is not an *opus operatum:* it is not mechanically operative. Only as we look away to Jesus in faith and love, only as we have Him at the core of our meditation, will we gain the priceless benefits of the ordinance. Let us approach the Table with "kneeling and praying hearts." We have read how men in lonely places in the Australian bush have been known to come to their Communion, after years of involuntary excommunication, with tears of joy streaming down their cheeks. May some such quenchless emotion subdue us now.[176]

Coming to a more recent statement we find that according to *God's Reign and Our Unity* the Lord's Supper is

1. a memorial;
2. an occasion of looking forward to God's coming Kingdom;

3. a means of communion "with one another and with the whole company of Christ's people in every age and place."[177]

Thus far the dialogue members are in accord with M'Naugher. However, the dialogue report is more explicit than most earlier Alliance writers and speakers at three points—two more "Catholic," one more "Protestant." Concerning the more "Catholic" emphases: first, a fuller attempt than elsewhere in Alliance literature is made to specify the nature of Christ's real presence at the Supper:

> There is a real presence of Christ which "does not depend upon the faith of the individual," even though, "to discern the body and blood of Christ faith is required" (BEM, p. 12, para. 13). The trouble begins, however, when we commence to argue whether this presence is associated with the outward, visible elements of bread and wine, or whether it is an inward, invisible presence received in the heart through faith; neither should be so asserted as to exclude the other.[178]

But this is not the whole "trouble." The question is whether the presence of the risen Christ is "associated with" the actual bread and wine in a manner different from his immanent "association with" everything else. And, where Roman Catholics and some Anglicans are concerned, the further question is whether the difference turns upon the actions of the (right sort of) minister.

Second, the Anglican/Reformed report strongly emphasizes the Lord's Supper as an offering, and the Roman Catholic/Reformed report is directly quoted to make the point: "Sanctified by his Spirit, the Church, through, with and in God's Son Jesus Christ, offers itself to the father. It thereby becomes a living sacrifice of thanksgiving through which God is publicly praised."[179] This is acceptable enough, provided that it be remembered that what we offer is our imperfect best, while what Christ offers is the one, full, perfect, and sufficient sacrifice for sin; what we are *given* is victory; what Christ *wins* is victory. To reiterate a point made earlier: any notion that at the Lord's Supper Christ is sacrificed *again* is ruled out in the Anglican/Reformed report—the finished work of Christ is in view throughout.[180]

The more "Protestant" emphasis which M'Naugher omitted, though he would have agreed with it, is this:

> There has . . . been a destructive polarization in our common history between emphasis on the preached word and emphasis on the sacrament. This is to put asunder what is given to us in Scripture and in the gospel as one. The gospel is news of the word made flesh. The preached word is an *anamnesis* of Christ just as is the eucharistic meal.[181]

If we now examine the Roman Catholic/Reformed report in relation to the foregoing discussion we find that here too it is taught that the Lord's Supper is a memorial. It is further pointed out that "when Christ gives the apostles the commission 'Do this in remembrance of me' the word 'remembrance' means more than merely a mental act of recalling."[182] The report might have explained that it means (after the Hebrew): "recalling something from the past into the present, so that it is effective now." Again, the Supper as *koinonia* is emphasized, and the eschatological note is struck. The statement on Christ's offering and ours is if anything more careful than that in the Anglican/Reformed report: Christ "is both Apostle from God and our High Priest (cf. Heb. 3:1) who has consecrated us together with him into one, so that in his self-offering to the Father through the eternal Spirit (cf. Heb. 9:14), he offers us also in himself and so through our union with him we share in that self-offering made on our behalf."[183]

On the real presence the Roman Catholic/Reformed report agrees with *God's Reign and Our Unity:*

> In the words of institution the emphasis is on the fact of the personal presence of the living Lord in the event of the memorial and fellowship meal, not on the question as to how this real presence (the word "is") comes about and is to be explained. . . .
>
> How Christ is present in the Eucharist, we may apprehend to a certain extent by looking at the work of the same Holy Spirit, e.g., in the birth of Jesus of the Virgin Mary and in his resurrection in body from the grave—although as acts of God they are explicable only from the side of God and not from the side of man.[184]

The Roman Catholic/Reformed report is further strengthened by emphasis upon the fact that "the whole saving work of God has its basis, centre and goal in the person of the glorified Christ,"[185] and by the place accorded to the concept of covenant: "In his person, his life, his death and his resurrection, Christ has established the new covenant."[186] Again, the understanding of the Lord's Supper as a "source and criterion for the renewal of the Church," entailing as it does the summons to unity and the call to mission, is most welcome.[187]

On presidency at the table the report has this to say: "The presidence of the commissioned church office-bearer at the celebration of the Meal effectively represents this unique role of Christ as Lord and Host. The commissioned office-bearer is there to show the assembled community that it does not have disposal itself over the Eucharist but simply carries out obediently what Christ has commissioned the Church to do."[188] With the report's question for further study on "the proper role of the ordained ministry in the celebration of the Eucharist"[189] we come to the Rubicon.

VIII. The Ministry: Reformed and Other Views

With the confidence of a man who knows that his opponents are beyond earshot, J. G. Mackenzie threw down the gauntlet at the fourth Congregational Council (1920): "Is the Church created by the presence of the Bishop?" The question expects a resounding "no!" "In other words, are we evangelical or cannonical [sic] and sacramental?"[190] By now it should be clear that the Reformed are sacramental, if not sacramentarian, and that their understanding of the sacraments derives from a prior hearing of the Word: "The Christian rites grew out of the Good News; they were not incantations to conjure it up from a void."[191] We need now to make clear that the Reformed are not sacerdotalists or sectarians, and that they have a positive understanding of ministry derived from their understanding of God's saving work in Christ.

Most of the points it is necessary to make may be introduced into a description of a careful paper by J. O. Dykes on "The Anglican View of the Church" that was delivered at the sixth Presbyterian Council (1896). What he says applies a fortiori to the Roman Catholic church—a body with which Presbyterians had little contact in 1896.

Dykes first points out that by the "Anglican" view of the church he does not mean the view of the nineteenth of the Thirty-nine Articles, an article which accords with the Reformed confessions. Anglicanism has changed. This is not to say that no connections remain between Reformed and contemporary Anglican thought:

> For us also the Church is a sacred body, Divine in its origin, founded by our Lord to be a permanent channel of saving grace to the world. We also hold the ministry to exist by Christ's will; and when our Anglican brethren claim that the Church, owing allegiance to her Divine Head alone, ought not to be subject in her sacred mission to any secular power, we go heartily along with them.[192]

The difficulty is that Anglicans hold other things as well:

> First, The supernatural grace of the Holy Ghost is communicated (on the Anglican view), not mainly through the Word of God heard and believed, but through the Sacraments; that is, by visible and external media.
>
> Next, Power to convey such sacramental grace is derived by the ministry from the Apostles, and transmitted from age to age through a visible and external act—the imposition of a bishop's hands.
>
> Third, The unity of the Church as the Body of Christ, at least within each local area, is not spiritual merely, but of necessity external and visible; a unity of administration marked by the obedience of all the faithful to the local diocesan.

These three positions hang together in the closest fashion.
(a) The cardinal point in the system is the bishop, since he is
the link which connects us with the historical Jesus. . . .
Where the episcopal order is absent, therefore, or where, if
present, its direct derivation from the Apostles has been
broken, there all security for salvation fails us.
(b) But this necessity for episcopal succession depends on the
double assumption, (1) that valid sacraments are the chief
media of saving grace, and (2) that sacraments are valid only
when power to administer has descended by imposition of
hands. . . .
(c) It is no less evident that on these assumptions the third
tenet of the system is easily justified: I mean the exclusive
pretension of the Church which holds by the lawful bishop
to be, within his diocese, the only body in which Christ dwells
and works, or at least has bound Himself to dwell and
work. . . .

Episcopal succession, sacramental grace, exclusive claim to be the
true Church—these three stand or fall together.[193]

Dykes maintains that the Anglicans compromised the formal principle of the Reformation when, by a canon of 1571, they added the
appeal to the Catholic tradition as expressed by the first six general
councils and by the consensus of the Fathers to the appeal to Scripture.
They also compromised the material principle of the Reformation,
justification by grace through faith. Its "essence is that the assured
reception by any individual of saving grace depends on no external or
visible rite whatever, but on something secret and personal, on the
religious attitude and actings of his soul toward God revealed in
Christ."[194] Dykes goes on first to show that the Anglican idea is not in
harmony with the spirit and ruling idea of the New Testament church:

As converts are won to the faith, they unite with the brethren, and are
grouped, or group themselves, into little societies, with or without
local officers. We see local groups where all the members do their best
to edify one another. They administer their own affairs. Priests there
are none anywhere, but all fulfil a spiritual priesthood. Life precedes
organisation and gives birth to it. When the qualifications of gifted
brethren to serve the brotherhood do come to receive official recognition, such officers are overseers merely. Even these are not met with
in every case.

Is not this on the face of it a singular contrast to the Catholic and
Anglican idea of the Church? Can two things be less alike than a rigidly

prescribed gradation of priests, on whose exclusive powers the very life of Christianity depends, and this elastic and fluid society of the New Testament?[195]

Second, the Anglican idea of ministerial orders is not adequately supported by the few ascertained facts concerning the early church's administration. We do not find monoepiscopacy as the rule in every community; or every bishop personally ordained by an apostle or by one whom an apostle had ordained; or a clear and firm distinction between bishops who have power to confer the sacerdotal office and priests and presbyters who can only receive it.

Lastly, the Anglican view accords ill with experience:

> Suppose it were true that valid sacraments are the only appointed method for generating, and the chief method for nourishing, Christian life, and that sacraments are valid only when dispensed by episcopally-ordained priests, what should we expect to find? Why, this: that the spiritual life of Christendom should be restricted to Episcopal communions, while beyond their pale, in the Churches of the Reformation, neither Christian faith nor Christian holiness should, for the last three hundred years, have been preserved. . . .

> Some Anglicans of the more Romanising type . . . admit that Christians who are beyond the true Church display characteristic Christian graces. But this they trace to the exceptional mercy of God, who, refusing to be limited by His own ordinances, does at times confer on persons who are outside His covenant and His household a precarious grace, on which they possess no claim, because He has given them no promise. . . . Thanks be to God, the blessing which He is pleased to send down upon Word and Sacrament in all our Churches is neither scanty nor occasional. It is perennial; it is widespread; it is abundant. . . . Loyalty to common facts and common sense forbids us to accept it as our Lord's will that transmission of the Holy Ghost through the laying on of a bishop's hands is "a fundamental law" of the Church's life.[196]

It must readily be granted that Dykes was writing against the background of aggressive, often sectarian, Anglo-Catholicism. It must also be remembered that most Anglicans hold only that episcopacy is of the *bene esse* of the church, not of its *esse*. Yet, to repeat what we said earlier, since there has so far been no reciprocal intercommunion recognized throughout Anglicanism, the Reformed and others may be forgiven for thinking either that practice has not yet caught up with theory, or that intractable, tacitly held theories are causing an impediment.[197]

Though most of the Reformed would accept the general lines of Dykes's case, some refinements would nowadays have to be made. First, neither Anglican nor Roman Catholic scholars of repute currently defend the view that their present church order is manifest in the New Testament in all its clear detail. Second, they do not maintain that an unbroken and otherwise uncomplicated line may be drawn from the Apostles to the bishops of today. Third, they are frequently more generous to nonepiscopal ministries than their forebears. From the Reformed side there may today be more general agreement that there can be no legitimate quarrel with *episkope* as such—or even with *episkopoi*. As Lovell Cocks told the seventh Congregational Council (1953):

> We have no insuperable objection to episcopacy as such, and in the united Church of the future we may come to understand and value it. Perhaps we may even find in the apostolic succession, when we come to share it, a very eloquent symbol of the continuity of the Church's life across the centuries. But I trust we shall go on denying, as we now deny, that it constitutes that continuity. By God's grace we already stand in the real apostolic succession, for it is in the contemporary Christ, the living Lord, that the Church's life across the centuries is summed up and secured. And as for the historical continuity—the outward succession—that is surely to be sought in the unchanging Gospel itself—the Word of God which generation after generation creates and replenishes the community of believers as it is proclaimed from faith to faith.[198]

This is the kernel of the Reformed case. The argument has nothing to do with "bad" bishops. In any case, every ecclesiology has its pitfalls, and if there can be ungodly, autocratic bishops, there can assuredly be autocratic presbyteries and recalcitrant Congregational diaconates. No, the case is that (a) the apostles had no successors in the sense required by the theory of historic continuity;[199] (b) bishops do not constitute the church; and (c) the true apostolic succession is the evangelical one. If it be the case that the bishop in approved orders alone can validly ordain, and that those who have been so ordained alone can administer valid sacraments, then we have not simply the unexceptionable view that the church requires to be decently ordered; we have the view that the grace of God is controlled by the structure of the church; a line is drawn between those who are of the true ministry and those who are not; the sacraments are elevated above the Word; and the result is sacerdotal sectarianism, the obverse of evangelical catholicism.

It is essential that we elucidate these points with some care, and we shall do so against the background of the Reformed understanding of catholicity expounded in the previous chapter.

First, although the Reformed have at their best honored order—sometimes almost to the point of allowing themselves to be impaired by it—they have always protested against the elevation of orders above the gospel. For the Reformed, order is never normative. More particularly, it is not the clergy who constitute the church. Even Fairbairn in 1891 did not quite state the position correctly: "It is the people," he said, "not the clergy who constitute" the church.[200] In fact, as we have seen, it is God's redeeming grace brought home by the Spirit that constitutes it—but Fairbairn lived in polarizing times! P. T. Forsyth (albeit not writing under Alliance or Council auspices) was more careful: "The true catholicity and the true succession are the evangelical—the catholicity and continuity of the Gospel, in its creative, self-organising, and self-recuperative power. . . . We do protest . . . against polity as a condition of Church unity."[201] As Leslie Cooke was to add in 1953, "Immediately an attempt is made to declare what organization is indispensable to a true Church the first step is taken to divide the Church."[202]

Second, there is the Reformed protest against sacerdotalism. This protest was regularly heard in earlier Presbyterian and Congregational Councils, and in the more recent address from which we have just quoted Cooke resumed the point. He declared that Congregationalists were witnesses to "a truly catholic doctrine of Grace. There seems to be a curious reluctance at times in discussions of Church union to face the fact that this is the crux of the problem. . . . One of the paradoxes of the so-called Catholics is that they hold in fact a limited doctrine of Grace—they are ever seeking to restrict Grace in some way by law."[203] None was shrewder or more pungent on this matter than Bernard Lord Manning. His criticism was for the most part directed against certain Anglican views of the ministry, and they were the more telling because of his deep affection for the Church of England:

> We decline still, as we have always declined, to have episcopalian ordination of ministers and episcopalian confirmation of Church members made into a sort of new circumcision within the limits of which alone is there full and valid and regular operation of God's grace.[204]

Still more crisply, he said that "the grace of God, we affirm, needs no legal machinery to protect it."[205] As for the analysis of "validity":

> The Supper of the Lord is either celebrated or not celebrated. The Body and the Blood of Christ are spiritually received or they are not received. We simply do not know what an irregular or an invalid

celebration is. We do not deal in percentages with the grace of God. . . . When we can botanise about the Burning Bush, either it has ceased to burn or it has been consumed.[206]

In full accord, a study group at the sixteenth Presbyterian Council (1948) bluntly stated:

It is our finding that in so far as the ministry of Presbyters and Bishops is concerned, the New Testament teaches the parity of these offices in the ministry of the Word and Sacraments. Therefore, in the light of this fact, the faith and polity of the Reformed and Presbyterian Church has no place for a sacerdotal episcopacy.[207]

Underlying this view is the doctrine of the priesthood of all believers—a doctrine conceived corporately by Presbyterians and Congregationalists at their best—some nineteenth-century pulpit autocrats and others notwithstanding.

Third, just as specific orders—not least episcopacy—are, however appropriate, not essential to the constitution of the church, so the Reformed cannot think of acceptance of the primacy of the pope as a necessary entailment of catholicity, still less as a prerequisite of it. John Owen put the point clearly long ago:

It is false that the union of the catholic church . . . *consists in subjection to any officer* or officers: or that it hath any peculiar form, constituting one church in relation to them, or in joint participation of the same individual ordinances whatever, by all the members of it; or that of the faith by which it is believed, and of the truth professed.[208]

At the first Congregational Council (1891), Fairbairn could speak with the confidence of one who is addressing the converted:

We do not, like the Roman Catholic, emphasize the visible head, the authority of the one man, which is but autocracy, or imperialism, or Caesarism in religion, nor do we, like the Anglo-Catholic, emphasize the apostolic descent of the clergy, which is the notion of an official and exclusive oligarchy transferred from civil to ecclesiastical polity; but we emphasize the people as the peculiar creation of God, inhabited and ruled by Him.[209]

Dr. McVicar was equally blunt when he told the second Presbyterian Council (1880) that "the unity of the Church under Christ, her only King and Head" is "the corner-stone of our polity. It is the central principle of Protestantism, and opposes effectually Roman Catholicism, which rests, from top to bottom, upon the dogma of the supremacy of the Pope."[210] It will be remembered that neither Fairbairn nor McVicar would have been regarded by Rome as "separated brethren."

As we suggested earlier the Alliance will sooner or later have to clarify its mind on the question of papal primacy—not least because our dialogue partners, the Anglicans and the Lutherans, are already investigating the matter. It does seem unlikely, however, that the Reformed could ever regard obedience to the bishop of Rome as an inseparable accident of "catholic."[211]

The three points reduce to one. The Reformed, though they have been regarded as sectaries by some, are not, at their best, sectarian. They are evangelical catholics who would find it paradoxical to have to become more sectarian in order to become more ecumenical.[212] It goes without saying that the varieties of sectarianism are legion, and Lewis Mudge specified some that transcend ecclesiological boundaries:

> The Church may not grasp the fact either practically or theoretically that in his appearance and work Christ has to do with all things (which means, in the first place, the whole world of men). The Church is uncatholic to the extent that it limits Christ's Lordship, as, for example, when it limits it to the soul, to heaven, to the elect, or (in the manner of liberalism) to a particular phase of historical and religious development. Or, on the other hand, the Church may not grasp the fact that all things uniquely and wholly belong to him. The Church may recognize other powers alongside his Lordship, which delimit his power or regulate it. Such powers may be natural theology, the laws of the "orders of creation," the autonomy of man, etc.[213]

Reverting to the possibility of sectarianism via the doctrine of orders which has principally concerned us, we would recall the advice of the prominent seventeenth-century ecumenist Richard Baxter, who regarded himself as a "meer Catholick." He urged his brethren not to "make a larger creed and more necessaries than God has done," and added, "All over-doing is undoing."[214] James Iverach reminds us of what the Reformed deem to be more than sufficient in this matter: "We say with the Romanist and the Anglican that there is no salvation outside of the Catholic Church of Christ; but then we add that Christ's Catholic Church embraces the whole people of God, that Christ has constituted His Church, not by visible organizations, or by external means, but by His grace flowing out to them, and by their living faith in Himself."[215] No doubt; but the thought cannot entirely be suppressed that Reformed protests against some doctrines of orders (however understandable they may have been in past ecclesiastical contexts—and even in some present ones) may betoken an inadequate appreciation of God's use of means and of his relationship to the created order. In fleeing sacerdotalism we should take care not to tumble headlong into deism.

IX. The Ministry in Alliance Literature

Having thus distinguished the Reformed approach to ministry from other positions, we must now outline the positive teaching on ministry which emerges from Alliance literature. For the last time we take our point of departure from Krafft:

> We confess that this true Church of Christ should be governed according to the order appointed by God in his Word, therefore there should be church officers (pastors, elders, and deacons), that the Word of God may be purely taught, the sacraments administered according to their institution, Church discipline rightly exercised, the office-bearers acting by way of warning or excommunication from the Table of the Lord according to the deserts of each case; also those appointed thereto should minister to the wants of the poor.
>
> We confess that the office-bearers of the Church (pastors, elder, deacons) should be called thereto in a lawful way by the Church, that they should be set apart to their offices by the laying on of hands, in the manner prescribed by God's Word, that those office-bearers form no distinct class from believers generally, and have all, in whatever place they may be, equal authority and power, under Christ their one Head.[216]

Here we have the biblical reference; the inferred nature of the offices (though we shall later note the empirical diversity of structures within the Reformed family); the association of ministry with the proclamation of the Word, church discipline, and the care of the poor; the requirement of an orderly call and setting apart; and a clear affirmation that officers and people do not represent species which differ in kind, and that officers and people are alike under the authority of Christ.

The theme of Christ's supremacy is reiterated on many occasions in Alliance literature, as, for example, at the seventeenth Presbyterian Council (1954): "We affirm that the Church, as the Body of Christ, participates in the Ministry of Her Lord, the sole Head of the Church and the Lord of history, by serving Him in word and deed. As Christ is Prophet, Priest and King . . . the Church in obedience to Him exercises also a prophetic, priestly, and kingly ministry. Every member of the

Church is called by God to take part in this three-fold ministry of witness and service with a willing and eager heart."[217] At the same council T. F. Torrance expounded Calvin on the matter:

The ministry of the Church is essentially corporate: in it the Church as Christ's Body participates in His whole prophetic, priestly and kingly ministry by serving Him. Christ exercises his ministry as Prophet, Priest, and King uniquely, vicariously, substitutionally, but the Church which is ingrafted into Him as His Body participates in His whole Ministry in a way appropriate to the Church as the Body of which He is the Head. The Church is essentially and only *servant*, and yet in its servant-way it is given to participate in Christ's prophetic, priestly, and kingly ministry, because through Baptism the Church is inserted into the functioning of His Body. Here then the Reformed doctrine of the ministry is at once so high that Calvin can speak of the ministers as exercising *vicaria opera* and yet as *repraesentant personam Christi*, and yet there is no hint at all of any relation of identity or prolongation between the ministry of the Church and that of Christ, and no thought of the Church as the extension of the Incarnation.[218]

The general character of the ministry has been well portrayed by Hendrikus Berkhof. Ministers "have to represent the Word of the crucified and risen Christ, which means they have to serve the double movement of incorporation and representation"; again, "they have to represent the Word in its totality, as *dabar*." Finally, "they have to represent the Word in the present world. This means that the names, numbers and functions have to vary according to the need of the period."[219]

On the question of ordination to the ministry, Glynmor John in 1966 summed up the Congregational view this way:

The ministry does not intervene from outside; it is not imposed upon a church. It does not appoint itself (for none appoints himself to any office in Congregationalism) and it is not at the disposal of any power extraneous to the church itself. It is exercised as within the *koinonia;* its spiritual milieu is the pastoral relationship. The primary qualification for the office of the ordained ministry, as for every other, is evidence of the Spirit's endowment and the sense of the Spirit's calling, both evidence and sense being recognized not only by the intending minister but also by the church. It is not as their creature but as God's gift to them that the church is presumed to call a man or a woman to minister to them. Ordination is the culmination of a whole series of procedures beginning with recognition and recommendation in the church where the candidate is a member, then at association, provincial, seminary and

denominational levels, so that when set apart to the office of minister in
a church the ordinand is also recognized as belonging to the corps of
ministers of the entire Communion of churches. Ordination therefore
is the act not of an elite standing above the Church but of the entire
membership of the Church.[220]

We have already alluded to a further strong emphasis in Alliance
literature; namely, to that of the priesthood of all believers. Time and
again this doctrine has been expounded in its true, corporate sense: the
covenanted fellowship of believers all together comprise the priesthood;
and time and again the warning has been issued that we must not abuse
this doctrine by construing it to mean that in the Church anyone can
do anything he chooses. As David Williams reminded the twelfth Presbyterian Council (1925), it is integral to the catholicity of the reconciled
community that all believers are "to reveal God to their fellows by word
and by life and to be the means of bringing them to God, and finally to
serve one another in love."[221]

Still, because of a diversity of gifts it is necessary that church life be
decently ordered; hence the special ministries of the church. Now it
follows from the sole headship of Christ over the church, and from the
fact that all believers are of the apostolate, members of the royal
priesthood, that there can be no distinction of status between those who
are ordained to special ministry and those who are not. To suppose
otherwise is to divide the reconciled family and to cast aspersions against
the baptism of all, which is, in effect, the sign of their ordination to
mission.[222] This point is underlined in *God's Reign and Our Unity:*
"Baptism means . . . the participation of believers through the Spirit in
what Christ has done for us as he shares with us his communion with
the Father and his mission to the world. . . . The one baptism is . . . our
common incorporation into Christ, into this common life of shared
worship and mission in him."[223]

From this point of view some doctrines of ordination are in danger
of reducing the significance of baptism. D. H. McVicar took no such
risks with his understanding of ordination presented at the sixth Presbyterian Council (1896):

> Ordination does not, *ipso facto,* impart spiritual gifts or special
> power; it is simply the solemn form by which the Church recognises
> Christ's call to office, and gives the persons ordained public author-
> ity to minister in His name. There is nothing in Scripture about
> ordination conferring special grace or an indelible ecclesiastical
> character, and qualifying a person to perform priestly acts—noth-
> ing as to deacons and presbyters being required to observe enforced
> celibacy.[224]

Clearly the ministers (and here we refer to the teaching elders) are ordained to the ministry of Word and Sacrament and to the pastoral office. But the question arises as to the admissibility of "lay" (an uncomfortable word!) celebration of the sacraments. Many Reformed churches allow this possibility, especially in pastoral emergencies, and the Anglican/Reformed dialogue report has this to say about it:

> The practice of "lay celebration" has sometimes been advocated because it was held to be a necessary witness to the "priesthood of all believers." This advocacy clearly rests on a misunderstanding, since it implies that it is the president who is alone the priest. The practice thus contradicts the doctrine which it is intended to support. On the other hand there have been and there still are situations where, because of a shortage of ordained ministers, or because of very rapid missionary advance, there are congregations which must either have the Eucharist without an ordained minister, or else have no Eucharist at all except on rare occasions. In some cases it may be said that this indicates a lack of proper foresight on the part of the Church's leadership, but this observation does not meet the immediate pastoral need. Reformed churches have therefore frequently taken the view that a lay person should be given authority by the Church to preside at the Eucharist in such circumstances. This is justified on the ground that the orderly modification of normal practice may meet particular pastoral needs, and fulfil the intention which the general practice is intended to serve. . . . The presidency of the ordained person does not depend upon his possessing a priesthood which others lack; it depends upon the good ordering which is essential to the life of the Church as it exercises corporately the priesthood given to it by the one who is alone the good [great] High Priest.[225]

But if no difference in status exists between the minister and the lay person; if we do not subscribe to the view that at ordination a special sacrament-validating *potestas* is mysteriously conferred that requires the restriction of presidency at the Lord's table to those thus ordained; if (as we increasingly say when wearing our liturgical hats) Word and sacrament belong together; if, as is very widely agreed, anyone may baptize provided it be done in the name of the Trinity and with water, then Robert Mackintosh was not so very wide of the mark in saying to the fifth Congregational Council (1930):

> A notable custom in some quarters among us is that of occasionally placing a layman, or a Christian woman of character and worth, in the place usually occupied by the minister at the distribution of the Lord's Supper. . . . By making a lay Christian the visible president at

some celebrations of the Lord's Supper, we do not disparage the ministry, but we testify our reverence for the membership when it is what it ought to be.

He went on to issue a warning: "Union with Methodists, or union with Presbyterians—to say nothing of union with Episcopalians—is likely to abolish this custom as a dangerous irregularity. New Testament ministries were charismatic; but the ministries of the more highly organized Church communities are terribly officialized."[226]

Mackintosh's word "visible" is important, for Christ is the real president at his table, and Mackintosh is no advocate of the slipshod. Congregational order does not permit anyone to do anything, as we have said; and those who have come to permit lay celebration (if only since about 1850) have their saints at Church Meeting who may in a solemn and orderly way set someone apart to serve at the Lord's table. Where this is done with prayer and out of a desire to honor God and minister to the people, and since Christ is present at his table, there is no reason to suppose that chaos will result, still less that God's grace will be withheld. If the Reformed do not *welcome* the possibility of lay celebration they may be smuggling into their ecclesiology more bogeymen than their catholicity can, or should, tolerate.

Turning now to the eldership, we must make several points. A major survey conducted for the Presbyterian Alliance by Dr. Robert W. Henderson[227] reveals that within the Reformed family a great variety of practice exists. For example, some churches ordain women as elders; others do not.[228] Most invite the participation of the congregation in the election of elders; a few do not. In some churches elders are ordained with the laying on of hands and the giving of the right hand of fellowship; in others only the latter forms part of the service. Here elders are ordained for life and serve for life; there they are ordained for life but serve only for specified terms. A committee of the United Church of Canada proposed in 1966 that elders should be admitted rather than ordained, since in that church service was not lifelong and elders' functions were performed vis-à-vis one congregation only.[229]

The duties assigned to elders vary considerably from place to place and can include pastoral visitation, judicial functions, the care of the poor, teaching in day schools, and fiscal and property responsibilities. When we further consider that in some Reformed churches the offices of pastor, elder, deacon, and doctor (that is, theological teacher) are retained, and that in Congregational circles the *deacon's* role frequently spans those of the Presbyterian elder and deacon (the latter normally being concerned with financial matters and works of charity), Anglicans may well wonder precisely what is being commended to them when their Reformed dialogue partners offer the eldership for consideration.[230] What must be maintained is that while in one sense the elders (and the Congregational deacons) represent the people, they are by no means the executive committee of a democratic assembly. They are God's appointees in a Christocratic body and they serve with (not below) the minister in the exercise of their duties.[231]

At least four matters arise on which further reflection is needed. First, the Anglican/Reformed dialogue report commends, but does not make a case for, the threefold pattern of ministry by bishops, priests, and deacons. However:

1. The threefold pattern is now universally conceded to be less than conclusively demonstrable from the New Testament.
2. Neither the Reformed nor the Anglicans actually display a convincing threefold pattern.
3. Both Anglicans and Reformed have numerous other official ministries—lay preacher, lay reader, deaconess, church social worker, Christian educationalist—to name but a few.[232]
4. The Anglican/Reformed report's commendation of a ministry which is personal, collegial, and communal in all its facets (or, as some would say, "at all levels") is not necessarily tied to a threefold pattern of ministry.

What is to be made of all this? And how seriously should the finding of a study section at the seventeenth Presbyterian Council be taken: "Organization and structure are necessary for the existence and witness of the Church. This does not mean, however, that any particular historical form of these is necessary for salvation."[233]

In this connection Alliance President W. Niesel warned in 1965 that

> our churches are in danger of having a complete ministerial structure imposed upon them. A *threefold ministerial system* is in future to be applied to us all. . . . The fact that the Vatican Council has recently been discussing these three offices . . . reminds us that this threefold ministerial system represents a typically western ministerial structure. The eastern Church has avoided narrowing the concept of the ministry to anything like this extent, and keeps much closer to the variety characteristic of the New Testament concept of the ministry.
>
> Why should we be tied to this Western ministerial system? What good reasons do our Anglican brothers have for wishing to impose this law upon us as well?[234]

These questions are not answered in *God's Reign and Our Unity*, and they are too important to be bypassed.

Second, there is the related question: "Whom should we ordain?" On the basis of the priesthood of all believers some suggest that every "minister"—the Sunday School teacher, the organist, the caretaker— should be ordained. When expressed, this view sometimes draws the retort, "They are ordained—we call it baptism!" On the other hand, and again on the basis of the priesthood of all believers, some in the Reformed family question whether any should be ordained. More work needs to be done on this question.

Our final two points have particular piquancy in the wake of the union of Presbyterians and Congregationalists within the Alliance. First, "Where does church power reside?" The question was raised in a paper by Dr. Harper of Allegheny which was read in his absence at the first Presbyterian Council (1877):

> In the seventeenth century, after the rise of Independency, this question, though not then a new one, was much debated, being deemed a sort of test question between Presbyterians and Congregationalists. The reply given by the latter in general was that the Church as a whole is the first receptacle of all Church power; while the former were inclined to qualify this statement by maintaining that office power is directly bestowed by Christ on those set apart to lawful office in the Church, and does not reach them indirectly through the body of the Church. I am disposed to think that there was a truth emphasised on either side in this controversy, and that neither party made the necessary distinctions. . . . I venture to suggest what I deem the proper solution of the problem,—a solution hinted, I think, though not clearly brought out by John Owen, in his valuable treatise on "Church Government."
>
> Officers are given by Christ to the Church for its edification.
>
> The officers thus given form a part of the Church, being members of it. On these grounds it may be proper to say that the Church is the first seat or receptacle under Christ of all Church power.
>
> But the phrase "Church power" is ambiguous, for it may mean at once certain rights, immunities, or privileges vouchsafed by Christ to the members of the Church in general . . . or it may mean the authority which attaches to officers according to Christ's institution. In the first sense the whole Church is the first subject or depository of Church power. In the second sense, those duly invested with office according to Christ's appointment are the immediate or first receptacle of Church power. Presbyterians, in maintaining that *office* power (for that was their favourite form of expression) is directly conferred by Christ on those lawfully chosen for office in the Church, were, we believe, right; but they do not seem to have admitted as frankly, as

none could do more consistently than they, that there is a certain kind of power of which the Church in general is the immediate depository.[235]

The differences of emphasis outlined here did not prevent the coming together of the international Presbyterian and Congregational bodies in 1970, but it must have exercised those united churches that are members of the Alliance. The Alliance would do well to discover what they have to teach us on the matter. It would be pleasant to think that Presbyterians and Congregationalists could now agree that power resides in the head of the church; that the power given to church officers is delegated by him and conferred through his people; and that there is a *mutual episkope* within the family of Christ both as among minister, elders (deacons), and people, and as between the local church and the wider (not higher) family of churches.

Finally, ought a minister to be a member of a local church? At the first Presbyterian Council (1877) William E. Moore quoted the constitution of the Presbyterian Church in the United States as saying that an elder must be " 'a member in full communion in the church in which he is to exercise his office.' . . . Hence a minister of the Gospel may not be chosen an elder, inasmuch as *he is not a member of a particular church.*"[236] Is this a tenable view? We suggest that grounds exist for saying that it is not. No doubt those who support the contested opinion wish to assert that the minister is a minister of the catholic church, not simply of a local church. But precisely for this reason the minister *ought* to be a member of a local church as are the elders with whom he works, for this, according to the Presbyterian and Congregational statements we have reviewed, is the way in which *everyone* becomes a member of the catholic church. If the minister is not a member of a local church, of what is he a member? The church invisible? Who can say? The presbytery? But the presbytery does not call him to minister; rather it sustains, or, more rarely, does not sustain the call addressed by a local church. If the minister is not a member along with those in the church of which he is minister, are we not making him into a separated person in an unwholesome way? Are we not removing the minister from the corporate discipline of those most closely associated with him in Christ's work? Ought not the minister to be subject, as every other member is subject, to the loving discipline of the local company? No doubt there is much to be said on this issue, but the issue ought to be a live one in a family that brings together those of the Presbyterian and Congregational families.

To close this chapter with a cautionary word: however important questions concerning sacraments and ministry may be, we must take care that the answers which they prompt are not such as to place order above the gospel of God's free grace. Otherwise, the catholic church— that company of those who are reconciled to God and to each other on the ground of Christ's finished work, and called by the Holy Spirit into his covenanted family—will continue to be torn asunder by ecclesiastical sectarianism.

5

The Philosophical-Apologetic Climate

In this chapter we shall discover that in the matter of responding to the philosophical-apologetic climate of the successive generations the record of the Alliance is uneven. Whereas in the early days both the Presbyterian Alliance and the Congregational Council made real attempts to evaluate their intellectual environment in the light of the gospel, in more recent years the Alliance has not devoted nearly so much time to this task. In particular, certain philosophical and methodological questions have not been faced by the Alliance as such.

No doubt it is partly a question of time and resources. Since the 1970s interconfessional dialogue has consumed both energies and finance, and ecclesiological discussion has been to the fore (as the very length of our fourth chapter indicates) in quest of signs of the unity which God has given his church. Again, as we shall see in the next chapter, clamant questions concerning peace and human rights have rightly occupied the Alliance's attention in recent years. Neither factor, however, accounts for the general absence from Alliance literature since 1920 of the kind of issues under review here.

Again, it may be that in many quarters the themes to which we shall now refer are not of pressing concern. Questions concerning the viability of religious language, the coherence of theism, the relations between faith and reason, and the like, may not be universally urgent. They are, however, real questions, and they have been pressed with considerable force and acumen—especially but not exclusively in Anglo-Saxon philosophical circles. Given that the bulk of Alliance literature still emanates from those circles, it is the more surprising that so little of these discussions has surfaced in the corpus.

Some may at this point be inclined to protest that Christians do not approach the world with arguments, but with the gospel. Indeed, an interesting exchange along these lines developed at the tenth Presbyterian Council (1913), before it became fashionable to say that one may not argue with unbelief, but only preach to it. In the course of a discussion of ministerial training D. J. Burrell said,

> Now, brethren, I suppose there is a place for dynamite in the economy of human affairs, but the study of explosives is a mighty poor preparation for a professional life in architecture. And I rise here, in the presence of academic brethren in schools of learning, and principally in theological seminaries, to say that it is my profound conviction that the whole work of the ministry is tremendously handicapped in these days by the undue emphasis laid on the necessity for apologetics . . . nine-tenths of the sermons that I hear these days are apologetic.[1]

In reply, James Iverach reminded Dr. Burrell of Paul, who was well skilled in the art of apologetics, and continued:

> I feel that we professors are not doing useless work when we are teaching our students what attitude the modern mind is taking towards God and man and the world, and when we are teaching them how to appreciate what is true in these modern views of evolution and everything else, so far as it seems to us. . . . I think a man would be ill-equipped for his ministerial work if he did not have some appreciation of what is in the atmosphere today. . . . I believe in the authority of the Gospel; I do not believe in apologetic sermons. I never apologize for God and His ways when I am preaching. I call upon my hearers to justify themselves to God and accept Him, but before I can say that, I must show myself acquainted with the state of mind of the people living in these modern days when everything is being questioned. If I know what these things are, I shall not preach the Gospel less simply and effectively than if I knew them not.[2]

The question presses: Could it be that if in some directions (notably the ecclesiological) the Alliance has become more ecumenical, in other directions it has become less so? We assume that if the church—not least in its Reformed expression—is genuinely concerned for the unity in Christ of the whole inhabited earth, then the questions posed by the world of thought cannot be sidestepped. It is, of course, possible to concede this point and then to argue that no one Christian world communion need address this issue on its own. This may well be so; and it is well known that the thought world of Marxism and of religions other than the Christian are engaged transconfessionally by the World Council of Churches. There is no reason in principle why the questions to which we shall refer might not receive similar treatment. This has yet to happen, however, and it may be that the Alliance is called to give a lead in the matter.[3]

Let us, then, examine the Alliance record in responding to the philosophical-apologetic challenges of the day. We shall begin by examining a major piece of stocktaking offered by D. W. Simon to the first Congregational Council (1891). We shall then provide some examples of the way in which Alliance writers and speakers approached intellectual issues in the early years.[4] Next, we shall note some contributions from the middle period, observing continuities and discontinuities with what went before. The somewhat desultory attention paid to intellectual movements since the Second World War will be considered next, and we shall conclude by suggesting that a number of issues, thus far neglected in Alliance circles, now cry out for attention.

I. The Early Years

Under the general heading "The Present Direction of Theological Thought in the Congregational Churches of the Several Countries Represented by the Council," D. W. Simon spoke to the first Congregational Council (1891) for Britain. He first draws attention to the lack of interest in—even contempt for—systematic theology:

> When prominent ministers refer in tones of mock humility to their ignorance of Systematic Theology, or earn cheap applause by denouncing dogma and contrasting it with life; when ministerial associations gaze wonderingly at a man who takes a deep personal interest in its study and thinks a knowledge of it necessary to true ministerial efficiency; when journalists rarely let pass an opportunity of flouting doctrine and dogma; when leading laymen exclaim, "We want practical preaching, not doctrine"; when the fact of a candidate for a pulpit having a sound knowledge of theology counts, as a rule, practically for little or nothing in his favour; and when it is easier to get a thousand pounds to build a college than a hundred to provide adequate teaching—what else can one say?[5]

He notes further that

> during the last thirty-five years only one "Systematic Theology" has been published by British Congregationalists; that out of some 600 registered Congregational publications during, say, twenty-five years, scarcely 50 are scientifically theological; and that out of upwards of

450 discourses by Congregational ministers printed during the last five years or thereabouts in *The Christian World Pulpit,* scarcely thirty were properly doctrinal.[6]

Simon grants that there is some interest in inspiration, the atonement, and future punishment, though even this interest "shows decided signs of giving place to the state of unreasoned sentimental conviction which is styled 'finding' or 'being found by' a truth." In "marked and cheering contrast" there is a growing interest, if not yet widespread active participation, in biblical studies. Preaching, if less doctrinal, is more ethical—though there is less appeal to the conscience than hitherto. There is "tenderness towards sceptics and outsiders, conjoined with scathing severity towards assured believers and insiders."[7]

As for theology proper, the old moderate Calvinism of Pye-Smith, Payne, and Wardlaw has disintegrated under the impact of ideas from Germany and the writings of Coleridge, McLeod Cambell, Maurice, Bushnell, Carlyle, and Robertson, and under the influence of "a changing evangelical consciousness." We now work towards "a Christocentric system, or perhaps to speak more exactly, towards one with the two foci of the Fatherhood of God and the Living Personality of Christ":

> Instead of laying stress on that which distinguishes God from the creature—as, for example, on His infinitude, His transcendence, His absolute authority and claims, His awful holiness, inflexible righteousness, and consuming anger—we dwell by preference on their essential affinities, as involved, for example, in the Divine Fatherhood, and immanence; in His love and yearning for man; and in the claims which men have on Him. The personal Trinity seems to have been practically dropped; and we have either fallen back on a sort of Sabellianism; or into the unity of Swedenborgianism; or are trying to rest in a duality of Father and Son,—little stress is laid on the personality of the Holy Spirit, even where He has not been reduced to impersonality; and His work has been nearly merged in that of Christ. Scarcely even a passing reference is now made to the theme of the Divine sovereignty on which our fathers used to touch with such awe. The divine decrees and predestination have been exorcised; election has been metamorphosed; and were such subjects as irresistible grace, effectual calling, adoption, and perseverance to be seriously expounded, most people would either wonder what was meant, or silently mutter, "Rip van Winkle." In dealing with *man* our starting-point is less and less distinctly the Fall, inherited depravity, guilt, and moral inability; instead thereof we dwell on his filial relation to God, either by nature or in Christ; on the good that is to be found even in

the worst; on his weakness, conflicts, sorrows, misfortunes; and assert either his freedom or blamelessness for lack thereof.

Instead of the humanity of Christ being overshadowed by his Divinity, His humanity under cover of phrases like "the Divine Man" is in some quarters supplanting His Divinity. The relation of the atonement to God is chiefly one of revelation: Christ propitiates man, not God. To speak of the Atonement as limited, or of saving grace as general and special, would strike most as a sort of blasphemy. Coming to the *ordo salutis*, conversion has been well nigh converted into decision for Christ; regeneration into a process of spiritual culture; with regard to justification by faith, that *articulus stantis et cadentis ecclesiae*, we are emphatically in a state of transition. In its forensic form it is almost surrendered; some are unwittingly drifting towards a view that smacks more of Rome than Geneva; and insight into its vital importance, when properly understood, is lamentably rare.

On the question of man's *future destiny*, we are in the main divided between Universalism, the doctrine of life in Christ, the Larger Hope, and various phrases of a non-commital position—the sterner views commonly held a generation ago have well-nigh disappeared. Other *eschatological* matters—even heaven, which preachers used to delight in depicting—awaken but languid attention. Such are the prominent features of the *status quo*.[8]

How does Simon react to his own somber catalogue of ills? First, he welcomes the reaction against dogma because it marks

the beginning of the end, among ourselves, of a struggle with one of the most grievous perversions of Christianity that have appeared during the history of the Church, namely, the transformation of the Gospel into a body of truths supernaturally received; with its correlate notion, that salvation hangs on the holding for true of certain saving doctrines. This is the error which found classical expression in the words of the Athanasian Creed, "Whosoever will be saved, before all things it is necessary that he hold the Catholic faith." . . . It is not mere truths or doctrines, not even if they were guaranteed by a perpetual Divine miracle, that can generate and nourish Christian life, but the personal action of the personal God, rendered possible through Christ's work and through faith in Christ—faith conditioned by testimony, proclamation, preaching.[9]

What is required is that theologians "go back to the great objective realities with which doctrines and theories are concerned."[10] Simon feels compelled to add that the error against which he protests "is the chief support of the ecclesiasticism, sacramentarianism and priestism which more than anything else hinder the progress of the kingdom of God."[11]

Simon is further disquieted by those who preach whatever seems *to them* true and up-to-date:

> All unwittingly these Melchizedeks are falling back . . . into the error that what saves men is truths about religion or Christianity or God; the only difference between them, and those they count antiquated, being, that the truths these latter taught were believed to have been supernaturally revealed and as such to possess authority; whereas the truths set forth by the former are those which each man has to discover for himself; and are taught, after the manner of the Scribes and Pharisees, without authority. If this sort of thing becomes general, I see nothing for it but relapse, for the more independent into agnosticism; for the weaker sort towards Romanism.[12]

There is still a further catalogue of disturbing features to come:

> A certain hankering after originality or novelty, which is sometimes rewarded by the discovery of mares' nests or the revival of ideas that have proved themselves unsound; in contrast thereto, a wonderful submissiveness to the behests of critical and scientific authorities, inside and outside the churches; an inclination, on the one hand, so to naturalise the supernatural, in the history of Israel, in the life of Christ, in the origin of our Scriptures, and in the rise and progress of the Christian life; and, on the other hand, to supernaturalise the natural in the ethnic religions, as to bring both under the evolutionary law according to which God is supposed to be realising the cosmic idea; the advocacy of a comprehension as regards membership, worship, and doctrine which will scarcely leave any one outside except the orthodox; disposition to reduce prayer to a sort of spiritual gymnastic or massage; and last, not least, a tendency to co-ordinate in the work of regenerating society, all sorts of cultural agencies, with the "Gospel, which is the power of God unto salvation," rooted more or less in the conscious conversion of Christianity, from a real spiritual dynamic, into a moral and religious regulative.[13]

Despite all, Simon believes that the majority of Congregationalists will remain loyal to "the central realities of 'the faith once delivered to the saints,'" and that they will in time share in the devising of "a theological science which will be accepted as the cornerstone of a true philosophy of the world."[14]

Simon's survey is illuminating in many respects, but not least because as early as 1891 he detected a shift in theology towards Christocentrism.

For him this is cashed in terms of the personality of Christ: we do not have here an inkling of the eschatological Christologies of later times. But the direction is perceptible, and later at the same council E. R. Conder drew further attention to it: "Everyone intimately acquainted with the sermons, the religious literature, and the evangelistic activity of the last 30 or 40 years must have become conscious of . . . THE PLACE PERSONALLY OCCUPIED BY OUR LORD JESUS CHRIST in theological thought, in preaching—especially evangelistic or mission preaching—and in Christian life."[15]

Conder further endorsed Simon's view that knowledge of the *method* of salvation was no longer the alleged prerequisite of salvation. Formerly,

> the knowledge of this Method was deemed essential to sound conversion. The intellectual view of faith, as *belief of the truth*—a view apparently simple, but thick-sown with perplexities—was pushed to the fore in place of the truly far simpler moral aspect of faith, as personal trust in Christ. In our day, instead of looking into himself to see whether he truly believes and understands the Gospel, the penitent is encouraged to bring his ignorance as well as his sinfulness and his impotence to Christ, and to put himself unconditionally in the hands of the living and loving Saviour who was delivered up for his trespasses and raised for his justification.[16]

The point must be pursued a little further. On the one hand, Simon and Conder were questioning an earlier scholastic rationalism. At the first Presbyterian Council (1877) Professor Godet had entered the lists too: "Let the Presbyterian Churches—which, since the sixteenth century have so gloriously defended the basis of the gospel, justification by faith, against the papacy—unite themselves to-day against Protestant rationalism and become the immoveable support of that which makes the crown of the gospel—the divinity of our Lord Jesus Christ."[17] On the other hand, as Iverach pointed out, the times called for an investigation of the place properly to be accorded to reason in matters of religious faith. This latter inquiry was undertaken in face of a hostile view suggesting that any idea of God, be it tenable at all, must be encompassable by human reason—human reason which, unavoidably, yields less than the absolute.[18] The demand for proof, the challenge to remove doubt—these are also aspects of the quest, and, to Robert Rainy, they were the explanation of the increasingly apologetic stance of theology.[19] In a paper of 1880 on "The Conflict between Faith and Rationalism in Holland," J. J. van Oosterzee went so far as to say that "Modern Rationalism assumes an air of triumph over the Christianity of the Gospel and the Church, as a thing that has had its day."[20]

The modern rationalism manifested itself above all in the attack upon the supernatural, as Simon saw. A. A. Hodge concurred: "The insurrection of reason against traditional superstitions and the usurped authority of the hierarchy, has been succeeded by the illegitimate insurrection of reason against all supernatural revelation and spiritual illumination."[21] Many joined in the protest. Rainy, for example, noted that "where the natural and supernatural come together, the utmost care is taken to give to nature everything that can in reason be ascribed to her. It is become a kind of punctilio. The natural, which used perhaps to be rather a stepchild in orthodox houses, is now become the spoilt child of the family."[22] The procedure, he continued, has altered the way in which doctrines are conceived and stated:

> Formerly doctrines used to be presented as the expression of revealed fact, or as divinely prescribed methods under which God deals with men, or men may deal with God. But they now appear rather as modes of human feeling and experience. They are moulds into which human thought may or ought to shape itself; they denote the character and movement which human experience may assume in certain relations.[23]

The prevailing influence of the "scientific outlook" was a major culprit in all of this, and Henry Calderwood and A. E. Garvie reminded their respective Councils in almost the same words that as long as it adheres to its own proper method science has no evidence with which either to substantiate or to deny the fact of the supernatural.[24] Science could not undermine the Bible for the same reason—their respective spheres were different. Calderwood maintained this position while at the same time arguing that theology is close to science insofar as the scientific quest has been and should be a matter of discerning the Creator's handiwork.[25] For his part Jean Monod pointed to the different aims of science and religion; we must, he said, distinguish between "Religion that aims at holiness, and Science, whether natural or philosophical or even theological, that aims at knowledge."[26]

The doughty Robert Watts remained unconvinced by those who sought to minimize this struggle by keeping science and religion in separate, non-conflicting compartments. He argued in 1880 that this was unscriptural in its denial of the truth that creation as such reveals God. He thought it was unscientific too, for "the scientist cannot complete his work within the limits prescribed."[27] This was a minority view, however, and was to remain so until it became more fashionable to think of the limitations of the scientific method, the place of imagination in the scientific enterprise, and the need for scientific humility in face of so fecund, mysterious, and potentially dangerous a universe.

The theme (more than the theory) of evolution was sounded loud and clear by the fathers of the Alliance. Among the oft-repeated notes were these: evolutionary theory may inform us as to the *method* of God the creator, but it is incompetent as a description of the *origin* of the universe. It was further defiantly affirmed that if Christians wish to construe evolution theistically—that is, as evidencing God's way of working—no sustainable scientific objection to this is possible. Again, it was regularly pointed out that the notion that higher forms of life develop from lower is preposterous and that evolutionary theory demands a superior— indeed a supernatural—Intelligence.[28] Theologically inspired skepticism was heaped upon any idea of the onward and upward education of the human race which would turn sins into unfortunate but surmountable obstacles. This, thought Rainy, was to deny the juridical aspect of things on which theology must always insist.[29]

From another direction than the scientific-materialist, theological thought was being influenced in an anti-supernaturalist direction. In the wake of Hegelianism came pantheizing immanentisms of various kinds. To Robert Watts pantheism was a "monstrous delusion." It invites us to believe on the one hand that the phenomenal is unreal, and on the other that "the only real being is manifested *in* and *through* this endless delusive flow." Watts would prefer us "to credit the testimony of our senses, as these philosophers themselves are wont to do when they are outside their studies, and to believe that both the organic and inorganic worlds are veritable realities."[30]

A. E. Garvie drew the theological consequences at the third Congregational Council (1908). If God and the universe are identified we have

a consequent denial of the personality of God and man, and of the reality of the opposition of human sin to divine holiness. That God is a mind which thinks, heart which feels, will which acts, self which gives itself to others, that God is Spirit, Light, Life, Love, in brief that God is personal, is a fundamental article of the Christian faith. Not less so is man's conviction that while in God he lives, moves and has his being, is God's offspring, yet he is not God, but is dependent on God. . . . Any attempt at doctrinal restatement with exclusive emphasis on divine immanence, the identity of God and man, must sacrifice essential features of the Christian faith. If God and man are one, and man cannot sin against God, then forgiveness and atonement become meaningless terms.[31]

As late as 1929 the Presbyterian G. W. Richards found it necessary to be equally clear on the matter:

The God of our fathers transcends the universe, yet He is not separated from it in such a way as not to be in full control of it. He is not an unfinished God, a God in the making, evolving with the world. He is in the world yet in such a way as not to be entangled with it, and in a manner subject to it. He works through the world to realize the reign of righteousness and love in the hearts of men, and yet He does not limit Himself to material or personal agencies in His redemptive activity. He works where and when and how He pleases. He is not an absolute substance into which men are merged by mystic ascent, or that is infused into our nature as a sort of medicine of immortality by sacramental transactions; nor is He submerged in the world in such a way that the distinction between creature and Creator is lost. He is not mere immanent will or reason which becomes self-conscious in men, and is progressively apprehended by men and recorded in the religious literature of the white and coloured races.

To distinguish Him from justifiable endeavours to define Him in modern terms, and to make Him more palatable to modern minds, I should say that he is more than "the immaterial reality," "the principle of concretion," "the sum-total of the forces of the universe," "the behaviour of the universe," "creative co-ordination," "will functioning through the world as becoming," "that feature of our total environment which most vitally affects the continuance and welfare of human life."[32]

Where Richards gives quotations, Robert Mackintosh in 1908 had no hesitation in naming names:

In the name of ultimate reason—Professor Bradley gives us a Pantheistic Absolute, and no human immortality; and Dr. McTaggart gives us an eternal society of interrelated spirits, and no absolute being as such; and Professor Royce gives us God and immortality, but without mention of Christ; and Professor Taylor finds that Royce's arguments are vitiated by reliance upon the relational form of thought, and himself gives us a fighting chance of immortality, and an Absolute that cannot be called personal or a self. Such differences do not prove that idealism is barren; but surely they prove that idealism is in no case to claim a monopoly of certainty. Dim movements of faith may be wiser than this shrill logical debate.[33]

Varieties of philosophy that were more obviously hostile to Christian faith were also subjected to close scrutiny at both Presbyterian and Congregational Councils. Thus, for example, Robert Flint treated the second Presbyterian Council (1880) to a detailed paper on "Agnosticism."[34] In reviewing this we must take care to notice the strong definition of agnosticism which Flint propounds. Whereas a contemporary philosopher, J. C. A. Gaskin, defines the term as "the view that there is not enough, or not good enough, evidence to decide whether God exists or not. Such a view admits the possibility that evidence may be forthcoming and hence that the existence of God or gods is a coherent possibility,"[35] Flint holds that the name "agnostic"

> is only appropriate to one whose refusal to believe in the existence of God, and of spiritual things, is rested on the allegation that the human mind is inherently and constitutionally incapable of ascertaining whether there is a God and spiritual things or not. But there is no kind of truth which may not be rejected, on the assumption that the human mind is inherently and constitutionally incapable of ascertaining whether there is such truth or not. . . . What is essential in Agnosticism is the reason on which it supports itself—the attitude towards truth and knowledge which it assumes; what is non-essential are the objects or propositions to which it is applied.[36]

Agnosticism is founded upon narrow and partial doctrines as to the nature of belief:

> Agnosticism must be the necessary result of overlooking or depreciating any element power or means of knowledge, any kind of evidence, or any natural and truthful criterion of evidence. Place, for instance, the criterion of truth exclusively in sense of sentiment, in the theoretical reason or the practical reason, in authority or universal consent; reduce it, with Locke, to the perception of the agreement or disagreement of ideas—with Leibnitz, to the absence of contradiction; with Herbert Spencer, to the inconceivability of the negative, etc.— and you must logically become, if only a partial agnostic, still an agnostic on a very large scale.[37]

Agnosticism finds fertile soil in the "critical spirit of the age," and churches need not think that agnostic criticism can be handled by "the mere exercise of discipline." Indeed, the churches, insofar as they have been one-sidedly dogmatic, are not guiltless vis-à-vis the spread of agnostic tendencies; and the misunderstanding of the relations between science and religion has been a further contributing factor.

Flint concludes with an appeal to his audience:

> Each one of you—fathers, brothers, sisters—by simply so living as to show that religion is supremely worth believing, may do far more to combat the spirit whence Agnosticism arises than I or any one could

do by a merely formal written attack upon it. The grand argument against anti-religious Agnosticism is the practical one of a consistent and vigorous Christian life—the argument which, through God's grace, we can all use.[38]

Here Homer nods, for while testimony (and it must be this rather than "argument" that Flint has in mind) can undoubtedly be impressive (and that in either direction—it can impress the skeptic with the irrationality of the witness!), it is not philosophically decisive. On the contrary, it opens up all the questions surrounding the alleged evidential character of religious experience.[39]

In 1908 Robert Mackintosh reviewed a number of other philosophical tendencies in an address entitled, "Recent Philosophy and Christian Doctrine." He detected an upsurge in empiricism—"given facts count for more, and necessary truths for less"[40]—and found unbelief widespread: "There is hardly now one wretched little freethinking undergraduate who will not tell you just where Jesus went wrong, and why."[41] He noted a recoil from intellectualism and an increase of voluntarism; the latter could go too far, however, for "if Voluntarism means that knowledge is the mere creation of will, the doctrine seems to be a sceptical renunciation of real knowledge."[42] As for the pragmatism of William James and F. C. S. Schiller:

> True, as the Germans remind us, it has been arranged that the trees shall not grow up into the sky; and no doubt it has also been arranged by a higher power that those who talk about philosophy shall usually be dull. It is hardly gracious, therefore, to quarrel with the amusing pages of Professor James or Mr. Schiller; yet one cannot help thinking that, at whatever sacrifice of literary effect they could have put their meaning more clearly, if they had chosen.[43]

For all their faults, however, the religiously minded empiricists do emphasize the moral aspects of religion, and this is an advance upon Calvinism's "determination that, whatever becomes of morality, or of God's character, it shall make sure of God's omnipotence."[44]

Amid the welter of available philosophies, what should be the attitude of the Christian thinker? James McCosh left the first Presbyterian Council (1877) in no doubt: We must maintain that truth can be discovered by man; that God can be known; that matter cannot explain the action of mind; that there is an essential distinction between good and evil; and that sin is not a mere negation, but a positive quality— "These are the foundation-stones of the temple of truth."[45]

At the Congregational Council of 1908 W. B. Selbie made reference to prevailing philosophical trends in his defense of "Historic Fact as a Paramount Necessity for Christian Doctrine." He reminded his hearers that "with the rise of a scientific historical method, arose also a new conception of the difficulty of arriving at historical certitude."[46] To this various responses have been made. On the one hand,

> to Lessing, Kant and Fichte the historical element in Christianity was purely accidental, and could only be held to represent religious truth in a symbolical fashion. History may exemplify ideas, but it is the ideas, we are told, that are important and not the form in which they become manifest to the mind. The form is always accidental. On these terms Christianity tends to become a metaphysical philosophy and is easily divorced from fact.[47]

On the other hand,

> those who believe with Harnack that "the tradition as to the incidents attending the birth and early life of Jesus Christ has been shattered," are compelled to find some new groundwork for their belief in Christ and for their doctrine concerning him. Hence the familiar apologetic of Ritschl and his school. The aim of these writers is to find a justification for Christian belief which shall be independent of historical criticism on the one hand and of metaphysic on the other. In order to accomplish this they draw a clear distinction between the theoretic knowledge that has to do with facts, and the religious knowledge that has to do with judgements. They believe in the "historic Christ," and they assert his divinity, but both belief and assertion are held to be independent of criticism on the one hand and of any philosophic interpretation of the Person on the other. They lay stress on the ethical content of the life of Jesus as over against its historical form. But their "historic Christ" is not really independent of criticism. Rather he is the Christ who is left to them as the result of a criticism with an anti-supernaturalistic bias. And their independence of metaphysic confines them to a religious knowledge derived from faith and experience alone. Their Christ is divine only in the sense that he has a certain religious value for the believer.[48]

The contention that Christian doctrine may be independent of historical fact is reinforced by pragmatism: "When Professor James asserts that 'The only meaning of truth is the possibility of verification by experience,' and that 'True is the term applied to whatever it is practically profitable to believe,' he is laying down propositions which strongly appeal to an age that loves to consider itself above all things practical."[49] For his part Selbie concurs with Professor Carveth Read that pragmatism is "a kind of scepticism, as any doctrine must be that puts the conviction of reason solely upon any other ground than cognition, whether it be action or feeling."[50]

Selbie is the first to admit that Christians have sometimes maintained a false relation of historic fact to doctrine: "For instance, it has sometimes been urged that the doctrine of the incarnation depends upon the fact of the birth of our Lord from a virgin, or that belief in the living Christ is impossible, apart from the belief in his bodily resurrection. But to deny this dependence of doctrine on a single isolated fact is not to deny that historic fact is no necessary basis for doctrine. It is merely to assume the obvious necessity of discriminating among the facts given, and of broadening the basis on which doctrine is built."[51] So far, so good; but then Selbie comes near to surrendering his case: "The force at the back of Christianity is the person of Jesus Christ, and our belief in the Person is not necessarily conditioned by the accuracy or otherwise of the reports we have received about incidents in his career. The historical testimony to the truth of the Christian origins does not depend on the degree in which we can authenticate every statement made in the Gospels."[52] But how many statements, and which ones, is it (in principle) necessary for us to be able to verify if we are not to fall into irrationalism, or if we are not, with Lessing and others, to remove Christ from the stage of history altogether?

Turning now to a related yet distinct field we must note that the Alliance had its origin in the period of the awakening academic interest in the great religions of the world. Alexander Stewart's article on "Christianity and the Science of Comparative Religion" appeared in the first volume of *The Catholic Presbyterian* (1879). In his opening question he drove to the heart of the matter: "Is Christianity a member of a series, one among many forms of religion, a stage in the development of the human mind, and nothing more?"[53] To this Stewart answered "yes" and "no." Christianity *is* a member of a series of movements which have met "the spiritual wants of man, and its authority and perfection may be expected, not to be compromised, but to be established, by a comparison of it with others."[54] On the other hand, "Christianity is the only system which has dared to probe to the bottom of the wound of which humanity is so sadly conscious, because it alone was provided with a perfect remedy. It can present the ideal at which men should aim without detraction, because it alone can hold out a prospect of its realisation."[55] The upshot is that "Christianity is at once an historical and a spiritual religion; it appeals at once to history and to conscience, and fears the verdict of neither."[56]

We may designate Stewart's view as the standard view; it was echoed by all the early Alliance writers and speakers who made reference to the other-than-Christian faiths by which people live.

II. The Middle Years

In the middle of our period (1925-31) we find a few pieces of intellectual stocktaking that merit attention.

When he addressed the Presbyterian Council in 1925 on "The Church and the New Age," George Galloway was relatively optimistic. True, there were lessons to learn from the principle of development which ruled out older, literalistic ways of construing the creation narratives; and the problem of religious authority had not yet been solved. Still, "the arrogant materialism of fifty years ago is dead, and the old dispute between science and religion is a thing of the past."[57] Again, the temper of New Testament criticism is less destructive than it was, and in the face of a mysterious universe people are more willing than before to admit the claims of faith.

Among the most serious problems confronting the church is the practical one: "The cult of amusement and pleasure, and the engrossing love of material goods have bred a shallow mind and a soul that is careless of the things of the spirit. Religion has no more dangerous foe than indifference of a merely conventional piety."[58]

What is missing from Galloway's address—and he was a philosopher of religion—is any indication of the importance for religious thought of the then-burgeoning process philosophies of Whitehead and Alexander, or of the rising threat of logical positivism represented by the Vienna Circle.[59] He did not even consider the widespread practical atheism (and its ethical consequences) to which J. D. Jones referred at the fifth Congregational Council (1930): "The vehemence of the attack a generation ago showed at any rate that there was a strongly entrenched belief to be attacked. The modern man doesn't attack, because the belief, for him, has simply dissolved. . . . Men no longer believe in a Sovereign God, a God who rules this world and who by the hand of Moses issued a moral code for His subjects, and therefore that moral code has lost its binding authority."[60]

If newer developments in philosophy were largely neglected, those in theology commanded somewhat more attention in Alliance literature during the middle period. Above all, Barth could not be overlooked. He is, chirruped one reviewer, "a new and a great light arisen on the religious and theological world."[61] In 1930 the Continental European Committee of the Presbyterian Alliance met at Eberfeld and heard an address by Dr. Kolfhaus of Vlotho on "The Situation of Theology in Germany at the Present Day." At that time he was able to bracket together Barth, Brunner, Thurneysen, and Gogarten as representatives of the new dialectical theology, the characteristics of which he enumerated:

1. The modern theology is not an entire innovation nor a simple turning back to the doctrines of the Reformation. It rather endeavors to grasp the fruits of the hitherto prevailing theology, and to handle the problems of modern life guided by the principles and persuasions of the Bible. . . .
2. Christian Religion is not a special case of the abstraction "Religion," but a reality not to be compared with other religions—absolutely conditioned by the *Deus dixit.* . . .
3. There is no knowledge of God without the Word God Himself is speaking. . . .
4. Revelation through the Word is given us not as a thing we can watch, nor as a matter we may dispose of, but as a challenge of God urging us to personal decision. . . .
5. It interprets God and man as two worlds that cannot be connected with one another except by the grace of God. . . . The optimistic faith in human progress and the Biblical-critical view of world and man are again crossing swords. . . .
6. The long-forgotten testimony of St. Paul, that justification and sanctification both are the work of God and that we are justified and sanctified only in Christ, is again acknowledged to-day. The problem of Ethics is identical with the problem of Dogmatics. . . .
7. We begin to understand again, that the interpreter of a Biblical book must hear his text as touching him in his personal situation.[62]

That not all were prepared to absorb the new theology uncritically is clear from an article by H. C. Lefever. He said that the result of Barthianism is "to cut Christianity completely off from the ordinary social and ethical life of the world."[63] Indeed, he continued,

> I am sorry about Barth. I think he is one of the tragic figures in the ranks of Christian theologians. Not because the Nazis deprived him of his Chair . . . but because I feel that he missed a great opportunity. As some of the nineteenth-century "liberals" stressed the manward side of the Incarnation so much that the Godward side was preserved only by a *tour de force,* Barth in his day was so filled with God that he had no room in his theology for man. I think he took too much from Kierkegaard. . . . If Barth, while re-calling his generation to belief in the Holy and Transcendent God, could at the same time have seen the image of God, however faint, in man and in all creation, I believe Christian theology throughout the world would have achieved a greater unity and power than it has had for centuries. But to that Barth would no doubt reply, in what Dr. Horton tells us is the one

English phrase Barth has learnt to repeat, "All the British are Pelagians."[64]

Lefever further records that at a seminar he asked Barth what place he gave in his theology to the "conception of human personality and received his succinct but shattering reply, 'None.' "[65]

Of course, Barth had by no means finished his work when Lefever wrote his article; and he was later to make much more of what he called the humanity of God.[66] We simply illustrate the fact that in the middle period of the Alliance's history spasmodic attempts were made to take stock of the prevailing intellectual climate, and that somewhat more attention was paid to the then-new theology of Barth and his followers.

III. The Flight from Philosophical-Apologetic Questions

As we approach our own time we find sporadic attempts to appraise some aspects of the philosophical and theological scene. Thus, for example, brief references can be found to Marxism[67] and existentialism;[68] rather more attention is paid to humanism[69] and secularization.[70] We have discovered only two paragraphs on the challenges posed to religious language by the logical positivists and the linguistic analysts![71]

It is not too much to speak of a general flight from the critique of the prevailing intellectual climate. One would not guess from reading Alliance literature that the question of God's existence has been the subject of widespread debate since the late 1950s, or that from the same period have come numerous writings which question the viability of religious discourse on the grounds that (a) its assertions are not really assertions at all; (b) religious statements, being unverifiable, are literally nonsensical; or (c) that no clear meaning can be accorded religious claims because those who make them will not permit criteria of falsification to be applied to them. And what of those who have placed religious discourse in the context of a unique and nonrelatable "language game"? Again, the disregard in Alliance literature of theodicy in the face of a threatened and divided world and in view of the considerable discussion of the theme since the 1960s is almost cavalier.

Quite apart from the more particular topics just referred to, some general matters cry out for the attention of the Reformed family. The Alliance (as we shall see in the next chapter) makes pronouncements on racism, peace, human rights—and rightly so. But what, philosophically and methodologically, is going on when these pronouncements are made? Is it possible to articulate a Christian view of the world, and if so, what would it look like? Ought we to presuppose the realist, evidentialist apologetic which traveled via Reid's Reformed sons to the "Old Princeton" where it was expounded by the Hodges and B. B. Warfield? Or ought we rather to believe with those who stand in the line of Kuyper and Bavinck that the "Old Princeton" approach yields too much to sinful man's reason, assumes too much epistemological common ground between believer and unbeliever, and that therefore we can proceed only along the lines of Christian presuppositionalism?

Or should we perhaps seek to breathe fresh life into natural theology? This would entail a fresh examination of the relations of faith and reason in the wake of the demolition of the classical arguments for the existence of God conceived as logical demonstrations. If Alliance statements assume, as they do, the God in whose name we speak, can we forever overlook the question of the coherence (at least) of theism?

If we decided that it is possible to adumbrate a Christian view of the world—one derived from the catholic-evangelical thrust in our theology and ever revisable by the Spirit through the Word—would we be helped in its construction by insights from older idealism, more recent process thought, existentialism, or Barthianism? If so, how should these insights be used—as providing the structure, or as offering analogies useful in communication?

Or is this entire line of questioning misguided? Ought we in fact to settle for the view that since Christianity is a way rather than a system we should be content to react as needed to contextual stimuli, and for the rest remain open-ended? What then would become of Christian communication? Are there no universals of the gospel? This question leads us into the next category of issues.

IV. Gospel Universals?

Implicit in the Alliance literature is the assumption that the gospel encompasses certain universals—God's gracious provision, our need—and that these ought to be the basis upon which Christians around the world stand. Implicit too is the assumption that this gospel is to be communicated, and here we come face to face with the perennial challenge, which takes on new forms in our day.

The question "How is the gospel to be *heard*?" is venerable indeed. Paul faced it at Athens, and we have elsewhere shown how it was faced in the second century by Justin Martyr, Clement of Alexandria, Irenaeus, and Origen, and through the centuries by those of the Platonist way.[72] We have also drawn attention to the "peril of reductionism" which confronts those who erroneously suppose that if a term appears in the discourse of two distinct worldviews, its *meaning* is identical.[73] We cannot rehearse the argument in detail here, but the point is that those who in the interests of communication seek to translate from one worldview to another are engaged in an *analogical* task, and they would do well to take particular care to distinguish between the points at which their analogies do and do not hold. Both the priest and the Levite would have agreed with the Samaritan that one should love one's neighbor, but they differed profoundly as to the meaning of "neighbor."

The question of communication in relation to the universals of the gospel takes on an exciting dimension at the present time because of the rapidly developing theologies to be found all around the world. In this connection Margrethe B. J. Brown raised two important questions:

> Will the consequences of such indigenous theological develop-ments necessarily induce the heretical type of limitations over against any universality of the Christian faith?
>
> Will such a theology abrogate its own legitimacy thereby, or is it possible to overcome this type of fragmentation?"[74]

In one's more surrealist moments (though in some quarters the reality is, perhaps, at hand), one can imagine the development of such attitudes as "I am of black theology" or "I am of feminist theology" just as easily as "I am of liberation theology" or "I am of Minjung theology." And all could be accompanied with the ritual unchurching of theologians of other persuasions. This would be the result of contextualization gone parochial, and that this might happen in the most sophisticated Western circles is suggested by the words of Don Cupitt: in view of the pluralism of society he declares that belief in God must bear "a specific meaning and is justified in relation to a particular religious community and its universe of discourse."[75] This seems to be the outworking in the re-ligious community of post-Wittgensteinian language games, and the result is conspicuously parochial. Where are the universals of the gospel?

The early volumes of the Presbyterian Alliance *Proceedings* contain a considerable amount of material on mission, including reports of mis-sion activity in many parts of the world, calls to evangelize the heathen, references to the world's need of the gospel, and reminders that the motive of Christian mission is gratitude for what God has done for us. But this material does not touch our present situation, nor does it for the most part betray that spirit of humble *listening* to those of other cultures which most contemporary missiologists recommend. At the heart of the newer situation lies the question, "How far are cultures themselves, and prior to Christianisation, witnesses to the activity of the one God?" This question is pressed by C. S. Song in a number of his writings, and it is beginning to appear in Alliance literature.[76] It is too soon to predict the outcome of the ongoing discussion, but it does seem important to keep two considerations in mind. First, that on the basis of God's nature as life-giving, creative Spirit, we cannot exclude him from any part of his created universe. But second, if we are not to fall into the immanentist trap we cannot bypass the scandal of particularity. Has or has not God acted decisively for the salvation of the world in Christ as nowhere else? It may be that in the coming years an important function of a world confessional family such as the Alliance will be to enunciate the universals of the gospel so that Christians will continue to be able to speak to each other. Such a task will be fulfilled only if as much attention is paid to the philosophical-methodological issues we have raised in this chapter as to the content of the gospel and the rich variety of the contexts in which the mission of the church is to be undertaken. The comparative neglect since 1920 of the challenge posed by secular philosophy and of the "meta questions" concerning theological discourse that philosophy has posed is in our opinion the most deeply disturbing finding revealed by our analysis. As new theologies proliferate and old foundations are radically questioned, ought not a primary function of such a body as the Alliance be to hold in lively debate those who are in quest of ways of presenting the one gospel to the many environments?

6

The Ethical Witness

In what must have been a powerful utterance, G. W. Richards reminded his hearers at the thirteenth Presbyterian Council (1929) of what we might call the catholicity of Reformed obligations:

> A Reformed congregation is a fellowship of men and women who believe themselves to be elect of God—chosen to do His will, elect to glorify God by serving their fellowmen. It is not a community of persons seeking to save themselves with laws and ordinances which God has provided through the Church as an instrument of salvation. It is not a fellowship merely of men and women who believe themselves to have been justified by grace alone; not a company of converted souls who have been suddenly transformed into sinless saints by the immediate action of the Spirit; not a school of sound doctrine and pure morals in which Jesus is master and example, and the Bible is the textbook on theology and ethics. A congregation of the Reformed Faith and Order is a community of persons called to do the will of God in all the relations of life, called to be co-workers with Him in the transformation of the world, not by might nor by power but by His Spirit. Here is a moral motive and a work-transforming dynamic more compelling than Kant's categorical imperative, *Thou shalt;* than the command of the Greek oracle, *Know thyself;* or of the mystic, *Submerge thyself;* or of the modern idealist, *Realize thyself;* or of the patriot, *Live for thy country;* or of the humanitarian, *Serve thy fellow-men.* Greater than any one, or all, of these motives of life and action, and comprehending all of them, is the imperative of the Reformed Churches, Glorify God! How shall we glorify Him? Let our great Reformer answer: "By putting our whole trust in Him, by obedience

197

to His will, by calling upon Him in every need which He offers, seeking from Him deliverance and all good, and that with heart and mouth we confess Him as the only source and origin of all good"; in short, if we are to live right among men in time, we must live for God in eternity.[1]

It must gladly be acknowledged (especially since we have noted, and shall note, lacunae in Alliance literature) that a deep concern for society at large has characterized the Alliance in both its ecclesial streams from the beginning. Indeed, so many specific topics have received attention that we can mention only some of them. Our selectivity is justifiable because we are not so much concerned with the detailed history of attitudes to particular moral and social issues as exemplified in Alliance literature, as with the general coverage given and the operating presuppositions, both of theology and of methodology.

I. Ethical Concerns of the Early Years

At the fourth Congregational Council (1920) an American commission traced the history of "Congregationalism and the Social Order"[2] from the colonial period to 1920, concluding with a review of such current agenda items as the church and the ownership of property, social unrest, democracy in industry, and rural welfare. At the same council a British commission reported on "The Contribution of Congregationalism to Civil and Religious Liberty,"[3] encompassing the ideals which had led Congregationalists in the sixteenth century and the struggles they had endured to realize those ideals. We shall not dwell on such predominantly historical studies, however. Rather, in the first half of this chapter we shall consider selected socioethical issues important in three periods of the Alliance's life: those which concerned the Alliance up to 1930; those which have been treated throughout the Alliance's history; and those which have come to the fore in the second half of the Alliance's life. Then in the second half of the chapter we shall indicate certain questions, so far undiscussed in Alliance literature, that are posed by the fact of ethical testimony and witness.

Among social issues regularly dealt with in Alliance circles up to 1930 we may note Sunday observance and temperance. As to the former, Hervey D. Ganse addressed the second Presbyterian Council (1880) on "The Sabbath's Claim on Christian Consciences." This claim, he argued, is established first by the very fact that the Sabbath exists—the idea of a day of rest transcends the barriers of religion and irreligion, for "unbelievers, atheists, and even Jews, in spite of their special tradition, in large measure observe the concerted rest-day."[4] Second, even those who deny it a divine origin declare the utility of the Sabbath. It meets the need of rest and refreshment, it "invites to religious thought and duty," and it is a necessity for the public worship of the whole community. Again, the Sabbath "supplies a most necessary opportunity for the religious education of the young in the family, the Sunday school, and the church."[5] Third, the obligation of Sabbath-keeping is laid upon us by the Decalogue itself. At the following Presbyterian Council (1884) H. B. Wilson spoke on "Sabbath Observance," paying particular attention to the transition in the Christian era from the seventh to the first day as being the appropriate day for worship and rest. In a nutshell: "The seventh day was commemorative of a completed work. . . . The first day of the week is commemorative of a completed work."[6] Wilson concluded by exhorting his hearers to "guard against Pharisaic restraints. Works of necessity and mercy are permissible." The Sabbath, he continued, on a rising wave of lyricism,

> should bring gladness and not grief to the household—sunshine rather than cloud; and to childhood and manhood, in the palace of the noble, the mansion of the rich, and the cottage of the poor, it should be the brightest, the happiest, the holiest and the best day of the week, and constitute the type of that eternal day of gladness, that rest that remaineth to the people of God.[7]

By 1921 W. G. Covert was found lamenting that "organized profanation of the Sabbath Day has as its supreme motive the making of money." His prescription was that "we must strike far more vigorously the note of genuine joy that legitimately should fill the hours of that day which commemorates the resurrection of our Lord."[8]

The early Congregational Councils were no less concerned about the Sabbath. Without the Sabbath, claimed A. Little in 1891, "the pulpit would [soon] become silent, houses of worship would close, Sunday-schools would be discontinued, the study of the Word would be neglected, the Church would languish and die."[9] To underline the point he borrowed three principles from Dr. Hopkins:

> *First.* That the religious observance of the Sabbath would secure the permanence of free institutions.
> *Second.* That without the Sabbath, religiously observed, the permanence of free institutions cannot be secured
> *Third.* That the civil, as based on the religious, Sabbath, is an institution to which society has a natural right, precisely as it has to property.[10]

Little called John Bright, Lord Beaconsfield, and the Presbyterian Philip Schaff in support, of whom the last had said, "The Church of God, the Book of God, and the Day of God are a sacred trinity on earth, the chief pillars of Christian society and national prosperity. Without them Europe and America would soon relapse into heathenism and barbarism."[11] Accordingly, the church must lead in defending the Sabbath, said Little, practicing what it preaches on the matter. He noted with some satisfaction that "those whose sole occupation it is to make money are gradually coming to see that it pays to keep Sunday"[12]—their workers perform more efficiently if they rest regularly. Into his more biblical treatment of the question at the third Congregational Council (1908) H. M. Scott introduced the following assertion:

> Revealed theology and natural theology, Christian ethics and secular ethics, unite in declaring that
>
> A Sabbath well spent
> Brings a week of content.[13]

Perhaps wisely from the point of view of rhetorical effect, he refrained from subjecting this tired non sequitur couplet to close scrutiny!

As to temperance, the Hon. William E. Dodge of New York referred to current American legislation and informed the second Presbyterian Council (1880) that "the principle of prohibition is growing more and more into public favour . . . it has proved the most successful of any attempt to stay the progress of this awful evil."[14] He appealed to statistics to support his anti-drink case and noted that among the causes of intemperance had been "the immense emigration from the lower classes of Ireland."[15] He pointed to the social costs of intemperance, invoked the "weaker brother" argument, and ended with a plea for total abstinence. At the following Presbyterian Council (1884) R. H. Lundie turned his spotlight upon Great Britain and listed crime, lunacy, pauperism, child neglect, disease and death, the deterioration of the race, economic disaster, and the ruin of men's souls as direct results of intemperance. Among the saddest results, he declared, was "the spread of the deadly curse in other lands. . . . Where the British flag is unfurled, Christianity and civilization enter, but alas, accompanied by the demon of drink."[16] That the Congregationalists were of similar mind is clear from their Council reports.[17]

In the early years of the Alliance "popular amusements" did not escape attention. A heavy hand was laid upon them by Theodore L. Cuyler at the second Presbyterian Council (1880). While allowing that "God never made man to be a monk, or this bright world to be a monastery," the cavortings in the modern ballroom filled him with horror. The news that the "popish archbishop of Quebec" had prohibited even round dances provoked the expostulation, "Shall popish morality exceed Presbyterian?" And he even had his stock converted actor, who "said to me while passing a theatre in which he had often performed, 'behind those curtains lies—SODOM!' "[18] So much for concerns which are almost entirely confined to the early years of the Alliance.

Apart from such isolated papers as that of W. G. Covert on Sabbath observance (1921), the emphasis upon that subject and upon temperance and popular amusements subsided dramatically after the First World War.

The old order, in which it appeared reasonable to hope for national consensus on such subjects, had collapsed never to return. Henceforth Sunday observance and temperance questions would be regarded much more as matters of private morality over which institutions—whether church or state—had no legitimate rights. Those who had fought for freedom were, for the most part, ill-disposed to having their freedom curbed by what came increasingly to be regarded as the petty sanctions of a former age. As the century wore on, increasing affluence gave many the opportunity of choosing to do things other then attend church on Sundays, and an increasingly materialistic, consumer age was not slow to suggest numerous ways in which more readily available money might be spent. With increasing family mobility old ties were, if not severed, more difficult to "police," and many of the younger generation went their more or less hedonistic way. These are, of course, broad generalizations. There was and still is poverty, even in the relatively affluent West; and there are still those who are organized to fight apparently rearguard (though sometimes successful) actions against the encroachments of commerce upon the Lord's Day and against alcohol. It remains the case, however, that dropping such matters from the agenda of the Alliance indicates a considerable social change in those countries that were the backbone of the Alliance earlier in the century. The fact that the subjects faded away without question (for no *decisions* were taken to speak no more upon them) is in itself suggestive of the extent of change.

Still, it is perhaps cause for mild surprise that the temperance question has not been quite forcefully raised in Alliance literature during recent years, in view of the prevalence of drug abuse and the well-established fact that alcohol and nicotine today are no less killers for being socially respectable in many circles. With growing numbers of alcoholics, both among Western adults and children and in the urban areas of developing nations, it would, of course, be the height of hypocrisy for Christians to fulminate only against those drugs in which most of them are not tempted to indulge.

II. Perennial Ethical Concerns

The Political Order

Three major areas of concern have been treated *throughout* our period. First, the political order has received considerable attention. Sylvester F. Scovel addressed the second Presbyterian Council (1880) on "Presbyterianism in Relation to Civil and Religious Liberty." At the sight of the banners of member churches which decorated the auditorium he enthused, "The blazonries about us at Horticultural Hall are magic mirrors in which we may see cabalistic lines and symbols into which we may read the sufferings and triumphs of Presbyterians for the noblest idea that ever kindled human enthusiasm—*liberty for men for the sake of loyalty to Christ.*"[19] Presbyterianism, he continued, exalts liberty of conscience as a gift from God; it exalts the idea of the equality of all under God; and its polity fosters fraternity. Indeed, both liberty and Presbyterianism spring from the Bible. Of course, liberty needs its "checks and balances," and these are provided by Presbyterianism's gradation of courts and its rights of appeal. As far as the state is concerned, Presbyterianism "demands such a relation, at least, as leaves the Church free to follow her sole Head in all her interior life and discipline."[20] Scovel proceeded to ransack history with a view to defending his thesis that "historians of liberty are sure to find the grafts which Presbyterian swords have stuck into the liberty tree."[21] What is now to be done in the cause of liberty? "Liberty has come only in a part of the world. It must be made to come everywhere."[22] There must be

1. Liberty for missionary propaganda of all descriptions. 2. Fulfillment of treaties in the interest of religious liberty. 3. Liberty of dissent from established churches, and of changing religions. 4. Liberty from every vestige of the Church and State combinations which oppress, or hamper, or dampen the life of the Church of Christ. 5. Liberty from cruel race-prejudice toward Jew, Indian, African and Chinaman. A *blazing pulpit,* and platform, and press for our despised races. 6. Liberty for Romanists against all Church spoilation, and all interference with their interior economy, and all expulsions. 7. Such liberty, even for atheists, as that they may not either sneer at the fear, or complain of the unfairness of Christian governments.[23]

Scovel went on to maintain that this liberty must be maintained "against all the encroachments of the modern State," and "against its first, oldest, and yet most active foe—the Church of Rome."[24] Most difficult of all, liberty must be defined

1. As against liberty misinterpreted into a false individualism.
2. As against liberty perverted into the crushing despotism of communism.
3. As against *laissez-faire* and indifference to morals, prostituting liberty into licence, and eating the heart out of the State as surely as stealthily.
4. As against the secularism that disarms the State morally by cutting the nerves that bind it to God and religion—a subtler danger than almost any other because it is Satan disguised as an "angel of light."[25]

Above all, "liberty must be based upon the Bible, or washed away from the shifting sands of human opinion."[26] Many variations were played upon these themes in Alliance literature, but among the more formal statements on the matter is this from the Presbyterian Council meeting two years before the outbreak of the Second World War:

We believe that Church and State have a common origin in the will of God, and that each has its distinctive place in the Divine economy. The Church needs the State and the State has need of the Church. Through their fellowship we may serve the purpose of God in the safeguarding of order and liberty and the establishment of justice.

The State exists not for its own ends but for the promotion of the common good by the enactment and administration of just laws, the discipline of the weak and sinful with a view to their reclamation, the right ordering of industrial and political life, the education of youth, the protection of the helpless, and the care of the poor. A nation which professes to be Christian is under obligation to realize the Christian ethic.

The State can serve these ends only as its life is purified, enriched and directed by men and women who acknowledge also the rule of God. Therefore the Church has a distinctive place within the life of society, providing opportunities for the worship of God, converting men and women to the obedience of Christ, instructing youth in religion, and extending within the State a spiritual community which ministers the things of God to men.

The State is called to serve the Church by the recognition of her distinctive character as a divinely ordered community, with distinctive

rights and obligations. The Church claims freedom in Christ to direct
and administer her own spiritual life, and to offer to the State her
counsels and admonitions. The Church does service to the State by
the evangelization of its citizens and by the building up of Christian
principles in her own membership. Thus Church and State render
mutual service according to the ordinance of God.[27]

This powerful statement, promulgated against the background of
gathering clouds over Europe, was entirely in harmony with the position
of those attending the concurrent conference at Oxford of the Universal
Christian Council of Life and Work. The latter body had as its theme
"Church, Community, and State," and its conference followed an extensive period of preparatory study.

Some of those present at Oxford might otherwise have been at the
Presbyterian Council. Indeed, the Presbyterian President W. A. Curtis
regretted that "valued leaders of our own Communion have had to give
[to the sponsors of the Oxford meeting] the assistance which would
otherwise have been at our disposal."[28] Still, the Council sent formal
greetings to the Oxford conference and wished it well.[29] The *Proceedings*
of the fifteenth Council (1937) contain a number of references to
menacing developments in Germany. Just as no German representatives had been permitted to attend the Oxford conference, so the
moderator of the Reformierte Bund was prevented from attending the
Presbyterian Council—a situation of which the Council formally disap-
proved. At the same council some articles of the Barmen Declaration
were read in the context of a detailed consideration of the German
situation, and the same resolution which regretted the absence of the
German moderator also expressed solidarity with the German Confessing Church. The resolution was unanimously adopted.[30]

Not surprisingly in view of their history and polity, the Congregationalists had a particular tale to tell where church-state relations were
concerned, and they told it, with historical illustrations, on more than
one occasion. Indeed, the fourth Congregational Council (1920) received
the report of a commission on "The Contribution of Congregationalism
to Civil and Religious Liberty," in which it was boldly affirmed that

the work of Congregationalism will *never be complete while a vestige of
the Establishment of religion by the State continues*. . . . Congregationalism
has ever been the most active of all Churches (with the exception of
the Baptists, who have been equally zealous) in the battle for religious
freedom, and for emancipation from State control. If they give up that
contest, there is no other agency that would be likely to continue the
struggle.[31]

With equal zeal Congregational papers were delivered on the Christian witness in civic and municipal life.[32]

More widely, the Congregationalists of the seventh Council (1953) heard two solid papers on "The Christian Doctrine of the State" and "The Freedom of the Church in the Modern State." The first was delivered by R. Tudur Jones, the second by Carl H. Schneider. Both papers echo the fact that although the Second World War was now past, the Cold War was at its height. Thus Jones affirmed that

> Christ is Lord. That is the standpoint of faith. Our Congregational Churchmanship has been concerned to express this conviction in the sphere of Church life and government. We have, side by side with this, a long tradition of political and social action, which has reflected our endeavour to see the implications of this Lordship in life generally. Christ, through His victory over death and evil, has been exalted above all powers and authorities. . . . The State is no longer free to do as it wishes. It is subject to Christ. . . . The instruments of oppression which the State may use against Christians have been robbed of their finality—Jesus is Lord of Life and Death, and so the prison and the firing-squad have been stripped of their real terror.
>
> This faith in the authority of Christ over the State will force Christians to take an attitude of criticism and opposition should the State seem to be contemptuous of its subjection to its divine Lord. On the other hand, when opportunity is given them, Christians will attempt to modify and mould the machinery of the State in order that they may, through it, express their faith that it is a servant and not a lord.[33]

Jones proceeds to review six responses to the question of church-state relations. First, there is the pietist answer that the state belongs to Satan, and that therefore Christians should withdraw from it. Jones rejects this response as a denial of the universality of Christ's victory. Second, the authority of the state has been identified with that of God—as in Caesaro-papalism and certain forms of the theory of the divine right of kings. This is a clear perversion of the Christian faith, and the Christian conscience cannot long remain satisfied with it. The third theory separates the kingdom of God from the state, and, as in Roman Catholic teaching, ascribes the origin of the state to the necessities of man's gregarious nature. "Inasmuch as it derives from the nature which has been created by God, the State has God's sanction. The State's purpose is thus ascertainable by reference to the nature of which it is a product, and man's reason is able to discern whether or not the State is performing the good which it should attain. . . . The standard by which it must

be judged is the Law of Nature."[34] Jones complains that by this theory
"The State is described as being unaffected by the redemption in Christ.
It is a natural society whose effectiveness can be appraised from that
creation which is as accessible to the non-Christian as to the Christian."[35]
In countering this position Jones expresses the conviction which we
endorsed in chapter 2 in connection with the work and person of Christ:
"But we come to the knowledge of God the Creator through the
knowledge of Him as Redeemer—the latter preceded the former in
point of time. So that this creation cannot be a neutral object of appraisal
as this doctrine supposes."[36] In any case, the human nature to which
Roman Catholic theologians refer us is very different from what God
meant it to be: "In some sense our human nature has lost its naturalness,
and so the nature on which the Roman Catholic Church builds is both
unknown and unknowable."[37]

Fourth, there is the doctrine of Orders, which attempts to distinguish
between the two realms—that of the kingdom and that of the state. This
approach has been used to justify both state absolutism and democratic
causes. It is ambiguous, for "if 'order' means no more than the *status quo*
the tendency will be for this theory to be manipulated in support of the
rights of the State against the people; if, on the other hand, the 'order'
which the State should preserve is the fair distribution amongst the
citizens of the wealth of the country, then the theory will be a means for
justifying far-reaching social changes."[38] Furthermore, "one cannot
acquiesce in the supposition that the Christian ethic is best restricted to
the area of private behaviour while leaving the State to follow an ethic
of its own . . . such a theory is in fact false to the teaching of Our Lord.
The State cannot be treated as though the Redemption had nothing
whatsoever to do with it."[39]

Fifth, there is Calvin's view that the true functioning of the state
depends on the church's freedom. The state must be taught God's law,
and rulers are to be obeyed when their conduct does not conflict with
that law. But there are weaknesses here:

> The very necessary emphasis that a body of earnest Christians is a
> means of curbing the dangers latent in the exercise of State authority
> was perverted to mean that the State should be subservient to the
> Church. The "saints" ought to rule. Both in Geneva and in the
> Nominated Parliament of 1653 in England, this type of experiment
> was a failure. Godliness is not enough to make a politician. Much of
> the difficulty arose from the attempt to turn Scripture into a system
> of positive law—with the result that such regulations as those dealing
> with witches were enforced in all their barbarity. On the other hand,

of course, the insistence that the State should observe the standards of justice demanded by God in the Old Testament created in men's consciences a sensitivity towards righteousness that had rarely appeared before. But there is a theological danger at the root of the Calvinistic theory. To think of the State merely in terms of the Old Dispensation entails a blunting of the Christian awareness of the demands of Christ upon them. Jesus came to fulfil the Law; and to organize the State on the basis of a doctrine which by-passes this crucial fact is a doubtful procedure.[40]

The sixth approach is that of those who claim that "the Kingdom of God is gradually being fulfilled by the process of social and political evolution. Care for the poor and the weak can be translated into legislation and enforced by law. And in so far as this is done, the Kingdom of God is brought nearer."[41] But "this theory is able to proceed only at the expense of caricaturing the human situation and perverting the obvious teaching of the Scripture. The demand of Jesus for an uncoerced and spontaneous love is the direct opposite of the coerced justice which alone the State can promote."[42] Undeniably, improvements can be made by the state which ease the lot of its subjects, but this is of justice and not love; it does not allow for the personal decision of faith, and, after all, "the Kingdom is God's Kingdom—it is not the production of human statecraft."[43]

The upshot is that tension between the claim of Christ and the claims of the state is inevitable, and this tension should be creative. There is much that cannot be achieved by state legislation, and Christians will recognize the fact. If Christians are responsibly to serve the state "they must be given responsibility in those manifold spheres where the interference of the state can be dispensed with."[44] The Christian will seek to ensure that the state remembers that people are not things, and that family life is to be maintained; and he will rebuke any state that uses its power against a weaker one. The conclusion is that "a Congregationalist will thus be aware at the same time of the claims of Christ and the possibilities of politics. This will cause him embarrassment, but out of his embarrassment he will create the laws and machinery of government as will ensure that the State does not abrogate to itself the honour and power which belongs to God alone."[45]

Carl H. Schneider set his scene autobiographically by pointing out that "I have lived under all possible forms of freedom or dependence of the Church in a State; first, in a strict State Church, i.e., a Church in a State which claimed to be Christian, with the King as the highest Bishop; then in a Church totally free from the State; then in a Church which the State tried to control completely, although the State was anti-Christian; and now I live in a free Church which, however, has to fight against a Church which regards the State as only a part of the Church, and which tries to over-rule State law the canonical law of the *codex iuris canonici.*"[46] Against this background Schneider examined the Byzantine idea that state and church are identical, the Roman Catholic notion that the church is over the state, and the Protestant idea of a partnership in tension. He rules out the first approach on the ground that Christian states, in the sense required by the theory, exist nowhere; the second is voided because in order to maintain its position the church has to forego the most vital Christian principles; and the third is not useful because, insofar as it appeals for an entirely free church, it overlooks the realities of the church's mission as prophet—and as a body with the freedom to suffer. The Christian church knows that "our citizenship is in heaven." But the state cannot think in this way, hence "there will be fundamental discrepancies always."[47]

What now of the international order? The sixth Congregational Council (1949) considered this, and in a message addressed to all its member bodies declared:

> We approach the disorder of society firm in the faith that Jesus Christ is the Saviour of men and the Lord of history. . . .
>
> The social message of the Christian Gospel has always recognized that all systems are formed by human nature, and therefore are conditioned by that nature. The Gospel comes to us, not to frame our temporary systems, but to confront us with eternal values. . . .
>
> All social systems must come under the directive, and the judgment, of the Gospel. . . .
>
> It is apparent that at present there exists a fundamental incompatibility between Christian principles and those forms of Communism which are built upon atheism and a denial of human freedom. . . . The primary Christian tactics in this situation is to press for the development of such constructive and creative programmes as will create areas of economic and social health throughout the world. . . .
>
> We recognize the permanent change brought about in the field of international relations by the discovery of atomic energy with its terrible immediate potency as a military weapon, and its long-distance potentialities of beneficent peace-time use. . . .
>
> The struggle which is now going on . . . is a conflict between the idea that the state is formed by man and must always be his servant, and the idea that man is the servant of the state. . . . Consequently, assaults against civil liberties, policies of racial discrimination and

segregation, and exploitation of peoples or support of political regimes which make serfs of their people, must be understood to be aids to the acceptance of an unchristian philosophy having world-wide ramifications.

The Church cannot resolve the debate between those who champion various forms of economic life as alternative economic systems to Communism. No one system will prove a panacea for all the social ills that befall mankind, and each will generate its own evils. . . . The free man in Christ, upon whom injustice must not be inflicted, and who cannot be unjust to other, is the basic unit of Christian society, and to that free society we pledge our loyalty.[48]

On the specific question of war and peace, we find that as early as the first Congregational Council (1891) the Honorable J. W. Patterson declared that "the Divine philosophy is that nations shall not 'learn war any more.' " He drew the consequence that "disarmament is the logical sequence to the teaching of both natural and revealed religion." At once, however, he had to add that "disarmament is impossible if not general"[49]—a conviction which has been underlined countless times from his day to ours. Nearer to our own time we find that none was more concerned about the potentialities of atomic power for good and evil than Sir Alfred Zimmers. Yet it is interesting to note that towards the end of an address on the subject he advised the sixth Congregational Council (1949) thus: "Certainly we Christians need to be concerned with world affairs. But let us not treat them as stones to be offered to Christian congregations in place of the Living Bread."[50]

The Presbyterian Council, no less than the Congregational, took the question of war and peace with due urgency. A public meeting on the subject was held at the twelfth Council (1925);[51] J. Y. Simpson spoke on "International Peace" at the thirteenth (1929);[52] and among the "Pronouncements on Matters of Faith and Life" made by the fifteenth Presbyterian Council (1937) was this on "The Church and War":

> We believe that recourse to war by the nations of the world is a heinous evidence of the sin of man's heart and an offence to God and to man. . . . The way of Christ is the way of love and reconciliation. The way of war is the way of hatred and enmity. War can neither establish justice and security, nor reconcile enemies. . . .
>
> While, in accordance with the Reformed tradition, we do not deny that war may lawfully be waged in defence against unjust and violent aggression, yet we recognize that among sincere Christians there is a divergence of opinion as to whether war can any longer find sanction in the Christian ethic. . . .

We believe that the peace of the world is endangered by reliance on the delusive security of armaments. . . . We call upon the nations of the world to support their professions and pledges of peace by mutual reductions in their armed preparations for war.

Finally, we call upon Christian people everywhere to work unremittingly for the removal of injustices and antagonisms between the nations, and, above all, to seek by the practice of Christian forgiveness, reconciliation, and love, to create lasting goodwill.[53]

Among many statements in a similar vein,[54] the most striking was that of the Alliance's executive committee which in 1983 called for a "Covenant for Peace and Justice." This statement declares that questions of peace and justice do not belong exclusively to the realm of politics; it finds no moral or theological justification of the use of nuclear weapons; it denounces the folly of the nuclear arms race, pledges support for trust- and peace-building initiatives, notes the destabilizing influence of poverty and the denial of human rights, and invites Alliance member churches to covenant together to work for peace and justice. The statement goes still further: "At the same time we dare to propose that all churches which confess Jesus Christ as God and Saviour whatever their tradition should form a covenant for peace and justice."[55] They can do this despite their differences on other issues, and as part of the process it is suggested that the World Council of Churches might convene a special ecumenical gathering at which all churches could combine to witness for peace and justice. The concluding paragraph of the statement appropriately combines human modesty with confidence in God, making clear that trust in God by no means absolves us from doing what lies at hand:

We know that we cannot determine the course of history. The future is not in our hands. God has his own ways of bringing about his kingdom. But as we pray "Your kingdom come" we need to do whatever we can to oppose the destruction of life. As long as we live we are called to be witnesses to God's love for all people and his whole creation.[56]

Though necessarily selective, our account of Alliance pronouncements upon peace and war has been based upon texts which are representative. These statements universally denounce war and advocate peace, but as we view them in sequence we cannot but detect the dramatic change of tone between, for example, the Presbyterian Council's affirmation of 1937 and the "Covenant for Peace and Justice" of 1983. Whereas in the former statement an appeal to the Reformed tradition supports just-war theory, the latter includes no such appeal. Faced by the weaponry now available in the world, the executive committee of the Alliance took the view that no theological justification exists for the use of nuclear weapons. This strong position is clearly influenced by the view that, even if it were ever tenable, older just-war theory is unsustainable when there can be no adequate application of force to the desired end, when there can be no "victors," and when the possible ecological devastation makes any "survival" uncertain and a doubtful privilege at best. Again, whereas the 1937 statement (not without good reason at that time) thinks in terms of one aggressive nation violating other nations, the 1983 affirmation drives more deeply into such underlying causes of war as poverty and the denial of human rights. In other words it closely relates the concepts of peace and justice and presupposes that without justice we shall not have peace. Its proponents are also in a position to call upon the World Council of Churches to coordinate a global Christian peace initiative—a position not enjoyed by the Presbyterians of 1937.

The Economic Order

The second sphere to have received fairly regular attention throughout Alliance history is that of the economic order (though it is striking that we do not find detailed Christian reflection on either capitalism or communism in the Alliance literature). At the second Presbyterian Council (1880) W. G. Blaikie spoke on "The Influence of the Gospel on Employers and Employed"[57]—the gospel, of course, emerging as a beneficent influence; and the Honorable Chief Justice C. D. Drake depicted Christianity as "The Friend of the Working Classes." After all, if the commands, precepts, and promises of God "were henceforth obeyed, lived out, and rested upon by all, the certain result would . . . be the speedy and lasting rise of the working classes in physical power, in intellectual strength, in material prosperity, in moral force, and, consequently, in influence in all the world's affairs."[58]

There was, nevertheless, "The Strife between Rich and Poor"—and Principal McVicar addressed this question at the fourth Presbyterian Council (1888). He apportioned blame evenhandedly: "The poor can be indolent, improvident, envious, unreasonable; and the rich can be proud, extravagant, heartless, oppressive."[59] He went on to urge the churches to work diligently for such legislative changes as would heal the rift in society (something which, as we saw, Tudur Jones much later thought that legislation alone could never do). In his speech on the same day Moses D. Hoge reminded his audience that "we do not find in the discources of our Lord any denunciation of an aristocracy of refinement and culture, or any condemnation of rich men because of their wealth."[60] He cited Jesus' acceptance of the extravagant gift of the widow's ointment and concluded that the cause of strife between wealthy employer and poor wage earner was greed. He looked for more "splendid benefactions" to remedy the situation. We cannot resist the reflection that this is one of the most dated speeches in the whole of the Alliance literature: what was sincerely said on the ground of high Christian principle now sounds so patronizing, and it seems to make the recipients of "splendid benefactions" somehow less than human—even though we know it was better that they should be helped than not helped. Among other topics addressed in Presbyterian circles were "The Land Question" and "The Wage Question."[61] The first and third Congregational Councils were concerned with similar themes.[62]

The fourteenth Presbyterian Council (1933) heard an address from Major Edwin J. Donaldson on "The Kingdom of God and the Economic Order":

> When God created man in His own image and placed him in the midst of the treasure-house of a fruitful earth, where everything was to be for his use and under his dominion, and where everything was "very good," a Kingdom of God was set up on earth and an Economic Order instituted on a Divine plan. But sin entered into the Kingdom; man, not content with his Maker's provision and plan, sought out many inventions. Then it was that all the world's problems, both social and economic, were born.[63]

Donaldson cannot understand why "there should be so marked a reluctance on the part of organized Christianity to endeavour to bring economic problems within the ambit of the Christian faith."[64] Some Christians say that the church should teach Christian principles, but not interfere in the economic sphere; others say that the church should work out detailed plans and offer precise advice. Donaldson agrees that the church must teach, but it cannot remain aloof from economic considerations since these directly affect the well-being of people. On the other hand the church should not be tied to particular policies without carefully testing them against "the standards of Christ's teachings."[65] Positively, the church "must preach in season and out of season the Gospel of Salvation through the shed blood of Christ."[66] It must be fully informed as to the implications of economic developments and must attack the moral evils of drink, gambling, and land monopoly—in which connection he wryly noted that "in the main, drink and gambling may be denounced, even in respectable churches, so long, of course, as not too much is said about brewery dividends, the Derby, the Dublin Sweep, or the Stock Exchange!"[67]

Next, the church must realize that as long as the world lives under the threat of war economic health is not possible; accordingly, the church must strive to eliminate the possibility of war. It must also accept the challenges thrown down by "the two greatest world forces towards materialism and reaction, namely, Roman Catholicism and Communism."[68] Donaldson did not blame Rome for doing what it believed in, but he did call for Protestant alertness to the fact that "where Rome holds sway economic conditions are never good." He also conceded that communism "has thriven largely because the Church in all lands has misinterpreted its mission and neglected its social opportunities."[69] Donaldson's concluding challenge concerned the question of increased leisure: What will the churches do? "If God does not get that extra time, the Devil will."[70]

Fifty years later, Charles C. West wrote a paper for the 1982 council of the Alliance. When we compare his approach with that of Donaldson (and our juxtaposition is intentional), we are conscious of a vast change in motivation and style. It is not simply that West brings to his exposition a sharper theological thrust; it is that he is more *urgent* in a world whose very foundations are threatened. In a paper on "Human Wealth and Power"[71] West notes the extraordinary expansion of wealth and power over the past two centuries, the limitations of the natural resources at our disposal, and the irrational human greed and lust for power which threaten the rational enterprises of science and technology. He outlines three principles and draws four consequences. The first principle is that "human beings live by being called into a covenant relation with a living and purposeful God who is lord of all creation. . . . No self-liberation establishes us as masters and planners of our fate. Rather we are placed by the Creator in a *relationship* with him, with each other, and with the non-human creation."[72] The second principle concerns our stewardship of creation whereby God calls us "to transform creation."[73] The third is that "economic drives tend to destroy the covenant" and hence the spirit of mammon must be controlled "so that wealth and power may serve and not destroy human community in its created environment."[74]

How can these principles be fulfilled? First, "The church can project a new vision of the promise of God for the transformation of the earth which will replace the goal of ever-expanding human wealth and power with which the world is obsessed."[75] Second, "the Church can project a fuller and deeper understanding of public justice for a technological age than the principles of individual rights or of peoples' solidarity. . . . The key to this understanding is divine justification, which brings the sinner and those sinned against into a new relationship with one another."[76] Third, "the Church can create new lifestyles in its own community, but on behalf of society as a whole."[77] Lastly, "the Church can engage in the struggle to direct the structures of human wealth and power into ways of justice, with a hope that is not based on the success of human management of human revolution."[78]

As with the question of peace and war, so here our representative selection of specimens of thought on the economic order clearly progresses from more local to more global considerations. In a way which is influenced by the biblical theology movement of the 1950s, and by such reflection on church and society as that engendered by the World Council of Churches, Charles West does not resort to specific biblical texts and illustrations in the manner of his forebears. Rather, he grounds upon the biblical concept of covenant and the doctrine of creation. Here we have an articulated theological worldview, not simply a series of principles supported by biblical references. Again, whereas in the earlier statements we have a more piecemeal approach to specific issues as various as workers' rights, drinking, and gambling, West realizes that wealth, power, justice, and the gospel of hope are inextricably interwoven. Finally, where Donaldson had no compunction in attacking the Christian hypocrisy of denouncing gambling while gambling at the Stock Exchange, West challenged the whole church as to lifestyle. It is clear that West's approach is consonant with the growing realization that in many ways—not least in view of the activities of multinational companies—the poverty of many and the wealth of relatively few are causally related in ways which should sting the church into a fundamental reappraisal of the gospel vis-à-vis the economic order.

Marriage and the Family

Ethical issues surrounding marriage and the family are the third consistently represented element in the Alliance literature. A paragraph from the "Manifesto and Appeal on Public Questions in Religion and Morals," which was adopted by the fourteenth Presbyterian Council (1933), may be taken as a summing-up of the "received view" within the Alliance family:

> Reverencing the home as the centre and spring of human life, and the family as the indispensable fosterer of human ideals of brotherhood and unselfishness, we deplore and condemn the pres-

ent-day assaults upon the holy estate of marriage, and regard the
advocacy or condonation of trial marriage, companionate marriage,
and easy divorce as essentially vicious, unworthy, and destructive of
the integrity of the family, of the sacred rights of childhood, and of
the highest interests of the community. Holding that, in accordance
with Holy Scripture and with the deepest instincts of humanity,
marriage is an ordinance of God essentially monogamous and permanent, we call for the stern repudiation of every tendency to cheap-
en its value or to lower the spirit of solemn responsibility in which it
should be entered by widening the facilities for divorce, and by
authorizing the remarriage of culpable partners who have been
divorced. While recognizing the existence of cases in which hardship,
outrage, and exasperation have been the occasions for legislative
relaxation of the traditional standards of marriage and divorce, we
are yet persuaded that the dangers and the social disorder which have
ensued have grievously outweighed the expected benefits, and have
aggravated the very evils from which escape was sought. We plead in
the name of Christ, the Guardian of purity and love, the Friend of
little children and the Ennobler of womanhood, for the restoration
and the vindication, both by public opinion and by legislative enactment, of His high ideal of marriage.[79]

No doubt some today would object to some of the phraseology here;
some might take exception to the emphasis upon the "nuclear family";
and there might be questions about the desirability and practicability of
invoking secular law to sustain a Christian view of marriage and family
life. The Alliance has other matters on its current agenda too, and from
a list given in *Called to Witness to the Gospel Today* we select three by way
of example:

How are the biblical insights on which the Christian and Reformed
view of the family and marriage rest reflected in the contemporary
teaching and practice of our churches?

For many churches in the countries of the Third World the question
of the Old Testament practice of concubinage and polygamy is one
which calls for clarification in the context of a Christian doctrine and
praxis of family and marriage. Has your church any light to throw on
this question?

How do churches respond to the new forms of relationships between
man and woman, parents and children, which are practised by many
young people today and who see no need for civil or religious rites
and sanctions?[80]

More specifically, a major international trilateral dialogue during the
years 1971-77 between the Lutheran World Federation, the Roman
Catholic Secretariat for Promoting Christian Unity, and the Alliance was
the first, and so far the only, occasion on which Alliance representatives
have been officially involved at the international level in discussing a
theological and socioethical question with colleagues of other Christian
communions. The results of the dialogue were published under the title
Theology of Marriage and the Problem of Mixed Marriages. This is a substantial document, and although we cannot here follow its close argumentation in detail, we must briefly indicate the main line taken. The report
speaks of three aspects of marriage:

> The first aspect shows the married couple in its own life, its history,
> and its fate. The second aspect brings the family as such into sharper
> focus: Children are an expression of both the nature of the institution
> and of personal love, they add nothing alien to the marriage but rather
> enlarge it to the other dimensions. Lastly, the third aspect throws the
> limelight on the importance of marriage for society. Marriage repre-
> sents the living cell, the fundamental element of both civil society and
> of the religious community.[81]

Thus far there is general agreement among the dialogue participants.
Divergent views begin to appear, however, in connection with Christ's
relation to marriage: "In the view of the Lutherans and the Reformed
Churches, the Catholic Church, in holding that marriage is a sacrament,
seems to forget that marriage does not of itself give grace but needs to
receive it . . . to the Reformation Churches it seems at least doubtful
whether Christ himself instituted this sacrament."[82] The suggestion
made towards overcoming the impasse is that the "relationship of grace
between the mystery of Christ and the conjugal state requires a name.
We all of us believe that the biblical term 'Covenant' truly characterizes
the mystery of marriage. It is this Covenant that the Catholic Church
calls a sacrament."[83]

All parties agree that marriage entails a commitment for life, but the
fact of actual marital breakdown exposes a further divergence between
the dialogue partners:

> In the Catholic Church marriage exists as a Christian marriage only
> in so far as it represents—must and can represent—in its fidelity the
> love of Christ for the Church. The Reformation Churches, on the
> other hand, consider that, since marriage needs to conform to the
> unity of Christ with the Church, the unity that the first marriage has
> not been able to realize, may possibly be realized in a second marriage

after a divorce. They do not therefore view divorce as a radical obstacle to a second marriage.[84]

Following a section on pastoral care as it applies to marriage and the family, the report comes finally to the vexed question of marriages between Roman Catholics and Protestants, so-called mixed marriages. The position of the Roman Catholic church is described in some detail, and its feeling is expressed that Lutheran and Reformed reservations concerning the force of current church regulations on the question had taken insufficient account of the pastoral intentions underlying those regulations. This, said the Roman Catholic participants, could lead to two forms of distortion:

—that of thinking that the various Churches are united in faith and doctrine concerning mixed marriages and of regarding ecclesiastical regulations as the sole source of differences on this matter;
—that of viewing ecclesiastical laws themselves as "the law" in the formalistic and legalistic Old Testament sense, and of pushing divergent ideas of law to the point of giving the impression that one wishes to reduce the radical character of the Gospel to a mere invitation by Christ which is not binding and which vanishes when confronted by the failure of man's weakness.

In the Catholic view, on the contrary, the laws of the Church are a function of theology and an expression of pastoral concern. They express in a practical manner the requirements of the doctrine of faith, and are intended to introduce Christian values into the life of the faithful.[85]

There thus arises an agenda for the future: the nature of Christian marriage should be clearly taught; Lutheran and Reformed churches should not, when remarrying the divorced, obscure their basic conviction that marriage is for life; and Roman Catholics should exploit the possibilities in the apostolic letter *Matrimonia Mixta,* which admits a certain flexibility in pastoral care where mixed marriages are concerned.

The Lutheran and Reformed participants then addressed two questions to the Roman Catholics: Could not the Roman Catholic church recognize as valid marriages performed by Lutheran and Reformed ministers? Could not the Roman Catholic church safeguard the obligation of the Roman Catholic partner in a mixed marriage to baptize and educate any children in the Catholic faith in a more pastoral and ecumenical manner, rather than by exacting a formal promise? While understanding these requests and expressing their hope that such steps would eventually be taken, the Roman Catholic participants could not justify taking such steps at the present stage of the dialogue.[86] It was agreed that further work should be done on the religious functions of canon law, the problem of Christian ethics (justification and sancti- fication; law and grace), the concept of humanity underlying marriage, the understanding of revelation and the role of Holy Scripture as a binding witness, and the relationship between sociological facts and Christian norms. At the time of this writing, these tasks remain on the table.

III. Ethical Concerns since 1933

In the second half of the Alliance's life—since 1933—the issue of human rights has received increasing attention, not that such issues were hitherto undiscussed in Alliance circles. We have already noted early affirmations concerning civil and religious liberties. What begins to happen in the 1930s is that questions of human rights become more urgent on the one hand (a fact by no means unrelated to the rise of Nazism in Germany), and less ecclesio-centric on the other. We are no longer dealing *only* with questions of church and state (though these questions persist), but with the rights of humans as humans.

Among a number of important addresses is one by the black Ameri- can A. D. Gray, who spoke to the seventh Congregational Council (1953) on "The Middle Wall of Partition."[87] Already this address includes an adverse reference to South Africa's apartheid policy, against which the Alliance has resolutely set its face. However, we must not give the impression that questions of human rights are coterminous with those of race. The underprivileged and threatened of all kinds have increas- ingly become the subjects of concern in the Alliance,[88] not least when the underprivileged are women.[89]

The most sustained reflection in Alliance circles prior to 1982 on the subject of human rights is found in a brief report of a consultation which took place in 1976. Jürgen Moltmann presented a paper entitled "A Christian Declaration on Human Rights" in which he strongly advo- cated the rights of God. "God's claim upon human beings was and is experienced in concrete events of the liberation of human beings, in their covenant with God, and in the rights and duties inherent in their freedom. *Image of God,* as destiny, points to God's indivisible claim upon human beings and therefore to their inalienable dignity."[90] Christians, he continued, must view human rights in the perspective of God's covenant. When this is done we see that because human beings as individuals, in community and in humanity are meant to reflect the image of God, all human rights are bound up with, and related to one another. One can neither curtail them, separate them from each other, or differentiate between them. Furthermore, all human rights are bound up with specific human duties. Rights and duties cannot be separated from each other; privileges should not grow out of rights nor empty demands out of duties.[91]

In light of the discussion of Moltmann's paper the members of the commission laid down their theological guidelines:

1. We understand the basic theological contribution of the Christian faith, in these matters, to be the grounding of fundamental human rights in God's right to, i.e., his claim upon human beings.
2. Our biblical faith commits us to a view of human life in its wholeness expressed in three basic complementarities: male and female, the individual and society, human life and its ecological context.
3. Our biblical faith also warns us about the destroying powers we face in the struggle for the realization of human rights.
4. We boldly confess the liberating power of Jesus Christ and affirm the Church's ministry of reconciliation and grace.[92]

With guidelines established, the report concludes with some reflections on their implications for the internal life of the churches, and for the already reviewed relations of the church to the state and to international affairs.

As to the question of human rights *within* the church, the greatest impetus behind the consideration of this matter has come from the Alliance's Caribbean and North American Area Council Theological Committee. That body's 1977 publication, *A Christian Declaration on Human Rights,* includes, for example, a paper by Margrethe B. J. Brown on "The Liberation and Ministry of Women and Laity" that is very much concerned with human rights within the church. Women, it is claimed, have traditionally been, and still are, an oppressed and isolated group within the church—especially where the ordained ministry is concerned. The author appeals for the amelioration of this situation, though it is noticeable that her discussion remains largely within what we might call "the human dimension" of human rights. That is to say, unlike Moltmann Mrs. Brown does not locate the issue within the idea of God's covenant or speak of God's rights. Yet one might have thought that no stronger theological case can be made for the ordination of women than this: if, by grace, and on the basis of Christ's finished work, God has called out a covenant people by the Spirit through the Word; if he has drawn them to himself and given them to each other in such a way that barriers of sex, race, and class are broken down; and if from this one family he chooses to call this woman or this man to be his minister, on what conceivable grounds does any part of the church deny God his right so to do?[93]

The covenant theme is resumed in a later work emanating from the Caribbean and North American Committee: *A Covenant Challenge to a Broken World* (1982). We have here a plethora of papers, to some of which we have already referred, and others of which are reprinted from extra-Alliance publications. The technological threats to nature's survival, the East-West and North-South tensions, male chauvinism, and the arms race—all these and other themes are represented in the collection. The overarching theme is God's gracious covenant, and it is treated both theologically and historically.[94]

IV. Underlying Principles

In the foregoing sections our aim has not been to chronicle everything the Alliance has said and done concerning the manifold socioethical issues that have come before it. Rather, in the light of the examples given we must concentrate upon the principles underlying the socioethical stances of the Reformed family. These have sometimes been implicit rather than explicit. Our view is that the issues are so important that the principles need more careful analysis in Alliance circles than they have so far received. We shall proceed by stages, mentioning first a basic assumption consistent throughout Alliance literature, no matter how variously it has been applied in Reformed circles. We shall then consider the sinfulness of structures and the question of collective responsibility. Next we shall ask how much common ground exists between Christians and others who together confront ethical problems in a threatened and divided world. Finally we shall seek to articulate the way in which the evangelical-catholic faith, grounded in God's atoning work, bears upon one issue in particular, that of apartheid.

The basic principle, nowhere questioned in Alliance literature, is that true Christian faith cannot but influence the whole of life, and accordingly that Christians have no option but to witness to God and serve their neighbors in the world. The characteristic Reformed emphasis upon God's sovereignty over all and the implications of the parable of the leaven have been reiterated on many occasions by Alliance writers and speakers. This is not to say, however, that they have all made quite the same emphasis, still less that they have without exception advocated identical practical responses to particular issues. We may illustrate differing emphases with two quotations—one from W. G. Blaikie, the other from Jürgen Moltmann—which between them span our period.

Blaikie opened his address on "The Influence of the Gospel on Employers and Employed" (1880) this way:

> I lay the foundation of this paper on the principle that the gospel of Jesus Christ is not only salvation for the individual, but regeneration for society. It was not souls only but society likewise that was shattered by the fall; and any remedy, equal to the disorder, needed to make provision for the restoration of both. In the prophetic announcements of the Redeemer and his work, the restoration of society is perhaps even more prominent than the salvation of the individual.[95]

Blaikie's goal is that employers shall be under the permeating influence of the gospel. For his part Moltmann writes:

> It is when Christianity is fulfilling its uniquely "Christian tasks" that it serves the humanness of all human beings. Conversely, it fulfils its uniquely "Christian tasks" inasmuch as it serves the humanness of all human beings. By proclaiming God's justifying grace, it proclaims the dignity of human beings. By practicing the right of grace, it practices basic human rights. Community with Jesus, the "Son of Man," leads it into suffering with the oppression of human beings, into resistance against tyranny and the sustaining prayer for the coming of God. Thus Christianity is not only externally and accidentally concerned with human rights, but internally, essentially, and with the whole of its existence.[96]

The change of key is most pronounced. No longer are Christian beneficence and Christian attitudes percolating from the church to the world around. Rather, the true church makes its proclamation from the midst of suffering humanity; the work is done by identification before it is done by influence; and the underlying theological motif is the creation of all people in the image of God. Clearly, the dramatic difference in emphasis between Blaikie and Moltmann is explicable only in relation to the change in relationship between the (Western) church and society at large. Blaikie, writing on the crest of the evolutionary wave, was right in correcting the individualistic approach to socioethical questions of some older writers. The concept of the kingdom is clearly present to his mind. But his optimism that the fellowship of employers and employed under the gospel is an attainable objective, though noble, is not, as we now see, justified by events. In any case, what if some employers and employees are Muslims, Hindus, Sikhs, Rastafarians, or

Moonies—a possibility Blaikie did not consider, but which has been realized in his own land now? The pluralism of society, the explosion of information concerning the plight and needs of people, the decline of the (Western) churches in strength and influence—all these are factors helping to account for the difference in tone between Blaikie and Moltmann. Both agree, however, that the church must fulfill its role and meet its challenge to be leaven in the lump of society.

But the question "how?" presses, and we may again turn to earlier and later Alliance literature in order to make the point. What R. W. Dale wrote in the introduction to the first volume of Congregational Council *Proceedings* (1891) must be quoted in full:

To some members of the Council the Thursday Evening Session at the Memorial Hall was of supreme significance and interest. The papers of Dr. Washington Gladden and Mr. Ben Tillett on the Labour Question, of Mr. Albert Spicer on the Land Question, of Mr. Gladstone on the Attitude of the Church to the Social Movements of Our Time, and of Dr. Cordley on the Liquor Laws, were listened to with close attention, which sometimes broke out into a passion of enthusiasm. They contained very much that deserves serious thought. But they did not in my judgment touch the practical question, as defined in the title of Mr. Gladstone's paper—The Attitude of the Church to the Social Movements of Our Time. That is a question on which large numbers of our people want guidance. I myself should like to know what is meant when it is said that the *Church* should assume a new position in relation to the claims of labour and the tenure of land. Is it meant that *as citizens* Christian men should take a more active part in all movements for social and economic reform? Or is it meant that *churches* should discuss these questions; should pass resolutions about them; should raise funds to maintain lecturers and to distribute literature in support of the "movement"; should form canvassing committees to secure the return to Parliament of candidates who accept an advanced programme? If all that is meant is that Christian men as citizens should do their utmost to improve the social and economic condition of the people, there is nothing new in the proposal. For thirty years I have been preaching that doctrine, and according to my strength and light have been endeavouring to practice it. Nor have Christian men generally been indifferent to the duty. In the agitation which secured the great, though imperfect, Education Act of 1870—an Act which has achieved an immense improvement in the social condition of the great masses of the people—a large proportion of the men who did most of the work, and who encountered most of the obloquy which has to be endured by all reformers, were ministers and members of churches in Birmingham, and in other parts of England. But we did our work as *citizens*. Our churches, as far as I remember, were not asked to pass resolutions in favour of a system of education "national, compulsory, unsectarian, and free," nor did we make collections for the League. I believe that the work was best done in that way. The Church should create in its members an eager desire to lessen the sorrow, the suffering, and the injustice, as well as the sin of the world; but it is not yet clear to my own mind that the Church, as a religious society, should take part in political, social, and economical agitation. In the Middle Ages the attempt was made to use the power of the Church to exert direct control over the social, and political life of Europe, and we do not look back upon the results of that policy with perfect satisfaction. I doubt whether in our own days the resumption of that policy would be at all more beneficial either to the Church or to the world.[97]

It is noteworthy that in his argument (with the general thrust of which many Christians in the Reformed family and elsewhere to this day generally agree) Dale jumps from the activity of the Christian citizen to the political control of life by the church. In the intervening years, however, many have come to see that these are not the only alternatives. Thus it has become possible for the Alliance, and for other similar corporate Christian bodies, to pass resolutions with clear political reference and implications—and this as part of their prophetic function—without seeking thereby to control the machinery of politics, or forgetting Sir Alfred Zimmers's point that Christians should not be offered world problems from the pulpit *instead of* the Living Bread.

The Alliance council report of 1982, for example, contains resolutions on Lebanon, on racism in South Africa, on the rights of native people in Canada, and on Lesotho.[98] With the terms of these resolutions we are not presently concerned. What must be observed is the change in attitude over the years as to the appropriate means of ensuring that the Christian voice is heard. The difference as to *means* between Dale and the recent resolutions parallels the difference of emphasis which we noted between Blaikie and Moltmann.

Difficulties of various kinds persist, however. The first is the problem of devising resolutions and statements which are not so platitudinous that they can safely be ignored by those to whom they are addressed, nor so specific in recommendations that they can be dismissed by secular experts as the work of the ill-informed. Again, the point Dale made concerns the adverse results of the church wielding political power in the Middle Ages. This suggests that the theological ground of churchly sociopolitical pronouncements must be spelled out clearly so that all concerned know that the churchly body is performing its prophetic function and not making a bid for government takeover.

But we have just used the term "churchly," albeit in a general context. Though the theological problem raised for the Alliance at this point is in what sense the Alliance is a churchly body, an ecclesial reality (a question to which we shall return), the practical and paradoxical difficulty is that the more competent the church representatives are who make statements and devise resolutions—especially where technical matters are concerned—the greater is the danger that in their decisions they will be far in advance of their constituency. National church assemblies accordingly have met with reflex action lately, and the problems are compounded when decisions are taken at the international level by a body such as the Alliance—its constituency is geographically, linguistically, historically, and culturally diverse. On the one hand, we must believe that God may speak by the Spirit through the Word to individuals, to local churches, to wider and national assemblies, and to those gathered for international consultation. On the other hand, we need to examine carefully the question of how far representatives are representative, and in what ways and to what extent they are accountable to their constituencies. The credibility of international Alliance resolutions and statements turns upon the positions reached on these matters.

Two further questions are raised by Christians—not least by Reformed Christians—in connection with sociopolitical witness. Those who adopt a "hands off" attitude vis-à-vis politics are not necessarily unconcerned about the world. They may consider that the primary duty of the church is to proclaim the gospel of redemption so that people become changed by grace. *Then* those converted people will help to change the world. Three replies may be offered. First, the argument proposed implies a truncated understanding of redemption of the kind from which we have just dissociated ourselves. Second, it is not explained why lawful pressure may not legitimately be applied in situations where, for example, inhumane policies are found. It would be fanciful to suppose that the conversion of all those employers who used child labor in Britain took place at all—still more that it occurred prior to the passing of the Factory Acts which ended the exploitation of the young. Nevertheless an important qualification remains to be made. If corporate Christian pronouncements are to be made in the name of the gospel, they must not be so identified with the gospel that those Christians who feel ill at ease with them feel alienated from the fellowship of saints. This would be subtly to make a Christian's sincerity turn upon the "work" of adopting a specific form of quasi-credal words, and it could lead to a further kind of sectarianism disruptive of the evangelical catholicity of the church. Hence these wise words of J. M. Lochman:

> Whenever the church of Christ follows Jesus it has clearly to take sides, but not in a party-political sense. It is aware of the "eschatological reservation" of the message of justification. It associates the politically penultimate with the ultimate of the kingdom of God; but it does not equate them. Above all it sees—even in the heat of controversy—those who hold different opinions in the perspective of the love and hope of Christ. The belief in justification while pressing for the enactment of justice protects this activity at the same time from any self-righteousness.[99]

Third, those who work to convert oppressors rather than to challenge them as they are may be under the subtle temptation of thinking that Christianity pays! That is, that once people become converted, the lot of all will improve. Against this view Hermann Johan Heering cautioned at the sixth Congregational Council (1949): "It is a happy discovery that Christian ethics, and Christian ethics only, open the way to a better, a responsible social order. But Christianity has to remain very alert never to identify itself with this coincidence, but only conscious of the fact that sacrifice is the most natural thing for a Christian in the social order."[100]

If the point just addressed arises in more conservative Christian quarters, the second question to be faced arises from the way some more radical Christians speak. It is sometimes said that Christians are called upon to oppose the sinful structures of society. In this connection the 1982 Alliance council report on "The Power of Grace and the Graceless Powers" includes these revealing sentences: "The application of the doctrine of Grace to groups and powers presented difficulties. A 'graceless power' was perhaps best identified as an unjust one, and such powers may be the result of a kind of idolatry when our ideals become distorted. The discussion focussed on theological formulations, but was constantly brought back to concrete situations, and the churches were urged to help those who suffered from injustice."[101] The definition in the second sentence here is satisfactory enough. The third sentence properly refers to the concern to assist *those who* suffer. They are people. But we need the same realism in reference to "sinful structures," which are kept in being by sinful people. Structures cannot obey, or disobey, the law—still less can they repent and turn from their wicked ways. People can do all of these things. It is significant that Alliance resolutions and statements are invariably addressed to people, not to structures.

At a deeper level, and long before the advent of theologies of liberation, P. T. Forsyth, speaking at the third Congregational Council (1908), answered those who said "We are more dull to individual sin because we are more alive to social sin. We have public compunction instead of personal repentance." He replied:

> First. Public compunction does not move to seek forgiveness, which is the prime righteousness of the Kingdom of God, but to pursue redress and reform. And redress and reform is not what makes Christianity. Christianity is a religion of redemption, but that is a religion of amelioration or assuagement. It is engrossed with the wrong done to our brother and not to our God, and is therefore to that extent the less religious.
>
> But second. The tendency is welcome in so far as this, that we cannot stop there. The more public it makes the sin, the more social and racial, so much the more does it drive us upon a treatment of sin which is ethical and not temperamental, racial as well as personal, and not only racial but divine. Now there is no treatment of it which satisfies these demands of the soul, the conscience, society, and God, but the atonement in Christ's cross. . . . A collective sin must have a central treatment.[102]

This strong statement properly reminds us of the rights of *God* and recalls us to our evangelical-catholic center; but it also raises the question of human solidarity vis-à-vis collective responsibility, and to this we must now turn.

V. Collective Responsibility

Underlying the Christian protest against sinful structures is a doctrine of humanity that was admirably summarized in the Alliance report on the *Theological Basis of Human Rights* (1976), and is here reiterated:

> *We understand the basic theological contribution of the Christian faith in these matters, to be the grounding of fundamental human rights in God's right to,* i.e., *his claim upon human beings.* This is to say that human rights are ultimately grounded not in human nature; nor are they conditioned by individual or collective human achievements in history. They reflect the covenant of God's faithfulness to his people and the glory of his love for the church and the world. No earthly authority can legitimately deny or suspend the right and dignity of being human. It is in the light of this covenant as fulfilled in the cross and resurrec-

tion of Jesus Christ and in the power of the Holy Spirit outpoured upon all flesh that Christians express solidarity with all those who bear a human countenance, and more particularly, a willingness to stand up for those whose fundamental rights and freedom are robbed.[103]

This excellent affirmation is foundationally trinitarian and covenantal. Later in the same document, as we saw, J. Moltmann writes:

> Because human beings as individuals, in community and in humanity are meant to reflect the image of God, all human rights are bound up with, and related to one another. One can neither curtail them, separate them from each other, or differentiate between them. Furthermore, all human rights are bound up with specific human duties. Rights and duties cannot be separated from each other; privileges should not grow out of rights nor empty demands out of duties.[104]

At this point we come to the issue raised by Forsyth and now reiterated by Moltmann, who properly conceives of people, individually and communally, as being under obligation; they are, accordingly, accountable; they have certain responsibilities. Now Christians will normally have no difficulty in agreeing that, individually and corporately, they are accountable to God. This is implicit in Reformed ecclesiology—indeed, in the Reformed understanding of the gospel. The area of difficulty may be defined like this: given covenant solidarity, what is the relation between individual and collective responsibility, and is there such a thing as collective *guilt*?

A section report presented at the Uniting General Council (1970) appears to assume the viability of the concept of collective responsibility in calling "upon our constituency to confess with us our common sin and individually those sins which are peculiar to each given situation."[105] This call, taken out of context, is innocuous. But the context is that of racism, and in such a context as this—quite apart from the philosophical question of the viability of collective responsibility—there is a serious pastoral problem represented by the elderly lady who said, "Our minister is such a *nice* young man, but I really cannot make myself believe that what is going on in South Africa is my *fault*." That the same question can arise in contexts which are not overtly Christian is clear from Julian Barnes's criticism of a television program by John Pilger on the plight of the Australian aborigines:

> Pilger unrolled his grim history of slaughter, land-theft and discrimination in his usual telling way: that's to say, by making the viewer feel incredibly guilty about things he has no control over. You may not even have been to Australia, but when Pilger fixes you with his basilisk

eye and tells you that many years ago "the billabongs ran with blood," you know that the footprints found beside the billabong exactly match your shoe size.[106]

What is happening, pastorally and liturgically, when we are invited to confess our implication in atrocities which are far away from our door, or far behind us in history? Could emphasis upon our part within sinful humanity actually *weaken* our sense of moral responsibility by providing us with a spurious exoneration: My involvement with sinful humanity has made me what I am, and I cannot help what I do. This would be to undermine our own humanity as well as to flout God. As if that were not enough, it would be illogical too, for to explain how one has come to be the sort of person one is is not the same as providing sustainable arguments for one's nonculpability in a particular situation.

Here is a line of investigation, not so far pursued in Alliance circles and of great importance in its own right, directly affecting the credibility of official Alliance pronouncements.

VI. Common Ground and Natural Law

An assertion made in the context of the twentieth council's report on "The Freedom of a Just Order" (1920) raises the question of common ground between Christians and others:

> But the question remains: How must the church go about making reconciliation effective in a given society where there is oppression and social injustice? Here the emphases among us differ. Some people think it wise to begin with the individual and spiritual aspect of the message of reconciliation, in evangelism toward personal conversion from which actions for justice and human development in society will result. Others, however, and these are more numerous among us, think that until now the church has been limited by this very attitude. Today therefore we should proclaim reconciliation with God in Christ by starting with acts of service, *often together with non-Christians*, which will result in authenticating our preaching of the Gospel and convincing the world of the sincerity of our faith.[107]

We may note in passing that here once again we have the alternative strategies proposed to which we have already given some attention. Our present concern is with the italicized words. The question is not, "Ought Christians to stand alongside non-Christians in the performance of acts of service?" We take it for granted that in a threatened and divided world they have no option here. The question is "Can the Christian stand on common ground with others?"—and the "can" here is a logical "can." Clearly Christians can stand with others in the sense of having the ability to do so, and many examples could be quoted to demonstrate the point. But can they consistently do so? If a Marxist thinks that by performing a piece of service he is advancing the revolutionary cause, whereas the Christian who joins him thinks that he is serving the kingdom of God, what are we to say? They cannot both be right; they may both be wrong; or one may be right and the other wrong—but does it matter, so long as the piece of service is rendered?

The question is, "How far is the concept of natural law viable?" Before coming directly to this question, and by way of a cautionary tale, we may recount what must surely be the most delightfully eclectic and contorted argument in the whole of the Alliance corpus. For this we are indebted to Dr. Clarence McCartney at the eleventh Presbyterian Council (1921). He was speaking on "The Place of Women in the Church," though his method of argumentation could be, and has been, applied much more widely; and it is his method of argument and not his views on women which concerns us here. Having noted that "women and the twentieth century are upon us," he presented some findings on the actual status of women in various parts of the Christian world. He then approached the question of the ordination of women to the ministry, paving the way by glutinous statements worthy of the most wan nineteenth-century poet (albeit he speaks in 1921): "Let me clear the floor of all irrelevant discussion by saying that we all agree in paying our tribute to the beauty and the intelligence of our women. I think the best theological mind I have come in contact with was the mind of a woman, and a woman who was very close to me in childhood. I believe in what St. Paul says, that henceforth there is neither bond nor free, male or female."[108] He refers to Thomas Gray, who was taught to pray by one of his aunts, and he quotes the following doggerel concerning "The Magdalene":

> Not she with traitorous lips her Saviour stung,
> Not she denied Him with unholy tongue;
> She, whilst apostles shrunk, could danger brave;
> Last at the Cross, and earliest at the grave.[109]

We turn the page and find ourselves in a different century, being treated to a misquotation of Samuel Johnson:

> We are not discussing the individual piety and intelligence of the women, but their place and office in the Church. Samuel Johnson once paused on the streets of London to listen to a woman preacher,

and Boswell, I think it was, asked him what he thought of it, and his answer is to the point today: "Why," he said, "it is like a bear dancing; it is not a question of whether it is done well or done poorly, but that the thing is done at all"—the eternal fitness of the thing.[110]

Here is the unvarnished eighteenth-century notion of the natural fitness of things. Then, and only then, McCartney comes to the Bible and discusses that "much warred-over passage of St. Paul in Corinthians." He considers three possible views: (a) that Paul meant what he said and that he was wrong; (b) that his advice concerned only his own time and context, and no longer holds today; and (c) that Paul's word stands for all time. Finding difficulties in all the options, McCartney resorts to natural law: "To my mind the whole subject is to be decided not by the exegesis of any difficult passage in St. Paul's letters, but by common sense, by expediency, and by a regard for the law of nature and by what the Church has found to be good in the past."[111] Here, as well as the resort to natural law, we have an appeal to tradition of a most un-Reformed kind. But worse is to come. McCartney sets his face against the ordination of women not only to the ministry, but to the eldership also, and he invokes a host of female specters to make the point:

> I am opposed to this measure [to ordain women as elders and ministers] because it will tend to increase heresy, fanaticism, the distortion and the perversion of Christian doctrine. What is the history of Christian Science, of New Thought, of Spiritualism, of all these fly-by-nights cults of which you read in the newspaper on Saturday evening? To ask that question is to answer it. They have been advocated by and floated upon the brain and the enthusiasm of women, and from Eve down to Mrs. Eddy and Mrs. Besant the place that woman has taken in Church doctrine and leadership is not an enviable one.[112]

The omission of any reference to those odder cults to which men have devoted their powers is more than somewhat glaring.

It is only proper to point out that McCartney was taken to task in the discussion of his paper. W. L. Robertson said, "I have sometimes heard ministers talk along that same line—which personally I utterly repudiate; and I notice that the same ministers, being married, cannot except at extreme peril maintain their position within their own home."[113]

But let us learn from McCartney. He is but an extreme example of one who worked his way towards a preselected conclusion by appeals of varying strength to whatever will suit him best. The resultant argumentative fog is a help rather than a hindrance if the auditors are philosophically unsophisticated—and this simply compounds the error, for improper advantage is taken of them. As to McCartney's overall strategy, in its appeal ultimately to natural law rather than to Scripture it is un-Reformed. But it does highlight the question, "How much reliance may we place on natural law?" Indeed, it thrusts to the fore the question, "Who is to determine what the natural law is?"

On the one hand, it would appear that it is only on the basis of some kind of natural law that Christian can stand with non-Christian in the service of humanity. On the other hand, the process of making deductions from the alleged deliverances of natural law is fraught with difficulties. McCartney, grounding on a conviction concerning the natural order of things, concludes against the ordination of women as being not fitting. This is typical of the procedure adapted in older-style Roman Catholic moral theology, which drew D. D. Williams' complaint that the Roman church not only puts its authority behind ultimate moral principles, but tends to treat "very complicated and debatable deductions from these principles as if they had the same authority."[114] He cites Maritain, who admits to "imperceptible transitions" from natural law principles to consequences in positive laws, and remarks: "It is just the 'imperceptibility' of these transitions which makes them suspicious. . . . Deciding what is natural is a naturally difficult question!"[115] He further complains that the natural law principle "puts a legalistic restriction upon the freedom of the Christian conscience in dealing with the unpredictable and always problematical stuff of actual social existence."[116] The latter point has been reinforced by Ronald Preston: "The very theology whose *raison d'être* was to deal with specific problems, proceeded by a deductive method of reasoning from the alleged self-evident deliverances of natural laws in a way which prevented it from dealing adequately with empirical data."[117] To these comments may be added the protest of Reinhold Niebuhr, that under natural law theory the law of love tends to be made an addendum to the natural law, so that one defines the determinate possibilities, and the other the indeterminate possibilities of good. Niebuhr contends, however, that no such neat lines may be drawn; for example, justice is an application of the law of love.[118]

A critique of natural law theory from a more theological perspective (which echoes the sentiments of Tudur Jones that we have already noted) was provided in Alliance literature by André Dumas:

> Who can determine what nature is, since sin has disordered and broken the creation? On what principle can we distinguish between mere observed facts and norms? How are we to ensure that the natural

law will not seem an even more subtle clericalism because it does not wear the outward garb of faith? And perhaps above all, what about some contents of natural law as declared in recent times, such as the 19th century private property or the procreative purpose of sexuality in the 20th century, when these contents do not meet with general acceptance in present-day societies and have considerable difficulty in presenting their rational or biological justification? The universal intention of natural law is plain, but the persuasiveness of its substantial content is open to doubt.

Here the problem is clearly set; and Dumas follows up at once with the dilemma—namely, that natural law is "the most comprehensive but also the most disputed enterprise at the present time, even though it is difficult to see what can take its place."[119] In the last resort it would appear that the doctrine of creation is at stake. As Paul Ramsey has said, "Any conception of the nature of man is so far a conception of the natural law."[120] But how, in view of the difficulties which we have indicated, is this to be worked out in ethical theory and practice? The more necessary it becomes for people of goodwill to stand together in the face of the abuses of people and of creation itself, the more urgent it becomes that sustained thought be given to this matter. Here, surely, is a task of primary importance for the Alliance and any others whom they may be able to interest in it. It may be that a particular obligation rests upon the Reformed family in this connection, for it is from within this tradition that most has been heard of natural man's blindness and inability— these being offset by God's common grace restraining sinners from their worst excesses and accounting for the good that they do on occasion seem able to do.

VII. Ethics: Catholic, Evangelical, and Reformed

We are in the end brought full circle to the recreating gospel and the illuminating Spirit—to that catholic, evangelical, and Reformed ground which it has been our purpose to exemplify from Alliance literature. For all that we may allow to natural morality, the Christian ethic entails the acknowledgment of God's holy *agape*, in the light of which our best efforts are imperfect, and our need of atonement is plain. Thus on the one hand we need to maintain that Christians by their obedient response to God's atoning *agape* are placed differently from those who make no such response: Christians seek God's glory and are empowered by the Spirit. On the other hand, Christianity does not repudiate the *content* of natural morality, or seek to annex natural morality from non-believing or differently believing humanity. The moral is the moral whoever is looking at it, but the Christian looks at it in a context that speaks of a goal unattainable in one's own strength, and of a need of grace to help: "Christian morality reaffirms and redeems natural morality."[121] It also sets it within an eschatological context, as the oscillation between deontological and teleological considerations in Christian ethical theory amply illustrates.

The atoning *agape* that provides the context of Christian ethical thought also provides the stimulus to Christian ethical action:

> Just as the "vertical" and the "horizontal" lines, the devotion of the Father to man and the devotion of the Son of Man to God, are inseparably linked together in the cross, so also are the spiritual-evangelistic and the human-social services of Christians. At the same time the cross indicates the direction and tendency of the social task: this task is only authentic when it is conceived of as *memoria passionis*, and takes into account those who suffer in specific situations.[122]

Thus we return for a concluding illustration to the Alliance's "Resolution on Racism and South Africa" (1982). We do not imply that this resolution is the Alliance's only significant recent ethical statement, and we are not here concerned with how the resolution will be followed up. Our purpose is simply to examine this text as an ethical-theological pronouncement in the light of what we have said concerning the Alliance's evangelical, catholic, and Reformed basis. We are not concerned with the detailed provisions of the resolution, but simply with the grounds on which it rests.

The opening paragraphs clearly spell out those grounds:

> God in Jesus Christ has affirmed human dignity. Through his life, death and resurrection he has reconciled people to God and to themselves. He has broken down the wall of partition and enmity and has become our peace. He is the Lord of His church who has brought us together in the one Lord, one faith, one baptism, one God who is the father of us all (Eph. 4:5, 6).
>
> The Gospel of Jesus Christ demands, therefore, a community of believers which transcends all barriers of race—a community in which the love for Christ and for one another has overcome the divisions of race and colour.
>
> The Gospel confronts racism, which is in its very essence a form of idolatry. Racism fosters a false sense of supremacy, it denies the common humanity of believers, and it denies Christ's reconciling,

humanising work. It systematises oppression, domination and injustice. As such the struggle against racism, wherever it is found, in overt and covert forms, is a responsibility laid upon the church by the Gospel of Jesus Christ in every country and society.[123]

Here, then, is an example of a Christian world communion reflecting the light of redeeming *agape* upon a situation in which some Christians, by supporting apartheid, violate the very *agape* they proclaim, and erect once again the barriers which Christ has broken down. The upshot is that "apartheid ('Separate Development') is a sin, and that the moral and theological justification of it is a travesty of the Gospel, and in its persistent disobedience to the word of God, a theological heresy."[124] There could scarcely be stronger language. Apartheid, it is declared, is utterly alien to God—it is a sin. Consequently, to propose a moral or a theological justification of it is to be guilty of heresy; for heresy is the distortion of Christian truth, and any justification of apartheid must turn upon the distortion, if not the outright denial, of at least the Christian doctrines of God, creation, humanity, redemption, the church. This is why the Ottawa Council declared that "this situation constitutes a *status confessionis* for our churches, which means that we regard this as an issue on which it is not possible to differ without seriously jeopardizing the integrity of our common confession as Reformed churches."[125]

It seems quite clear that those who would divide the church along racial lines are radically untrue to the Reformed catholic-evangelical heritage. They introduce, perpetuate, and justify a most sinister form of sectarianism alien to the gospel and sustained by brutal means. But let us beware of hypocrisy—and that not only vis-à-vis racism (and on this point the resolution cautions us). We cannot suppress the thought that any form of sectarianism which breaks the body of Christ and divides those whom he has made one—and divides them supremely and most tragically at the Lord's table—is ugly. Accordingly, sectarian ecclesiological divisions are ugly, and the fact that they are not normally in these days maintained by force and by loveless legislation makes them no less ugly. To break apart those whom God has called to himself and given to each other is never justifiable. Secession and schism may, sadly, occur on doctrinal or other grounds; but to bar those who are Christ's from the fellowship of his table on grounds of race or church order (questions of discipline apart) is never a defensible act.

At this point we may fittingly refer once again to the Anglican/Reformed dialogue report, *God's Reign and Our Unity*. The authors of that report resisted those who advocated strong disjunctions between either church unity and evangelism or peace and justice. They declared that "evangelism, social justice and church unity are not conflicting concerns, but are complementary aspects of the one mission of God in which we participate as accountable stewards. To restrict our concern to any one of them would be to abridge the gospel."[126] It is by now also clear that any one of them can be vitiated by the sectarian spirit, in profound violation of the catholic, evangelical, and Reformed heritage.

Here are two further reflections. First, we have concentrated on the presuppositions of the Alliance's "Resolution on Racism and South Africa." Earlier, however, we raised in passing the question of the status of such resolutions. How is the Alliance acting when it drafts and passes such resolutions—as a churchly body, an ecclesial reality? Traditionally within the Alliance—and this was essential to the views of both the Presbyterian and the Congregational founders—the Alliance's deliverances have been advisory only, and not binding upon any member church. But in the South Africa case it would appear that the Alliance has not simply spoken like a quasi-ecclesial reality, it has acted like one vis-à-vis the Nederduitse Gereformeerde Kerk (in the Republic of South Africa) and the Nederduitse Hervormde Kerk van Afrika: it has suspended them. Given the grounds of this action and the motives underlying it, we do seem to have here something remarkably similar to an act of church discipline. Given the grounds and the motives, this seems not to be an association simply suspending some misbehaving members according to its rules. What are the ecclesial implications of the action taken at Ottawa? This question was urgently posed by Richmond Smith, the third theological secretary of the Alliance, at the close of his eighteen years' service in that post,[127] and it will occupy the Alliance for some time to come.

Second—and this resumes a point made earlier—the strength of the Alliance's "Resolution on Racism" is its enunciation of the universals of the gospel and its being a declaration of the fellowship. The needs of this threatened and divided world are universal in scope, and they are supremely matched by the gospel, itself universal in scope. It is not fitting for the Reformed family—or any other Christian family—so to partition reality that Christians can proclaim only a local message and perhaps find it difficult or even impossible to communicate with their remoter brothers and sisters.

Those who have by grace been grasped by the vision of evangelical catholicity that is integral to the Reformed tradition, those who really believe in being reformed by the Spirit through the Word discerned within the fellowship—such have no alternative but to affirm their gospel and to live by it in all spheres: ecclesiastical, intellectual, sociopolitical. Nor is this simply a matter of getting our theory straight

as individuals or of living consistently as individuals. It is a matter of
fellowship, as Lovell Cocks so wisely reminded the sixth Congregational
Council (1949):

> Men must learn their Christian responsibilities in the local fellowship
> before they can be good citizens of the world or fruitful members of
> the ecumenical church. . . . Only a community can witness to a com-
> munity. This is the significance of our high churchmanship which
> insists that the church is not only an agency for the proclamation of
> the Gospel but is itself a part of the Gospel.[128]

7

Conclusion

We have now reviewed and analyzed a considerable body of material produced under the auspices of one Christian world communion. We hope to have made good the claim that, taken as a whole, and blemishes notwithstanding, the Alliance's theological corpus may justly be characterized as catholic, evangelical, and Reformed. Although the choice of themes has been necessarily selective, we have not found any major strand of material published under Alliance auspices which would deny this threefold claim. The corpus is catholic in that it is in the line of the apostolic faith of the ages; in that, when true to itself, it is nonsectarian in content and spirit, acknowledging the one Head of the one church; and in that it is concerned for the whole of life and for the whole created order. It is evangelical in that its foundation and inspiration is the good news of God's gracious initiative whereby, on the ground of Christ's once-for-all finished work, he calls out a people for his praise and service, binds them to himself and to each other in a covenant that cannot be broken, and dispatches them in mission and service to the world. It is Reformed in that it has continual recourse to the authoritative Word as that is discerned under the Spirit in fellowship, and in relation to the tradition of the ages and the context of the times; and in that it knows its need of constant reformation under the Word. We reiterate the warning of our first chapter: in speaking as we just have we refer to the prevailing atmosphere of the *Alliance* literature, not to the position of every *Reformed* church, congregation, or Christian. It remains only to enumerate four general findings, and then to turn to specific points raised by the study.

I

1. The theological work published under the auspices of the Alliance since 1875 represents a significant contribution to the theological discussion of the past century. If individual items are not always weighty or original, taken as a whole the corpus enables us to monitor trends and to assess the theological temperature of a prominent Christian family's most widely representative body. Given that until the 1950s the Alliance's theological work was for the most part undertaken in occasional bursts of activity associated with councils, and that for the first eighty years of its life there was no ongoing policy for theological work, the comprehensiveness of coverage we have found is the more remarkable.

2. The Alliance's utterances and publications reveal a communion which is catholic, evangelical, and Reformed. Its view of catholicity derives from its understanding of the gospel, and, at its best, the communion is ever open to reformation by the Spirit, through the Word received in fellowship. It must be confessed, however, that since about 1920 the emphasis upon the doctrine of the atonement has declined. This is not, of course, a feature of Alliance theology alone. In many quarters, and under such various influences as post-Hegelian immanentism, the mid-nineteenth-century rediscovery of Alexandrian theology, and evolutionary and process thought, some theologians have come to speak of incarnation and of Christ's victorious omnipresence without much reference to his atoning work. As a reaction against undue concentration upon the "mechanics" of the atonement and its "application," this is welcome enough. But the scandal of particularity may not be obliterated: God's once-for-all work in the cross and resurrection remains the basis of our reconciliation with him and therefore with one another. It is thus the basis of Reformed Catholic churchmanship and also of the Reformed family's socioethical witness.

3. In our second and third chapters we provided ample evidence that the Alliance literature reveals a communion which maintains the apostolic faith, whatever the precise attitude of its several members to creeds and confessions per se. We saw that every major doctrine of the Christian faith has been articulated in the corpus, though they have not all received equal attention. Were it otherwise the result would be astonishing indeed, given that the Alliance's theological work, however detailed in parts, is overall of an "occasional" character. Nevertheless, the *relative* lack of emphasis upon the Trinity and upon eschatology—a deficiency which is by no means confined to Alliance literature—is disquieting. More recent signs that the balance is being redressed are

welcome. We have seen that the Trinity and eschatology have always been implicit in Alliance literature.

4. True to its ecumenical vision, the Alliance has played and continues to play its part in the bilateral dialogues of the post-1970 period. It has also encouraged responses from its member churches to the multilateral dialogue which has produced the document *Baptism, Eucharist and Ministry*. It is now possible to analyze the relations between these responses and the bilateral reports to which the Reformed have contributed. To the extent that the Reformed responses are discordant this question is raised: How far are those engaged in the work of dialogue corporately representative of their respective communions? The alienation of those within the several communions who are on the "liberal" and "conservative" wings is a danger, and were it to happen in the absence of attempted remedies it would call into question the way in which the term "ecumenical" is used.

One problem with both bilateral and multilateral dialogue reports is reception. How are the results of dialogues to be communicated to regions and localities in such a way that any challenges to fresh thinking and any encouragements to positive action towards greater unity can be accepted, and not appear as attempted impositions from on high? The problem is the more acute in so varied a family as the Alliance, in which, as we saw in our introduction, linguistic, cultural, and ecclesiological distinctions, together with the difficulty of representing the whole family in theological work and the lack of regional unity, make coherent and consistent global responses to dialogue reports more difficult. It would seem that the only way forward is to regard international dialogue reports as checks, balances, and stimuli to regional unity efforts; for in the last resort Christian unity is a matter of "all in each place," and the suggestions of others must, to be productive, become *our own*. This is easier said than done, however, for, on their own admission, the content of dialogue reports is beyond the reach of many local congregations—even beyond the reach of many pastors— around the world, and not only in the developing nations. In the more mobile and consumer-oriented lands, where the church allegiance of so many has so little to do with a confessional stance, the content of dialogue reports can appear as remote, even antiquarian. Clearly the problems outlined here will occupy the Alliance, and other similar bodies, for some time to come.

We cannot suppress the feeling that a measure of lateral thinking may be required in ecumenical dialogue circles. For long enough we have asked, "What are the beliefs which unite Christian people?"—and we can produce an impressive list of these; but universal fellowship at the Lord's table which is mutual and reciprocal continues to elude us. So then we wonder whether the reconciliation of ministries will obviate this difficulty; and at once we land in that impasse which results when one side construes its ministerial orders as necessary to the God-given structure of the church, and when the other will not repudiate its ordination or deny the divine blessing manifestly bestowed upon its ministries. Ought we perhaps now to ask, "What is the ecclesiological significance of the fellowship which God has given us, and which we actually enjoy, in Christ?" As we have elsewhere asked, "Are there ways of pursuing this question which would avoid both such 'new circumcisions' (overt or implicit) as, 'If you do not assent, or order yourselves, in our way you are somehow deficient,' and such erroneous notions as that because actions (allegedly) speak louder than words we can believe and order the Church as we like?"[1] On what grounds should we determine that a perennial Christian diversity is here an obstacle, and there a gift? What are the ecclesiological implications of God's un-merited grace which has accepted even us?

II

We turn now to specific points raised by our study. In the course of our work we noted a number of lacunae in the literature, and we have suggested reasons for them: notably the occasional nature of the Alliance's theological output for so much of its life, the two world wars, and the lack until the late 1950s of a coordinated theological policy, in addition to the fact that such matters as Christian-Marxist dialogue and the questions of missiology and dialogue with people of other faiths have been treated in the wider arena of the World Council of Churches. Not all lacunae are blameworthy. It now remains to enumerate the lacunae, all of which suggest areas of work which require attention. At once two caveats must be made. First, we by no means suggest that an agenda for the future should be derived exclusively from the lacunae of the past.[2] Each succeeding age brings the Christian church fresh challenges— though even as we make this obvious point we are conscious of a "family likeness" between the challenges: for example, Arianism is ever with us; or again, if we think in terms of such diabolical novelties as germ warfare, the basis of a Christian response will still be the eternal gospel. Second, the Alliance family is large and its permanent structure is small. It could not conceivably attend to all the points to be listed. However, some of the points are of wider-than-Alliance interest: we have found them arising from Alliance theological literature, but they arise elsewhere too.

For this reason we shall attempt to classify our suggestions for future consideration under two headings: "theological tasks for the Alliance," and "theological tasks for the wider Christian community."

Theological Tasks for the Alliance

1. A fresh examination is needed of the atonement as basic to ecclesiology and witness, and this in relation to the trinitarian understanding of God and the eschatological perspective of the gospel. We noted the relative lack of attention to the atonement in the recent Alliance literature, and we can well understand why some, having escaped harsher views of penal substitution, should wish to keep this doctrine at arm's length. Nevertheless, as we saw, the atonement is the ground of our reconciliation. It is on the basis of God's once-for-all redeeming act in Christ that the church is called into being. Hence the atonement (not church structure) is at the root of our ecclesiology. But, of course, the whole Trinity is involved in this atoning work. We might take Romans 8:26-39 as a *locus classicus* here: in his triune being God graciously provides for a people; the Father calls them to himself by the Spirit who intercedes for them, and the Son works the victory on the stage of human history that entails the vanquishing of death and the eternal security of those who are justified by grace through faith. Though we have stated the matter crudely we can see that the themes of the Trinity, the person and work of Christ and of the Spirit, ecclesiology, and eschatology are all there, and that all are inextricably linked together. Our study of the Alliance literature suggests room for a fresh consideration of these doctrines in their mutual interrelations, and the Alliance would perform a useful ecumenical task were such a study to be undertaken. Here is the ground of evangelical catholicity.

2. In 1970 the World Presbyterian Alliance united with the International Congregational Council. We have enumerated the grounds on which this union took place: the fact that Presbyterians and Congregationalists had already come together in united churches; and the convictions that if ecumenism was to be taken seriously churches should continue in separation only for significant theological reasons and that between the Alliance and the Council there were no such obstacles. But the questions arise: "How far have the two strands really come together?" "Has the Alliance really reckoned with the ecclesiological diversity within its own family?" We have seen that church establishment is one issue that demands attention. Among Reformed, Presbyterians, and Congregationalists this is a question that raises the ecclesiological question—indeed, it raises the question, "Who is a Christian?" For on

the one hand we have a few Reformed/Presbyterian churches that are state churches; some of them are to some extent funded by the state, others are not. On the other hand, the Alliance embraces Congregationalists who, in fidelity to the idea of the gathered church (albeit conceived as catholic at its best!), believe that the church comprises enrolled believers whose initiation—baptism, nurture, and profession of faith—is complete. We have found no sustained treatment of this matter, despite its importance—especially in a period of the decline of many state churches.

3. The literature prompts a number of ecclesiological questions which take on a particular coloring within the Reformed family. There is the question of admission to the Lord's table vis-à-vis baptism on the one hand and church discipline on the other. Who may come to the table? In the increasingly mobile societies of today, how viable is the concept of the church as covenant fellowship? Again, the questions of ordination in relation to the doctrine of the priesthood of all believers, and the necessity of a threefold ministry, were raised by the material analyzed in chapter 4. The Reformed will need to pay continued attention to these questions, as well as to the essentialist versus existentialist views of ordination. Nor will the Reformed forever be able to delay taking a position on papal primacy: the Reformed Alliance is, after all, in dialogue with the communion that regards obedience to the bishop of Rome as a mark of catholicity, and at least two of the Alliance's other dialogue partners, the Anglicans and the Lutherans, have paid some attention to the matter.

Then there is the question of the eldership. One cannot help but reflect during some bilateral dialogue discussions that if our partners knew us better, or were less polite, they would ask many more searching questions than they do when we commend that venerable office to them. We have seen that there is not one uniform view of the eldership within the Reformed family, and that the duties assigned to elders around the world are manifold.[3] Here is an office which cries out for fresh attention within the Reformed family.

4. The Alliance's 1982 "Resolution on Racism and South Africa" has not only borne witness to the fundamental Reformed concern for the catholicity of the evangel, but has also raised afresh the question of the ecclesial status of the Alliance. This question requires careful consideration vis-à-vis the "churchly" disciplining of members, and also in relation to the accountability of council and other representatives to the Alliance on the one hand and to their home churches on the other. If Alliance forums are to be regarded, like denominational assemblies, as churchly gatherings in which God the Holy Spirit may speak a *new* word

to his people, then those attending can only be representatives, not mandated delegates, and ways must be found of dealing pastorally with those occasions when a council decision runs counter to the stance of a member church or churches.

5. We have hinted on more than one occasion that we are perhaps at the threshold of an exciting period of theological activity in which contributions from all cultures will increasingly be shared with the wider family. Our hope is that the Alliance may serve as a "sounding board" for its members as indigenous theologies are developed: this in the interest of the universals of the gospel and the fact of God's extensive covenant with people of all races and cultures. If in one sense the context of theology is the environment in which the Christian lives, in another sense the context of theology is, for example, the trinitarian provision of Romans 8:26-39, to which we have just referred.

Theological Tasks for the Wider Christian Community

Certain matters arising from Alliance literature may well command wider-than-Reformed interest. They can be divided into (1) philosophical and (2) ethical matters.

1. We saw in chapter 5 that until about 1920 both the Presbyterian and Congregational Councils regularly took stock of the philosophical-theological climate of their times, and that this activity has since lapsed. The Alliance is by no means the only guilty party in this respect. True, Christian-Marxist dialogue has occurred, and so have dialogues between Christians and people of other faiths. We are not aware, however, that there has been ecumenical consideration of such philosophical problems as those posed by logical positivism and analytical philosophy; yet these concerns have been as prominent in the post-1930 period as post-Hegelian idealism, evolutionary thought, and materialism were in the first fifty years of the Alliance's life. One would hardly think from reading Alliance literature that serious doubt has been cast upon the meaningfulness of religious language, or upon the coherence of theism. There is the question of the viability—even the possibility or impossibility—of natural theology, a matter on which positions are taken by some of our dialogue partners, but which the Alliance itself has never probed. The weakness to which we here point is endemic in the ecumenical movement; yet ought not concern for the *oikoumene* to include concern for intellectual no less than for religious and social needs?

2. We have seen that real attempts have been made throughout the life of the Alliance to view socioethical concerns in the light of the gospel.

It has become clear, however, that this branch of the Alliance literature poses questions of wider-than-Reformed importance. What are we to make of the concept of collective responsibility underlying so much ecumenical writing in the socioethical field? Is the concept of natural law viable? Its ubiquity is plain for all to see, not least, as we saw, in Alliance literature. What provides the common ground on which, in a threatened and divided world, people of goodwill may consistently stand? Finally (and now in relation to a specific issue, the satisfactory resolution of which depends upon a common mind on the theoretical issues just raised), is it not time to take up the agenda bequeathed to Roman Catholics, Lutherans, and Reformed by the trilateral dialogue on *Theology of Marriage and the Problem of Mixed Marriage?*

III

The suggested agenda items for the Alliance could be disposed of in many ways: by consultations, by the publication of requested papers, by member churches acting on the Alliance's behalf. For those items which are of wider-than-Reformed interest, our first point of reference, in fidelity to the Lund principle, must be the World Council of Churches. It will be interesting to see how many of the matters arising from the Alliance literature up to 1982 appear on the agenda to come.

We may conclude that the Alliance's interest in relation to future tasks should be to work towards the clear articulation of the reconciling gospel of the grace of God, with the aims of making a credible confession, stimulating Christian reflection and action, and protesting against barriers erected on ecclesiological, social, or racial grounds between those whom God has joined together. An important step in the desired direction was taken at the Ottawa Council of 1982, when it was resolved to challenge all member churches to ask themselves what it means to witness to Christ today in their several contexts. The booklet *Called to Witness to the Gospel Today* was published as a stimulus to such questions, and it constitutes the Alliance's major current study text. Given the goodwill and the active participation of its member churches, the Alliance may increasingly become a lively forum for theological reflection leading to creative action. To repeat the challenge: the Alliance is called to live by and witness to the gospel of the atoning grace of the triune God, who ever addresses and reforms his people by the Spirit through the Word discerned in fellowship. If member churches are faithful to this evangel they will not fail to be catholic and apostolic; they will minister compassionately and joyously to the religious, material, and intellectual needs of their several constituencies, and to the needs of the greater family beyond their borders.

We cannot predict the future, though we have some grounds for supposing that the way may not be easy. But we march on as pilgrims following the victorious Christ; and as we go we may ponder some words of W. G. Blaikie in the very first issue of *The Catholic Presbyterian*. He there appropriately combines eschatological longing with Scottish realism:

> The Church, it would seem must pass through a somewhat creeping, caterpillar existence before she is developed into her bright, soaring condition. Let us learn all that we have to learn while we are in the chrysalis state, *but think longingly all the while of the brighter day to come!*[4]

Appendix I

Alliance Councils

Presbyterian Councils:

1. 1877 Edinburgh
2. 1880 Philadelphia
3. 1884 Belfast
4. 1888 London
5. 1892 Toronto
6. 1896 Glasgow
7. 1899 Washington, D.C.
8. 1904 Liverpool
9. 1909 New York
10. 1913 Aberdeen
11. 1921 Pittsburgh
12. 1925 Cardiff
13. 1929 Boston
14. 1933 Belfast
15. 1937 Montreal
16. 1948 Geneva
17. 1954 Princeton
18. 1959 São Paulo
19. 1964 Frankfurt

Congregational Councils:

1. 1891 London
2. 1899 Boston

3. 1908 Edinburgh
4. 1920 Boston
5. 1930 Bournemouth
6. 1949 Wellesley
7. 1953 St. Andrews
8. 1958 Hartford
9. 1962 Rotterdam
10. 1966 Swansea

Alliance Councils

(numbered here and in our notes consecutively from 1877):

20. 1970 Nairobi (the Uniting General Council)
21. 1977 St. Andrews (the Centennial Consultation)
22. 1982 Ottawa

Appendix II

Biographical Notes

We here list some of those who made significant theological contributions to the work of the Alliance. As explained in the preface, all those listed are now deceased, and this cannot but underline the fact of British and North American dominance in the affairs of the Alliance until 1948. The Librarians of The Congregational Library, Boston, Massachusetts, and The Philip Schaff Library, Lancaster Theological Seminary, Lancaster, Pennsylvania, are warmly thanked for supplying some of the following information.

BLAIKIE, William Garden (Presbyterian).
Born at Aberdeen, Scotland, 1820. Arts at Aberdeen; Divinity at Edinburgh. D.D. (Edin.); LL.D. (Aber.). Licensed 1841. Minister, Drumblade, 1842-43; Pilrig, Edinburgh, 1844-68; Professor, New College, 1868-97. Moderator of the General Assembly of the Free Church of Scotland, 1892. First president of the Presbyterian Alliance, 1888-92. Numerous publications, notably on Old Testament, biographical, and social themes. Died 1899.
  See *William Garden Blaikie: An Autobiography*, edited and with an introduction by Norman L. Walker. London: Hodder & Stoughton, 1901.

BOMBERGER, John Henry Augustus (German Reformed, U.S.A.).
Born at Lancaster, Pennsylvania, 13 January 1817. Marshall College and Mercersburg Theological Seminary. D.D. (Franklin and Marshall College). Minister of German Reformed churches in Pennsylvania, 1838-70; President, Ursinus College, Collegeville, Pa., 1870-90. Publications include *Infant Salvation in Its Relation to Infant Depravity, Infant Regeneration, and Infant Baptism* (1859); *The Revised Liturgy: A History and Criticism of the Ritualistic Movement in the German Reformed Church* (1867);

248

Reformed Not Ritualistic: A Reply to Dr. Nevin's "Vindication" (1867). Edited *The Reformed Church Monthly*. Died 19 August 1890. See the *Rev. J.H. Bomberger*, Philadelphia: Publication and Sunday School Board of the Reformed Church in the U.S., 1917.

COCKS, Harry Francis Lovell (Congregationalist).
Born at Uxbridge, England, 2 August 1894. Hackney College, London (under P. T. Forsyth, q.v.). D.D. (Lond.) for *By Faith Alone* (1943). Minister, Winchester, 1917-22; Hove, 1922-27; Headingley Hill, Leeds, 1927-32; professor, Yorkshire United Independent College, Bradford, 1932-37; principal, Scottish Congregational College, Edinburgh, 1937-41; principal, Western College, Bristol, 1941-60; chairman, Congregational Union of England and Wales, 1950-51; moderator, Free Church Federal Council, 1962-63. Other publications include *The Faith of a Protestant Christian* (1931); *The Nonconformist Conscience* (1943); *The Wondrous Cross* (1957); *The Religious Life of Oliver Cromwell* (1960). Died at Amersham, 15 January 1983.

CURTIS, William Alexander (Presbyterian).
Born at Thurso, Scotland, 1876. Arts and Divinity at Edinburgh. D.Litt. and D.D. (Edin.); D.Theol. (Paris and Debrecen). Licensed 1901. Ordained 1903. Professor of Systematic Theology, Aberdeen, 1903-15; Professor of Biblical Criticism, Edinburgh, 1915-46; Dean of the Faculty of Divinity, 1928-46; principal, New College, Edinburgh, 1935-46; president, Presbyterian Alliance, 1933-37. Publications include *A History of Creeds and Confessions of Faith in Christendom and Beyond* (1911). Died 30 September 1946.

DALE, Robert William (Congregationalist).
Born at Bermondsey, England, 1 December 1829. Spring Hill College, Birmingham, 1847-53. M.A. (Lond.); D.D. (Yale); LL.D. (Glasgow). Carrs Lane, Birmingham: assistant, 1853-54; copastor, 1854-58; pastor, 1858-95. Chairman, Congregational Union of England and Wales, 1869. First president, International Congregational Council, 1891. Publications include *The Atonement* (1898); *Christian Doctrine* (1903); *History of English Congregationalism* (1907). Died 13 March 1895.
See A. W. W. Dale (son), *The Life of R. W. Dale of Birmingham*. London: Hodder & Stoughton, 1899; *Dictionary of National Biography*, 1901f.

DOUGLASS, Truman Bartlett (Congregationalist).
Born at Grinnell, Iowa, 15 July 1901. Union Theological Seminary, New York. Minister, Union Church, Montclair, New Jersey (asst.), 1926-30; Pilgrim Church, Pomona, California, 1930-35; Pilgrim Church, St.

Louis, Missouri, 1935-43; vice-president, Board of Home Mission, 1943-68. Died at New York, 27 May 1969.

DYKES, James Oswald (Presbyterian).
Born at Point Glasgow, near Greenock, Scotland, 14 August 1835. Edinburgh University and New College, Heidelberg, Erlangen. D.D. (Edin.). Ordained East Kilbride, 1859. Colleague of Dr. Candlish at Free St. George's, Edinburgh, 1861-64 (resigned through ill health). Without charge for a time in Melbourne, Australia. Regent Square, London, 1869-88; Principal and Barbour Professor of Divinity, Theological College of the Presbyterian Church in England, 1888-1907. Publications include various books on biblical and devotional themes; and *The Divine Worker in Creation and Providence* (1909). Died 1 January 1912.

FAIRBAIRN, Andrew Martin (Evangelical Union/Congregationalist).
Born at Inverkeithing, Fife, Scotland, 4 November 1838. Edinburgh University (did not take degree). D.D. (Edin., Yale, Wales); D.Litt. (Oxon); LL.D. (Aberdeen); Fellow of the British Academy, Evangelical Union Theological Hall, Glasgow, 1857-60. E.U. Bathgate, 1860-72; St. Paul's Congregational, Aberdeen, 1872-77. Principal, Airedale College, Bradford, 1877-86; first principal, Mansfield College, Oxford, 1886-1909. Chairman, Evangelical Union, 1870; Congregational Union of England and Wales, 1883. Publications include *Studies in the Philosophy of Religion and History* (1876); *The City of God* (1882); *The Philosophy of the Christian Religion* (1902); *Studies in Religion and Theology* (1910). Died 9 February 1912.

See *Dictionary of National Biography,* 1912-21; W. B. Selbie, *The Life of Andrew Martin Fairbairn.* London: Hodder & Stoughton, 1914; Robert S. Franks, "The Theology of Andrew Martin Fairbairn," *Transactions of the Congregational Historical Society* 12 (1937-39): 140-50; A. P. F. Sell, "An Englishman, an Irishman and a Scotsman . . ." (i.e., W. B. Pope, R. Watts, and A. M. Fairbairn), *Scottish Journal of Theology* 38 (1985): 41-83.

FORSYTH, Peter Taylor (Congregationalist).
Born at Old Machar, Aberdeenshire, Scotland, 12 May 1848. Aberdeen University, New College, Edinburgh, and Göttingen. D.D. (Aber.). Tutor to a lord's family, 1874-76. Minister, Shipley, 1876-79; St. Thomas's Square, Hackney, 1879-85; Cheetham Hill, Manchester, 1885-88; Clarendon Park, Leicester, 1888-94; Emmanuel, Cambridge, 1894-1901. Principal, Hackney College, London, 1901-21. Chairman, Congregational Union of England and Wales, 1905. Numerous publications include *The Person and Place of Jesus Christ* (1909); *The Work of*

Christ (1910); *Faith, Freedom and the Future* (1912); *The Principle of Authority* (1915); *The Justification of God* (1917); *The Church and the Sacraments* (1917). Died 11 November 1921.
    See Gwilym O. Griffith, *The Theology of P. T. Forsyth.* London: Independent Press, 1948; W. L. Bradley, *P. T. Forsyth, The Man and His Work.* London: Independent Press, 1952; John H. Rodgers, *The Theology of P. T. Forsyth.* London: Independent Press, 1965; A. M. Hunter, *P. T. Forsyth: Per crucem ad lucem.* London: SCM Press, 1974; Donald G. Miller et al., *P. T. Forsyth, The Man, The Preacher's Theologian, Prophet for the 20th Century.* Contains a bibliography of writings by and on P. T. Forsyth, together with a reprint of his *Positive Preaching and the Modern Mind.* Pittsburgh: The Pickwick Press, 1981.

GOODWIN, Edward Payson (Congregationalist).
Born at Rome, New York, 31 July 1832. Amherst College and Union Theological Seminary, New York. D.D. (Western Reserve University; Amherst). Home missionary pastor, East Burke, Vermont, 1859-61; First Congregational Church, Columbus, Ohio, 1861-67; First Church, Chicago, 1868-1900. Published numerous sermons, pamphlets, and addresses. Died 15 February 1901.

HODGE, Archibald Alexander (Presbyterian).
Born at Princeton, New Jersey, 18 July 1823 (son of Charles and Sarah, née Bache). College of New Jersey and Princeton Theological Seminary. D.D. (College of New Jersey); LL.D. (Wooster University). Missionary, Allahabad, India, 1847-50 (ill health caused his return). Minister, Lower West Nottingham, Maryland, 1851-55; Fredericksburg, Virginia, 1855-61; Wilkes-Barre, Pennsylvania, 1861-64. Professor of Theology, Western Theological Seminary, Allegheny, Pennsylvania, 1864-77 (and for eleven years pastor, North Church, Allegheny); Professor of Theology, Princeton Theological Seminary, 1877-86. Publications include *Outlines of Theology* (1860); *The Atonement* (1868); *Life of Charles Hodge* (1880). Died 11 November 1886.

HORTON, Douglas (Congregationalist).
Born at Brooklyn, New York, 27 July 1891. Hartford Seminary Foundation. Minister, Middletown, Connecticut, 1915-25; Leyden Church, Brookline, Massachusetts, 1925-31; United Church of Hyde Park, Chicago, 1931-38. Minister and secretary, General Council of Congregational Churches, 1931-38. Minister and secretary, National Council of Congregational Churches, 1938-55; Dean of Harvard University Divinity School, 1955-60. Died at Randolph, New Hampshire, 21 August 1968.

HROMADKA, Josef Luki (Czech Brethren).
Born at Hodslavice, Moravia, 8 June 1889. Professor at the Comenius
Faculty, Prague. Founder (1958) and president (1958-69) of the Chris-
tian Conference for Peace. Collaborated with Thomas Masyryk to found
the first Czechoslovak Republic. Supported the Spanish Republic. Lenin
Peace Prize, 1958. Died at Prague, 26 December 1969.
    See article by C. C. West in *Sons of the Prophets,* ed. H. T. Kerr.
Princeton: Princeton University Press, 1963.

KRAFFT, Wilhelm Ludwig (Reformed).
Born at Cologne, 8 September 1821. Universities of Bonn and Berlin.
D.D. (Bonn). Toured Europe and the Middle East; studied at Rome.
Privatdocent, Lutheran Theological Faculty, Bonn, 1846; extraordi-
nary professor, 1850; full professor, 1859. Lectured on the geography
of Palestine, and later on church history. Published *Die Topographie
Jerusalems* (1846); *Briefe und Dokumente aus der Zeit der Reformation* (1876);
Die Deutsche Bibel vor Luther (1883). Died at Bonn, 11 March 1898.

McCOSH, James (Presbyterian).
Born at Carskeoch Farm, Ayr, Scotland, 1 April 1811. Universities of
Glasgow and Edinburgh. D.D. (Edin.); LL.D. (Dublin and Harvard);
D.Litt. (Queen's University, Ireland). Minister, Abbey Church, Arbroath,
1835-38; Brechin, 1838-43 (Church of Scotland) and 1843-52 (Free
Church of Scotland). Professor of Logic and Metaphysics, Queen's Col-
lege, Belfast, 1852-68; president of Princeton College, U.S.A., 1868-88. A
founder of the Presbyterian Alliance and of the Evangelical Alliance. His
numerous publications include *The Supernatural in Relation to the Natural*
(1862) and *Christianity and Positivism* (1875). Died 16 November 1894.
    See J. David Hoeveler, Jr., *James McCosh and the Scottish Intellectual
Tradition,* Princeton: Princeton University Press, 1981; id., "Evangelical
Ecumenism: James McCosh and the Intellectual Origins of the World
Alliance of Reformed Churches," *Journal of Presbyterian History* 55
(Spring 1977): 36-56.

MACKINTOSH, Robert (Congregationalist).
Born at Dunoon, Scotland, 23 May 1858. Glasgow University, 1872-77
(M.A., D.D.); New College, Edinburgh, 1877-81. Minister, Dumfries,
1890-94. Professor, Lancashire Independent College, Manchester, 1894-
1930. Publications include *Essays Towards a New Theology* (1889); *Hegel
and Hegelianism* (1903); *Christianity and Sin* (1913); *Albrecht Ritschl and His
School* (1915); *Historic Theories of Atonement* (1920). Died 12 February
1933.
    See A. P. F. Sell, *Robert Mackintosh: Theologian of Integrity.* Bern: Peter
Lang, 1977.

SCHAFF, Philip (German Reformed/Presbyterian).
Born at Chur, Switzerland, 1 January 1819. Tübingen, Halle, and Berlin Universities, 1837-40. Travels in Italy and Sicily while tutor to Baron Kröcher. Privatdocent at Berlin, 1841-43. Professor at the German Reformed Seminary, Mercersburg, Pennsylvania, 1843-63. Secretary of the Sabbath Committee, New York City, 1863-70. Professor of Theological Encyclopaedia and Christian Symbolism (1870-73), of Hebrew and Cognate Languages (till 1874), of Sacred Literature (till 1887), and of Church History (till 1893) at Union Theological Seminary, New York. Schaff selected the American scholars who participated in the translation of the Revised Version of the Bible. He founded the American Society of Church History (1888), and edited the series of *Nicene and Post-Nicene Fathers* (28 vols.), and the first edition of the *Encyclopaedia* which bears his name. His numerous publications include *The Creeds of Christendom*, 3 vols. (1877) and *A Companion to the Greek Testament and the English Version* (1883). Died at New York, 20 October 1893.
See D. S. Schaff, *The Life of Philip Schaff*. New York, 1897; George H. Shriver, *Philip Schaff, Christian Scholar and Ecumenical Prophet*. Macon, Ga.: Mercer University Press, 1987.

STAFFORD, Russell Henry (Congregationalist).
Born at Milwaukee, Wisconsin, 1890. Drew Theological Seminary. Assistant, Central Congregational Church, Brooklyn, New York, 1912-15. Ordained 1914. Minister, Open Door Church, Minneapolis, Minnesota, 1915-18; chaplain, U.S. Army, 1918; minister, First Congregational Church, Minneapolis, 1919-23; Pilgrim Church, St. Louis, Missouri, 1923-27; Old South Church, Boston, Massachusetts, 1927-45. President, Hartford Theological Seminary, 1945-58. Died at Hartford, Connecticut, 31 July 1971.

WATTS, Robert (Presbyterian).
Born at Moneylane, Dundrum, N. Ireland, 10 July 1820. Lafayette College, Pennsylvania, and Washington College, Virginia. LL.D. (Washington and Lee College). Princeton Theological Seminary, 1849-52. Minister, Philadelphia, 1853-63; Gloucester Street Church, Dublin, 1863-66. Professor of Theology at The Assembly's College, Belfast, 1866-95. Moderator of the General Assembly of the Presbyterian Church in Ireland, 1879-80. Publications include *The New Apologetic, or the Downgrade in Criticism* (1879); *The Newer Criticism and the Analogy of Faith* (1881); *The Rule of Faith and the Doctrine of Inspiration* (1885). Died 26 July 1895.
See A. P. F. Sell, article under "Fairbairn" above; *Dictionary of National Biography*.

Appendix III

Bibliography

The following is a list of the more theological works published under the auspices of, or in association with, the World Presbyterian Alliance, the International Congregational Council, and the World Alliance of Reformed Churches.

A. Serials

Proceedings of the Councils of the WPA, the ICC, and the WARC for the
  dates given in Appendix I above.
The Catholic Presbyterian, 1879-83.
The Quarterly Register, 1886-1936.
The Presbyterian Register, 1937-48.
The Presbyterian World, 1949-55.
The Reformed and Presbyterian World, 1956-70.
The Reformed World, 1971- .
World Congregationalism, 1959-65.
Congregational Studies, 1965-70 (occasional).
The Bulletin of the Department of Theology, 1960-84. (From 1960 the quarterly
  Bulletin had appeared only in French and German. From 1984 theolog-
  ical articles were reprinted as translations eleven times per year in
  French, German, and Spanish in a new magazine, *Reformed Perspectives.*)

B. Studies from the World Alliance of Reformed Churches

1. *Called to Witness to the Gospel Today,* 1983.
2. *Confessions and Confessing in the Reformed Tradition Today,* 1983.
3. *Responding to "Baptism, Eucharist and Ministry": A Word to the Reformed
   Churches.* Ed. Alan P. F. Sell, 1984.
4. *Baptists and Reformed in Dialogue,* 1984.

5. *Testimonies of Faith* (Taiwan). Ed. Choan-Seng Song, 1984.
6. *Reformed and Disciples of Christ in Dialogue.* Ed. Alan P. F. Sell, 1985.
7. *Mennonites and Reformed in Dialogue.* Ed. Hans Georg vom Berg, Henk Kossen, Larry Miller, and Lukas Vischer, 1986.
8. *Reformed Theology and the Jewish People.* Ed. Alan P. F. Sell, 1986.
9. *Against Torture.* Ed. Jill Schaeffer and Adrienne Reber, 1987 (French edn. 1986).

C. Dialogue Reports (and see also Studies from the World Alliance of Reformed Churches, nos. 4, 6, and 7 above)

(a) International

Theology of Marriage and the Problem of Mixed Marriages: Dialogue between the Lutheran World Federation, the World Alliance of Reformed Churches and the Secretariat for Promoting Christian Unity of the Roman Catholic Church, 1971-77. Geneva: Lutheran World Federation; Geneva: World Alliance of Reformed Churches; Vatican City: Secretariat for Promoting Christian Unity, 1977.
The Presence of Christ in Church and World. Dialogue between the World Alliance of Reformed Churches and the Secretariat for Promoting Christian Unity, 1970-77. Vatican City: Secretariat for Promoting Christian Unity; Geneva: World Alliance of Reformed Churches, 1977.
God's Reign and Our Unity: The Report of the Anglican-Reformed International Commission, 1981-1984. London: SPCK; Edinburgh: The Saint Andrew Press, 1984.
Theological Dialogue between Orthodox and Reformed Churches. Ed. T. F. Torrance. Edinburgh: Scottish Academic Press, 1985.
(For more recent titles, see n. 2 of Conclusion.)

(b) Regional (in which the Alliance's regional bodies have formally been involved)

Reconsiderations. Roman Catholic/Presbyterian and Reformed Theological Conversations, 1966-67. New York: World Horizons, 1967.
The New Man. An Orthodox and Reformed Dialogue. Ed. John Meyendorff and Joseph McLelland. New Brunswick, N.J.: Standard Press, 1973.
The Unity We Seek. A Statement by the Roman Catholic/Presbyterian-Reformed Consultation. Ed. Ernest L. Unterkoefler and Andrew Harsanyi. New York: Paulist Press, 1977.
An Invitation to Action. The Lutheran-Reformed Dialogue Series III. Ed. James E. Andrews and Joseph A. Burgess. Philadelphia: Fortress Press, 1984. This work includes *Marburg Revisited* (1966), which is Series I (1962-1966) of the American Lutheran–Reformed dialogue;

The Report of Series II (1972-1974); and the European Leuenberg Agreement (1973).

D. Miscellaneous Books and Pamphlets (Note: Pamphlets preparatory to general and other councils whose content has been reproduced in *The Reformed World* and its forebears are not listed here.)

Albert Peel, *The Noble Army of Congregational Martyrs*. London: Independent Press, 1948.

Albert Peel and Douglas Horton, *International Congregationalism*. London: Independent Press, 1949.

Ralph Calder, *To Introduce the Family*. London: Independent Press, 1953.

Ralph Calder, ed., *A Review of World Congregationalism 1953-1957*, 1957.

Norman Goodall, *Congregationalism Plus*. London: Independent Press, 1953.

Lewis S. Mudge, *One Church: Catholic and Reformed*. London: Lutterworth Press, 1963.

The Creator Spirit in Secular Society. Reports of Task Forces, North American Area Council of the World Alliance of Reformed and Presbyterian Churches. Philadelphia: General Assembly Office of the United Presbyterian Church, U.S.A., 1966.

Reconciliation in Today's World. Ed. Allen O. Miller. Grand Rapids: Eerdmans, 1969.

Robert W. Henderson, *A Profile of the Eldership*. Geneva: World Alliance of Reformed Churches, 1974.

Marcel Pradervand, *A Century of Service: A History of the World Alliance of Reformed Churches, 1875-1975*. Edinburgh: Saint Andrew Press, 1975.

Theological Basis of Human Rights. Geneva: World Alliance of Reformed Churches and Lutheran World Federation, 1976.

A Christian Declaration on Human Rights. Ed. Allen O. Miller. Grand Rapids: Eerdmans, 1977.

Living in Covenant Fellowship. Reports from the European Area Council. Geneva: World Alliance of Reformed Churches, 1980.

A Covenant Challenge to Our Broken World. Ed. Allen O. Miller. Study by the Caribbean and North American Area Council. Geneva: World Alliance of Reformed Churches, 1982.

Alan P. F. Sell, *Saints: Visible, Orderly and Catholic: The Congregational Idea of the Church*. Geneva: World Alliance of Reformed Churches; Allison Park, Pa.: Pickwick Publications, 1986.

Have No Fear, Little Flock. Budapest: Reformed Church in Hungary, 1987.

Peace, War and God's Justice. Ed. Thomas D. Parker and Brian J. Fraser. Toronto: The United Church Publishing House, 1989. (See also n. 2 of Conclusion.)

Notes

Abbreviations

B: *Bulletin of the Department of Theology,* World Alliance of Reformed Churches (1960-1984)

C: *Proceedings* of the International Congregational Council (ten volumes, 1891-1966)

CP: *The Catholic Presbyterian* (1879-1883)

P: *Proceedings* of the Councils of the Presbyterian Alliance (nineteen volumes, 1877-1964; and see WARC below)

PR: *The Presbyterian Register* (1937-1948)

PW: *The Presbyterian World* (1949-1955)

QR: *The Quarterly Register* (1886-1936)

RPW: *The Reformed and Presbyterian World* (1956-1970)

RW: *Reformed World* (1971-)

WARC: *Proceedings* of the Councils of the Alliance from the Uniting General Council of 1970 (i.e., from volume 20 of the series under P above)

WC: *World Congregationalism* (1959-1965)

1. Introduction: The Reformed Alliance and Its Theological Work

1. For the development and ethos of the Reformed tradition see John H. Leith, *Introduction to the Reformed Tradition,* rev. ed. (Atlanta: John Knox Press, 1981).

2. P 7, 1899, app. 15.

3. P 17, 1954, final (unnumbered) page.

4. Figure computed from Albert Peel and Douglas Horton, *International Congregationalism* (London: Independent Press, 1949), pp. 65-89.

5. See M. Pradervand, *A Century of Service: A History of the World Alliance of Reformed Churches, 1875-1975* (Edinburgh: The Saint Andrew Press, 1975). In chapter 12 the origins of the Congregational Council are sketched. For the origins see also William G. Blaikie's "Introductory Narrative," P 1, 1877, pp. 1-13.

6. See Peel and Horton, *International Congregationalism.* For the origins see

also Alexander Mackennal's "Preface" to C 1, 1891, pp. xxiii-xxv, and A. W. W. Dale, *The Life of R. W. Dale of Birmingham* (London: Hodder & Stoughton, 1899), chap. 23.

7. See John Waddington, *Surrey Congregational History* (1866), pp. 124-25, 314; Edward E. Cleal, *The Story of Congregationalism in Surrey* (1908), p. 212.

8. See Albert Peel, *These Hundred Years: A History of the Congregational Union of England and Wales, 1831-1931* (London: CUEW, 1931).

9. *The Presbyterian* (Edinburgh), May 1868, quoted in P 1, 1877, p. 2, and by Pradervand, *A Century of Service*, p. 13. For MacGregor (1830-1894) see Hugh Watt, *New College Edinburgh: A Centenary History* (Edinburgh: Oliver & Boyd, 1946), p. 229.

10. For McCosh and Schaff see Appendix II.

11. With a view to planned missionary effort on the American frontier the Presbyterian Church had entered into a Plan of Union with the Congregationalists in 1801. The plan met with considerable success, but an increasing number of Presbyterians came to feel that the federated churches could not be adequately controlled by church courts; that the Presbyterian Church should have its own church boards and not work through cooperative ventures; and that action should be taken against doctrinal "impurities" which were being absorbed from Samuel Hopkins (1721-1803) and Nathaniel W. Taylor (1786-1858).

In 1834 the Presbyterian General Assembly expelled the Synods of Western Reserve, Utica, Geneva, and Genesee. Many were affronted by this action, left the church, and joined those expelled to form the Presbyterian Church, U.S.A., New School. The term "Old School" came to be applied to the expelling party. See Lefferts A. Loetscher, *A Brief History of the Presbyterians* (Philadelphia: Westminster Press, 1958), ch. 10; Gaius Glenn Atkins and Frederick L. Fagley, *History of American Congregationalism* (Boston: The Pilgrim Press, 1942), chap. 10.

12. P 1, 1877, p. 3. For Blaikie see Appendix II.

13. Ibid.

14. Ibid.

15. From the point of view of our study, it is interesting to note the strongly philosophical motive which underlay McCosh's advocacy of the council. He was a product of the Scottish common sense school of philosophy, whose founder was Thomas Reid (1710-1796). Against Hume and others Reid urged that the phenomena of the world have a reality independent of the experiencing mind— hence the label "intuitional realism" which has been applied to his thought. Reid's views were transmitted by Dugald Stewart and modified by McCosh's teacher, Sir William Hamilton. It fell to McCosh to attempt to steer a course between British empiricism (epitomized in his day by J. S. Mill) and materialism on the one hand, and German post-Kantian agnosticism and post-Hegelian idealism on the other. He was especially distressed by the "pantheism" to which he was sure Hegelianism led, and he lamented the fact that this brand of philosophy was taking root in his homeland, notably through the influence of John and Edward Caird. When theology was thus influenced, the result was a weak doctrine of sin, and, consequently, of the atonement. See further the works by J. David Hoeveler, Jr., listed under "McCosh," Appendix II.

16. World Alliance of Reformed Churches Archives, WPA-HA 1.

17. See Peel, *These Hundred Years,* p. 106.

18. For Dale see Appendix II.

19. For the memorial tribute to Dexter and Hannay see C 1, 1891, pp. 335-36.

20. P 6, 1896, pp. 227-28.

21. For a fuller discussion of the points just made see A. P. F. Sell, *Theology in Turmoil: The Roots, Course and Significance of the Conservative-Liberal Debate in Modern Theology* (Grand Rapids: Baker Book House, 1986).

22. C 4, 1920, p. 350. But some Congregational covenants were heavily doctrinal!

23. P 11, 1921, p. 93.

24. C 5, 1930, p. 162.

25. For Curtis see Appendix II.

26. P 15, 1937, p. 112.

27. Ibid., pp. 252-54.

28. Many of Forsyth's books were reprinted between 1946 and 1964. His *Positive Preaching and the Modern Mind* (1907) was reprinted five times during that period. For Forsyth see Appendix II.

29. P 17, 1954, p. 75.

30. C 8, 1958, p. 21.

31. WARC Archives: correspondence with the International Congregational Council.

32. *Minutes,* World Presbyterian Alliance executive committee, 1956, App. II, p. 4.

33. For the reflections of the first theological secretary on his period in office see Lewis S. Mudge, "The Theological Work of the Alliance: 1957-1962," *Journal of Presbyterian History* 55 (Spring 1977): 101-6.

34. P 19, 1964, p. 224. This was reaffirmed by the executive committee at its meeting in Strasburg, 1966. See *Minutes,* p. 14.

35. Pradervand, *A Century of Service,* p. 286.

36. Though more modest than a council the consultation is nevertheless numbered 21 in the sequence from 1877. The papers presented are in RW 34, 1976-77.

37. WARC 21, 1982, p. 178.

38. RW 33, no. 7, Sept. 1975, p. 320.

39. However, in December 1985 the first of a series of international dialogue meetings between the Alliance and the Lutheran World Federation was held. The intention was to review the present Lutheran-Reformed situation in the light of regional developments between the two communions over the previous ten years.

40. The report of the first dialogue session was published under the title *Marburg Revisited: A Reexamination of Lutheran and Reformed Traditions,* ed. Paul C. Empie and James I. McCord (Minneapolis: Augsburg Publishing House, 1966). This report, together with the reports of the second and third sessions, together also with the European Leuenberg Agreement, may be found in *An Invitation to Action, The Lutheran-Reformed Dialogue Series III,* ed. James E. Andrews and Joseph A. Burgess (Philadelphia: Fortress Press, 1984).

41. See Thomas F. Torrance, ed., *Theological Dialogue between Orthodox and Reformed Churches* (Edinburgh: Scottish Academic Press, 1985).

42. The reports, respectively, are *The Presence of Christ in Church and World* (Vatican City: Secretariat for Promoting Christian Unity; Geneva: World Alliance of Reformed Churches, 1977); *Baptists and Reformed in Dialogue,* Studies from the World Alliance of Reformed Churches, no. 4 (Geneva: WARC, 1984); *God's Reign and Our Unity* (London: SPCK; Edinburgh: The Saint Andrew Press, 1984).

43. Since 1982 consultations have been held with the Mennonite World Conference, the World Methodist Council, the Disciples' Ecumenical Consultative Council, and the Orthodox churches. A second phase of dialogue with the Roman Catholic church began in 1984.

44. The Cumberland Presbyterian Church's application for membership was declined on the ground of insufficient "evidence that the Cumberland Church now accept the doctrinal basis of the Alliance" (P 2, 1880, p. 24). Article 2 of the constitution restricted membership to churches "whose creed is in harmony with the Consensus of the Reformed confessions." However, that consensus had not at that time been determined. In the event the Cumberland Church was received into membership at the third Presbyterian Council (P 3, 1884, p. 161), and no further attempts were made to apply doctrinal tests to aspiring members. See Hubert W. Morrow, "Admission of the Cumberland Presbyterian Church to the World Alliance of Reformed Churches," *Journal of Presbyterian History* 55 (Spring 1977): 58-73.

45. Classical Reformed Confessions include the following: Zwingli's Sixty-Seven Articles (1523); the Ten Theses of Berne (1528), the First Basel Confession (1534); the First Helvetic Confession (1536); the Geneva Confession (1536); the French Confession (1559); the Scottish Confession (1560); the Belgic Confession (1561); the Second Helvetic Confession (1566); the Westminster Confesssion (1647).

Prominent larger catechisms include Calvin's (1541); the Heidelberg (1563); Craig's (1581); the New (1644); and the Larger (1648). Among shorter catechisms are the Little (1556); Craig's (1592); A Catechism for Young Children (1641); the Shorter (1648).

Congregational declarations and statements of faith include the following: Browne's Statement of Congregational Principles (1582); the First Confession (1589) and the Second Confession (1596) of the London-Amsterdam Church; the Cambridge Synod and the Platform (1646-48); the Savoy Declaration of Faith and Order (1658); the English Congregational Union Declaration (1833); the "Burial Hill" Declaration (1865); the Constitution of the National Council and the Oberlin Declaration (1871); the "Commission" Creed (1883); the Declaration of Faith of the Congregational Church in England and Wales (1967). This last is included among a number of confessions of the past thirty years in *Reformed Witness Today: A Collection of Confessions and Statements of Faith Issued by Reformed Churches.* ed. Lukas Vischer (Bern: Evangelische Arbeitsstelle Oekumene Schweiz, 1982).

While neither Presbyterians nor Congregationalists have been reluctant to declare the faith commonly held among them, the former have normally required confessional subscription of at least ministers and elders; the latter have not. Moreover, Congregationalists have in their local church covenants experienced corporate confessing at its most intimate.

46. For an account of the successive journals see Edmond Perret, "Signposts for a Centennial," RW 35, no. 5, 1979, pp. 195-99. The journals were *The Catholic Presbyterian* (1879-83); *The Quarterly Register* (1886-1936); *The Presbyterian Register* (1937-48); *The Presbyterian World* (1949-55); *The Reformed and Presbyterian World* (1956-70); *Reformed World* (1971-).

47. Peel and Horton, *International Congregationalism*, p. 23.

48. Pradervand, *A Century of Service*, p. 190.

2. The Faith of the Ages

1. P 1, 1877, pp. 42, 43.

2. Ibid., p. 44.

3. C 2, 1899, pp. 45-50.

4. Cf. A. P. F. Sell, *Theology in Turmoil* (Grand Rapids: Baker Book House, 1986), chap. 3.

5. WARC 20, 1970, p. 211 (RW 31, 1970-71, pp. 118-22).

6. Ibid., p. 212. Cf. J. Moltmann, "The Future of Creation: Creation as an Open System," in *A Covenant Challenge to Our Broken World*, ed. Allen O. Miller (a study by the Committee of Theology of the Caribbean and North American Area Council of the Alliance) (Geneva: WARC, 1982), pp. 178-79. Moltmann's paper is a chapter from his book, *The Future of Creation* (Philadelphia: Fortress Press, 1979).

7. John H. Reisner, "Reconciliation and Creation," in *Reconciliation in Today's World*, ed. Allen O. Miller (papers prepared for the North American Area Theological Committee of the Presbyterian Alliance) (Grand Rapids: Eerdmans, 1969), p. 81.

8. RW 31, 1970-71, p. 53.

9. RW 34, 1976-77, pp. 311-12.

10. P 1, 1877, p. 44.

11. RW 34, 1976-77, p. 315; for a biblical-theological exposition of man as steward of the created order see Peter Pokorny's Bible studies on the theme of the Alliance's Ottawa Council of 1982: *Thine Is the Kingdom, the Power, and the Glory*, RW 36, 1981, pp. 245-74.

12. P 12, 1925, p. 253.

13. Ibid., p. 254.

14. Ibid., p. 257.

15. Ibid.

16. Ibid., p. 259, quoting the Scottish metrical version of Psalm 104:31.

17. Ibid., p. 260.

18. P 15, 1937, p. 32.

19. P 13, 1929, pp. 34-35.

20. C 3, 1908, pp. 28-29.

21. Hence the theme of the Ottawa Council; see n. 11 above, and WARC 21, 1982, *passim*, and RW 37, Sept.-Dec. 1982, *passim*.

22. In a paper, "The Church—God's Glory in His People," presented at the St. Andrews Centennial Consultation, 1977; see RW 34, 1976-77, p. 309.

23. P 1, 1877, p. 45.

24. Sixty-seven Articles of 1523, 3. Other concurring authorities to which Krafft refers include the First Helvetic Confession (1536), 11; the French Confession of Faith (1559), 18; the Belgic Confession of Faith (1561), art. 21; and the Second Helvetic Confession (1566), chap. 11. The assertion of "no other way" is present by implication only in *Reformed Witness Today*, ed. Lukas Vischer (Bern: Evangelische Arbeitsstelle Oekumene Schweiz, 1982).

25. With reference to the comparative study of religion, Eric J. Sharpe has said that Friedrich Max Müller's *Introduction to the Science of Religion* (1873) "might well be called the foundation document of the discipline." See his "Comparative Religion at the University of Manchester, 1904-1979," in *Seventy-fifth Anniversary Papers 1979*, ed. David A. Pailin (Manchester: Victoria University Faculty of Theology, 1980), p. 26.

26. P 2, 1880, p. 357.

27. Ibid., p. 361.

28. P 2, 1880, p. 366.

29. Ibid., pp. 366-69.

30. C 3, 1908, p. 30. Revised and reprinted in *The Cruciality of the Cross* (1909) (London: Independent Press, 1949), chaps. 1 and 2.

31. C 3, 1908, p. 30.

32. Ibid., p. 37.

33. Ibid., pp. 45-46. In *The Cruciality of the Cross*, p. 39, the word "on" is used as here suggested.

34. C 3, 1908, p. 52n.

35. Ibid.

36. WARC 20, 1970, pp. 63-76. The theme of the church as a reconciled and a reconciling community also appears in Choan-Seng Song, "Reconciliation and the Church: The Freedom of Christian Witness," RPW 31, 1970-71, pp. 65-70.

37. Allen O. Miller, Introduction to *Reconciliation in Today's World*, p. 7.

38. Donald G. Miller, "God Reconciles and Makes Free," in *Reconciliation in Today's World*, p. 21.

39. P. T. Forsyth, C 3, 1908, p. 34.

40. Ibid., p. 33. That not all Reformed theologians of an earlier generation were happy with this emphasis is clear from the address of Professor Godet at the first Presbyterian Council (1877). He regretted that "this supreme point of the gospel, the eternal divinity of Christ, has not been *especially* marked in the confessions of faith of the sixteenth century," and he felt that against Protestant rationalism the doctrine of the incarnation should be emphasized: "Esteemed brothers, shall we abandon to the Church of the Pope the honour of upholding in the face of Protestant unbelief the two pillars of gospel salvation, the incarnation and the expiation?" (P 1, 1877, p. 40). Forsyth was by no means *anti*-incarnation, but he was decidedly pro-atonement and against "the Christ idea" which would remove Christ from the plane of history and reduce atonement to spiritual influence (cf. W. Radcliffe, P 10, 1913, p. 90). Nor would Forsyth have disagreed with Thomas G. Apple that "What [Christ] has done for fallen man receives its true value from what he is" (P 2, 1880, p. 492).

41. P 1, 1877, 45.

42. See, e.g., James Orr's review of the matter in *The Virgin Birth of Christ* (London: Hodder & Stoughton, 1907). For Orr see A. P. F. Sell, *Defending and*

Declaring the Faith: Some Scottish Examples, 1860-1920 (Exeter: Paternoster Press; Colorado Springs: Helmers & Howard, 1987), chap. 7. At the ninth Presbyterian Council (1909) Louis M. Sweet came down in favor of belief in the virgin birth as an actual event to which the biblical testimony is entirely accurate. See P 9, 1909, pp. 199-202. In the following paper (pp. 202-10) William P. Armstrong similarly sought to rehabilitate the resurrection of Jesus as an actual historical event: "The Resurrection of Jesus stands with His death in the centre of the Gospel of salvation by grace" (p. 209).

43. P. T. Forsyth, C 3, 1908, p. 47.

44. P 1, 1877, p. 29.

45. See *Called to Witness to the Gospel Today*, Studies from the World Alliance of Reformed Churches, no. 1 (Geneva: WARC, 1983), p. 7; P 2, 1880, p. 492.

46. C 2, 1899, p. 464.

47. Ibid., p. 465.

48. Ibid., p. 467.

49. See P 18, 1959, on the theme "The Servant Lord and His Servant People."

50. P 10, 1913, p. 91.

51. Ibid., p. 93. We recall James Denney's dry remark: "Arianism and Athanasianism both give answers to a question which multitudes of genuine Christians never ask. . . . The question which Jesus asks . . . is Who say ye that I am? not, How think ye that I came to be?" See his *Jesus and the Gospel* (London: Hodder & Stoughton, 1909), pp. 403, 405.

52. RPW 32, 1972-73, p. 300.

53. P 19, 1964, p. 99.

54. P 1, 1877, p. 44.

55. Ibid., p. 29. See further, A. P. F. Sell, "Augustine versus Pelagius: A Cautionary Tale of Perennial Importance," *Calvin Theological Journal* 12 (1977): 117-43.

56. P 1, 1877, p. 56.

57. P 13, 1929, pp. 33-34.

58. P 19, 1964, p. 150.

59. C 3, 1908, pp. 34-35.

60. Donald G. Miller, "God Reconciles and Makes Free," in *Reconciliation in Today's World*, p. 24. Martin H. Cressey writes interestingly on "Changing Understandings of Man and Their Bearing on Theology," RW 33, 1974-75, pp. 291-99. This is an edited version of a paper prepared for the Baptist/Reformed dialogue (1973-77), for which see chap. 4.

61. P 1, 1877, p. 45.

62. Ibid., p. 46.

63. Ibid.

64. Ibid., p. 47. This working is further specified in relation to baptism and the Lord's Supper in articles 28 and 29.

65. RW 27, Sept. 1963, p. 301.

66. C 3, 1908, p. 238.

67. Ibid., p. 239.

68. Ibid.

69. Ibid.

70. Ibid.

71. Ibid., pp. 240-41.

72. Ibid., p. 245.

73. Ibid.

74. P. T. Forsyth, *The Work of Christ* (1910) (London: Independent Press, 1938), p. 15.

75. P 2, 1880, p. 546.

76. Ibid., p. 548.

77. Ibid.,.p. 551.

78. Ibid., p. 552.

79. Ibid., p. 553. Bomberger taught at Ursinus College, Pennsylvania. See Appendix II.

80. Though in an important article on "The Holy Spirit and the Sanctification of Christians" Jacques de Senarclens preserved the needed emphasis. See RPW 28, June 1964, p. 61.

81. P 19, 1964, p. 108.

82. P 5, 1892, pp. 1-12, and P 10, 1913, pp. 272-77, respectively.

83. J. Tibbe, P 19, 1964, pp. 204-5.

84. C 3, 1908, p. 32.

85. P 19, 1964, p. 96.

86. Ibid., pp. 140-42.

87. Ibid., p. 166.

88. Ibid., p. 125.

89. Ibid., p. 158.

90. Ibid.

91. P. T. Forsyth, *The Church and the Sacraments* (1917) (London: Independent Press, 1947), p. 83.

92. P 19, 1964, p. 163.

93. Ibid., p. 168.

94. Ibid., p. 171.

95. Joseph McLelland, P 19, 1964, p. 195.

96. WARC 20, 1970, p. 180.

97. Ibid., pp. 180-81.

98. P 19, 1964, p. 208.

99. WARC 20, 1970, p. 182.

100. Mudge, *One Church: Catholic and Reformed* (London: Lutterworth Press, 1963), p. 73. It is perhaps surprising, in view of rapid church growth in many parts of the world, that so little appears in the Alliance literature of the past twenty years on the charismatic phenomenon. The most substantial contribution in this field is that of William Klempa, "Ecstacy and the Experience of the Holy Spirit," RPW 32, 1972-73, pp. 110-21. From this we learn that Klempa, with good reason, prefers the *Holy* Spirit to the *happy* spirit. He does not, however, address the objection lodged by one prominent strand within the Reformed tradition, namely, that the message of the apostles having been authenticated, the charismata gradually disappeared from the church. See B. B. Warfield, *Counterfeit Miracles* (1918) (London: The Banner of Truth Trust, 1972).

101. CP 31, 1881, pp. 1-9.

102. Ibid., p. 9.

103. P 1, 1877, p. 48.
104. P 17, 1954, p. 158.
105. Ibid., p. 167.
106. C 4, 1920, p. 426.
107. Ibid., p. 427.
108. C 1, 1891, pp. 319-20.
109. P 17, 1954, pp. 140-41.
110. Ibid., p. 143. In the chapter cited in n. 6 above J. Moltmann views creation from an eschatological perspective.
111. C 4, 1920, p. 424.
112. QR 11, Nov. 1919, p. 219.
113. P 1, 1877, p. 43.
114. R. W. Dale, C 1, 1891, p. 35.
115. Paul Jacobs, RPW 27, June 1962, pp. 63-64.
116. T. F. Torrance, P 19, 1964, p. 156.

3. The Evangelical-Catholic Heritage

1. See Jan Milič Lochman, "Not Just One Reformation: The Waldensian and Hussite Heritage," RW 33, 1974-75, pp. 218-24; Amadeo Molnár, "Chanforan 1532," RW 37, 1983, pp. 189-95. From time to time both the Presbyterians and the Congregationalists took stock of the Reformation as an event. This entailed emphasis on the Reformation as a recovery of the gospel which had been obscured by Rome. In earlier days it incorporated condemnations of Roman practices, together with discussions of the Calvin-Servetus episode. Since our interest here is more theological and doctrinal we shall not review the strictly historical surveys. We should, however, note that in the context of current dialogue with the Roman Catholic church the question of the way in which both sides now view the Reformation is prominent.

2. See Stephen Mayor, "Congregationalism and the Reformed Tradition," RW 33, 1974-75, pp. 196-208. Dr. Mayor goes too far in stating that "even in the classical Congregationalism of the seventeenth century there was little sense of the wholeness and authority of the Church Catholic" (p. 202). The local church was the Church Catholic to the Congregationalist. Moreover, as William Bartlet said, "A universall visible Church militant on earth, is not denied. . . ." See Ἰχνογραφια, or a Model of the Primitive Congregational Way (ca. 1658), p. 51. See further, Alan P. F. Sell, *Saints: Visible, Orderly and Catholic: The Congregational Idea of the Church* (Geneva: World Alliance of Reformed Churches; Allison Park, Pa.: Pickwick Publications, 1986).

3. P. T. Forsyth, *Faith, Freedom and the Future* (1912) (London: Independent Press, 1955), pp. 336, 347.

4. C 1, 1891, p. 62.

5. Ibid., pp. 62-63.

6. Goodwin here overstates his case. Notably, chap. 20 of Savoy contains four sections "Of the Gospel, and of the extent of the Grace thereof" which are absent from Westminster, and chap. 15, "Of repentance unto life *and salvation*," is

rewritten and rearranged. We should be warned that Goodwin selectively refers only to the Congregational fathers of the Calvinistic sort, thereby excluding, for example, his namesake John Goodwin (1594-1665) the Arminian.

7. C 1, 1891, p. 64.

8. Goodwin mangles the Robinson quotation which is here given accurately. On the main point he is correct, and has H. M. Dexter behind him. See the latter's *Congregationalism of the Last Three Hundred Years as Seen in Its Literature* (New York: Harper, [1879]), pp. 402-10.

9. C 1, 1891, p. 65.

10. Ibid., p. 66.

11. Ibid., p. 68.

12. Ibid., p. 69.

13. For a paper on "The Influence of the Protestant Reformation on the Civil and Political Institutions of Communities and Nations" by Henry M. Baird, see P 5, 1892, pp. 60-68. In his address to the first Presbyterian Council (1877), Philip Schaff reminded his hearers that "in the age of the Reformation the Anabaptists and Socinians were the only Christians who advocated toleration from principle. The burning of Servetus for heresy and blasphemy is the one dark stain on the fair fame of the great and good Calvin, but it was justified even by the gentle Melanchthon," P 1, 1877, pp. 35-36. On the other hand General R. E. Prime, speaking at the ninth Presbyterian Council (1909) on "Calvin and Servetus" was, according to one's viewpoint, either more generous to, or more whitewashing of, Calvin. See P 9, 1909, pp. 131-36.

14. C 1, 1891, p. 74.

15. Ibid., p. 76.

16. Ibid., pp. xxx-xxxi. The question of how far their councils and the like are genuinely representative of their constituencies continues to haunt the Alliance and similar bodies, and we shall return to it in chap. 7. An ecumenical mainstream can, paradoxically, be somewhat parochial.

17. P 5, 1892, pp. 41-42.

18. Ibid., p. 43.

19. Ibid., p. 44.

20. Ibid., p. 46.

21. Ibid., p. 52.

22. Ibid., p. 54.

23. P 1, 1877, p. 43. Among numerous other addresses on the Bible see James Kidd, P 6, 1896, pp. 308-14; A. C. Zenos, ibid., pp. 314-19; and a series of speeches in P 8, 1904, pp. 38-85.

24. P 1, 1877, p. 75.

25. Ibid., p. 33. Schaff found his position to be consistent with that of the Reformed confessions, which do not propose a theory of inspiration. He noted that the Helvetic Consensus Formula, according to which even the Hebrew vowel points are inspired, never commanded general assent (p. 34). At the same council Alexander Mitchell presented "The Harmony between the Bibliology of the Westminster Confession and That of the Earlier Reformed Confessions" (ibid., pp. 48, 371-77).

26. P 2, 1880, p. 494.

27. For the papers and discussion see P 2, 1880, pp. 104-26.

28. P 7, 1899, p. 14. Though as early as the third Presbyterian Council (1884) Talbot W. Chambers and Lucien Gautier had spoken favorably of modern critical methods in papers under the title, "Biblical Criticism: Its Proper Function" (P 3, 1884, pp. 67-81). See further A. P. F. Sell, *Theology in Turmoil* (Grand Rapids: Baker Book House, 1986), chap. 2.

29. C 3, 1908, p. 352.

30. P 12, 1925, p. 244.

31. Ibid., pp. 248, 245.

32. P 3, 1884, p. 60.

33. P 10, 1913, p. 48.

34. P 15, 1937, p. 220.

35. See C 9, 1962, pp. 43-53. For the use of a similar position to devotional ends see the series by Max Dominicé delivered at the seventeenth Presbyterian Council (1954): PW 23, 1955, pp. 6-14, 59-67, 105-13, 153-60.

36. C 9, 1962, p. 44. Though he does later point out that while the exclusiveness of Christianity's claim is of God's appointing, in another sense Christianity is most inclusive, for God may not be excluded from any part of his creation. Thus Christians have no cause to lord it over others.

37. Ibid., p. 45.

38. Cf. A. P. F. Sell, "John Wyclif (d. 1384): Anniversary Reflections," RW 38, Mar. 1985, pp. 290-300.

39. RW 33, June 1975, p. 250.

40. Ibid., p. 255.

41. C 2, 1899, pp. 59-60.

42. P 1, 1877, p. 27.

43. Ibid., p. 37.

44. Ibid.

45. Ibid.

46. P 2, 1880, pp. 965-1123. The report is a mine of information on the then current status of confessional statements in those churches whose views and practices the committee sought to discover.

47. P 3, 1884, p. 32.

48. Ibid., p. 36. It is, however, somewhat ironic that the second Council should have refused the application for membership of the Cumberland Presbyterian Church on the grounds of insufficient evidence that that church "now accepts the doctrinal basis of the Alliance" and has a creed which is "in harmony with the Consensus of the Reformed Confessions" when the same council had to appoint a committee to inquire what such a consensus might be! At the third Council the Cumberland Church was admitted, though the council did not (as it could not) make itself "accountable for their particular views." See P 2, 1880, pp. 24, 235-43, 333-34, 460; P 3, 1884, pp. iv, 13.

49. P 12, 1925, p. 28.

50. Ibid., pp. 102-4.

51. Ibid., p. 116.

52. Ibid., p. 143. Parts 2 and 3 of Barth's paper are in P 12; part 1 is in QR 13, Feb. and May 1926; cf. n. 71 below. Professor Lang of Halle opened the discussion by introducing the absent Barth, this "comparatively young man of Swiss origin," none of whose works had been translated into English, to the

audience. How comforting to lesser theological lights to know that there was a time when even Barth had to be introduced as one almost unknown!

53. P 12, 1925, p. 149.

54. P 13, 1929, pp. 387-88.

55. See *Confessions and Confessing in the Reformed Tradition Today,* Studies from the World Alliance of Reformed Churches, no. 2 (Geneva: WARC, 1983); and the collection, *Reformed Witness Today,* ed. L. Vischer (Bern, 1982).

56. P 16, 1948, p. 38.

57. Ibid.

58. P 8, 1904, p. 88.

59. P 10, 1913, p. 173.

60. P 2, 1880, p. 265.

61. P 16, 1948, p. 41; cf. P 2, 1880, p. 267.

62. *Confessions and Confessing,* p. 5. A point illustrated by Stephen Mayor, who refers to the fact that despite the Westminster Confession, the English Presbyterians went Arian in the eighteenth century; see RW 33, 1974-75, p. 202. On the other hand, it would appear that after the greetings of the American Unitarian Association were brought to the fourth Congregational Council (1920) by Samuel A. Elliot, and the reminder given that "most of the old Puritan churches of eastern Massachussetts have now for many years acknowledged a Unitarian fellowship," Unitarian greetings were never again sought! See C 4, 1920, p. 208.

63. P 8, 1904, p. 114.

64. P 10, 1913, pp. 180-81.

65. Ibid., p. 170. The point was underlined in homely fashion by Donald Fraser: "What strikes us is, that the old Confessions still cover the Protestant theology, but fit clumsily. They are like garments made for men of a former generation. They are tight at the wrong place, and roomy at the wrong place. They are too long, and not broad enough" (CP 3, April 1880, p. 247).

66. Alliance Executive Committee *Minutes,* 1966, p. 14.

67. *Called to Witness to the Gospel Today,* Studies from the World Alliance of Reformed Churches, no. 1 (Geneva: WARC, 1983), p. 9; cf. RW 32, 1972-73, p. 311.

68. *Confessions and Confessing,* p. 17.

69. A point made by J. H. S. Burleigh, "Our Common Faith," QR 15, May 1933, p. 272.

70. P 1, 1877, p. 29; cf. Burleigh, "Our Common Faith," p. 270.

71. QR 13, Feb. 1926, p. 101. It may be that Barth had local Congregational covenants in mind, but the classical theory concerning these does not support him. At the sixth Congregational Council the 17th-century Richard Mather was quoted as follows: A covenant is "a solemne and public promise before the Lord, whereby a company of Christians, called by the power and mercy of God to fellowship with Christ, and by His providence to live together, and by His grace to cleave together in the unitie of faith and brotherly love, and desirous to partake together in all the holy Ordinances of God, doe in confidence of His gracious acceptance in Christ, binde themselves to our Lord and one to another, to walk together by this assistance of His Spirit, in all such wayes of holy worship in Him, and of edification one towards another, as the Gospel of Christ requireth

of every Christian Church and the membership thereof" (C 6, 1949, p. 38). Nor should it be overlooked that the Westminster Assembly of Divines included the distinguished Independents Thomas Goodwin, Philip Nye, Jeremiah Burroughes, William Bridge, and Sidrach Simpson. See the magisterial study by Robert S. Paul, *The Assembly of the Lord* (Edinburgh: T. & T. Clark, 1985).

72. Geoffrey F. Nuttall, *Congregationalists and Creeds* (the 1966 W. M. Llewellyn Lecture, Memorial College, Swansea) (London: Epworth Press, 1967), pp. 11-15. Cf. the following from J. A. Macfadyen's 1879 address from the Chair of the Congregational Union of England and Wales: "As a matter of history, so far is it from being true that Congregationalism has no confession, there is no body of churches in Christendom which is richer in confessions than our churches are. Every member of a church before being received into fellowship makes his confession. Every student before entering college makes a confession. Every minister before accepting his pastorate makes a confession. Every congregation in laying the foundation stone of its meeting-house makes a confession. As circumstances have arisen that seemed to necessitate it, the churches have united to raise their testimony, and to leave it embodied in declaration or confession. We claim for Congregationalism the merit of having preserved to this day the first and only legitimate use of creed or confession." See Alexander Mackennal, *Life of John Allison Macfadyen* (London: Hodder & Stoughton, 1891), p. 184. See further Alan P. F. Sell, "Confessing the Faith in English Congregationalism," *The Journal of the United Reformed Church History Society* 4 (1988): 170-215.

73. W. Gordon Robinson, "Congregationalism and the Historic Faith," *The Congregational Quarterly* 29 (July 1951): 213.

74. Ibid., pp. 212-13. He remarks (p. 204) that even the Savoy Declaration "had little influence in England, though it had much in American Congregationalism." R. F. G. Calder makes the same point in C 8, 1958, p. 33. See further W. G. Robinson, "The Savoy Declaration of 1658 and Today," *Congregational Historical Society Transactions* 18 (Aug. 1958): 75-88; B. L. Manning, *Essays in Orthodox Dissent* (1939) (London: Independent Press, 1953), p. 187; WC 7, Jan. 1965, pp. 1-11. It should not of course go unremarked that churches which are not formally tied to the doctrinal forms of the past can be thoroughly hidebound by past *custom* in their church life. Neither the presence nor the absence of formally subscribed creeds is a panacea in this matter. Indeed, "We believe in the way we have always done things" is the primary article in the creed of some, were they never so creedless! For a useful statement of the mainstream Congregational position on the subject see C. S. Duthie, "Affirmations of Faith," B 7, Spring 1967, pp. 1-8.

75. C 9, 1962, p. 34.

76. C 3, 1908, p. 268.

77. C 6, 1949, p. 38.

78. *The Savoy Declaration of Faith and Order*, ed. A. G. Matthews (London: Independent Press, 1959), pp. 51-53.

79. C 5, 1930, p. 47.

80. Ibid., p. 125.

81. C 1, 1891, p. 68.

82. P 12, 1925, p. 179; and in QR 13, Nov. 1925, p. 92.

83. C 1, 1891, pp. 107-16.

84. P 1, 1877, p. 28.

85. C 1, 1891, p. 108. For a later survey of Congregational practice in the matter see Norman Goodall, *Congregationalism Plus* (London: Independent Press [for the International Congregational Council], 1953), chap. 3. Bradford himself came down in favor of the (sentimental) view that "creeds divide, life unites," C1, 1891, p. 112. This view still surfaces from time to time in Reformed circles and elsewhere. Thus in the recent past John W. de Gruchy felt compelled to analyze it carefully in "The Role of Doctrine in the Church," RW 34, 1976-77, pp. 250-55.

86. P 1, 1877, pp. 46-47.

87. The "loss" of discipline is noted by W. G. Blaikie in "The Old 'Marks of the Church': Why Were They Superseded?" QR 3, May 1894, pp. 163-66. He offers two answers: (a) the difficulty of deciding when the Word and sacraments were faithfully handled; (b) since Christ gave ordinances to a church he had already founded, the church cannot be defined by what is posterior to itself. We shall shortly note the important distinction to be drawn between defining the church and empirically recognizing the church by its "notes" or "marks." For some contemporary considerations see A. P. F. Sell, *Church Discipline* (London: United Reformed Church, 1983).

88. P 12, 1925, p. 24.

89. P 15, 1937, p. 52.

90. Ibid., p. 51.

91. P. T. Forsyth, *The Church and the Sacraments* (1917) (London: Independent Press, 1953), p. 83.

92. P 1, 1877, p. 285.

93. P 5, 1892, pp. 72-76. The literature contains a number of articles and addresses on Presbyterian polity. See Samuel J. Wilson, "The Distinctive Principles of Presbyterianism," P 2, 1880, pp. 148-56; G. B. Strickler, "The Scriptural Authority for the Presbyterian System," P 7, 1899, pp. 53-59. In rehearsing the prominent characteristics of Presbyterianism—loyalty to Christ, witness-bearing, catholicity, love of civil liberty, educational concern, and missionary zeal—it might almost seem as if William M. Paxton studiously avoided the *differentia* of Presbyterianism. See P 2, 1880, pp. 25-26.

94. CP 3, 1880, p. 47.

95. CP 1, 1879, p. 190.

96. QR 6, 1901-3, p. 360.

97. PW 21, Dec. 1952, p. 339. For Cairns's comment see P 1, 1877, p. 52. Flint's sermon on John 27:20, 21, was not printed in P. It may be seen in his *Sermons and Addresses* (Edinburgh, 1899), pp. 11-27. His offending remark (p. 26) was: "Most Presbyterians probably, while claiming for Presbytery that it is 'founded on the Word of God and agreeable thereto,' will not deny that the same may be said of other forms of Church government."

98. P 9, 1909, pp. 89-90.

99. Ibid., p. 143.

100. W. G. Blaikie, QR 3, May 1894, p. 165.

101. Blaikie, CP 5, 1881, p. 112.

102. CP 9, 1883, p. 2.

103. P 16, 1948, pp. 154-57.

104. L. Mudge, *The Servant Lord and His Servant People* (Geneva: World Alliance of Reformed Churches, 1959), pp. 2, 3.

105. RPW 25, June 1958, pp. 66-68.

106. Ibid., Dec. 1958, p. 158.

107. Ibid., p. 159.

108. Ibid., pp. 159-60.

109. P 18, 1959, p. 78.

110. P 17, 1954, p. 76.

111. C 10, 1966, p. 23. For a study of the Congregational idea of the church see A. P. F. Sell, *Saints: Visible, Orderly and Catholic.*

112. A. Peel, *The Noble Army of Congregational Martyrs* (London: Independent Press [for the International Congregational Council], 1948), p. 11.

113. Cf. Alfred Bentall, C 3, 1908, pp. 253-59; F. J. Powicke, ibid., p. 266. None was more adept at this kind of apologetic than Dr. A. J. Grieve. In an address on "The Congregational Tradition" delivered at Carrs Lane Church, Birmingham, England, on 1 June 1948, he said: "Do not therefore be misled by any assertion that all derive from and broke away from Episcopacy. Both it and Presbyterianism are offshoots from us and from the New Testament Church. The Early Church Universal was a Congregational type. Two points are decisive: (i) the exercise of discipline as the act of the whole body of church members. . . . (ii) the manner in which the ministry of the church was conceived and applied. Each Congregational 'bishop' or pastor was elected by the whole people. . . . Not only so, but when he was ordained the Christian people assembled and said, 'We choose him,' and proceeded in prayer that God would strengthen the man whom He had prepared for them." Quoted by Charles Surman, *Alexander James Grieve* (Manchester: Lancashire Independent College, 1953), p. 48. Cf. Grieve's colleague Robert Mackintosh in "Christian Unity and Church Union," *Holborn Review* (Jan. 1921): 38. For Mackintosh see A. P. F. Sell, *Robert Mackintosh: Theologian of Integrity* (Bern: Peter Lang, 1977), and Appendix II.

114. Alonzo H. Quint supplied a paper on "The Place of Ecclesiastical Councils" to the first Congregational Council; see C 1, 1891, pp. 100-102.

115. C 4, 1920, p. 388.

116. C 7, 1953, pp. 48-49, 51-52. Cf. P 12, 1925, pp. 173-80; and QR 13, Nov. 1925, pp. 88-93: the Congregationalist A. E. Garvie on "The Reunion of Non-Episcopal Churches from the Standpoint of Congregationalism," especially pp. 174-75 and 89.

117. Cf. C 4, 1920, p. 383.

118. C 5, 1930, pp. 253-54.

119. C 8, 1958, p. 45.

120. Quoted by T. B. Douglass, ibid., p. 48. See D. Jenkins, *Congregationalism: A Restatement* (London: Faber, 1954), p. 44.

121. C 7, 1953, pp. 46-47.

122. Ibid., p. 24.

123. C 10, 1966, p. 73. This International Congregational Council study was also published as a pamphlet under the title, *Congregationalism in an Ecumenical Era* (London: Independent Press, 1967).

124. H. F. Lovell Cocks, C 7, 1953, p. 53.

125. C 6, 1949, pp. 80-81.

126. C 4, 1920, p. 143.

127. Ibid., p. 431.

128. C 1, 1891, pp. 201-2.

129. C 7, 1953, p. 60.

130. C 2, 1899, p. 443.

131. C 5, 1930, p. 246.

132. C 7, 1953, p. 26.

133. Ibid., p. 54.

134. Ibid., pp. 70-71.

135. For a typical case along these lines see W. J. F. Huxtable in WC 3, Sept. 1961, pp. 11-14. For the contrary view see Harry R. Butman, WC 4, May 1962, pp. 35-39; and WC 6, Jan. 1964, p. 7. As early as 1920 J. G. Mackenzie declared: "My own impression is that our real contribution to the promotion of Christian Unity at the present moment will lie in the unification of the churches of our own order. We lack a church consciousness. We are a collection of churches, not a church. We have too great a tendency to live in the freezing atmosphere of isolation; the connecting channels become frozen; the collective outlet to society becomes blocked, and our corporate witness is lost. . . . Let us realize that just as the individual citizen has no rights against the state, but only within the state, so the individual Christian and the local church have only rights and liberties within the church; otherwise the local church becomes sectarian and ceases to be catholic, manifesting at one point the whole church.

"It is this, I think, the older Independency has still to learn. Congregationalism in the sense I have heard older men use the term will only work when we are perfect, and then it will not be needed" (C 4, 1920, p. 179).

136. WC 5, May 1963, p. 27; cf. W. A. Visser 't Hooft: "It belongs to the very nature of the Church that it expresses itself in a concrete, local congregation of believers gathered to hear the Word of God, to receive the sacraments, and to live in fellowship with each other" (WC 3, May 1961, p. 27).

137. C 6, 1949, pp. 2-3. Cf. the section on "Congregationalism and Councils" in the "Message to the Churches" delivered by the seventh Congregational Council, C 7, 1953, pp. 159-60.

138. P 1, 1877, p. 54.

139. Ibid., p. 67.

140. P 7, 1899, p. 263.

141. P 4, 1888, p. 53.

142. QR 11, Aug. 1919, p. 196.

143. C 5, 1930, pp. 170, 171.

144. C 10, 1966, p. 26. John Huxtable's address is reprinted in abbreviated form in B 7, Winter 1966-67, pp. 5-10. See further A. P. F. Sell, "Anabaptist-Congregational Relations and Current Mennonite-Reformed Dialogue," *The Mennonite Quarterly Review* 61 (July 1987): 321-34.

145. M. Pradervand, *A Century of Service* (Edinburgh: The Saint Andrew Press, 1975), pp. 220-22.

146. P 15, 1937, p. 53. Macgregor also applauded Archbishop Söderblom, who, when a friend introduced to him a Roman priest at Stockholm in 1925 as "the only Catholic present," expostulated, "All of us who are here are Catholics!"

(ibid., p. 50). When reading older divines it is well to note that "catholic" is often used as the antonym of "bigot." Thus, for example, Philip Doddridge (1702-1751) describes the lectures of his tutor John Jennings (d. 1723) at Kibworth Academy as follows: "He furnishes us with all kinds of authors upon every subject, without advising us to skip over the heretical passages for fear of infection. It is evidently his main care to inspire us with sentiments of Catholicism, and to arm us against that zeal which is not according to knowledge" (*Correspondence and Diary of Philip Doddridge*, ed. J. D. Humphreys [1831, vol. I, p. 198]).

147. P 1, 1877, p. 46.

148. CP 1, 1879, p. 6.

149. P 1, 1877, p. 81. This is plagiarized by Robert H. Fleming in P 10, 1913, p. 137.

150. C 1, 1891, p. 28. When we recall that this sermon was preached less than two months after the promulgation of *Rerum Novarum* we may suspect that there is cheek as well as lyricism here!

151. Ibid., pp. 302-3. In his remark that "The history of a State is not the history of its statesmen" Fairbairn appears as an unwitting harbinger of those who in our own time speak of "the underside of history"—the Minjung theologians of Korea, for example.

152. C 7, 1953, pp. 81-82.

153. P 2, 1880, p. 346.

154. Ibid., pp. 344-53.

155. P 10, 1913, p. 135.

156. See D. H. McVicar in P 2, 1880, p. 346: "We are . . . unable to see how . . . Congregationalism, with its want of organized unity and inadequate executive power for purposes of discipline, can hope to become universal. But it is otherwise with Presbyterianism. We rest it solely upon divine truth." Congregationalists might have pointed out that despite their alleged "wants" they managed to remain more orthodox than the English Presbyterians of the 17th and 18th centuries, most of whom ended in unitarianism; they also managed to pioneer the modern missionary movement along with others. But they can speak for themselves—as John K. M'Lean did: "Our polity is the only one under heaven or which even heaven can produce, ample enough and free enough, and fit enough to furnish union ground for the denominations" (C 1, 1891, p. 137).

157. See B 1, nos. 3 and 4, 1960-61; and B 2, nos. 1 and 2, 1961; and the resulting book: Lewis Mudge, *One Church: Catholic and Reformed* (London: Lutterworth, 1963).

158. P 2, 1880, pp. 151-52.

159. B 2, no. 1, 1961, p. 6.

160. Ibid.

161. Ibid., p. 11.

162. T. F. Torrance, review in *The Scottish Journal of Theology* 5 (1952): 91, 93, 95.

163. P 19, 1964, pp. 221-22.

164. *Called to Witness to the Gospel Today*, p. 24.

165. As a contribution to the debate on catholicity the Alliance's European

Theological Committee wrote seven theses on the subject. See B 2, Autumn 1961, pp. 11-12. See further B 6, Autumn 1965, pp. 1-9. Cf. also J. L. Hromadka, who said with reference to the Third World Conference on Faith and Order (Lund 1952), "We cannot answer the question, What is the Church? without first asking, Who is Jesus Christ?" (P 17, 1954, p. 126).

166. C 7, 1953, p. 50.

167. P 17, 1954, p. 134.

4. The Ecumenical Vision

1. G. D. Henderson, P 13, 1929, p. 272. Cf. Roswell D. Hitchcock: "This our Presbyterian Alliance of course emphasizes Presbyterianism; but in no hard, narrow, narrowing way. It looks out in all directions, and is actually leading out, into wider fellowships. Its next logical consequent had already in fact preceded it: I mean the ecumenic *Protestant* Alliance, Evangelical we call it, which, in 1552, John Calvin, as he wrote to Cranmer, would have crossed ten seas to assist in consummating. In time we shall see that still better ecumenic *Christian* Alliance, of which there is scarcely a sign as yet. And then, at last, in God's own time, far down the horizon now, we shall have not union only, but unity, the real unity, for which our Lord prayed and the ages wait" (P 2, 1880, pp. 71-72).

2. P 1, 1877, p. 34.

3. RW 37, Mar. 1983, p. 157, quoting Calvin's commentary on *Hebrews* (10:25). For a detailed study of "Calvin and Ecumenism" see W. Nijenhuis, RPW 25, Dec. 1959, pp. 343-54.

4. Quoted by G. W. Richards, P 13, 1929, p. 291.

5. Ibid., p. 280.

6. Letter to Melanchthon, 21 January 1545, quoted by H. P. Van Dusen, P 17, 1954, p. 150.

7. Quoted by F. H. Henderson, P 9, 1909, p. 395, by H. P. van Dusen, P 17, 1954, p. 151, and by W. G. Blaikie on the first page of P 1, 1877.

8. P 1, 1877, p. 9.

9. C 4, 1920, pp. 345-48.

10. Ibid., p. 478.

11. C 1, 1891, p. 210.

12. Ibid., p. 245.

13. Ibid.

14. Ibid., p. 247.

15. When, in defense of the view that "human consciousness resents it," Allon returns with approval to Kant's view "that knowledge is entirely dependent on subjective conditions," he is both inaccurate vis-à-vis Kant and unduly concessive.

16. C 1, 1891, p. 248.

17. Ibid.

18. P 9, 1909, pp. 393-94.

19. Ibid., p. 395.

20. Ibid., pp. 404-5.

21. P 4, 1888, p. 154.

22. P 10, 1913, p. 216; cf. ibid., p. 161.
23. P 13, 1929, pp. 260-61. Prior to the Lausanne Conference Alliance representatives held a conference at Geneva in September 1926, and offered their suggestions "to all whom it might concern." They include the following: "4. In any scheme of reunion for Christendom a reasonable freedom should be conserved (a) in respect of the Church's constitutional autonomy and liberty to develop its life through orderly progress; and (b) in respect of the thought and action of its individual ministers and members. . . . 7. It is suggested that care be taken to secure that adequate definition be obtained of the *representative* and *constitutional* character of the episcopate as a proposed element in the future organisation of the Church; and that in the light of history and scholarship it be acknowledged openly as a basis for reunion that the Church of the future is not pledged or bound to hold that the episcopate is in itself necessary to the *esse* of the church. The future relation of the episcopate to the presbyterate in actual practice, apart from theory, needs to be explored in the interest of a settlement, so that Episcopal and Presbyterian usages may be co-ordinated at all points, and neither submerged" (QR 13, May 1927, p. 232).
24. P 13, 1929, pp. 261-62. Sixty years later the Alliance continues to wrestle with the problem. See the paper of the 1984 executive committee on "Unity and Union in the Reformed Family of Churches," and the consultation on that subject at New Delhi, 1985. For the consultation report see RW 39, Sept. 1986, pp. 582-88.
25. P 14, 1933, p. 236.
26. P 15, 1937, p. 221.
27. P 18, 1959, pp. 21-22.
28. P 19, 1964, pp. 220-21.
29. The Christological development in the understanding of "catholic" which we traced in the previous chapter facilitated the Christological understanding of church unity.
30. P 19, 1964, p. 180.
31. PW 23, March 1955, p. 3.
32. B 6, Winter 1965-66, p. 3.
33. C 7, 1953, p. 88.
34. P 17, 1954, p. 122.
35. P 16, 1948, p. 111.
36. Ibid., p. 96.
37. B 6, Winter 1965-66, p. 2. Cf. J. A. Mackay, B 8, Summer 1968, p. 7.
38. RW 27, March 1983, p. 150.
39. C 10, 1966, p. 76.
40. The list of Reformed Christians who helped to promote the modern ecumenical movement includes (not to mention those still living) A. Lang, J. Vernon Bartlet, Charles Merle d'Aubigné, J. Ross Stevenson, William Paton, W. A. Visser 't Hooft, Eugene Carson Blake, Marc Boegner, Pierre Maury, John Mackay, Alphonse Koechlin, Henry Smith Leiper, John Baillie, Leslie Cooke, and Norman Goodall. See Norman Goodall, "Some Congregational Pathfinders in the Ecumenical Movement," *Congregational Historical Society Transactions* 20 (Oct. 1967): 184-99. For an example of a criticism of Pan-Presbyterianism from within the family see A. B. Bruce, as quoted by J. M'Naugher: "In

recent years the phenomenon of Pan-Presbyterianism has made its appearance. It is to be feared that this movement will not serve the cause of catholicity, but will rather work in a purely antiquarian direction, and serve the purpose of those who would bind the reformed Churches to the seventeenth century." On which M'Naugher remarked, "How happily the forebodings of my distinguished and greatly loved preceptor have fallen by the wayside!" (P 12, 1925, p. 408). In recent years it has become customary to speak of "Christian world communions" rather than of "confessional" bodies. This is appropriate as far as the Alliance is concerned, for, as we have seen, membership in it does not turn upon confessional subscription. Ralph Calder made the point for Congregationalists at the last Congregational Council (1966): "Confessional" is "not an appropriate term to us for the relationship which binds Congregationalists together. Our particular kind of unity is not a 'confessional' one, but a mixture of shared history and common conviction about the nature of the togetherness of Christian people in Christ's Church" (C 10, 1966, p. 91).

41. Quoted by J. McCord in M. Pradervand, *A Century of Service* (Edinburgh: The Saint Andrew Press, 1975), p. viii. For the remarks of the third general secretary of the World Council of Churches, Philip Potter, see the report of his address to the WARC Executive Committee, 1975, in *Reformed Press Service*, Feb. 1975.

42. P 16, 1948, p. 210.

43. P 1, 1877, p. 1. Blaikie quoted James McCosh, a pioneer of the Alliance, as saying that there might be a Grand Council which "should have authority to see that their fundamental principles of doctrine and of government are carried out in each of the Churches, and might cut off those that deliberately departed from them in act or in profession" (ibid., p. 2). This would have necessitated a more definite doctrinal consensus than, as we have seen, it proved possible to reach.

44. Ibid., p. 5.

45. Ibid., pp. 4-6.

46. P 1, 1877, p. 19; cf. pp. 13, 23; P 9, etc. For a pioneer's view see J. David Hoeveler, Jr., "Evangelical Ecumenism: James McCosh and the Intellectual Origins of the World Alliance of Reformed Churches," *Journal of Presbyterian History* 55 (Spring 1977): 36-56.

47. P 2, 1880, p. 19.

48. C 4, 1920, pp. 50-51. W. G. Blaikie testified as follows at the first Congregational Council (1891): "I do not think our Presbyterian alliance has contracted our sympathies with other churches. I think the result has been in the other direction. I think it has given us altogether a wider outlook, and made us realise more the great work and the great battle in which all the churches are engaged. . ." (C 1, 1891, p. 45).

49. C 9, 1962, p. 23.

50. P 17, 1954, p. 77. This was endorsed by the next Presbyterian Council; see P 18, 1959, p. 221. For the executive committee statement adopted at Basle, 1951, see RPW 27, March 1962, pp. 11-14.

51. P 17, 1954, p. 176. At the same council J. A. Mackay declared, "We are not, and we should never become, an ecclesiastical power block" (ibid., p. 115).

52. P 19, 1964, p. 221.

53. Ibid., p. 260.

54. C 6, 1949, p. 67.

55. WARC 20, 1970, p. 248. For a paper by Lukas Vischer on "The Ecumenical Commitment of the World Alliance of Reformed Churches" see B 24, Summer 1984, and RW 38, March 1985, pp. 261-81. The latter contains responses by Frank Nichol, John W. de Gruchy, and Lewis S. Mudge.

56. *The Report of the Third World Conference on Faith and Order at Lund, Sweden* (Aug. 15-28, 1952) (London: SCM Press, 1952), p. 6.

57. P 17, 1954, p. 36.

58. *Minutes* of the Presbyterian Alliance Executive Committee, 1966, app. 5b, p. 72.

59. See the executive committee paper cited in n. 24 above.

60. P 17, 1954, p. 117.

61. Ibid., p. 118. Cf. idem, RPW 27, March 1962, p. 18.

62. P 13, 1929, p. 276.

63. Ibid., p. 294.

64. Cf. Leslie Cooke at the eighth Congregational Council, C 8, 1962, pp. 70-71.

65. RPW 27, March 1962, p. 13.

66. Vittorio Subilia in RPW 29, March 1966, p. 11.

67. RPW 27, Dec. 1963, p. 353.

68. Though cf. R. J. Drummond's reminder of the view of Thomas Chalmers: "How could the Congregationalist expect the Episcopalian at one leap to descend to his level, or the Episcopalian expect by one pull to drag up the Congregationalist to his lofty eminence? Presbytery was the meeting point — a midway station given for happy spirits to alight betwixt the earth and heaven" (P 12, 1925, p. 99).

69. The first theological secretary was Lewis S. Mudge, for whose reflections on his time in office see "The Theological Work of the Alliance: 1957-1962," *Journal of Presbyterian History* 55 (Spring 1977): 101-6. Cf. also the view of the then Alliance President William P. Thompson: "Developing Relationships with Other World Confessional Bodies and with the World Council of Churches Require a Strong Alliance," RW 34, Sep.-Dec. 1977, p. 294.

70. RW 32, Dec. 1973, p. 341.

71. Ibid., p. 346. Cf. N. Ehrenström, "A Bird's Eye View of Bilateral Dialogues," RW 33, Dec. 1975, pp. 339-46.

72. *The Presence of Christ in Church and World* (Vatican City: Secretariat for Promoting Christian Unity; Geneva: WARC, 1977); *Baptists and Reformed in Dialogue*, Studies from the World Alliance of Reformed Churches, no. 4 (Geneva: WARC, 1984); *God's Reign and Our Unity* (London: SPCK; Edinburgh: The Saint Andrew Press, 1984). We do not overlook Lutheran-Reformed conversations which have taken place. In Europe a conversation was initiated by the Faith and Order Commission of the World Council of Churches in which the department of studies of the Lutheran World Federation and the Alliance's department of theology were involved. A report entitled *Lutheran and Reformed Churches in Europe on the Way to One Another* was published in 1967. Meanwhile, the report of Lutheran-Reformed conversations in North America had been published under the title *Marburg Revisited* (Minneapolis: Augsburg Publishing

House, 1966). From 17-22 March 1975 seventeen theologians from the two communions met in Strasbourg for a world-level consultation (see RW 33, Sept. 1975, pp. 314-20). Their recommendations concerning further study and regional fellowship and action were not followed through by the world bodies, which became increasingly preoccupied in other (notably the Roman Catholic) directions. However, the report of the fully fledged Lutheran-Reformed International Dialogue Commission (1985-88) is now available: *Toward Church Fellowship* (Geneva: Lutheran World Federation and World Alliance of Reformed Churches, 1989). This is the first thorough and sustained examination at the international level of Lutheran-Reformed relations.

73. The themes echo the title of the so-called Lima text of the World Council of Churches, *Baptism, Eucharist and Ministry* (1982). The Alliance has not so far pronounced upon this text but is encouraging its member churches to submit their findings on the document by the due date both to the Faith and Order Department of the World Council of Churches and to the Alliance. In order to assist the discussion process the Alliance has published *Responding to "Baptism, Eucharist and Ministry": A Word to the Reformed Churches*, Studies from the World Alliance of Reformed Churches, no. 3 (Geneva: WARC, 1984); reprinted in B 24, no. 1, 1984, and RW 38, Sept. 1984, pp. 187-200. The further regional work which Alliance representatives have done in the field of dialogue should not be overlooked. Important studies have been undertaken jointly by the Caribbean and North American Area Council of the Alliance and the (Roman Catholic) Bishops' Committee for Ecumenical and Interreligious Affairs. See *Reconsiderations* (New York: World Horizons, 1967). The publications *Marburg Revisited* (1966), *Lutheran-Reformed Consultation, Series II, 1972-74* (1974), and *An Invitation to Action* (1984) grew out of the joint studies of the Caribbean and North American Area Council of the Alliance and the USA National Committee of the Lutheran World Federation. In Europe the far-reaching Leuenberg Agreement was reached between Lutherans and Reformed in 1973. Finally, the Caribbean and North American Area Council joined with North American Orthodox representatives in conversations which resulted in the publication of *The New Man* (New Brunswick: Standard Press, 1973). Regional, bi-, and multilateral conversations in which the Reformed have been engaged under extra-Alliance auspices are too numerous to mention.

74. P 1, 1877, p. 58. For an early perspective on the Roman church see Robert Knox, "The Evangelization of Ireland," P 2, 1880, pp. 419-25. "Romanism in the United States" and "in Canada" were among topics treated at the third Presbyterian Council (1884). "Ireland: Its Special Difficulties and Claims" was considered, and the Rev. Charles L. Morell's view was summed up by his title, "Presbyterianism, the Best Remedial Agency for Ireland." "The Conflict with Rome" was among the subjects discussed at the fourth Presbyterian Council (1888). The fourteenth Presbyterian Council (1933) heard C. Merle d'Aubigne's reminder that "after the Conference of Lausanne, the Pope's Encyclical letter of 1928 forbade all loyal sons of that Church from taking part in any Conference having for its topic Christian unity, and reaffirmed the absolute necessity of other Churches accepting all the tenets of Rome, before anything could be said of union" (P 14, 1933, p. 287). For a more theological paper on "The Roman Catholic Idea of the Church" by Henri Bois see P 6,

1896, pp. 55-60. As late as 1934 Adolf Keller could say that "the Roman Church remains an irreconcilable enemy of the Protestant Church, especially when the anti-Protestant order of Jesuits has power." See QR 16, May 1934, p. 54. For comments and articles on the Second Vatican Council see, e.g., C 10, 1966, pp. 43-50; WC 5, Jan. 1963, pp. 4-8; RPW 26, June 1961, pp. 252-58; RPW 27, March 1963, pp. 197-201, June 1963, pp. 248-53; RPW 28, March 1965, pp. 200-214, Sept. 1965, pp. 305-14; RPW 26, March 1966, pp. 6-22; 30, June 1969, pp. 251-65.

75. P 19, 1964, p. 242. A statement by Latin American representatives, presented too late for discussion, was "received with appreciation" by the executive committee on 14 August 1964. It was printed in P 19, 1964, pp. 275-76. It welcomes signs of renewal within the Roman Catholic church but is more guarded than the Council as a whole, pointing out that "we reaffirm and continue to maintain the principles of the Reformation, such as: the supremacy of the Holy Scriptures as the only rule of faith; justification by faith; the universal priesthood of all believers; free access to God; the sovereignty of Jesus Christ as the only head of the Church; and the catholicity of the Church of Christ which is not the exclusive possession of any ecclesiastical institution" (p. 275). Matters were not helped when, on 6 January 1964, Pope Paul VI sent a telegram to the general secretaries of the World Council of Churches and of the Christian world communions in which he said, "The door of the fold is open" (and he did not mean that the faithful should *exit* through it!). See M. Pradervand, *A Century of Service*, p. 249. See further, P. Ricca, "Some Reflections on *De Oecumenismo*," RPW 28, Sept. 1965, pp. 305-14, especially pp. 306-7, where he opines that although in its new decree the Roman church "now offers a new ecumenical programme to the other Christian Churches, one no longer centred on the idea of a 'return to Rome,' " nevertheless that church continues to understand itself as "an obligatory transition point for all."

76. *The Presence of Christ,* p. 7.

77. Ibid.

78. Ibid., pp. 8-9.

79. Ibid., p. 7.

80. Ibid.

81. *Decree on Ecumenism (De Oecumenismo)* (London: Catholic Truth Society, 1965), p. 21n.

82. RW 28, Sept. 1965, p. 309.

83. Ibid., p. 310.

84. *Decree on Ecumenism,* p. 27 (our italics).

85. From the text of the address as translated from the original French, World Council of Churches, 1984.

86. See P. T. Forsyth, *The Charter of the Church* (London: Alexander and Shepheard, 1896), p. 39.

87. *The Presence of Christ,* p. 10.

88. Ibid.

89. Ibid., p. 12.

90. Ibid., pp. 12-13.

91. Ibid., p. 13.

92. Ibid., pp. 13-14.

93. Ibid., p. 14.
94. *Decree on Ecumenism,* p. 28.
95. *The Presence of Christ,* p. 15.
96. Ibid., p. 16.
97. Ibid.
98. Ibid., p. 17 (our italics).
99. Ibid., p. 16.
100. Ibid., p. 18.
101. Ibid., p. 17.
102. Ibid., p. 19.
103. Ibid.
104. Ibid.
105. RPW 28, March 1965, p. 201. Cf. W. Niesel, "Our Witness in the Ecumenical Movement Today," RPW 28, Dec. 1965, pp. 345-46.
106. *God's Reign and Our Unity,* p. 83. In this section and the next we draw upon our article, "Ecclesiology in Perspective: Conversations with Anglicans and Baptists," RW 38, Sept. 1984, pp. 168-76, and *Reformed Perspectives* (in French, German, and Spanish), Sept. 1984.
107. *God's Reign and Our Unity,* p. 5. We have already noted that the Presbyterians have not normally required subscription of any but ministers and elders. The present report does not make this point.
108. Ibid., p. 6.
109. Ibid.
110. Ibid., p. 7.
111. Ibid., p. 11.
112. Ibid., p. 15.
113. Ibid., p. 16.
114. Ibid., p. 19.
115. Ibid., p. 22.
116. Ibid., p. 29.
117. Ibid., p. 39.
118. Ibid., p. 46.
119. Ibid., p. 51.
120. Ibid., pp. 55-56.
121. Ibid., p. 57.
122. Ibid., p. 72.
123. Ibid., p. 82.
124. *The Presence of Christ,* p. 30.
125. See A. P. F. Sell, "Dubious Establishment? A Neglected Ecclesiological Testimony," *Mid-Stream* 24, 1 (1985): 1-28. As long ago as 1920 an English commission on the promotion of Christian unity reported: "In all these discussions on the question of reunion one element of difficulty seems to have been left out of account and will need to be reckoned with before any practical steps can be taken. We refer to the question of Establishment. Congregationalists generally feel that union with an Established church is almost an impossibility. . . . So far . . . the question has been shirked but it will need to be faced in the not very distant future" (C 4, 1920, p. 483).
126. *God's Reign and Our Unity,* pp. 33, 44.

127. *Baptists and Reformed in Dialogue*, p. 8.

128. In 1981 one set of such considerations resulted in the union of most of the believer-baptizing Churches of Christ with the United Reformed Church to form the United Reformed Church in the United Kingdom.

129. *Baptists and Reformed in Dialogue*, p. 11.

130. Ibid., p. 17.

131. Ibid., pp. 19-20.

132. Ibid., p. 23.

133. Ibid., p. 26.

134. Ibid., pp. 27-28.

135. Ibid., p. 38.

136. *The Final Report* (London: CTS/SPCK, 1982), p. 36.

137. *The Presence of Christ*, p. 33.

138. The Congregation's response is printed in full in *Ecumenical Trends* 11 (Dec. 1982): 165-71.

139. See further J. Michael Miller, *What Are They Saying about Papal Primacy?* (New York: Paulist Press, 1982). As it turns out, *Toward Church Fellowship* does not address the matter.

140. P 13, 1929, p. 278.

141. P 1, 1877, p. 47.

142. Ibid., p. 31.

143. P 6, 1896, p. 180.

144. C 3, 1908, p. 225.

145. Ibid., p. 233.

146. Ibid., p. 236.

147. P 6, 1896, p. 183.

148. Ibid., pp. 186-87.

149. P 13, 1929, p. 270. For the view that the difference between Word and sacrament is one of degree, not of kind, see David Williams, P 12, 1925, p. 219.

150. C 5, 1930, p. 140. Mackintosh was also characteristically pungent concerning the Council of Trent: "During the Middle Ages the Western Catholic Church, in strangely haphazard fashion, raised the number of sacraments to seven, and succeeded in imposing its arbitrary will upon the Church of the East. The Council of Trent proceeds to affirm as *de fide* that all these seven sacraments were founded by Christ! A theology that will say that will say anything" (ibid.).

151. Ibid. See further A. P. F. Sell, *Robert Mackintosh* (Bern: Peter Lang, 1977), chap. 3.

152. P 6, 1896, pp. 186-87. Cf. P. Carnegie Simpson, "The Sacramental Significance Is Godward and Evangelical before It Is Manward and Ethical," QR 16, Aug. 1934, p. 66.

153. C 3, 1908, p. 229.

154. P 1, 1877, p. 47.

155. C 7, 1953, p. 49; cf. J. H. Cockburn in P 16, 1948, p. 105.

156. P 2, 1880, pp. 530-31.

157. P 17, 1954, pp. 137-38.

158. C 3, 1908, p. 226.

159. QR 16, Aug. 1934, p. 67.

160. *God's Reign and Our Unity*, p. 33.
161. P 2, 1880, p. 528.
162. P 6, 1896, pp. 181-82.
163. C 5, 1930, p. 141.
164. P 1, 1877, p. 47.
165. P 2, 1880, p. 510. Bannerman quotes Stoddard's *Works* (London, 1834), pp. clviiff. Solomon Stoddard (1643-1729), a Congregationalist, taught that "the Lord's Supper is instituted to be a means of regeneration," and that even those who know that they are in a "natural condition" should be encouraged to attend. See especially his *An Appeal to the Learned, Being a Vindication of the Right of Visible Saints to the Lord's Supper, though They Be Destitute of a Saving Work of God's Spirit in Their Hearts* (1709). We should note (as Bannerman does not) that it is visible saints who are thus encouraged—that is, those who are on the roll of a local church, but who have not had the saving experience. On the one hand this shows a retreat from the earlier Independent view that the church comprises converted people; on the other hand it serves as a dissuasive against undue introspection in quest of assurance. What it does not countenance is the table open to any and everyone. In this connection, and since John Wesley has come to be regarded by many as the pioneer of the open table because of his statement that "experience shows the gross falsehood of that assertion, that the Lord's Supper is not a converting ordinance" (*Journal*, 27 June 1740), we should note that this comment was made in the context of the denial by the Moravian, Philip Henry Molther, that apart from "full assurance of faith" a person should not use any of the means of grace. Wesley was no more advocating the open table than was Stoddard. See John C. Bowmer, "A Converting Ordinance and the Open Table," *Proceedings of the Wesley Historical Society* 34, 5 (March 1964): 109-13. The Gospel Standard Baptists are among those who have denied that the gospel may be offered to any but "sensible sinners." Article 26 of the Gospel Standard Trust states, "We reject the doctrine that men in a state of nature should be exhorted to believe in, or turn to God." See A. P. F. Sell, *The Great Debate: Calvinism, Arminianism and Salvation* (Worthing: H. E. Walter; Grand Rapids: Baker Book House, 1983), pp. 82-83, 129-30, 135.
166. *God's Reign and Our Unity*, p. 45.
167. P 2, 1880, pp. 508-9.
168. Ibid., p. 509.
169. Ibid., p. 515. Bannerman cited (p. 512 and note) the Congregationalists as theoretically holding the "purity" line, though "the *practice* of very many Independent churches is substantially identical with our own."
170. Thus, for example, whereas *God's Reign and Our Unity* (p. 30) declares that "the practice of Christian baptism . . . looks back to [the] decisive event" of Jesus' baptism by John, Robert Mackintosh concludes on exegetical grounds that the direct origin of Christian baptism with water lay in Peter's action on the day of Pentecost (C 5, 1930, pp. 137f.). This, of course, is to say that there is no positive evidence that Jesus instituted the sacrament of baptism.
171. P 16, 1948, p. 91.
172. P 17, 1954, p. 75.
173. Ibid., p. 117.
174. C 5, 1930, p. 139.

175. P 14, 1933, p. 198.

176. Ibid., p. 201.

177. *God's Reign and Our Unity*, p. 44.

178. Ibid., p. 42. "BEM" in parentheses is *Baptism, Eucharist and Ministry* (Geneva: World Council of Churches, 1982).

179. Ibid., p. 43, quoting *The Presence of Christ in Church and World*, p. 23.

180. *God's Reign and Our Unity*, p. 39. See in this connection Pierre-Yves Emery, "The Teaching of Calvin on the Sacrificial Element in the Eucharist," RPW 26, Sept. 1960, pp. 109-14.

181. *God's Reign and Our Unity*, p. 42.

182. *The Presence of Christ*, p. 21.

183. Ibid., p. 25.

184. Ibid., pp. 21, 24.

185. Ibid., p. 23.

186. Ibid.

187. Ibid., p. 26.

188. Ibid., p. 22.

189. Ibid., p. 28.

190. C 4, 1920, p. 178.

191. Bernard Lord Manning, *Essays in Orthodox Dissent* (London: Independent Press, 1939), p. 69.

192. P 6, 1896, p. 61.

193. Ibid., pp. 61-62.

194. Ibid., p. 63.

195. Ibid., pp. 64-65.

196. Ibid., pp. 67-69. Dykes quotes Charles Gore, *The Mission of the Church*. Cf. I. J. Roberton's illustration at the thirteenth Presbyterian Council: "Long ago I had as a fellow-student at Edinburgh University, F. G. Tait, soon thereafter open Golf Champion of the world, killed alas! at Magersfontein. His father, our Professor of Physics, was illustrating to us the Law of Kinematics from the flight of a golf ball; and one day he told us of two things a golf ball could not do in its flight; we really were made to feel that the entire scientific universe would crash in chaos did a golf ball do either of these two things. So said Father Tait on Tuesday; but on Saturday Son Freddy just went down to North Berwick and persuaded and enabled a golf ball to do both things which had been proved by his father to be impossible. Which is just for example what our narrowly sacerdotal friends have to learn, that their conscientious beliefs crash badly against solid reality" (P 13, 1929, p. 267). Cf. also J. D. Jones at the fifth Congregational Council: "But I imagine I speak for all Congregationalists when I say that we could never assent to the suggestion that Episcopal Ordination is necessary to the validity of a ministry. To assent to any such suggestion would be much more than a case of flouting our own history, and doing dishonour to some of the greatest princes of the Christian pulpit—it would be to blaspheme the Holy Ghost. . . . To doubt the validity of our ministries and the reality of our Sacraments would be to fly in the face of our most sacred religious experiences" (C 5, 1930, pp. 45-46).

197. On this point *God's Reign and Our Unity*, p. 82, issues a clear challenge. A further illustration of Roberton may be noted: "To Presbyterians the

Lausanne discussions must have been fairly exciting, and occasionally amusing; when, for example, it was sincerely laid down that for authority we must add tradition to Scripture; or—that your Ministry—to be a Ministry, must be in Apostolic Episcopal succession, Presbyterians may have been reminded of the cathedral with the exquisite chapter-house, which chapter-house had been built with so daringly wide a span of roof, that timid antiquity hastened to secure it by a central supporting pillar. Recent examination, however, showed that now, and apparently for centuries, the pillar had sunk down into the foundations; so that, unseen from beneath, there was a clear gap of several inches between the top of the pillar and the great roof it was supposed to support. Which thing is an allegory" (P 13, 1929, pp. 63-64). K. L. Parry was blunt and to the point at the fifth Congregational Council: "We are asked to accept the fact of episcopacy but not a theory. But the *necessity* of episcopalian ordination *is* a theory" (C 5, 1930, p. 175).

198. C 7, 1953, p. 53. R. H. Stafford described the theory of apostolic succession (in the sense of the continuity of orders) as "the deistic idea as it is applied to the Church" (ibid:, p. 68). As early as 1888 Principal Caven advocated the appointment of persons to supervise ministers and sessions (P 4, 1888, p. 71). At the seventeenth Presbyterian Council T. F. Torrance advocated the institution of a reformed episcopate "in which the corporate episcopate is given collegiate or corporate expression and in which the presbytery is the prime locus of *episcopatus*, although *episcopatus* might be administered *in presbyterio* by a presiding Presbyter" (P 17, 1954, p. 144). See also the "Report on the Study of *episcope*" prepared by J. K. S. Reid in consultation with Richmond Smith, WARC 20, 1970, pp. 184-95. James Whyte poured some Scottish cold water over inordinate desires to read too much into, or to make too much use of, the term *episcope*. See "That Blessed Word *episcope*," B 9, Spring 1969, pp. 5-8.

199. See T. W. Manson, *The Church's Ministry* (London: Hodder & Stoughton, 1948).

200. C 1, 1891, p. 304.

201. Forsyth, *The Church and the Sacraments* (London: Independent Press, 1947), pp. 45-46. For the distinction drawn between catholic unity as holy or moral, and as canonical, see his *Congregationalism and Reunion* (London: Independent Press, 1952), pp. 21-23. See further Daniel Jenkins, "Reformation and Catholicity," in *Thine Is the Kingdom, the Power, and the Glory* (study guide for the Ottawa Council) (Geneva: World Alliance of Reformed Churches, 1981), pp. 30-35; and his early work, *The Nature of Catholicity* (London: Faber, 1942).

202. C 7, 1953, p. 86.

203. Ibid., p. 83.

204. Manning, *Essays in Orthodox Dissent*, p. 133.

205. Ibid., p. 114; and C 5, 1930, pp. 258, 259. At the seventh Presbyterian Council Samuel Smith spoke on "Sacerdotalism." At the end of his address he moved "that the Alliance of Presbyterian Churches deplores the rapid spread of sacerdotal and sacramentarian doctrine throughout the English-speaking nations, and urges the Presbyterian ministers to instruct their congregations fully in the scriptural principles of the Protestant Reformation." The motion was referred to the business committee, whose deliverance was unanimously adopted: "While we deplore the tendencies referred to, and while encouraging

free discussion in our meetings, it is not customary for the Council to take formal action on questions which may be construed as an interference with the internal doings of any Church" (P 7, 1899, pp. 64, 197-98).

206. Manning, *Essays in Orthodox Dissent*, pp. 116, 117; and C 5, 1930, pp. 258, 259.

207. P 16, 1948, p. 215.

208. J. Owen, *Of Schism*, in his *Works*, 1850-53, ed. William H. Goold (London: The Banner of Truth Trust, 1967), vol. 13, p. 161.

209. C 1, 1891, p. 304.

210. P 2, 1880, p. 350.

211. In "The Reformed Tradition and the Papacy" Ross Mackenzie made bold to outline the "Requisites of a Reformed Papacy," while reaffirming that the Reformed "are not willing to concede that any particular order is necessary to all churches in all periods." See *Journal of Ecumenical Studies* 12 (1976): 359-67.

212. Accordingly we record with incredulity the statement of Russell H. Stafford: "I dare say that most of us Congregationalists are broad-minded enough—certainly I am, for one—to accept episcopal reordination for our ministers, if that were asked of us by a competent congregation of the world, as a brotherly gesture towards its right wing" (C 9, 1962, p. 25). Here eirenicism is carried to the point of betrayal. Consider, for example, the classic reply of John Howe (1630-1705) to his friend Seth Ward, Bishop of Exeter: "Why pray Sir, said the Bishop to him, what hurt is there in being twice Ordain'd? *Hurt,* my Lord, says *Mr. Howe* to him; the Thought is shocking; it hurts my Understanding; it is an absurdity: For nothing can have two Beginnings. I am sure, said he, I am a Minister of Christ . . . and I can't begin again to be a Minister." See E. Calamy, *Memoirs of the Life of the Late Revd. Mr. John Howe, M.A.* (1724), p. 39. On the wider issue we may compare Howe with Baxter as quoted below. Replying to Bishop Stillingfleet's "Sermon of Schism," Howe declared that "without all controversy the main inlet of all the distractions, confusions, and divisions of the Christian world, hath been by adding other conditions of church communion than Christ hath done." See Howe's *Works*, vol. 5 (London: The Religious Tract Society, 1863), p. 226. On the other hand, the results of a survey (B 2, Winter 1961-62, pp. 9-15) revealed that the Dutch Reformed Church of the Netherlands, the Reformed Church of France, and the Waldensian Church at that time required the reordination of Roman Catholic priests who desired to enter their ministries. Egbert Emmen of the Dutch church baldly stated that "no ordination in the Roman Catholic Church has ever been accepted in our church as valid." For the French church Pierre Lestringant said that failure to reordain a Roman Catholic priest would entail affirming that the call to the Roman priesthood is identical to the call to the Reformed ministry, and this is not the case. The commentator rightly notes that these views turn upon an essentialist understanding of ministry, whereas those who would not reordain adopt an existentialist view. How are these to be combined in a consistent theology? The fact that this answer has yet to be given within Alliance circles may indicate that the essentialist churches have in the meantime changed their view, or that the question has not been faced, or that it has been faced and that no answer is within reach. In our opinion essentialist teaching accords ill with

the Reformed tradition at large, and insofar as it is held today it undermines from within the Reformed understanding of catholicity and of the parity of ministers. "Even the catholic priests," declared Calvin, "would greatly please us if they tried to maintain themselves in their position for we would willingly concede to them that they have a holy and honourable office, *provided that they exercise it.*" Quoted by Amadeo Molnár, RW 34, Dec. 1976, p. 172.

213. See B 2, Autumn 1961, p. 7.

214. R. Baxter, *The Reformed Pastor* (1655) (London: SCM Press, 1956), p. 101; id., *Reliquiae Baxterianae,* ed. M. Sylvester (1696), I, pp. 40, 27.

215. P 10, 1913, pp. 62-63. For matters relating to the Lambeth Quadrilateral, see QR 12, May 1921, pp. 388-94; RPW 26, Sept. 1961, pp. 303-9. For further counters to sacerdotalism see CP 1, March 1879, pp. 200-207; CP 5, May 1881, pp. 321-31. For episcopacy see P 1, 1877, pp. 53-54; QR 11, Feb. 1918, pp. 57-59; QR 11, Nov. 1918, pp. 127-29; PW 21, June 1951, pp. 62-72. For F. W. Dankbaar's surprise at the Presbyterian "sacrifice" in accepting episcopacy in the Church of South India see PW 20, Sept. 1950, p. 104. For Anglican-Presbyterian relations see RPW 25, March 1958, pp. 5-22; RPW 28, June 1965, pp. 246-49. For the view that in the Lima text on the eucharist "the ecclesiastical situation prevails over exegesis," see P. Ricca, RW 37, Sept. 1983, pp. 239-47.

216. P 1, 1877, pp. 46-47. For a more recent discussion see R. McAfee Brown, "Order and Ministry in the Reformed Tradition," in *Reconsiderations,* pp. 107-38.

217. P 17, 1954, p. 85. For recent theses on the ministry by the Council of Theological Seminaries in the USA, see RW 36, no. 3, 1980, pp. 117-21. For the history of the Reformed understanding of the ministry, see QR 13, May 1927, pp. 224-27; and P 9, 1909, pp. 95-103.

218. P 17, 1954, pp. 143-44.

219. B 7, Summer 1967, pp. 4-5.

220. C 10, 1966, pp. 75-76.

221. P 12, 1925, p. 216. Otto Weber's call for "The Renewal of the Church's Common Ministry," P 19, 1964, pp. 122-35, should be noted.

222. Dr. Kerr, however, when lamenting the "downgrade" from the purest Presbyterian ideals, gave his diagnosis thus: "He was sorry to confess it, that Congregationalism was to an extent creeping into congregations of all denominations, and what was needed was a stiffening rather than a relaxing of the reins" (P 1, 1877, p. 119).

223. *God's Reign and Our Unity,* pp. 32-33. C. S. Duthie made the point in relation to Congregational anti-clericalism: "If we have not erected the ordained ministry into an order sharply divided from the laity (a word we have never loved), it was not that we set little store by God's gift to his Church but that we know how easily clericalism can usurp the place and authority of Christ and prevent the fullest use of that primary ministry which is the ministry of the whole Church" (C 6, 1949, p. 81).

224. P 5, 1892, p. 287. Cf. W. M. Clow, P 10, 1913, pp. 217-21.

225. *God's Reign and Our Unity,* pp. 52-53.

226. C 5, 1930, p. 143.

227. *Profile of the Eldership 1974* (Geneva: World Alliance of Reformed Churches, 1975).

228. Henderson points out (ibid., p. 20) that the report to the third Presbyterian Council on the eldership made no reference to female elders. At the first Presbyterian Council Vincent Dusek stated that the Unity of the Brethren had female elders "Ere John Calvin was born" (P 1, 1877, p. 121).

229. *Profile of the Eldership*, p. 33.

230. See *God's Reign and Our Unity*, pp. 75-77. Similarly, the Reformed may wonder where the Anglican threefold ministry is. Bishops we see; priests we see; but deacons seem to be somewhat more insubstantial beings. Whereupon informed Anglicans might, by a *tu quoque*, retort that in some places the Presbyterian diaconate has but a shadowy existence. For references to elders see P 2, 1880, pp. 165-76; P 3, 1884, pp. 373-84, 391-401, app. 131-36; PW 22, Dec. 1953, pp. 145-48; RW 22, Dec. 1973, pp. 363-73; RW 33, Mar. 1974, pp. 10-17. The last two mentioned are by R. Henderson. For references to deacons, see, e.g., CP 7, Apr. 1883, pp. 267-82; CP 7, June 1883, pp. 443-50; RPW 24, March 1957, pp. 212-17.

231. Cf. P 1, 1877, pp. 107, 115; RPW 28, June 1965, p. 248.

232. See P 17, 1954, pp. 87-88. As long ago as the second Presbyterian Council J. Marshall Lang appealed for flexibility in ministry, having the need for evangelists especially in mind. Cf. P 2, 1880, pp. 646-63.

233. P 17, 1954, p. 86.

234. RPW 28, June 1965, p. 247; cf. B 6, Winter 1965-66, p. 4.

235. P 1, 1877, pp. 115-16.

236. Ibid., p. 111, our italics.

5. The Philosophical-Apologetic Climate

1. P 10, 1913, p. 229.

2. Ibid., p. 231.

3. The Reformed family itself would benefit from serious engagement with the question, "How far is inner-Reformed unity hindered by the ecclesiastical results of conflict between philosophical and/or theological presuppositions?"

4. We here omit questions concerning biblical criticism, for these have been noted in chapter 3 above.

5. C 1, 1891, p. 77. The trends outlined in this section are treated in more detail in the first four chapters of A. P. F. Sell, *Theology in Turmoil* (Grand Rapids: Baker Book House, 1986.

6. C1, 1891, p. 78.

7. Ibid.

8. Ibid., pp. 78-79.

9. Ibid., p. 79.

10. Ibid., pp. 79-80.

11. Ibid., p. 80.

12. Ibid.

13. Ibid.

14. Ibid., p. 81.

15. Ibid., p. 195.

16. Ibid., p. 196.

17. P 1, 1877, p. 40.

18. Cf. ibid., p. 74.

19. P 2, 1880, p. 79.

20. Ibid., p. 920. This paper was sent to the meeting, van Oosterzee being unable to attend.

21. P 1, 1877, p. 58.

22. P 2, 1880, p. 86.

23. Ibid., pp. 86-87.

24. Ibid., p. 201; C 3, 1908, p. 95.

25. P 2, 1880, pp. 198-201.

26. P 3, 1884, p. 94.

27. P 4, 1888, p. 133.

28. See P 3, 1884, pp. 82-95, 249-54; P 4, 1888, p. 107; C 2, 1899, p. 46.

29. P 2, 1880, p. 84.

30. P 1, 1877, p. 198.

31. C 3, 1908, p. 96. The point might have been put more strongly. If God and the universe are identified, the doctrine of creation has no place. Further, if the universe/God is the ultimate reality—i.e., if it is all there is—we are perilously close to classical atheism. See J. C. A. Gaskin, *The Quest for Eternity: An Outline of the Philosophy of Religion* (Harmondsworth: Penguin Books, 1984), p. 113.

32. P 13, 1929, p. 285.

33. C 3, 1908, p. 83.

34. Flint was later to give his 1887-88 Croall lectures on this theme. See his *Agnosticism* (Edinburgh: Blackwood, 1903). For Flint, see A. P. F. Sell, *Defending and Declaring the Faith: Some Scottish Examples, 1860-1920* (Exeter: Paternoster Press; Colorado Springs: Helmers & Howard, 1987), chap. 3.

35. Gaskin, *The Quest for Eternity*, p. 189.

36. P 2, 1880, p. 244.

37. Ibid., p. 246.

38. Ibid., p. 250.

39. Analogously, F. F. Ellinwood said, "Were the members of the Church leading a supernatural life, unbelief in the supernatural would become impossible" (P 4, 1888, p. 111). This is, of course, philosophically a non sequitur; homiletically it represents an unwarrantable heaping of guilt upon one's hearers. Were the living experience of the church exactly as it ought to be there would still be reasons (if not necessarily good grounds) for unbelief.

40. C 3, 1908, p. 76.

41. Ibid., p. 77.

42. Ibid., p. 79.

43. Ibid., p. 80.

44. Ibid., p. 82. It should be remembered that Mackintosh regarded himself as a "refugee" from Calvinism.

45. P 1, 1877, pp. 193-94.

46. C 3, 1908, p. 63.

47. Ibid.

48. Ibid., pp. 63-64.

49. Ibid., p. 65.

50. Ibid., p. 66.

51. Ibid.
52. Ibid.
53. CP 1, 1879, p. 447.
54. Ibid., p. 452.
55. Ibid., p. 455.
56. Ibid.
57. P 12, 1925, p. 369.
58. Ibid., p. 370.
59. It is only proper to point out that Galloway was typical rather than unusual in his neglect.
60. C 5, 1930, p. 37.
61. Quoted in QR 15, May 1931, p. 39.
62. QR 14, Nov. 1920, p. 338.
63. PR 18, Dec. 1943, p. 173. This article was reprinted from *The South India United Church Herald.*
64. Ibid., pp. 174-75. A delightful misprint occurs on p. 177, where Lefever refers to the patronizing praise accorded by Anglo-Saxon theologians to the theology of continental Europe: "I venture to suggest that the praise is fulsome because it is more than a little patronising and it is patronising because, though fully appreciative of the ability shown in the Continental theological *circus,* English theologians as a whole show little desire to acquire that ability for themselves."
65. Ibid., p. 178. It is not, perhaps, irrelevant to point out that Lefever was a pupil of A. E. Garvie, who wrote in 1929 that Barthianism was "a minor evil product of the war." See *The Congregational Quarterly* 7 (1929): 21. For a hagiological attitude towards Barth see Jacques de Senarclens, RPW 30, March 1969, pp. 206-14. Among the surprises here is the remark that in February 1968 Barth "successfully combined, in the following unique way the two adjectives which had been irreconcilable for centuries: the true church is 'a catholic and evangelical church, or, and this amounts to the same thing, evangelical and catholic'" (p. 206). But, e.g., the Reformed scholar P. Carnegie Simpson published *The Evangelical Church Catholic* in 1934.
66. Though we do not think that his concessions on this point extricate him from the methodological wood, or answer the charge of N. H. G. Robinson in *Religious Studies* 7 (1972): 325: "The inevitable result of [Barth's] intransigent attitude [to human truth] is to represent truth of revelation, not as something inescapable, but as thoroughly esoteric and as quite irrelevant to all human problems and all human questions. It becomes indeed, humanly speaking, a language-game which one may or may not be called upon to play. Consequently, this theological stance involves, as Barth himself later admitted, a radical inhumanity; but what he did not see is that this inhumanity, this irrelevance, cannot be corrected by a new emphasis upon the humanity of God or upon the new humanity of what is in the absolute sense a new creature. There is no escape from these implications, and the indispensable correction can be achieved only by tracing the fault further up the line of argument to its source in the fundamental presuppositions, in the basic theological strategy of fencing off divine truth, truth of revelation, on all sides, from every possibility of alliance or conflict with human truth."

67. P 14, 1933, pp. 26-27.

68. RPW 27, June 1962, pp. 60-67.

69. P 14, 1933, pp. 262-78; P 16, 1948, p. 203; C 9, 1962, pp. 70-78.

70. RW 32, June 1972, pp. 51-62 (by the Baptist, Paul Ballard).

71. C 9, 1962, pp. 97-98. For an account of the lacunae see A. P. F. Sell, *The Philosophy of Religion 1875-1980* (London: Croom Helm, 1988).

72. See A. P. F. Sell, "Theology and the Philosophical Climate: Case Studies from the Second Century A.D.," *Vox Evangelica* 13 (1983): 41-65, and 14 (1984): 53-64; idem, "Platonists (Ancient and Modern) and the Gospel," *The Irish Quarterly* 44 (1977): 153-74.

73. See A. P. F. Sell, "The Peril of Reductionism in Christian Thought," *Scottish Journal of Theology* 27 (1974): 48-64.

74. RW 31, Dec. 1971, p. 364.

75. Don Cupitt, *The Leap of Reason* (London: Sheldon Press, 1976), pp. 106-7.

76. See RW 38, June 1984, *passim*. Collected here are papers presented at the Cairo Consultation of 1984 on the Alliance's study booklet, *Called to Witness to the Gospel Today* (1983). C. S. Song was the director of this study program from 1983 to 1986.

6. The Ethical Witness

1. P 13, 1929, pp. 288-89.

2. C 4, 1920, pp. 321-41.

3. Ibid., pp. 395-417.

4. P 2, 1880, p. 560.

5. Ibid., p. 561.

6. P 3, 1884, p. 421.

7. Ibid., p. 422.

8. P 11, 1921, p. 354.

9. C 1, 1891, p. 271.

10. Ibid., p. 272.

11. Ibid.

12. Ibid., p. 275.

13. C 3, 1908, p. 383.

14. P 2, 1880, p. 570.

15. Ibid., p. 571.

16. P 3, 1884, p. 436. Cf. P 11, 1921, pp. 194-210.

17. See C 3, 1908, pp. 482-505; C 5, 1930, pp. 264-78.

18. P 2, 1880, pp. 584-90.

19. Ibid., p. 312.

20. Ibid., p. 316.

21. Ibid., p. 319.

22. Ibid., p. 321.

23. Ibid.

24. Ibid.

25. Ibid., p. 322.

26. Ibid., p. 323.
27. P 15, 1937, p. 225. Other treatments of the theme include P 14, 1933, pp. 303-12; P 17, 1954, pp. 90-93, 196-204; CP 1, 1879, pp. 17-26; PW 21, March 1951, pp. 2-12.
28. P 15, 1937, p. 29.
29. Ibid., p. 157.
30. Ibid., pp. 252-54.
31. C 4, 1920, p. 415. It will be recalled that in chap. 4 above we drew attention to the lack of serious discussion of the establishment question in current bilateral dialogues. See also C 1, 1891, pp. 158-73; C 3, 1908, pp. 119-30.
32. See C 2, 1899, pp. 335-57; C 3, 1908, pp. 434-44.
33. C 7, 1953, pp. 99-100.
34. Ibid., p. 102.
35. Ibid., pp. 102-3.
36. Ibid, p. 103.
37. Ibid.
38. Ibid.
39. Ibid., p. 104.
40. Ibid., pp. 104-5.
41. Ibid., p. 105.
42. Ibid.
43. Ibid.
44. Ibid., p. 106.
45. Ibid.
46. Ibid., p. 107.
47. Ibid., p. 115.
48. C 6, 1949, pp. 4-6; cf. ibid., pp. 146-59; C 2, 1899, pp. 79-88; P 15, 1937, pp. 135-43.
49. C 1, 1891, p. 238.
50. C 6, 1949, p. 178.
51. P 12, 1925, pp. 314-30.
52. P 13, 1929, pp. 302-10.
53. P 15, 1937, pp. 226-27.
54. See RPW 30, Sept. 1968, pp. 108-19; RW 35, no. 2, June 1978, pp. 65-71; RW 38, March 1984, pp. 13-34. This last is a valuable presentation of Christian and secular statements under the heading, "Peace and War: The Challenge of the Churches to the Present International Order." The author is Olle Dahlén, a former Swedish ambassador. In three volumes edited by Allen O. Miller the Caribbean and North American Area Council Theological Committee has paid much attention to these themes. See *Reconciliation in Today's World* (Grand Rapids: Eerdmans, 1969); *A Christian Declaration on Human Rights* (Grand Rapids: Eerdmans, 1977); *A Covenant Challenge to Our Broken World* (Geneva: WARC, 1982). See also *Called to Witness to the Gospel Today* (Geneva: WARC, 1983), pp. 40-41.
55. RW 37, June 1983, p. 182.
56. Ibid.
57. P 2, 1880, pp. 180-89; cf. pp. 223-25.

58. Ibid., p. 197.
59. P 4, 1888, p. 142.
60. Ibid., p. 155.
61. P 5, 1892, pp. 343-63; cf. ibid., pp. 86-88. See also QR 11, Nov. 1917, pp. 43-44.
62. C 1, 1891, pp. 173-92; C 3, 1908, pp. 132-42, 411-34.
63. P 14, 1933, pp. 250-51.
64. Ibid., p. 251.
65. Ibid., p. 254.
66. Ibid., p. 255.
67. Ibid.
68. Ibid., p. 257.
69. Ibid.
70. Ibid., p. 259.
71. See the council's preparatory study booklet, *Thine Is the Kingdom, the Power, and the Glory* (Geneva: World Alliance of Reformed Churches, 1981), pp. 49-56.
72. Ibid., pp. 51-52.
73. Ibid., p. 52.
74. Ibid., p. 54.
75. Ibid.
76. Ibid., p. 55.
77. Ibid.
78. Ibid.
79. P 14, 1933, p. 239; cf. P 7, 1899, pp. 330-38; P 9, 1909, pp. 370-77.
80. *Called to Witness to the Gospel Today*, pp. 33-34.
81. *Theology of Marriage and the Problem of Mixed Marriages* (Geneva: Lutheran World Federation; Geneva: World Alliance of Reformed Churches; Vatican City: Secretariat for Promoting Christian Unity, 1977), p. 11.
82. Ibid., p. 13.
83. Ibid., p. 14.
84. Ibid., p. 17.
85. Ibid., p. 31.
86. Although Mgr. Jozef Tomko dissented. See pp. 34-35n.
87. C 7, 1953, pp. 116-20.
88. See P 15, 1937, pp. 163-78; C 4, 1920, pp. 114-19; RW 31, March 1971, pp. 195-202; RW 31, Dec. 1971, pp. 348-57; RW 33, June 1975, pp. 268-74; RW 34, June 1976, pp. 50-72; RW 24, Sept.-Dec. 1977, pp. 324-27; RW 35, March 1978, pp. 30-33; RW 36, Dec. 1981, pp. 370-75; RW 37, Dec. 1983, pp. 292-300.
89. In earlier volumes of *Proceedings* we hear of "Women's Work in the Church," of deaconesses, and even, from time to time, of the ordination of women. This last is, however, generally ruled out on mixed (and confused) grounds, the argument centering now in the Bible, now in natural law. We shall refer to such an argument below. The council of the Congregational Union of England and Wales approved in principle the ordination of women to the ministry in 1909. QR 11, Nov. 1917, p. 44, noted the case of Mrs. Constance Mary Coltman, who, having completed her theological course with distinction,

was now seeking ordination. Mrs. Coltman became the first female Congregational minister in England, being ordained in 1917. See Elaine Kaye, "Constance Coltman—A Forgotten Pioneer," in *The Journal of the United Reformed Church History Society* 4 (1988): 134-46. The emphasis upon the *rights* of women in this matter came later, as we shall see.

90. *Theological Basis of Human Rights* (Geneva: World Alliance of Reformed Churches, 1976), p. 9. The entire document, including Moltmann's paper, is reprinted in the collection *A Christian Declaration on Human Rights*; see n. 54 above.

91. Ibid., p. 16.

92. Ibid., pp. 1-2.

93. We by no means suggest that simply because an individual "feels a call" the church must automatically endorse it. Precisely because of the covenant, ministry is the concern of the whole body. Hence, calls to any special service are brought before the church and tested, and, if endorsed, those concerned are trained in whatever ways may be deemed appropriate.

94. William Klempa contributes a particularly lucid and concise account of one of the more notoriously difficult parts of the history: "The Concept of the Covenant in Sixteenth- and Seventeenth-Century Continental and British Reformed Theology," *Covenant Challenge to Our Broken World*, pp. 130-47.

95. P 2, 1880, pp. 180-81.

96. Quoted by J. M. Lochman in *Christian Declaration of Human Rights*, pp. 23-24.

97. C 1, 1891, pp. xxxi-xxxii. Cf. B 9, Spring 1969, pp. 9-14.

98. WARC 22, 1982, pp. 158, 176-80, 207, 208.

99. RW 32, Dec. 1973, p. 350.

100. C 6, 1949, p. 118.

101. WARC 22, 1982, p. 184.

102. C 3, 1908, pp. 35-36.

103. *Theological Basis of Human Rights*, pp. 1-2.

104. Ibid., p. 16.

105. WARC 20, 1970, p. 226.

106. *The [London] Observer*, 26 May 1985. See further, A.P.F. Sell, *Aspects of Christian Integrity* (Calgary: University of Calgary Press, 1990; Louisville: Westminster/John Knox, 1991).

107. WARC 20, 1970, p. 225, our italics. On the question of common ground in ethics see A. P. F. Sell, "Christians, Humanists and Common Ground," *Journal of Moral Education* 1 (June 1972): 177-85; idem, *Aspects of Christian Integrity*, chapter 3.

108. P 11, 1921, p. 159.

109. Ibid.

110. Ibid., p. 160. On 31 July 1763 James Boswell told Johnson that he had been that morning to a Quaker service and had heard a woman preaching. Whereupon Johnson expostulated, "Sir, a woman's preaching is like a dog's walking on its hind legs. It is not done well; but you are surprised to find it done at all" (Boswell, *The Life of Samuel Johnson* [London: Dent Everyman edn., 1925], vol. 1, pp. 286-87).

111. P 11, 1921, p. 162.

112. Ibid., p. 163.

113. Ibid., p. 164. A. J. Brown said, "As a matter of fact, the women of the Presbyterian and Reformed Churches are not asking for ordination to the ministry and do not care a copper whether it is granted or not" (ibid., p. 165). By this time, as we have seen, the Congregationalists had already received their first female minister.

114. D. D. Williams, *Interpreting Theology 1918-52* (London: SCM Press, 1953), p. 74.

115. Ibid.

116. Ibid.

117. R. H. Preston, "The Study of Christian Ethics," *Theology* 67 (1964): 146.

118. See his "Reply to Interpretation and Criticism," in *Reinhold Niebuhr: His Religious, Social and Political Thought*, eds. Charles W. Kegley and Robert W. Bretall (New York: Macmillan, 1956).

119. RW 34, Dec. 1976, p. 158.

120. P. Ramsey, *Nine Modern Moralists* (Englewood Cliffs, N.J.: Prentice Hall, 1962), p. 112.

121. N. H. G. Robinson, *The Groundwork of Christian Ethics* (London: Collins, 1971), p. 305.

122. J. M. Lochman, RW 32, Dec. 1973, p. 349.

123. WARC 22, 1982, p. 176.

124. Ibid., p. 178.

125. Ibid., pp. 177-78.

126. *God's Reign and Our Unity* (London: SPCK; Edinburgh: The Saint Andrew Press, 1984), p. 22.

127. See Richmond Smith, "Taking Stock . . . The Department of Theology of the Alliance," RW 37, June 1983, pp. 208-9, 211-12. For the same author's review of the work of the department of theology from the Uniting Council of 1970 to 1982, see RW 37, March 1982, pp. 63-99.

128. C 6, 1949, p. 143.

7. Conclusion

1. A. P. F. Sell, "Doctrine, Grace, Gospel and Unity," *Life and Work*, May 1987, p. 23.

2. Thus, since 1982 (and therefore outside the scope of this study), the following theological concerns, among others, have been treated in Alliance circles either for the first time or with renewed intensity: unity and union within the Reformed family (RW 39, Sept. 1986, pp. 582-88); the ordination of women in the member churches of the Alliance (RW 38, Dec. 1985, pp. 434-43; RW 39, March 1986, pp. 484-95); the Lord's Supper in the Reformed family (RW 39, June 1986, pp. 518-38); the Congregational idea of the church (A. P. F. Sell, *Saints: Visible, Orderly and Catholic* (Geneva: WARC; Allison Park, Pa.: Pickwick Publications, 1986); Reformed responses to *Baptism, Eucharist and Ministry* (A. P. F. Sell, *Responding to Baptism, Eucharist and Ministry: A Word to the Reformed Churches* [Geneva: WARC, 1984]; RW 37, March 1983, pp. 131-40; RW 37, Sept.

1983, pp. 239-47; RW 38, Sept. 1984, pp. 187-200; RW 38, June 1985, pp. 341-46; RW 39, Sept. 1986, pp. 549-65; RW 39, March 1987, pp. 683-92; *Sola Scriptura*, a study by the European Committee of the Alliance in RW 39, March 1986, pp. 455-73); conversations with the Mennonites (*Mennonites and Reformed in Dialogue*, ed. H. G. vom Berg et al. [Geneva: WARC; Lombard, IL.: Mennonite World Conference, 1986]; A. P. F. Sell, "Anabaptist-Congregational Relations and Current Mennonite-Reformed Dialogue," *The Mennonite Quarterly Review* 61 [July 1987]: 321-34); conversations with the Disciples of Christ (*Reformed and Disciples of Christ in Dialogue*, ed. A. P. F. Sell [Geneva: WARC, 1985]; RW 39, Dec. 1987; *Towards Closer Fellowship: Report of the Dialogue between Reformed and Disciples of Christ* [Geneva: WARC, 1988]; cf. *Mid-Stream* 27 [April 1988]); conversations with the Methodists (RW 38, Dec. 1985, pp. 444-47, 452; RW 39, Dec. 1987, pp. 823-29; A. P. F. Sell, "Some Reflections on Reformed-Methodist Relations," *Epworth Review* 13 [Jan. 1986]: 30-40; *Reformed and Methodists in Dialogue* [Geneva: WARC, 1988]); continuing discussions with the Roman Catholic church (*Toward Church Fellowship* [Lutheran-Reformed Joint Commission] [Geneva: Lutheran World Federation; Geneva: World Alliance of Reformed Churches, 1989]); preparations for international conversations with the Orthodox churches (*Theological Dialogue between Orthodox and Reformed Churches*, ed. T. F. Torrance [Edinburgh: Scottish Academic Press, 1985]; *Reformed Theology and the Jewish People*, ed. A. P. F. Sell [Geneva: WARC, 1986]); peace and justice (RW 37, June 1983, pp. 179-82; RW 38, March 1984, pp. 13-34; RW 39, Dec. 1986, pp. 617-24; *Peace, War and God's Justice*, ed. T. D. Parker and B. J. Fraser [Toronto: United Church Publishing House, 1989]); gospel and cultures (RW 38, June 1984; RW 38, June 1985, pp. 309-40; RW 38, Sept. 1985, pp. 357-84); confessing the faith today (RW 39, March 1987, pp. 645-60); *Covenanting for Peace and Justice* (Geneva: World Alliance of Reformed Churches, 1939).

3. See Robert W. Henderson, *A Profile of the Eldership* (Geneva: WARC, 1974).
4. CP 1, 1879, p. 6.

Index of Persons

(See also Appendix III: Bibliography)

Select Index of Subjects

agnosticism, 186-88, 258
American Unitarian Association, 268
Anabaptism, 17, 64, 102-3, 266, 295
Anglican Consultative Council, 19
Anglicanism/Anglicans, 109, 137-42, 145, 147, 148, 161-64, 242, 277, 287
apartheid, 18, 218, 233-35
apologetics, chap. 5
Arianism, 240, 263, 268
Arminianism, 48, 106
atonement. *See* Christ: work of
Augsburg Confession, 74
authority, 70-71, 116, 182

baptism, 64, 103, 110, 120, 131, 139, 143-44, 147, 149-54, 170, 242, 263, 282, 294
Baptists, 142-46
Baptist World Alliance, 19, 74, 130
Barmen Declaration, 13, 77, 204
Bible, 13, 24, 51, 54, 57, 61, 62, 65-71, 74, 75, 76, 78, 87, 88, 89, 93, 95, 103-4, 106, 111, 116, 118, 143, 146, 148, 153, 156, 168, 169, 182, 184, 197, 202, 203, 215, 224, 230, 235, 237, 244, 266, 270, 272, 279, 281, 292, 294

Calvinism, 54, 61-62, 63, 65, 79, 106, 147, 180, 288
catechisms, 260
catholicity, 1, 14, 20, 33-34, 46, 85, 90, 94, 100-101, 104-11, 112, 120, 128, 135, 140, 144, 165, 167, 170, 176, 237, 238, 245, 265, 271, 272, 273, 276, 284
Chalcedonian formula, 37, 41-43
Christ: person of, 36-43, 181, 238, 262, 263; work of, 30-36, 181, 196, 238, 241, 258, 262
Christocentric emphasis, 10, 68-71, 88, 109, 111, 120-22, 132, 160, 168-69, 173, 180, 182-83, 275

Church, 34-35, 36, 46, 50-52, 77-78, 81-111, chap. 4, 236, 242, 262, 265, 271, 272. *See also* Congregationalism, polity, Presbyterianism
church and state, 64, 145, 203-9. *See also* establishment
Church Meeting, 99, 100, 104, 155, 172
collective responsibility, 226-28, 244
common ground, 228-32
common sense philosophy, 258
confessions of faith, 9, 12, 13, 20, 37-39, 44, 65, 71-83, 95, 105, 114, 138, 238, 260, 262, 267, 268-69, 295
Congregationalism, 9, 11, 17, 34, 69, 86, 91-104, 106-7, 124, 169, 174, 259, 260, 265-66, 269, 270, 271, 272, 273, 277, 286, 294, 295
conscience, 64, 66, 82
covenant(s), 89, 90, 91, 97, 112, 135, 150-51, 160, 176, 210, 219-20, 259, 260, 268, 292
creation, 25-27, 44, 52, 110, 212, 288
creeds, 24, 76-83, 95, 99, 238, 260, 267, 269, 270
Cumberland Presbyterian church, 20, 260, 267

deacons, 85, 168, 172, 287
"decisionism," 50
Declaration of Faith (1967), 79
dialogues, 16, 18-19, 129-46, 177, 216-18, 239-40, 244, 259-60, 263, 278, 295
Disciples' Ecumenical Consultative Council, 260
Disciples of Christ, 260, 295
discipline, 84, 145, 168, 242, 270
divorce, 216-17
Dort, Canons of, 73

economic order, 211-14
ecumenism. *See* unity

302